0 1341 04377137

W9-AHQ-037

THE POWER OF GOLD

THE POWER OF GOLD

THE HISTORY OF AN OBSESSION

PETER L. BERNSTEIN

JOHN WILEY & SONS, INC.
New York • Chichester • Weinheim • Brisbane • Singapore • Toronto

This book is printed on acid-free paper. ♾

Published by John Wiley & Sons, Inc.
Published simultaneously in Canada.

Library of Congress Cataloging-in-Publication Data:

Bernstein, Peter L.
The power of gold : the history of an obsession / Peter L. Bernstein.
p. cm.
Includes bibliographical references and index.
ISBN 0-471-25210-7 (cloth : alk. paper)
1. Gold—Folklore. 2. Gold—History. 3. Gold—Social aspects. I. Title.

GR810.B47 2000
398′.365—dc21 00-036647

Printed in the United States of America

10 9 8 7 6 5 4 3 2

For Barbara, once again and always.

They wonder much to hear that gold, which in itself is so useless a thing, should be everywhere so much esteemed, that even men for whom it was made, and by whom it has its value, should yet be thought of less value than it is.

Sir Thomas More (1478–1535). *Utopia of Jewels and Wealth*

Acknowledgments

Ninety-one years ago, Lytton Strachey observed that "Every history worthy of the name is, in its own way, as personal as poetry, and its value ultimately depends upon the force and the quality of the character behind it."* True enough, but writing history is also hard work. It involves organizing masses of facts—many of them unfamiliar—into a coherent story, developing ideas that bear some logical relationship to the facts, and communicating the results in a fashion that will interest more people than just the writer. As a result, the task cannot be a solitary one. I know whereof I speak.

The first of my acknowledgments goes to my wife, Barbara, who is also my business partner. Her contribution to this book was significant on all levels. Her many positive suggestions, her equally valuable criticisms, her diligent editing, and her unfailing inspiration were all essential to the completion of the task. It never would have happened without her.

This book was my third partnership with my editor, Peter Dougherty. Peter creates a unique intellectual adventure that is challenging, exciting, and great fun. He has once again showed me how to transform a heap of jumbled ideas into a coherent whole. His brilliant insights, his ready grasp of the subject matter, and his total commitment as friend and guide to this project are visible on every page. He is the editor that all writers wish for, and I can only hope that the future holds many more of these stimulating and rewarding opportunities to work with him.

*"A New History of Rome," *Spectator* 102 (January 2, 1909), pp. 20–21.

Charles Kindleberger, my great friend and comrade-at-arms in World War II, became indefatigably engaged in this work from the very beginning. His generosity to me was boundless. He provided inestimable guidance to research sources and shared his own research materials and notes without stint. He was tireless in supplying suggestions, criticisms, and fresh viewpoints. He showered the full benefit of his extraordinary knowledge of economic and financial history upon every part of the manuscript. It was a rare privilege to have him as mentor and intellectual companion.

I was also most fortunate in having Richard Sylla's bountiful assistance from beginning to end. Dick's authoritative criticisms and recommendations provided many significant improvements to the book by protecting me from oversimplifications in interpretation and omissions of essential facts.

Throughout the entire process, Edward Klagsbrun's counsel and support were essential in enabling Barbara and me to keep our eye on the ball.

Myles Thompson deserves my gratitude for his unremitting enthusiasm, editorial assistance, and important support, as well as many valuable suggestions about the content and development of the undertaking.

Three friends and colleagues were also kind enough to read the full manuscript. My two-time co-author and great friend, Robert Heilbroner, as so often in the past, gave me the benefit of his historical expertise, his deep understanding of economics, and his great talent for literary quality. Peter Brodsky led me to important clarifications in areas that suffered from undue fuzziness in the early drafts. Elliott Howard drew my attention to a long list of flaws and offered helpful comments on the subject of gold.

The team at Wiley under Jeff Brown's confident leadership went to the limit on our behalf, with enthusiasm, skill, and gracious responsiveness to our needs. In addition to Jeff, this group included, in alphabetical order, Sylvia Coates, Mary Daniello, Peter Knapp, Livia Llewellyn, Meredith McGinnis, Joan O'Neil, Lori Sayde-Mehrtens, Rachel Salzman, and Jennifer Wilkin. Special thanks are due to Adrian Weston's outstanding contribution.

Everett Sims's conscientious editing has added polish, grace, and clarity to many rough edges. I am also grateful to Ev for proposing that I should write a book about gold. Although there were many moments when I wished I had not listened to him, I am confident that no other topic would have captured my interest as this one has.

I was fortunate to work with a group of skillful, imaginative, and indefatigable research assistants. They saved me many hours of labor and made useful contributions at the same time. Here they are, in the sequence in which they served: Michelle Lee, Susan Cohen, Steven Sherrifs, Betsy Wallen, and Linda Chang. Our business associate, Barbara Fotinatos, saw to it that the project kept moving along, not least by contributing her expert guidance in the language and habits of the Greeks.

I am pleased to express special gratitude to Andrew Freeman, who arranged for the staff of *The Economist* in London to permit Barbara and me to spend several hours in the privacy of their Directors' Room reading issues of their invaluable publication from the 1920s and 1930s. As readers will note in Chapters 17 and 18, this fascinating material brought the times to life as nothing else could have.

The following people also provided significant assistance along the way and deserve my warmest thanks: Barbara Boehm, Ulla Buchner-Howard, Mike Clowes, Barclay Douglas, Hans Falkena, Rob Ferguson, Benjamin Friedman, Milton Friedman, Alan Greenspan, James Howell, Henry Hu, Steve Jones, Dwight Keating, Leora Klapper, Benjamin Levene, Richard Rogalski, Paul Samuelson, Ronald Sobel, and Gentaro Yura.

Convention dictates that the author relieves all of the above from any responsibility for errors that may remain in the manuscript. Charlie Kindleberger decries this convention, pointing out that the author, after all, depended on the authority of these individuals in preparing the work and should not be expected to check out the accuracy of their suggestions. The quality of the assistance I have received on this occasion assures me that, just for once, Charlie is mistaken. All errors that remain in the manuscript are mine. May we hope that they are few and far between.

P. L. B.

Contents

THE DESCENT FROM GLORY

THE POWER OF GOLD

Prologue
The Supreme Possession

About one hundred years ago, John Ruskin told the story of a man who boarded a ship carrying his entire wealth in a large bag of gold coins. A terrible storm came up a few days into the voyage and the alarm went off to abandon ship. Strapping the bag around his waist, the man went up on deck, jumped overboard, and promptly sank to the bottom of the sea. Asks Ruskin: "Now, as he was sinking, had he the gold? Or had the gold him?"[1]

This book tells the story of how people have become intoxicated, obsessed, haunted, humbled, and exalted over pieces of metal called gold. Gold has motivated entire societies, torn economies to shreds, determined the fate of kings and emperors, inspired the most beautiful works of art, provoked horrible acts by one people against another, and driven men to endure intense hardship in the hope of finding instant wealth and annihilating uncertainty.

"Oh, most excellent gold!" observed Columbus while on his first voyage to America. "Who has gold has a treasure [that] even helps souls to paradise."[2] As gold's unquenchable beauty shines like the sun, people have turned to it to protect themselves against the darkness ahead. Yet we shall see at every point that Ruskin's paradox arises and challenges us anew. Whether it is Jason in search of the Golden Fleece, the Jews dancing around the golden calf, Croesus fingering his golden coins, Crassus murdered by molten gold poured down his throat, Basil

Bulgaroctonus with over two hundred thousand pounds of gold, Pizarro surrounded by gold when slain by his henchmen, Sutter whose mill-stream launched the California gold rush, or modern leaders such as Charles de Gaulle who deluded themselves with a vision of an economy made stable, sure, and superior by the ownership of gold—they all had gold, but the gold had them all.

When Pindar in the fifth century BC described gold as "a child of Zeus, neither moth or rust devoureth it, but the mind of man is devoured by this supreme possession," he set forth the whole story in one sentence.[3] John Stuart Mill nicely paraphrased this view in 1848, when he wrote "Gold thou mayst safely touch; but if it stick/Unto thy hands, it woundeth to the quick."[4] Indeed, gold is a mass of contradictions. People believe that gold is a refuge until it is taken seriously; then it becomes a curse.

Nations have scoured the earth for gold in order to control others only to find that gold has controlled their own fate. The gold at the end of the rainbow is ultimate happiness, but the gold at the bottom of the mine emerges from hell. Gold has inspired some of humanity's greatest achievements and provoked some of its worst crimes. When we use gold to symbolize eternity, it elevates people to greater dignity—royalty, religion, formality; when gold is regarded as life everlasting, it drives people to death.

Gold's most mysterious incongruity is within the metal itself. It is so malleable that you can shape it in any way you wish; even the most primitive of people were able to create beautiful objects out of gold. Moreover, gold is imperishable. You can do anything you want with it and to it, but you cannot make it disappear. Iron ore, cow's milk, sand, and even computer blips are all convertible into something so different from their original state as to be unrecognizable. This is not the case with gold. Every piece of gold reflects the same qualities. The gold in the earring, the gold applied to the halo in a fresco, the gold on the dome of the Massachusetts State House, the gold flecks on Notre Dame's football helmets, and the gold bars hidden away in America's official cookie jar at Fort Knox are all made of the same stuff.

Despite the complex obsessions it has created, gold is wonderfully simple in its essence. Its chemical symbol AU derives from *aurora*, which means "shining dawn," but despite the glamorous suggestion of AU, gold is chemically inert. That explains why its radiance is forever. In Cairo, you will find a tooth bridge made of gold for an Egyptian 4500 years ago, its condition good enough to go into your mouth today. Gold is extraordinarily dense; a cubic foot of it weighs half a ton. In 1875, the English economist Stanley Jevons observed that the £20 million in transactions that cleared the London Bankers' Clearing House each day would weigh about 157 tons if paid in gold coin "and would require eighty horses for conveyance."[5] The density of gold means that even very small amounts can function as money of large denominations.

Gold is almost as soft as putty. The gold on Venetian glasses was hammered down to as little as five-millionths of an inch—a process known as gilding. In an unusually creative use of gilding, King Ptolemy II of Egypt (285–246 BC) had a polar bear from his zoo lead festive processions in which the bear was preceded by a group of men carrying a gilded phallus 180 feet tall.*[6] You could draw an ounce of gold into a wire fifty miles in length, or, if you prefer, you could beat that ounce into a sheet that would cover one hundred square feet.[7]

Unlike any other element on earth, almost all the gold ever mined is still around, much of it now in museums bedecking statues of the ancient gods and their furniture or in numismatic displays, some on the pages of illustrated manuscripts, some in gleaming bars buried in the dark cellars of central banks, a lot of it on fingers, ears, and teeth. There is a residue that rests quietly in shipwrecks at the bottom of the seas. If you piled all this gold in one solid cube, you could fit it aboard any of today's great oil tankers;[8] its total weight would amount to approximately 125,000 tons,[9] an insignificant volume that the U.S. steel industry turns out in just a few hours; the industry has the capacity to turn out 120 million tons a year. The ton of steel commands $550—2¢ an ounce—

*Where in the world did the Pharaoh of Egypt obtain a bear, much less a polar bear, over two hundred years before the birth of Christ? My source cites "the contemporary Greek writer Athenaeus, who grew up in Egypt."

but the 125,000 tons or so of gold would be worth a trillion dollars at today's prices.*

Is that not strange? Out of steel, we can build office towers, ships, automobiles, containers, and machinery of all types; out of gold, we can build nothing. And yet it is gold that we call the precious metal. We yearn for gold and yawn at steel. When all the steel has rusted and rotted, and forever after that, your great cube of gold will still look like new. That is the kind of longevity we all dream of.

Stubborn resistance to oxidation, unusual density, and ready malleability—these simple natural attributes explain all there is to the romance of gold (even the word *gold* is nothing fancy: it derives from the Old English *gelo*, the word for "yellow"). This uncomplicated chemistry reveals that gold is so beautiful it was Jehovah's first choice for the decoration of his tabernacle: "Thou shalt overlay it with pure gold," He instructs Moses on Mount Sinai, "within and without shalt thou overlay it, and shalt make upon it a crown of gold round about."[10] That was just the beginning: God ordered that even the furniture, the fixtures, and all decorative items such as cherubs were also to be covered in pure gold.

God issued those orders many thousands of years ago. What is the place of gold in the modern world of abstract art, designer jeans, complex insurance strategies, computerized money, and the labyrinths of the Internet? Does gold carry any significance in an era where traditions and formality are constantly crumbling beyond recognition? In a global economy managed increasingly by central bankers and international institutions, does gold matter at all?

Only time can tell whether gold as a store of monetary value is truly dead and buried, but one thing is certain: the motivations of greed and fear, as well as the longings for power and for beauty, that drive the stories that follow are alive and well at this very moment. Consequently,

*In most instances, I have calibrated weights of gold in metric tons, even though convention more frequently uses millions of ounces. It is not difficult to conceive of a few thousand tons—about as large as the numbers get—whereas millions of ounces convey little meaning.

the story of gold is as much the story of our own time as it is a tale out of the past. From poor King Midas who was overwhelmed by it to the Aly Khan who gave away his weight in gold every year, from the dank mines of South Africa to the antiseptic cellars at Fort Knox, from the gorgeous artworks of the Scythians to the Corichancha of the Incas, from the street markets of Bengal to the financial markets in the City of London, gold reflects the universal quest for eternal life—the ultimate certainty and escape from risk.

The key to the whole tale is the irony that even gold cannot fulfill that quest. Like Ruskin's traveler jumping off the boat, people take the symbolism of gold too seriously. Blinded by its light, they cashier themselves for an illusion.

The following chapters proceed in roughly chronological order, but the story is neither a complete history of gold nor a systematic analysis of its role in economics and culture; detailed histories of money and banking abound. Instead, I explore those events and stories involving gold that most appealed to me because they display the desperation and ultimate frustrations that have inflamed human behavior. Beginning with the magical and religious attributes of gold, the history proceeds to the transformation of gold into money. As that transformation progresses, however, we shall never lose sight of the magical qualities of gold or the ironies of its impact on humanity.

My hope is that what I have chosen to include will illuminate and occasionally infuriate the reader about how the fascination, obsession, and aggression provoked by this strange and unique metal have shaped the destiny of humanity through the ages.

A METAL FOR ALL SEASONS

1

Get Gold at All Hazards

If gold were more plentiful on earth—say, as abundant as salt—it would be far less valuable and interesting, despite its unique physical attributes and beauty. Yet gold has been discovered on every continent on earth. That sounds like a contradiction, but it is not. Although gold deposits are widespread, in one form or another, no one area has yielded its gold easily. Finding and producing gold demands immense effort relative to the amount of glittering yellow metal that makes its appearance at the end of the process.

For example, in order to extract South Africa's annual output of around five hundred tons of gold, some seventy million tons of earth must be raised and milled—an amount greater than all the material in the pyramid of Cheops.[1] The South African mines are the worst, but we are all familiar with the tales of the Forty-Niners panning day after day in the waters of California and ending up with nothing but a few driblets of gold. As Will Rogers put it after returning from a visit to the Klondike, "There is a big difference between prospecting for gold and prospecting for spinach."[2]

This radically distorted ratio of effort to output appears to have done little to discourage people from pursuing the worldwide search for gold—perhaps the most telling evidence of how highly prized, vital, essential, and irresistible gold has been from the earliest of times. Even in myths, as this chapter relates, the quest for gold was gluttonous.

Although gold does not mix with other metals, thin veins of it are scattered throughout the mountains where granite and quartz have filled in cracks in the earth's crust and have been pressed together by fierce heat over millions of years. The elements have washed, blown, and scattered these deposits over the years, but gold has retained most of its purity even as it has suffered the ravages of nature's dynamics. Much of this gold has flowed downward in mountain streams. Gold's high density and weight tend to separate it from the other material in the waters, where it drifts to the bottom as nuggets or flows along as fine as dust.

Relative to the needs for it, gold does appear to have been more plentiful in ancient times, especially in Egypt and the Near East, than it has been since the Roman era. A little bit of gold goes a very long way when it is used only for adornment and decoration and not for coinage or hoarding: mining by the Egyptians produced only about one ton annually.[3] Until the development of coinage, which put gold into the hands of the masses and greatly expanded the need for it, most of the available gold was owned by monarchs and priests. Its use was ceremonial in large part, a medium for advertising power, wealth, eminence, and proximity to the gods. Whatever was left over was used for jewelry and other forms of personal adornment.

When Moses came down from Mount Sinai to deliver the Ten Commandments to his people, he found the Jews in a delirium worshipping a golden calf. He was so enraged to see them bowing to an icon like those worshipped by the hated Egyptians that he smashed the tablets inscribed with the Word of God—the Ten Commandments—which he had just brought down from Mount Sinai. The story reveals that the Jews, even as slaves, had ample amounts of gold on their persons. It never occurred to them to use their gold to bribe themselves out of captivity in Egypt; as gold was not yet perceived as money, they would have found few takers. Until they melted their gold into the golden calf, they adorned their ears, arms, and necks with it.

The more than four hundred additional references to gold in the Bible confirm how plentiful gold was at that time. Poor Job declaims, "If I have made gold my hope, or have said to the fine gold, 'Thou art my confidence'; If I rejoiced because . . . my hand had gotten much. . . . This also were an iniquity to be punished by the judge; for I should have denied the God that is above."[4] Abraham, the founder of the Jewish nation, is described in Genesis 13 as "rich in cattle, and in silver, and in gold." He furnished the servant who went to fetch Rebecca with vessels of gold, including a nose ring.

When Moses climbed Mount Sinai to receive the Word from God, God gave him a lot more to do than just transmit the Ten Commandments and many associated rules and obligations. God also issued precise directions for the construction of a sanctuary where the Jews were to worship Him, together with a tabernacle to go inside the sanctuary. God began right off by specifying that "thou shalt overlay it with pure gold, within and without shalt thou overlay it, and shalt make upon it a crown of gold round about." That is just the beginning: God even ordered that the furniture, fixtures, and all the decorative items such as cherubs were to be covered in pure gold. The instructions, as they appear in Chapters 25–28 of Exodus, persevere for some eighty paragraphs of painstakingly detailed measurements and designs.

Once settled in the Promised Land, the Jews must have accumulated masses of gold, primarily from plundering the tribes they had defeated in battle. Moses and his troops took over three hundred pounds of gold from the Midianites, "jewels of gold, ankle-chains and bracelets, signet-rings, earrings, and armlets."[5] Gold gleamed from the walls of the interior of Solomon's great temple (located near the Wailing Wall of modern Jerusalem), which was 135 feet long, 35 feet wide, 50 feet high, and divided into three chambers. Solomon enjoyed lavishing gold on his personal possessions as well: his shields were made of gold, his ivory throne was overlaid with gold, and he sipped his wine from golden vessels.[6] When the queen of Sheba came to visit Solomon, she brought him an amount of gold (coals to Newcastle?) that has been estimated at as much as three tons—worth over $20 million at today's prices.[7]

The sanctuary and tabernacle that Moses built to God's protracted specifications have disappeared, and Solomon's massive gold-encrusted temple has been defaced. But in AD 532, after ten thousand men working for six years had used more than twelve metric tons of gold in building the church of Saint Sophia in Constantinople, the Byzantine emperor Justinian—who supervised the entire operation—could exclaim, "Solomon, I have surpassed thee!"[8] Justinian was well versed in the uses of gold. He inherited 320,000 pounds of gold, used it all up, and then taxed his subjects to pay mercenary armies, to finance public works, and, most of all, to bribe his enemies to refrain from invading his domains. The process of using gold to proclaim the power of the church would be repeated in gleaming golden mosaics and decoration throughout Italy, in Spain, and even on the wildest steppes of Russia.

Neither Solomon nor Jehovah himself were the first to use gold to inspire reverence. The ancient Egyptians probably set the style for later religions, including the Jews, to emulate. The Jews, with one god, had it easy compared with the Egyptians, who had two thousand deities to worry about, many of whom bore some relation to the all-powerful Sun God. You can consume a lot of gold convincing everyone how powerful and all-knowing two thousand deities are. Christians, with only one god to worship but several thousand saints to pray to, have faced similar problems.

The use of gold in Egypt was a royal prerogative, unavailable to anyone but the pharaohs. That constraint facilitated the way that the pharaohs assumed god-like roles and authenticated their heavenly character by adorning themselves with the same substance that embellished their gods. Creating gold jewelry in Egypt was a high art, lavished upon dead monarchs as well as live ones.

An impressive demonstration of the use of gold to project power was carried out by a fascinating pharaoh who happened to be a woman, described by the Egyptologist James Henry Breasted as "the first great lady of the world." Hatshepsut was the daughter of Thutmose I, who was the first pharaoh to be buried, about 1482 BC, in the Valley of the Tombs of the Kings at Thebes. After Hatshepsut seized power from her nephew-stepson around 1470 BC, she sat on the throne as king until her death about 1458 BC and was known by approximately eighty titles, including Son of the Sun and Golden Horus (the Egyptian god of light). Although she passed up the opportunity to add the traditional royal title of Mighty Bull, she was nevertheless depicted in most contemporary art as a man.[9]

Hatshepsut was an impressive woman by any standard. She managed a major increase in Egyptian trade with Palestine, Syria, and Crete, which had withered during the preceding 150 years when Egypt was occupied by Asian invaders known as the Kyksos. The explorations for gold during her reign were ceaseless, reaching farther and farther south, probably well into Zimbabwe.

Hatshepsut's demand for gold was enormous, because she was a builder on a scale that would put Louis XIV and his Versailles to shame. She was also fond of gilding her face with a mixture of gold and silver dust. When she decided to erect a great monument for Amon Re, the chief god of Thebes, her original design included two gold pillars one hundred feet high that would be seen above the walls of the Karnak complex, which covered an area larger than the Vatican. When her chancellor prevailed on her to be a little more economical, she built the pillars of granite and covered only their peaks with gold. But even that required generous amounts. When the job was complete, she declared, "Their height pierces to heaven. . . . Their rays flood the Two Lands when the sun rises between them. . . . You who after long years shall see these monuments will say, 'We do not know how they can have made whole mountains of gold.' "[10]

Most of the gold of biblical times and ancient Egypt—approximately four thousand years before Christ—came from the bleak and forbidding landscape of southern Egypt and Nubia; *nub* is the Egyptian word for gold. Nubia continued to supply gold to the Western world well into the sixteenth century. According to one authority, the output of the Nubian mines "far exceeded the quantity which was drawn from all the mines of the then known world in subsequent ages, down to the discovery of America."[11]

The Egyptians had developed these mines from shallow ditches, but in time they cut complex underground shafts deep into the hills. The deeper the mines were cut, the greater the human pain that went on inside. The best description we have of the horrors experienced by the workers in these mines has been provided by Diodorus, a Greek who visited Egypt about the time that Caesar ruled Rome. The air in the shafts was fetid, constantly depleted by the tiny candles that barely illuminated the terrible darkness. The heat was intense, the earth frequently gave way, and subterranean water was a constant hazard. The fires used to crack the quartz in the rock released arsenic fumes that caused excruciating deaths among the many who inhaled them. The slaves had to work on their back or side and were literally worked to death if they were not crushed to death by falling rocks before they expired from exhaustion.[12]

No wonder slavery was so prevalent—and warfare so important—as military victories brought fresh supplies of slaves to work the mines. Diodorus informs us that the kings of Egypt did not limit the slave population to notorious criminals or captives taken in war, but even their "kindred and relations" as well—men, women, and children under the lash of the whip and without housing or care of any kind.[13] In an ingenious arrangement, the slaves were guarded by mercenaries drawn from many different nations. As none of them spoke the language of the slaves, there was little opportunity for the slaves to corrupt or to conspire with their guards in order to effect escapes.[14]

The employment of human labor was the standard mining technique right up to the twentieth century, except for a process that the Romans had devised in Spain, whose gold-stuffed hills served as the backbone of the Roman economy. The Romans originally used human labor to dig as deep as 650 feet to extract the ore from the Spanish countryside, but with a new method, called hydraulicking, they used powerful jets of water to break up the rock and expose the gold-bearing earth. The water came from great holding tanks situated as much as four hundred to eight hundred feet above the site. The method, though wonderfully efficient and productive, washed away entire mountains, destroyed farmland, and silted many rivers and harbors.[15]

Hydraulicking was used in spotty fashion in other parts of Europe as well, but its most notable reappearance was in California in 1852, at the height of the gold rush. The Roman technique was faithfully reproduced in the Sacramento area, with water under pressure of up to thirty thousand gallons a minute smashing into the rocky hillsides and mountains. The environmental damage was awful. Forests and farmland disappeared in short order, the detritus even pouring into San Francisco Bay and leaving the landscape dotted with piles of rock and barren mountainsides. Nevertheless, hydraulicking was the primary method of gold extraction in California until 1884, when angry citizens finally had it outlawed.

Today, in the great gold mines of South Africa, the shafts reach down as far as twelve thousand feet and the temperature reaches 130° F. As one source describes it, "To produce one ounce of fine gold requires thirty-eight man-hours, 1400 gallons of water, electricity to run a large house for ten days, 282 to 565 cubic feet of air under straining pressure, and quantities of chemicals including cyanide, acids, lead, borax, and lime." The labor force employed in the South African mines exceeds four hundred thousand men, about 90 percent of whom are black.[16]

King Ferdinand of Spain coined immortal words in 1511 when he declared, "Get gold, humanely if possible, but at all hazards—get gold."[17]

Not all gold has to be mined. When gold is carried down by mountain streams, the prospector can wade in and sieve up the fragments of gold-bearing ore that have broken loose from the mountainside. Gold was collected long ago in this fashion in Asia Minor, where gold coinage first made its formal appearance. Some 3500 years later, the California gold rush of the nineteenth century began on the banks of the Sacramento River, when the Forty-Niners crowded into the river with their crude equipment to "pan" the gold out of the rushing waters.

They were following a practice that had come down from the ancient Greeks, who used woolly sheepskins for panning gold from the rivers—the tight curls of the sheep's coat did an excellent job of capturing and holding the fragments of gold as the waters came rushing down the mountainsides. The mention of fleece and gold together immediately evokes Jason and the Golden Fleece, a legend that is worth a brief digression for its moral.[18]

Phryxus, the son of the king of Boeotia, an area in eastern Greece, had been badly treated by his stepmother, so his own mother arranged for him and his sister to escape on the back of a winged ram whose fleece was pure gold, a handsome gift that she had received from Hermes (for services undefined). The trip could hardly have been smooth, because the Golden Fleece must have weighed heavily even on a ram delivered by Hermes. Phryxus's sister, Helle, was apparently susceptible to air sickness, and, lacking the facilities of modern aircraft, became dizzy and fell off the ram into the sea; the point where she landed was named after her as the Hellespont.

Phryxus held on. After a trip of over one thousand miles, he was finally delivered by his ram to Colchis on the far eastern side of the Black Sea. Happy to be safe and alive, he sacrificed the ram to Zeus and presented the fleece to the local king, Aeetes. Aeetes was delighted, as he had been told by an oracle that his life depended upon his possession of this fleece. Consequently, he nailed the Golden Fleece to a tree in a sacred grove and hired a huge, bloodthirsty dragon to guard it.

Meanwhile, back in northern Greece a king named Pelias decided he had better get rid of his handsome and popular nephew Jason, who was trying to assert his family's claim to the throne. Pelias told Jason that he could have the throne if he would first perform a deed "which well becomes your youth and which I am too old to accomplish. . . . Fetch back the fleece of the golden ram. . . . When you return with your magnificent prize, you shall have the kingdom and the sceptre."[19] Pelias never dreamed that Jason would succeed and return one day with his magnificent prize; on the contrary, he fully expected Jason to perish along the way or at least in the jaws of the guardian dragon.

Jason did take the Golden Fleece, with the help of his Argonauts, but only after an extensive and prolonged series of hair-raising adventures. Even then, he would have failed had it not been for the assistance he received from Aeetes's daughter Medea, who possessed magic powers. Medea had been hit with a dart thrown by Eros and had fallen madly in love with Jason, so she used all her wiles to catch his fancy. Jason was sufficiently tempted by her to offer to take her back to Greece with him, but on the condition that she support his efforts to take the Golden Fleece. Much as she loved him, Medea was unwilling to yield to what might well have been a seductive ruse. "O stranger," she cried, "swear by your gods and in the presence of your friends, that you will not disgrace me when I am alone, an alien in your land."[20] Jason swore to make her his "rightful wife" as soon as they returned to Greece. As such oaths were guarantees as reliable as written contracts in our time, Medea delivered the goods by singing the dragon into drowsiness while Jason seized the Golden Fleece from the tree.

The story does not have a happy ending, because Jason was a compulsive social climber. From the outset, he was determined to become king of his homeland. He risked his own life and those of his friends in search of a sheepskin dusted with gold. He used a king's daughter to bear children and promised to marry her. When he returned to Greece and found that he could not succeed to the throne, he fled with Medea to Corinth. There he proceeded to woo the daughter of King Creon but he told Medea what he was up to only after Creon had agreed to his betrothal to the princess. When Medea, inconsolable, recalled to him his solemn oath in Colchis, Jason justified himself by saying that their children would be better off because his newly betrothed had better social and political connections in Corinth than Medea did. The only solace he offered her was some gold and a request to friends to provide her with hospitality.

Medea fixed him. With a fine touch appropriate to the occasion, she created a gorgeous gown made of cloth of gold and drenched it in poison. She then presented it as a gift to the bride-to-be. Delighted at the sight of this beautiful garment, the poor young woman wrapped herself in the radiant fabric, twined the golden wreath into her hair, and died a horrible death. Medea then completed her act of revenge by killing her own sons and flying off in a dragon-drawn chariot she had conjured up. Jason threw himself on his sword and died on the threshold of his home.

The gold of Aeetes's fleece had promised Jason power. That power gained him a princess who promised him a throne. But in the end, it was the gold that snuffed out both his bride and his future.

2

Midas's Wish and the Creatures of Pure Chance

Though the crowns of gold that monarchs wear on state occasions must weigh heavy on their heads, no monarch has ever chosen zinc or plastic as an alternative. Rulers for centuries have also been fond of stamping their likeness on gold coins, to circulate throughout their kingdom and beyond. The tension between gold as adornment and gold as money developed early in history and has continued up to the present time. The everlasting radiance of gold, together with its scarcity, suggested such exceptional value that its route from the golden calf, the gilded phallus, and the Golden Fleece to its use as money was probably inevitable. The process works both ways: gold's massive purchasing power adds to the lustre we see when we look at gold jewelry or the gilded dome on a state capitol.

This chapter is about the nature of money and how gold coinage came into being. We shall see that gold's association with power and magic linked it to the wide range of monetary functions that emerge when trade and business flourish. Money serves cultures and also reflects their basic values, and that may best explain gold's longevity as a form of money. Indeed, gold has played the most important role as money in those cultures that hold business and exchange in highest repute.

Value alone is insufficient for a substance to qualify as money. Lots of things have value that do not serve as money. In fact, the most effective forms of money have developed from objects that were otherwise quite useless, such as paper and computer blips.

In early Britain, cattle and slaves served as money. Their value was set by law—although the church, eager to discourage slavery, refused to accept slaves in payment of penances.[1] Pepper was popular in medieval times. In some areas, hoarding cattle to serve as wealth instead of as a food supply is a practice that has continued into modern times; this practice has led to serious ecological degradation in parts of Africa, where the sheep and goat population shrank by over 66 million from 1955 to 1976.[2]

That is a rare case. In modern times, nothing useful has ever functioned as money for very long. For example, the cigarettes accepted as currency in Germany in the early days after World War II ultimately went up in smoke. Gold, in contrast, has always been useless for most practical purposes that call for metal, because it is so soft. With only 125,000 tons of it in existence, gold is also too scarce to have many uses.

But gold has clear advantages as money compared to other kinds of useless substances that people have used for the purpose. Unlike cowrie shells, which were the main form of money for centuries in parts of Asia, gold is remarkably durable and does not easily fragment. Every single piece of gold, no matter how small or how large, is instantly recognizable everywhere as a receptacle of high value. Furthermore, every piece of gold is valued only by its weight and purity, attributes that are inconveniently applied to cattle.

Seen from the perspective of uselessness, the electronic blips on computer screens that comprise most of the money in the modern world are the best form of money—we have no other use for them, they are readily recognizable as money, they weigh a lot less than gold or even paper, they are easily transferable, they can be broken down into any amount we choose from a penny to trillions of dollars and even beyond, they are as durable as we wish them to be, and they have a kind of magic that commands our respect.

Yet gold endures as a standard of value. From the Golden Rule to Olympic gold, it has commanded far more respect than any other substance in history.

But we should hesitate before admiring the sophistication of our contemporary currency while snickering about currencies in societies supposedly more primitive than ours. Consider the monetary system on the small island of Yap in the Caroline Islands, as charmingly described by an American anthropologist named William Henry Furness III, who spent several months on Yap in 1903.*[3]

Furness points out, "In a land where food and drink and ready-made clothes grow on trees and may be had for the gathering, it is not easy to see how a man can run very deeply in debt for his living expenses." Nevertheless, people like some tangible representation of the labor they have expended that can be accumulated as wealth.

The medium of exchange, or, more properly, the store of value on Yap at that time was called *fei*. *Fei* consisted of thick stone wheels with diameters ranging from saucer-size pieces to twelve-foot millstones. The stones from which these *fei* had been fashioned came from limestone quarries found on the island of Babelthuap, one of the Pelao Islands about four hundred miles away, and brought to Yap long ago, piece by piece, in canoes and on rafts by some venturesome natives described by Furness "as persuasive as . . . the most glib book-agent."

The smaller and more portable *fei* served as a medium of exchange and were handed around in payment for fish or pigs. The larger *fei*, however, received different treatment. The natives punched holes in the center of these *fei* to facilitate moving them about, but most of these big stones weighed so much that they remained permanently in one spot. On the rare occasions when a major transaction took place, the

*Furness spelled it Uap.

process went through with a simple acknowledgment of change of ownership while the "coin" continued to sit undisturbed wherever it happened to be.

In fact, the wealthiest family in the community owned an enormous *fei* that no one could see or had ever seen. According to this family, their *fei* lay on the bottom of the sea. Many generations past, while an ancestor was towing it on a raft attached to his canoe, a terrible storm came up. Unlike the protagonist of Ruskin's story, this man had decided that life came first and money second: he cut the raft adrift and watched the huge stone sink below the waves. But he survived to tell the tale and to describe to everyone the extraordinary size and quality of the stone he had lost. Nobody had ever doubted the veracity of his testimony. As Furness described it, "The purchasing power of that stone remains, therefore, as valid as if it were leaning visibly against the side of the owner's house."

Furness goes on to tell what happened when the German government bought Yap from Spain in 1898 and wanted to transform the island's rocky coral paths into proper roads for modern transports. The natives had no interest in spending their time doing that kind of work, despite repeated commands from the Germans to get busy. The Germans finally decided to levy a fine that would be lifted only when the task was completed. A German official went through the island, marking the most valuable *fei* with a black cross that confirmed the government's claim to that stone. According to Furness, "This instantly worked like a charm: the people, thus dolefully impoverished, turned to and repaired the highways . . . that they are now like park drives." Then the government erased the crosses, and "Presto! the fine was paid, the happy *failus* resumed possession of their capital stock, and rolled in wealth." In other times and other places, we call this sequence of events taxation and government spending.

This story reminds me of an experience of my own early in my career in 1940 when I went to work in the research department of the Federal Reserve Bank of New York in the heart of the city's financial district. One day, as a treat, my boss took me down to see the gold stored in the antiseptic vaults of the bank, five stories underground—sunk below bedrock to discourage thieves from tunneling through the outside walls. We entered the area through a ponderous airtight and watertight cylindrical door of stainless steel that unlocked automatically at nine in the morning and locked automatically at five in the afternoon. Just inside was a lunchbox, replenished daily with fresh sandwiches, to provide for any hapless member of the staff who got stuck inside when the automatic locks slammed shut at the end of the day. A little further on, there was a scale for weighing the gold, a scale so sensitive that a pea would send it rocking. With gold, even dust matters.

The gold was stored in oversized closets, about ten feet wide, ten feet high, and eighteen feet deep. The closets were filled to the ceiling with towering piles of gold bricks, each brick the size of three large candy bars. The bricks weighed about thirty pounds apiece—four hundred troy ounces—and were worth $14,000 in those days, when gold was officially priced at $35 an ounce. At those prices, $2 billion was stacked up there, a sum of money that was sufficient to buy four days' worth of the *total* production of goods and services in the United States at that time but was crowded into just one small space five stories below the busy New York City streets. Seeing over one hundred thousand gold bars, stacked to the ceiling and ablaze under the electric lights, is an unforgettable and chilling sight.

That gold did not belong to the United States. It belonged to France, England, and Switzerland, and to many other countries as well. Those countries had for a long time stored their official gold holdings at the New York Federal Reserve for both safekeeping and convenience. Each bar consigned in this manner was impressed with its owner's seal or a similar mark for identification. This process was known as earmarking gold, an expression that may date back to a method of indicating ownership of domesticated beasts. Earmarking enabled each nation to avoid all the care and expense of moving gold cross-country or across the seas when one country had cause to transfer gold to another. For example, if England lost gold to France, a guard at the Federal Reserve had merely to bring a dolly to England's closet, trundle the gold to the French closet, change the earmark, and note the change on the bookkeeping records.

These movements of just a few feet from one closet to another often reflected a major change in wealth between countries, with broad ramifications on economic well-being. Yet the citizens of each country never saw the gold to which their government held a claim.* If the

*Americans are in the same boat. In the process of doing research for this book, I tried to obtain access to the U.S. official gold reserve at Fort Knox, Kentucky. I was told that it is an army base and no visitors are allowed. The U.S. Treasury reports that we own $11 billion

gold had sunk into the Hudson River but the bookkeeping had progressed just the same, the economic and financial consequences to each nation would have been just as far-reaching as when the gold was shifted from one closet to another.

This procedure bears a striking resemblance to what went on at the island of Yap, with its transfers of ownership of assets that never moved and with the agitated economic activity that resulted when the Germans marked a black cross on the *fei*. As we shall see, the resemblance between so-called primitive and so-called modern uses of money did not stop at the shores of Yap and the cellars of the Federal Reserve.

The *fei* of Yap were stores of wealth. Stores of wealth sit. Money moves. It travels from one pocket to another. A store of wealth is mass; money is measurement of wealth.

Gold's durability, density, and glow made it a natural choice as a store of wealth long before people thought about using it as money. Like everything that has served as a store of wealth, gold in ancient times was a passion, a blatant expression of power, a means to provoke envy among enemies or people of lower status, or a vehicle for currying favor—as when the queen of Sheba showered gold on King Solomon.

Gold deployed as money becomes something different. People who go out to spend or lend money have to be cool-headed, calculating, precise, strategic in their vision. Before gold could be used as money instead of as a store of wealth, people had to become sufficiently productive to have something to trade, travel had to become more routine, and measurement had to be defined for the purpose.

In short, money comes into being when people are doing business. Not much business was transacted at Yap, where economic life was communal rather than commercial. We need money when we want to hire someone or because we want to offer the money to someone else in exchange for something we do not own. We use money when we want something today rather than tomorrow. Then we borrow from someone

---

in gold, but if nobody can get down there to have a look, how do we know that the gold is really there?

willing to wait until later to spend their money. Money moves from buyer to seller, from lender to borrower, and from borrower to lender. It seldom sits still very long and someone else is always involved.

When gold was only a store of wealth, payments from one party to another were infrequent. The process was cumbersome and time-consuming. Like cattle and the stones of Yap, no two gold bars or rings in ancient times were ever precisely the same size and fineness. As a result, every transaction involved testing for purity and putting the gold on a scale to determine its exact weight.

Coins were an ingenious innovation designed to get around the tedious business of weighing and checking purity, but they did not come upon the scene until around 700 BC, a good two thousand years or more after gold was first launched on its monetary career. Although coins enabled people to skip the measurement process and get right down to business, coins could serve this purpose only if they were genuine—they had to be worth precisely what their inscriptions represented them to be worth for this purpose.

Even at the very beginning, therefore, a widely accepted method for gauging the purity of gold and determining its weight was essential before gold could be used as money. Gold has acquired its own measuring system for these purposes, although versions of this system are now used on other precious metals and the most valuable jewels.

We define the purity of a piece of gold in terms of its carats. For example, 24-carat gold is 100 percent pure. Carat—the word derives from the Greek word *keration*, *qirat* in Arabic, and *carato* in Italian—was originally a measure of weight rather than purity, however, and for a delightful reason. Carats are the fruit of the leguminous carob tree, every single pod of which weighs one-fifth of a gram.

Today the carat has been replaced by the grain as the conventional unit of weight. Grains of barley or wheat in the middle of the ear have the same remarkable attributes as the carat—a standard weight regardless of the size of the ear. The troy ounce, which comes from the French town of Troyes where the measure was first put into use, weighs 480 grains, and twelve troy ounces equal one pound, which is the same as one sixteen-ounce pound avoirdupois. Thus, troy ounces are heavier than the ounces we are used to employing. The modern convention is to express the weight of gold in grains, but the price is expressed in troy ounces.

The Egyptians were casting gold bars as money as early as 4000 BC, each bar stamped with the name of the pharaoh Menes. The Egyptians even had a defined ratio between gold and silver. Throughout most of history, silver has been valued at only 5 percent to 8 percent of gold's value—ratios of 12 to 20 parts of silver to 1 part of gold—but the Egyptians set silver equal to 10 percent as much as gold because they had no indigenous silver supply.[4] It is also possible that the arithmetic was easier at that ratio, but we have no evidence of that. In any case, this step was the beginning of a complex, incestuous, and occasionally violent cohabitation of gold with silver in the money stock, a battle that haunts most of the history of gold as money.

The awkward process of weighing gold and checking its purity in every transaction sounds like more of a nuisance than it was in reality. These ancient civilizations bore a greater resemblance to the island of Yap than to an industrialized society like ours. When most property belonged to the monarch, when economic activity was primarily agricultural, and when transportation was so difficult that most communities were self-sufficient, long-range trade and commercial transactions were either rare or of minor importance.

As the need for money grows, it rapidly inspires innovation to make it function more efficiently and conveniently. The Assyrians and Babylonians were more active traders than the Egyptians, and they developed more elaborate and uniform gold bars. They stamped lions on the heavier bars, about thirty pounds in weight, and put ducks on the smaller bars that weighed about half as much. The lions and the ducks were a help in signifying value, but until about 600 BC people still wanted to weigh each piece of gold rather than accept the stamped indications at face value. The Mesopotamian peoples also broke their gold monies into smaller denominations known as talents, minas, and shekels; these denominations soon became common throughout Asia Minor and the Greek cities and settlements throughout the Mediterranean basin. The shekel has survived to this day in Israel.

The process of weighing the precious metals in each transaction was indeed a nuisance for everyone concerned, but these ancient arrangements had one great advantage that would vanish once coinage arrived upon the scene. When money was just pieces of metal of varying weights, it had no nationality. Even the Egyptian bars traded on the basis of their weights, not because they carried a pharaoh's name. In Chapter 38 of Genesis we read that Joseph's brothers sold him to total strangers from another land for thirty shekels of silver, without any concerns about rates of exchange or acceptability of the silver in the foreign country. Thus, while our ancient forebears functioned with the one form of money that was acceptable everywhere, modern experts—having experienced the original sin of national monies—dream of a supranational currency but have no idea how to implement it.*

The prosaic sequence of events that led from crude gold bars to a full-fledged system of coinage developed from a romantic and dramatic sequence of events that took place in the eastern part of Asia Minor, now Turkey. This story, which is admittedly part legend, begins in Phrygia, a kingdom whose capital city by that name was located on the banks of a small mountain torrent called the Pactolus. The first king of Phrygia, about 750 BC, was Gordius, a poor man with nothing to his name but a pair of oxen. Gordius was succeeded by his son Midas, thereby initiating a curious tradition for the Phrygian dynasty, who named themselves alternately Gordius and Midas.

This first King Midas was poor like his father, but we are told that he was a good man who wanted to be generous to others despite his poverty. One stranger whom Midas invited into his home turned out to be the foster father of Bacchus. Bacchus was so impressed with Midas's hospitality to his foster father that he granted the king any wish of his own choosing.

That irresistible offer was what got poor Midas into trouble. Midas's wish to have everything he touched turn to gold is usually held up as illustrating the dire consequences that stem from being overly greedy. Money isn't everything, as the saying goes. We should hesitate, however, before assuming that money was an obsession with Midas. If, according to the story, Midas inherited from his father Gordius nothing more than

*I am grateful for this insight to a sprightly and illuminating unpublished manuscript by Andrew Meadows, the curator of Greek coins at the British Museum.

two oxen, he must have been a poor man, especially for a king. If he was a good man, why then should we assume that he was greedy? Perhaps his wish simply reflected a desperate desire to find a shortcut out of his dire poverty, a choice made without regard to the consequences.

Midas discovered his error in short order. When his food turned to gold as he tried to eat it, and even his beloved daughter became a golden statue when he embraced her, Midas begged Bacchus to throw the damned wish into reverse. Bacchus must still have held a high opinion of Midas, for he immediately obliged by instructing Midas to bathe in the Pactolus River. Midas thereby transferred his golden touch to the Pactolus, the legend continues, which is why that river turned out to be such a rich source of gold for the Phrygians and their close neighbors the Lydians. Midas thereby ended up with the best of both possible worlds—the gold in the Pactolus made him rich, but he was once more able to eat and touch his loved ones without turning everything and everybody into solid gold. The actual location of the Pactolus is no longer visible, but geographers believe that it was a stream carrying alluvial gold from the slopes of Mount Tmolus in Anatolia. By the time the Romans took over this area, perhaps half a millennium later, the mountain had been eroded by rushing water and had no more gold to yield.

Midas did not live happily ever after. The Cimmerians, a powerful nomadic tribe from southern Russia, invaded Phrygia and overthrew Midas, who committed suicide by taking poison to escape the savage hordes at his gates. Midas was not forgotten, however, for his chariot remained tied to a post by a complex knot in the main temple of Gordium for three hundred years. An oracle predicted that whoever could untie the knot would become king of Asia; this was none other than the Gordian knot that young Alexander of Macedon would cut through with his sword in 334 BC, on his way to conquer the lands all the way from Egypt to India.[5]

Most of the reliable history about this area of Asia Minor, as opposed to blends of fact and fiction, comes down to us from Herodotus, the Greek historian who lived around 500 BC. Herodotus's *Histories* comprised the first extended narrative in prose in Western civilization and set a tough act for later historians to follow. He emerges from these accounts as consistently perceptive, wise, and entertaining, with a sharp eye for gossip as well as the foibles of the characters whose chronicles he chose to record.

Herodotus's history begins in about 700 BC in Lydia, an area to the northwest of Phrygia; Lydia occupied most of the center of Asia Minor from the Aegean Sea inland approximately two hundred miles.[6] Sardis, the capital city, had the good fortune of sitting on great supplies of alluvial gold, most of which streamed down from the mountains into the Pactolus River—thanks presumably to Midas. Lydia also mined a metal called electrum, often referred to as "white gold," which was about two-thirds gold and one-third silver. The word derives from the ancient Greek word *Ηλεκτωρ* (elector), which means "he who shines" (the Greek word for sun is *Helio*, as in heliotrope) and is the root from which we derive the modern word *electric.* With all that wealth bestowed upon them, the Lydians frequently engaged in wild orgiastic dances in honor of Cybele, the goddess of the mountains and guardian of ores and metals.[7]

According to Herodotus, the kings of Lydia traced their ancestry from Hercules and had ruled for 22 generations, or 550 years, at which time their king was named Candaules. Candaules was madly in love with his beautiful wife. He was also a show-off. One day he hid with his favorite bodyguard Gyges to give Gyges the opportunity of observing the lady undress and display her lovely body. Unknown to the two men, the queen noticed what had happened. She called Gyges to her the next day and told him that either the man who had planned this violation must die or the man who had illegally seen her nakedness must perish. She let Gyges choose between making the event legal by killing his king and then marrying her and leading the kingdom, or being killed immediately by her instead. That choice is what is known today as a no-brainer.[8] And so began the dynasty known by the tongue-twisting title of Mermnadae.

Although the Lydians were outraged at the murder of their king, Gyges persuaded them to wait to hear what the oracle at Delphi had to say on the matter. The oracle declared in favor of Gyges, perhaps not coincidentally because of the generous gifts of gold and silver that he subsequently lavished upon her, including six golden bowls that weighed about eighteen hundred pounds (over $6 million at today's prices).

Nevertheless, the oracle also predicted that Gyges's dynasty would perish in the fifth generation, when Candaules's descendants would finally claim their revenge on the Mermnadae. Gyges and the Lydians took little notice of her prophecy—at that moment.

The first three descendants of Gyges—Ardys, Sadyattes, and Alyattes—ruled for a total of 118 years, of which 57 were accounted for by Alyattes alone.* These three kings of Lydia spent most of their time making war on their southern and western neighbors in an effort to extend their domain to all of western Asia Minor out to the Ionian coast of the Aegean, although Ardys (660–637 BC), like Midas, had his hands full holding off the invading Cimmerians. Unlike most empire-builders through history, however, the Mermnadae refrained for the most part from destroying the homes and holy places of the defeated peoples, who were also left to enjoy loyal autonomy. The Lydian kings simply wanted monetary tribute and assured supplies of food and other materials, reasoning that they would be better off with a peaceful empire than one filled with people eager to take revenge against them.

Croesus, son of Alyattes and the great-great grandson of Gyges, ascended the throne in 568 BC at the age of 35.[9] This Croesus was the man who most people wished they were as rich as, which was a good thing, but he was also the fifth generation of the Mermnadae, which was an unfortunate thing. Regardless of the double-talk usually offered by the oracle at Delphi, the prediction the oracle gave to Gyges about the fifth generation being the last would turn out to be correct. Nevertheless, during his reign, Croesus completed most of the conquests that his predecessors had begun. He succeeded in occupying nearly all of western Turkey, including Phrygia, and even made an alliance with the Spartans on the Peleponnesus.[10]

Herodotus tells some entertaining stories about Croesus. The most revealing involved a visit by Solon, who had just written a code of laws for the Athenians, who promised to obey them for ten years. Solon took those ten years off to go sightseeing. When he arrived at Sardis, Croesus was impatient to show him the treasury with its immense wealth in gold. Then he turned to Solon, asking whether Solon had so far seen anybody,

*For a fascinating description of the great burial mounds of Alyattes and possibly of Gyges, see Tassel, 1998.

in all his far-flung travels, whom he considered to be "more fortunate than all men." Solon mentioned a great war hero of Athens and a couple of prizewinning athletes and their devoted mother. Dumbfounded, Croesus exclaimed, "As far as you are concerned, our prosperity amounts to nothing, and you do not even consider us on a par with private citizens!"

Solon agreed. "When you ask me about human affairs," he replied, "you ask someone who knows how jealous and provocative god is. . . . My dear Croesus, humans are the creatures of pure chance." He admitted that rich men can gratify their desires and have the resources to absorb misfortune, but he then pointed out that the lucky man does not have to concern himself with misfortune: "He suffers no bodily harm, he doesn't get sick . . . he has good children, and he is handsome."[11]

Herodotus tells us that the Lydians "are the first people we know of to mint and use gold coins and silver coins, and they were the first retail tradesmen."[12] Sardis had a marketplace with a cluster of small shops offering a wide variety of goods ranging from meat and grain to jewelry and musical instruments. Herodotus had a word for this: καπηλοι (*kapeloi*), which translated literally means "merchant" or "seller"; in Greek slang, it means "man with a big hat" and could be read in more modern terms as "huckster."* The Lydians were so busy converting almost everything into salable merchandise that, as Herodotus reports, "Except for prostituting their female children, the Lydians observe the same customs as the Greeks."[13] As the women accumulated coinage, however, they created their own dowries and as a result had unusual freedom in choosing their husbands.

These Lydian innovations in the development of money and trade were no coincidence. In addition to its location on the banks of the Pactolus, streaming with alluvial gold, the Lydian capital of Sardis sat astride the great east–west highway that linked the Aegean Sea to the Euphrates and more distant Asia, a span of nearly seventeen hundred

*Was this the equivalent of Napoleon's derogatory characterization of the English as a nation of shopkeepers?

miles.[14] Trade and commercial activities were a natural development, and they brought with them the need for weights and measures and, most important of all, money in a convenient form for doing business. Money, in turn, created a demand for goldsmiths, money changers, and ultimately bankers. Sardis grew into a major urban center filled with wealthy families living in the highest luxury.

One ingenious Lydian innovation was the use of a local black stone, similar to jasper, for testing the purity of the lumps of gold received in payment for commercial transactions. This stone came to be known as the touchstone, because goldsmiths rubbed gold objects against it and then compared the mark against a set of 24 needles containing varying proportions of gold and silver, gold and copper, and all three metals. The 24th needle was pure gold, just as 24 carats measure pure gold.* All of this contributed to the development of a well-functioning coinage system, but we cannot appreciate what the Lydians accomplished and what Croesus in particular achieved without a brief step backward about 150 years.

At the beginning of the seventh century BC, Lydian money consisted of bean-shaped lumps of electrum, called *dumps*. These dumps were too heavy for easy exchanges, as they had no uniformity in size or weight and bore no stamp to indicate their value.[15]

Gyges, the first of the Mermnadae, made a revolutionary reform in Lydia when he suppressed private issuance of metallic money (primarily electrum) and established a state monopoly over the issuance of dumps. The official monopoly of the state over the creation of money has persisted throughout history. Article I, Section 8 of the Constitution of the United States, for example, declares that "The Congress shall have power to coin money, regulate the value thereof, and of foreign coin." These concepts dominated the control of money supplies—note the U.S. reference to "coin"—as long as money was hard, but they began to diminish in importance as we progressed to modern times.[16] The development of negotiable credit instruments during the late Middle Ages and the increasing use of commercial bank liabilities as money—the modern checking account—bypassed the state's monopoly over the creation of money and diluted the importance of gold as a means of

*A century later, a Greek philosopher named Chillon observed that "Gold is tried with a touchstone, and men by gold" (Kemmerer, 1944, p. 178).

payment for daily transactions. The role assigned to gold gradually changed into a kind of governor of the monetary system, a backing that was intended to set limits on the issuance of all other forms of money.

When Ardys succeeded Gyges on the throne in 660 BC, he too was interested in creating a more efficient monetary system. He began stamping the electrum ingots with marks to guarantee their weight and value, providing different ingots for different folks: Lydia had one set, the Babylonian towns to the east had a different set, and the Ionian coast towns to the west still another.[17] In time, however, the dumps became more uniform in size, and less than fifty years passed before the lumps and dumps became recognizable coins: round, uniform, and clearly stamped. A lion's head—the logo for the dynasty launched by Gyges—appeared on every one of them. The innovation spread rapidly in a western direction toward Greece, where coinage soon became an integral part of a system of rapidly developing trade all around the Mediterranean basin. If the Lydians were the first people to invent and use coins, the Greeks were the first to make coinage an art form; for the Greeks, beauty was an aim in designing money as much as it was in virtually everything else they touched.

The story is probably only a rough approximation of what actually happened, for nothing that took place that long ago is ever beyond controversy. Some modern experts had believed that full-fledged Lydian coinage originated before 700 BC, perhaps fifty years earlier than that, even though Herodotus had set 687 BC as his estimate of the date. But in 1951, a group of archeologists working in the great Ionian city of Ephesus came upon a huge hoard of Lydian money buried under the ruins of the temple of Artemis, which had been built about 600 BC. Over three thousand items came into view, including unstamped dumps, stamped dumps, and a mass of coins with the lion's head struck upon them, in addition to a substantial pile of jewelry and statuettes fashioned of gold and silver. Careful examination confirmed that the first true coins dated from around 635 BC, which in turn confirmed that Herodotus was right in the first place and should not have been doubted.[18] This dating would place the beginning of coinage around the end of the reign of Ardys, the son of Gyges, or at the beginning of the reign of his son, Sadyattes.

Croesus played the climactic role in this process. Although we shall see that he turned out to be a disaster as a military strategist, thereby fulfilling the oracle's prophecy about the fifth member of the Mermnadae, he was a master innovator when it came to monetary affairs and in his appreciation of the economic and political power packed into the precious metals. He was not kidding with Solon: he was convinced that money and happiness were inseparable.

Croesus's father Alyattes had been the first of the line to issue gold coins, which developed into a lucrative source of exports for Lydia and paid for much of their imports; the Lydian standard of living thereby enjoyed the advantages of trading something useless for something useful. Recognizing the value of these gold coins to his country's prosperity, Croesus called in all the outstanding electrum coins, melted them down, and minted new coins in the new style of pure silver and gold. In 1964, modern archeologists succeeded in uncovering the fire-resistant pots where Croesus's men extracted the impurities from the gold and silver from electrum by heating the metals with a mixture of lead and salt—a method that has not been found in excavations elsewhere.[19]

The coins of Croesus were stamped on one side with the foreparts of a lion and a bull, the arms of the city of Sardis. The opposite side had oblong and square punch marks, or depressions—the technical numismatic expression is that the coins were "incused"—to show their value. Most important, Croesus made the denominations and weights of his new coins conform as closely as possible to the weights and denominations of the old currency. The basic denomination, already familiar to everyone in that area of the world, was called the stater, which was subdivided into smaller denominations of thirds, sixths, and twelfths. The coins were minted with great care in order to maintain the uniformity of their size and weight.[20] As a result, they were immediately acceptable throughout his kingdom. The division of the staters into twelfths carried forward to the development of the troy ounce, composed of 24 carats of pure gold, and reappears again in the English shilling, which—until the relatively recent conversion into the decimal system—consisted of twelve pennies.

In the process of putting his reform into action, Croesus had launched the bimetallic currency system that would prevail in most countries over most of subsequent history. The silver coins were needed to serve as the denominations that were too small for the use of gold; most of the gold was used to finance foreign trade. Like the Egyptians, Croesus set the ratio of gold to silver at 10:1 as a matter of convenience, although he made no legal ruling to that effect.[21] This bimetallic system had its useful features, but, as we have seen, monetary systems based on two metals were seldom stable, because changing supplies of the two metals over time caused their relative values to fluctuate.

Nevertheless, when his reform was complete, Croesus had established the first imperial currency in the history of the world. His beautiful coins of gold and silver were immediately accepted—indeed, demanded—throughout Asia Minor and were circulated in Greece on the western side of the Aegean as well. This universally accepted currency played a critically important role in adding to the entire area's prosperity and economic development: it stimulated trade both within the Lydian Empire and with the nations to the east, west, and south, which in turn encouraged the free interchange of people and ideas.[22] Croesus's accomplishment was equivalent to the establishment of the euro in western Europe in our time. If that revolutionary step of creating a common currency for communities that had always had their own money can succeed, the euro will have achieved precisely what Croesus had consummated: increased trade within Europe and with the rest of the world, with populations more mobile, and enjoying a robust rate of economic growth.

By the time he was done, Croesus had created a great innovation that has reverberated through history up to our own era. It was not just the establishment of a rational, systematic, and widely acceptable form of money, a step that was momentous in its own right. There were many other materials that he could have used as a base for his monetary system—copper, shells, or beads, for example. The focus on gold and silver, however, transformed those metals into the ultimate standards of wealth and money. In time, these attributes would prove to be more valuable than the reverence accorded them as objects of religious worship or as articles of beauty.

Fifteen years into his reign, Croesus began to worry about the growing power of the Persians, whose king Cyrus had already led his troops into the eastern parts of Asia Minor along the shores of the Black Sea. Croesus was well aware of Cyrus's expectation to gain great economic power as well as valuable territory by subduing the Lydians.

Croesus decided that he should take the offensive and cut down the Persian power before it became invincible. Under similar circumstances, most leaders throughout history have sat down with their generals and other advisors and mapped out a strategy to confront the approaching enemy. Not Croesus. Rational and ingenious when it came to money and gold, Croesus worked out his military strategy by consulting oracles; he sent messengers to the oracle in Delphi, to six other Greek oracles, and even to one in Libya. He tested the forecasting accuracy of the oracles by instructing each messenger to count one hundred days from their departure, visit the oracle, and ask the oracle what Croesus was doing on that day. He then chose something to do that he was convinced no one would be able to guess: he chopped up a turtle and a lamb and boiled them together in a bronze pot.

When all the messengers had returned with the responses of the various oracles, he was astonished that one of them had actually guessed right: the oracle in Delphi. Croesus had always been partial to that oracle, because it had legitimized the reign of his great-great grandfather Gyges. The Delphic oracle prophesied that Croesus would be eating "strong-shelled tortoise seething in bronze with the flesh of lambs."[23]

Croesus lost no time in plying the oracle with gifts, including 117 ingots of pure gold, each weighing 150 pounds, to say nothing of a lion of pure gold that weighed six hundred pounds, plus a golden vat of 522 pounds that could hold five thousand gallons for mixing wine and water. He also ordered all Lydians to make a sacrifice for the oracle. The oracle, in return, conducted business with Croesus in thoroughly modern fashion. Croesus received "rights of first consultation without a fee, front-row seats at Pythian games and festivals, and the right, in perpetuity, for any Lydian who so desired to become a citizen of Delphi."[24] That is a literal quote from Herodotus.

The oracle also advised Croesus that if he made war on Cyrus, he would "destroy a great empire." Happy and confident, Croesus took off to do battle with the Persians, even though they outnumbered his forces.

The first engagement was a fierce one but ended in a standoff. Croesus figured he had better withdraw to Sardis and wait until he could gather his allies before attacking Cyrus a second time. Cyrus, aware of Croesus's intentions, hurried toward Sardis, forcing Croesus to face him on the great plain that lies before the city. When Cyrus saw that Croesus had placed his powerful cavalry in the front ranks, he transferred his own horsemen to the camels usually employed in carrying food and equipment. Horses are afraid of camels and cannot stand the sight or the smell of them. The Lydian cavalry was thrown into confusion by the camel charge and the whole Lydian army had to retreat into the city, where they suffered a siege that lasted fourteen days before the Persians finally broke through and claimed victory. The Delphic oracle had got it right again: a mighty empire had been destroyed, but it was the empire of Croesus that fell, not the empire of the Persians.

Cyrus decided to celebrate his victory by burning Croesus at the stake as an offering to the Persian gods. As the flames were mounting, the soldiers heard Croesus call out the word *Solon* three times. When asked what he meant, Croesus told them that Solon was "a man I would give a great fortune to see talking with all the tyrants of the earth." Cyrus was so moved by what Croesus told him about Solon's visit that he ordered the fire put out and Croesus untied. As they sat together as friends, Cyrus pointed out to Croesus that the crowd they could see in the distance was "looting [his] city and carrying off [his] wealth." Croesus still had his wits about him, despite all he had been through. "It's not my city or my wealth they are looting," he pointed out. "None of it is mine anymore. What they are looting and leading away belongs to you."[25]

With those poignant words, Croesus fades from view.

The most challenging feature of the Croesus story is in its curious intermixture of luck and skill. Croesus was lucky enough to rule a domain on the banks of the Pactolus, blessed by Midas with an apparently endless supply of gold. As Solon reminded him, "Humans are the creatures of pure chance." Croesus was also helplessly superstitious in the critically important role of military commander-in-chief. Yet he was a masterful ruler and a memorable innovator in finance who launched gold on its long career as money. He may not have earned the assets he deployed, but he used them to his greatest advantage.

There is a sour current observation about lucky people like the Lydians: that they were born on third base and thought they had hit a triple. J. Kenneth Galbraith has phrased the same thing more eloquently: "Men possessed of money, like men earlier favoured by noble birth and great title, have infallibly imagined that the awe and admiration that money inspires were really owing to their own wisdom or personality."[26] Galbraith's characteristically acerbic wit contains much truth, but Croesus and the Lydians may be the exception that proves his rule. The political and financial innovations of the Lydians were remarkable enough in their own time. Viewed from the perspective of the 2500 years since the death of Croesus, however, their accomplishments were truly extraordinary. It was their wisdom and personality that inspired the awe and admiration for their money, not the other way around. Most important, they demonstrated that you don't have to be bad just because you are rich.

Other nations in the past had conquered their neighbors but never with the benign touch of the Lydians. Other nations in the past had developed monetary systems but never with the systematic structure and wide acceptability of the Lydian currency. The Greeks, the Persians, the Romans, and ultimately the nations of Europe and the New World all walked in the footsteps of the imperial Lydians, and most of them with a far heavier tread. Although the sun may never have set on Queen Victoria's global empire of the late nineteenth century, the Lydian model defined the character and even the shape of the political and economic relationships between the center and the colonies, including the colonial financial assets that were accumulated in deposits in the London banks and were both denominated and transacted in sterling.

Nevertheless, without the Midas touch, the Lydians might have been nobodies. As the economists like to say, the gold was probably a necessary even if not a sufficient condition for their ascendancy. The origins of Lydian power and dominance—indeed, their views of their earthly mission—were rooted in the golden fruits of the Pactolus River and the electrum ores that coursed through the mountains around them. Other nations in other times have set out on conquests to become rich; the Lydians achieved their empire in large part because they were rich—as rich as Croesus.

3

Darius's Bathtub and the Cackling of the Geese

The defeat of the Lydians by the Persians greatly accelerated the transformation of gold from a means of adornment into a central role as money. Despite their remarkable innovations in coinage, the Lydians thought that it was their gold, not their money, that mattered. When Solon came to visit, Croesus did not say, "Look how much money I have!" He showed Solon his "treasure." Nor did he use his handsome golden stater coins to compensate the oracles whose services he so voraciously consumed. He sent them gifts of magnificent objects crafted from gold. Nevertheless, the services the oracles offered in return, such as rights of first consultation without a fee and front-row seats at the Pythian games, would normally be forthcoming today only in response to a monetary accommodation.

That viewpoint was soon to come about. Croesus's ingeniously designed monetary system would lead to a profound social transformation, although he was totally unaware of the genie that he was letting out of the bottle. The radiant purity, malleability, and density that made gold so appropriate for objects of worship—including its general uselessness for anything other than adornment—were precisely the attributes that made it such an extraordinarily convenient material for coins.

The result was the development of a curious kind of feedback in the role of gold in society. Gold would never have attained its position as supreme monarch of monetary systems without its unique physical attributes, yet the demand for gold became so insatiable over time because it *was* used as money. The demand for gold to embellish religious objects and our own bodies has a limit somewhere; the demand for gold as money is infinite. This has caused all kinds of havoc throughout history, as men were provoked to risk the wildest deeds in search of new sources of gold or to plunder the supplies that belonged to others.

In a sense, the transformation of gold into money democratized it. Thanks to coinage, the ownership and use of gold after Lydia was no longer a royal prerogative. It was now literally in the hands of common citizens, even if only the most wealthy, who could touch and feel it, hoard it in their homes, buy things with it, and pay their debts with it—even as they continued to put their gold through their ears and noses and to wrap it around their necks, wrists, and fingers. Before long, they would be paying their taxes with it. The notions of power and wealth thus blended into one.

The Greeks provide a moving example of the merging of gold as adornment and gold as money. In accord with the tradition that gold imparts godliness to inanimate objects, Phidias clothed his great statue of Athena in the Parthenon in a cloak of gold, even though gold was much rarer than silver in Greece. This cloak was, in effect, the official treasure of the city-state of Athens, in full display for all to see, unlike the U.S. gold stock buried in Fort Knox—that is, until the wars with Sparta, when the Athenians had to peel the golden treasure from their goddess and convert it into money to finance their military operations.[1]

Although Greek coinage was primarily silver, the use of Lydian-style gold coins proliferated elsewhere and ultimately provided the model for the coinage system that would function throughout the entire Roman Empire. Long before Rome, however, Cyrus (558–529 BC), the victor over Croesus at Sardis, and his successor, Darius (521–485 BC), had promptly adopted Croesus's international system of coinage and put it into operation throughout the great Persian Empire. Darius also outdid Croesus and his staters: instead of a local logo, Darius stamped his own likeness on his coins and labeled them darics. But then a monarch who calls himself the King of Kings would be likely to do something like that.

Darius's money—and his likeness—spread far and wide. His coinage has been found from the Baltic to Africa and throughout central Asia. In addition to using their gold to mint coins that financed trade across such a wide span of lands, the Persian government was also the first in history to collect taxes in coin rather than in kind.[2] The world has never been the same. In fact, the kinds of money that governments have been willing to accept in payment of taxes throughout history have been a primary influence on what forms of money become most acceptable to society at large. We shall see instances in which even debased money with minimal purchasing power has enjoyed some broad acceptability when governments have permitted their citizens to use it to discharge their tax liabilities.

The Persians emulated the Lydian system of coinage with great success, but they also knew how to use gold as a manifestation of power. For example, after Alexander the Great had finally smashed the Persian Empire by defeating the King of Kings at Issus in 331 BC, he entered Darius's huge field tent and examined the golden chariot, the golden throne, and the golden bathtub, all elaborate objects of great beauty—and these were only Darius's traveling equipment. "So this is what it meant to be a king," observed Alexander.[3]

Impressed as he may have been by Darius's golden bathtub, Alexander was already fully familiar with the use of gold as money as well as for adornment. Some time after 360 BC, Alexander's father, Philip II of Macedon, had opened up rich sources of gold and silver in Macedonia and Thrace—northward in the Balkans toward modern Bulgaria—and was soon minting both metals into coins in sufficient number to meet all his current needs and to finance his plans for future military conquests.[4]

Establishing substantial monetary wealth was just one of this brilliant man's achievements in the course of transforming the backwater countryside of Macedonia into the greatest power of his age. If Philip were alive today, he would be in constant demand as an expert consultant on both the economics and the politics of developing nations. He had an innate sense of priorities, of how to set his ideas in motion in the most effective and efficient manner, and of how to deploy power to maximum advantage.

When Philip ascended the throne of Macedon in 359 BC at the age of 23, his mountainous kingdom consisted of a small population of mixed tribes, who were poorly fed and occupied their time primarily by making war against one another. By the time Philip was through, he had established Macedonia as a great power and himself as the dominant personality in all of Greece, even though many Athenians considered him a provincial upstart.

He began where he should have begun: with agriculture. Through irrigation, canal construction, land drainage, and flood control, he turned the alluvial plains of his kingdom into a breadbasket. His ample and growing food supply helped him make peace among his pesky constituency, attracted a growing population of southern Greeks, led to the building of new towns, and provided an expanding pool of manpower for his armies. In addition to feeding the increasing populations, Philip's agricultural reforms significantly enhanced Macedonia's military power by generating feed and pasture for horses and cattle. Like the German panzers, Philip's abundance of horses would give his army fearsome mobility in combat. In addition, the meat from the cattle gave his men strength and endurance over his enemies, a feature that attracted Napoleon's attention many centuries later. His local campaigns around Macedonia also augmented that absolutely essential economic resource: slaves—slaves to work the mines, slaves to work the fields, slaves to keep the whole economy humming.*

Philip also made full preparation for his succession, hiring Aristotle from Athens to tutor his son Alexander from the ages of thirteen to sixteen, the equivalent of sending the young teenager to Harvard as an undergraduate and Cambridge or Oxford for graduate work. When Philip was assassinated in 336 BC, after a reign of 23 years, Alexander reminded his people that "My father took you as nomads and paupers, wearing sheepskins, pasturing a few sheep on the mountains . . . he made you inhabitants of cities and brought good order, law, and customs into your lives."

*Slaves really mattered. At its height, the population of Athens amounted to about five hundred thousand people, of whom 350,000 were slaves.

Philip set the value of his gold coins at ten times the value of his silver coins, a convenient piece of arithmetic that differed from the unwieldy Persian ratio of 13½:1; his choice also probably reflects the relative increase in gold supplies from newly discovered mines. He decorated his highest-value coins on one side with a chariot to celebrate his victory in the chariot race at the Olympic games of 356 BC, and with a head of Zeus on the other side; many wondered whether that head was Zeus's or really Philip's.

Philip's keen financial instinct led him to produce more coins than he needed for current transactions and army pay. He hoarded the balance as a reserve to finance the wide-ranging military campaigns against the Persians that were on the drawing boards at the time of his assassination.

After Philip was killed and Alexander inherited the throne from his father, he kept all of Philip's Macedonian mints busy pouring out coinage, in addition to the output of mints in Greece, Asia Minor, Syria, Egypt, and Mesopotamia. Supplying gold and silver to feed the mints was no problem. In addition to Philip's hoard and the current output of the Macedonian and Thracian mines, Alexander captured huge amounts of treasure during the course of his victorious campaigns to the east. Alexander followed his father's policy of making gold the prime monetary standard, and, being a man of action and splitter of Gordian knots, he stayed with the 10:1 relationship, adjusting the supplies of each metal from his substantial reserves in order to make the simple ratio function without difficulty throughout his immense empire.

Although Alexander had so much gold available to him that he could afford to be prolific in minting coins, the demand for coins ran high. Alexander wanted to be certain that his men would find his coinage acceptable, no matter where they were serving. The troops under his command were primarily mercenaries, and he paid them well to discourage them from looting. He paid many of their civilian debts, gave wedding presents of money to some troops, and distributed separation bonuses when they went home. In his vision of himself as a bearer of Greek civilization rather than as a conqueror, Alexander also brought along with him scientists, engineers, and explorers, and these people had to be paid as well. In addition, he expanded his civilian rule over conquered territories by establishing more than seventy new towns in a great arc from Egypt to India; this, too, created an additional demand for acceptable money. Finally, his vision included prosperous trade among the many areas of his diversified empire, an objective that needed a common currency. Alexander was convinced that trade would promise higher living standards for all.

Alexander and Philip both understood the propaganda and public relations value of gold coinage. Whereas Philip's *philippeioi* had the head of Zeus stamped upon them, Alexander stepped down a notch. He used Hercules, a god ranking below Zeus but symbolizing the greatest physical strength; like Philip's Zeus, the portrait of Hercules stamped on the coins bore a striking resemblance to Alexander himself. Alexander did not change the name of the gold coins established by his father: they remained *philippeioi*. His followers, however, kept Alexander's designs but changed the name of the coins from *philippeioi* to *alexanders*!

Alexander's coinage system prevailed for over 150 years, from India in the east to most of the Greek and Egyptian areas to the west, until the Roman general Quinctius Flaminius defeated Philip V at Cynocophalae in 197 BC and brought closure to the Macedonian hegemony. Flaminius had learned his monetary lessons well: his first step to commemorate his victory was to transform some of Philip's tribute into new gold coins bearing his portrait—the first time a living person had appeared on Roman coins.

The Romans had been using metallic money for a long time. During the fourth century BC, they were in the habit of keeping their treasure in the temple of Jupiter. This choice was made for the purpose of security, but it was also an interesting blend of temporal wealth and heavenly religion. In 390 BC, so the legend runs, the cackling of the geese that lived around the temple alerted the Romans to a surprise attack by the Gauls, who were invading Italy at that point. The Romans were so grateful for this notice of impending danger that they constructed a shrine to their goddess of warning, whose name was Moneta; *moneta* in turn became the derivation of "money" and of "mint."[5]

That was not all in the way of money that we have inherited from the Romans. The Romans also gave us the monetary denomination of pound—*libra*—which is why the pound sterling is identified by the symbol £. In addition, the Latin word *denarius* came to stand for penny and was conventionally abbreviated as *d* in English usage. Finally, the term *solidus*, which meant that a coin was pure gold or silver, was worth one-twentieth of a pound of silver and was equivalent to twelve *denari*. English money was built up from these ratios. A pound was equal to twenty shillings and a shilling was equal to twelve pence—a system that lasted from Norman times until the 1970s, when Britain finally yielded and adopted the decimal denominations long in use everywhere else.*

Although the Romans may have started using the word *moneta* in 390 BC, their gold stock at that moment was small. The Elder Pliny mentions an amount in the Roman treasury that contained less than half the gold that Phidias had lavished fifty years earlier on his statue of Athena in the Parthenon and only one-seventh as much as Croesus had delivered to the oracle at Delphi 150 years earlier. Even as the Romans opened up additional gold supplies by extending their territories, and even when their victory over Carthage in the Punic Wars brought them control over the massive reserves of gold in the Spanish mountainsides, they still perceived gold as a reserve but not as something spendable.[6]

The Roman need for gold grew rapidly after about 150 BC as the empire expanded at an accelerated pace, which meant rising military requirements at the same time. Gibbon's *The History of the Decline and Fall of the Roman Empire* reports, "The golden eagle which glittered in front of the legion, was the object of their fondest devotion; nor was it esteemed less impious, than it was ignominious, to abandon that sacred ensign in the hour of danger."[7] Later, he tells us, "The Emperor Domitian [who ruled from 81 to 96] raised the annual stipend of the legionaries to twelve pieces of gold, which, in his time, was equal to about ten of our guineas."[8] Ten guineas in Gibbon's time was the equivalent of about $53, or roughly $2500 in 1999 purchasing power—but

*The British made a stab at decimalization in 1847, when they introduced a two-shilling coin called the florin; the florin was thus one-tenth of a pound. This coin continued to circulate along with its slightly larger near-cousin, the half crown, which was equal to two shillings sixpence. There were no crown coins at that time or thereafter.

there was far less to buy in Roman times and a soldier received shelter, food, and medical care in addition to compensation. Hence, $2500 was a generous annual stipend.

Indeed, the Romans used coinage-money to a far greater extent than any of their predecessors in history. Thousands of soldiers throughout the empire had to be paid, and some Roman generals even minted their own gold coins to distribute to their troops. Furthermore, bread and circuses did not come for free, but promoting domestic tranquility among the Roman *politii* was essential if emperors hoped to remain in power. The doles were distributed in cash on occasion, but even the more frequent payments in kind, the *alimenta*, or bread rations, were largely imported from outside Italy and had to be paid for with coinage.

These recurrent and growing needs for coins were accompanied by an increasing demand for replacement coinage as many coins simply disappeared, some worn beyond usefulness as coins, some in shipwrecks, and some due to plunder by barbarians. A significant amount of gold went to the East in exchange for spices from India and silks that took a circuitous route but that originated in China; once the metal arrived in India, it stayed there and did not return to the channels of trade.[9] At the same time, the highest-quality ore was being depleted, so the level of mining activity had to expand even more rapidly than the need for metal to mint.

There seemed to be no limits to the demand for gold. After Caesar conquered Gaul, the Romans imported over one hundred thousand slaves from that territory to work the mines in Italy, to say nothing of the slaves they employed to work away their short lives as miners within Gaul itself. We have already seen how the Romans used slaves to exploit the mineral riches of Spain, at a level of cruelty and disdain for the environment that readily matched the appalling record of the Egyptians.

Wealthy Romans showed off to one another by generously lavishing gold on their bodies, their women, and their homes, but they measured their wealth by their accumulations of gold coins. In the Roman Republic, and the empire that followed, golden money was essential to grease the way to political power. Unlike all the monarchies that had ruled nations since the beginning of time, in Rome it was how much gold you had, rather than who your father was, that defined how much say you had in the affairs of state. How much you had to say, in turn, defined how much bribery and other loot came your way from others in similar pursuit of power and riches.

For example, when Julius Caesar returned from service in Spain as *quaestor* (provincial official for financial affairs), he had harvested sufficient Spanish gold to buy him attention as a leader, but not enough to take him as far as he had hoped to go. He therefore combined his interests with two other ambitious Roman citizens, one a fabulously rich man named Crassus and the other a military commander named Pompey.

Crassus had begun accumulating his fortune by organizing a fire brigade that put out fires only if paid in advance. In those cases where the owner failed to pay and the building was destroyed by fire, Crassus would buy up the burned-down ruin at a fraction of its worth as a standing structure. He acquired a large number of tenements in this fashion, restored them, and let them out at fancy rents.[10] In addition, Crassus lent money at interest and acquired ownership of silver mines, agricultural estates, and slaves in great numbers. He even educated his slaves to become readers, stewards, and cooks.[11] The huge income that accrued to Crassus from all this wealth enabled him to bribe officials so that he could buy up additional confiscated estates at depressed prices.

Although Pompey ended up with his head cut off, in all likelihood as a result of a contract on him taken out by Caesar, Crassus was destined for an even more horrible end. Crassus was eager to show that he was more than a moneybags and that, like Pompey and Caesar, he could successfully command troops in battle. Accordingly, he provoked a war with the Parthians in Mesopotamia and set off on his campaign with 44,000 troops under his command, foot soldiers for the most part. At the battle of Carrhae in 53 BC, the Parthians attacked the Romans with ten thousand horse archers and a corps of one thousand Arabian camels, making quick work of the job at hand. Crassus attempted to negotiate a surrender, but the Parthians set upon his troops with such ferocity that only ten thousand of the original forty thousand managed to escape. For Crassus, the Parthians reserved a special fate that expressed their disdain for the money-mad Roman civilization that he represented. They finished him off by pouring molten gold down his throat.[12]

Up to this point in our story, the supply of gold has been taken for granted or the opening up of new supplies more or less kept pace as the demand for gold expanded. The Jews escaping from slavery, the Egyptians, the Lydians, the Persians, and Philip and Alexander all appear to have had enough gold to do with it whatever struck their fancy, from crafting objects of worship and beautification to coining elegant coins as means of exchange and stores of wealth. From today's perspective, we can see that they were in the happy position of owning an indefatigable printing press bestowed upon them by nature, whose output, because it happened to be shiny, dense, and malleable into beautiful things, was accepted without question everywhere.

Now everything changes. With an empire that reached from the Mediterranean to the Black Sea, and from the border of Scotland to the southernmost areas of Egypt, the Romans found that their supply of gold for coinage constantly fell short of their needs despite mining output of at least five tons a year.[13] Quite aside from governmental expenditures that had to be financed, the emperors spent money on themselves with a degree of abandon that their citizens could only envy. Yet nature sets the ceiling on the supply of gold and silver: you cannot create metal out of nothing. The alchemists in later times were to learn that lesson over and over again.

A society that uses metal for money will always be constrained by the supply of that metal. The random location of mineral deposits makes countries such as Lydia rich as a matter of good luck and other countries greedy for gold as a consequence of bad luck. History teaches us that natural advantages are not an automatic formula for success, but having a head start endowed by nature never did anybody any harm.

When a nation's supply of metal is insufficient to meet the needs for coinage, and, in many instances, even when coins are no longer the only acceptable form of money and paper substitutes are in use, there are three ways out. One is to live with an insufficient supply of money, so the demand for goods at current prices chronically falls short of the supply of goods offered for sale, and downward pressures on the price level persist over extended periods of time. This painful process has often occurred as a default solution, with dire political and social consequences. The Great Depression of the 1930s is the most vivid but by no means the only example of this policy that we shall encounter in later pages.

A second method of overcoming a shortage of monetary metals is to import gold from other areas, either by plunder or by trade. These solutions have motivated both great adventures and complex economic policies, not always with happy outcomes. The third method is the simplest but is unlikely to be successful over the long run, namely, to use the same amount of metal to produce a greater supply of coins.

That solution is known as debasing the currency, which used to mean literally reducing the metallic base from which coins are minted, or mixing base metal with the precious metal, while leaving the face value unchanged. Over the years, debasement has come to mean any irresponsible, or at least ill-advised, effort to create new money out of nothing—a process at which governments have become increasingly ingenious with the passage of time. All three of these approaches will occupy our attention in the pages that follow.

The monetary innovation of debasement has a long history. For example, Dionysius of Syracuse (405–367 BC) had borrowed heavily from his citizens and was hard put to figure out how he could pay them back. He ordered all coins in the city brought to him, under penalty of death. He restamped the coins so that each one-drachma coin now read two drachmas. After that, paying off his debts was easy.[14] Dionysius's methods were drastic, but the essence of the process—like many things Greek—was classic in its execution.

The Roman emperors learned to make debasement a routine procedure. One might argue that the Romans had no choice, given the dynamics of their society and their empire. Even though they succeeded in developing abundant supplies of gold throughout their empire—and, in fact, expanded their empire in some directions primarily to acquire new sources of gold—their financial requirements and their insatiable demand for adornment in gold grew so rapidly that they simply never had enough gold to satisfy their needs. Most important, they never acquired a sufficient sense of rectitude to choose between government spending and the good things in life.

The Romans set an example for debasement that later rulers throughout history have followed in many different formats, but on a scale that few have matched. The usual method of debasement was to mint coins with an unchanged face value but smaller in size and with a reduced metallic content, thereby stretching the available supply of metal to produce a larger number of coins. Debasement worked best when people were fooled into thinking that nothing untoward had occurred with newly issued coins, but you can't fool all of the people all of the time. Debasement on many occasions did lead people to melt down the old coins and bring the unadorned metal to the mint; they would walk away with more coins of a given face value than those that had been melted down. It was the state that benefited from the increased inflow of precious metals that this process brought about. In view of the primitive nature of tax systems in those days, the debasement process was an important source of governmental revenue.

Nero was the first emperor to take the route to debasement—a development that should come as no surprise. Nevertheless, Nero was a piker at the task, despite his mindless pursuit of luxury. The heavy spending by his successors on personal goodies and the maintenance of the armies and bureaucrats over the wide stretches of the empire strained government finance to the limits. As paper money and bank credit had not yet been invented, debasement was the only available method to create enough purchasing power to satisfy the constantly expanding needs.

By the time that Gallienus became emperor in AD 260, silver coins had 60 percent less metal than they had when Augustus became emperor. Gallienus then threw discretion to the winds. He ruled for only eight years, but he managed to cut the silver content of the coins down to a mere 4 percent. The outcome was inevitable: wild price inflation. One expert has estimated that prices increased at the negligible pace of 0.4 percent a year over the 250 years between the reign of Augustus and when Gallienus was emperor; but during the 34 years after Gallienus began his machinations with the coinage and Diocletian became emperor, prices rose over 9 percent a year—which means that in AD 304 prices were twenty times higher than in AD 260.[15] Roman money was now not just a financial wreck; it was a physical wreck as well. The copper coins had so little metal content and had become so thin and frail that their imprint could be placed on only one side.

Although the small-denomination Roman coins had become essentially worthless, the gold coins had fared better. The Romans did reduce the gold content and size of the coins over time so that more coins could be produced with a given amount of gold, but they resisted the temptation to mix the gold with alloys, the technique that destroyed the ability of Roman copper coins, and even some silver coins, to function as anything more than curiosities.

After Diocletian came to power in AD 284, he spent some twenty years trying to reform the currency and, under a bewildering variety of price and output regulations, to bring inflation under control. Diocletian was also wary of how gold could lead a nation into trouble. According to Gibbon, in AD 296 Diocletian caused a diligent inquiry to be made "for all the ancient books which treated of the admirable art of making gold and silver [i.e., alchemy], and without pity committed them to the flames; apprehensive, as we are assured, lest the opulence of the Egyptians should inspire [the Romans] with confidence to rebel against the empire."*[16] What with everything, Diocletian was exhausted by the burdens of being emperor. In 305, he retired voluntarily and set himself up in a lovely palace on the Dalmatian coast, where he lived more or less happily for the rest of his life.

Diocletian's successor was Constantine, who reigned from 306 to 337 and who immediately set out to improve the acceptability and respectability of the Roman currency by issuing a new gold coin called the gold solidus, which later became known as the bezant. When Constantine issued the first bezants, they weighed 4.55 grams—heavier than any other gold coin in existence—and were 98 percent pure. At $300 per ounce of gold, the bezant in today's money would be equal to $42.66, but the purchasing power of gold in Constantine's time was much greater than it is today. Clearly, this was a coin with high current value. The bezant continued in production, with unchanging weight and purity, for about seven hundred years, long after Rome had fallen to the barbarians. The gold bezant thereby deserves a place in the *Guinness Book of Records*, as no other coin in all of history can match its longevity.[17]

The supply of gold for minting was not a problem for Constantine. His conquests eastward brought massive inflows of tribute. Building in part on what he had learned about government fiscal policy from Diocletian, Constantine also levied new taxes payable only in gold or silver and employed the proceeds to feed his mints for transformation into the new coinages.

*Gibbon indicates that alchemy existed as early as the Egyptian Empire. He goes on to comment that Diocletian's act is "the first authentic event in the history of alchemy" (Vol. I, p. 411).

But the richest source of gold came about as a result of Constantine's conversion to Christianity, which he established as the state religion in 313. Inspired by his vision of a shining cross and the words *"In hoc signo vinces"* ("In this sign, I shall conquer"), Constantine proceeded to strip all the pagan temples throughout the empire of the gold and other treasures they had accumulated over hundreds of years.[18] Some of this gold resided almost permanently on top of his head: he wore his bejeweled golden crown at all times.[19] About twelve hundred years after Constantine, in another religious revolution, Henry VIII of England—a famous debaser of the coinage—solved part of his fiscal problems by pillaging the Catholic churches and monasteries in the name of suppressing the "pagan" faith. Henry copied Constantine in other ways as well: he enjoyed showing off his power by covering his person with a gold crown, gold chains, and gold sewn into his garments.

And so the story comes full circle. Gold as religious adornment and gold as money converge once again. Unlike the more ambiguous relation between the two in the time of Croesus, however, money now emerges as the clear winner not only over gold as adornment but over gold itself. The possession of gold from this point forward is no longer a matter of right, privilege, or hierarchical position in society. It is earned or it is plundered or discovered anew in the rivers and mountains. Whatever the source, an increase in the stock of gold provokes high excitement, because that gold is an instant path to money—and to power.

4

The Symbol and the Faith

As we move along, past the fall of the Roman Empire and toward the rise of new empires to the east, gold becomes even more important than it had been in earlier times, both as adornment and as money. Powers come and go, monetary systems wax and wane, new sources of gold open up, but the focus on gold is a constant that links one era to the next. Nothing else serves better for a nation seeking power.

In AD 200, when the Roman Empire was about the same age as the United States of America in AD 2000, the capital of the empire was losing its control over the outer territories, but Roman coins were still in circulation everywhere. Like the U.S. dollar, Roman money had lost purchasing power and, in some areas, the deep respect it had once deserved, but it was nevertheless the only money that circulated throughout the empire.

Then, as Rome's European dominions succumbed to the invasions and depredations of the barbarians, Rome's common currency vanished.

It did not stop circulating because of any decree or agreement among the new rulers who proliferated within the borders of the old empire. Roman money dropped out of sight because money itself virtually dropped out of sight.

There was little use for money in the terrors and ravages of the early years of the Dark Ages. Trade and travel throughout Europe fell to a trickle. Urban life disintegrated as people huddled as close as possible to food supplies; the barbarians themselves came from rural communities and the way of life in cities and towns was unfamiliar to them. As the magnificent Roman roadways deteriorated into ruts, even bricklaying skills grew scarce. The need for money for soldiers' wages also dried up as government-supported armies were replaced by roving bands of ruffians who lived off the land.

But coins are hard. Unlike dollars on a computer screen, they were not about to disappear into thin air. The Roman coins of gold continued to exist as though nothing had happened, although they seldom circulated as money. So where did they go?

People hoarded the coins and other golden objects against the terrifying insecurity and loneliness of the times. Archeologists have discovered substantial amounts of buried treasure from the Dark Ages throughout Europe, even in far north Scandinavia. Sometimes as crudely as this, sometimes in more elaborate forms, hoarding gold at times of uncertainty and fear would persist throughout most of future history. There is little difference in principle between the burying of gold in the backyard during the Dark Ages and, as we shall see, the desperate effort to build and preserve gold reserves at the Bank of England in 1930 and 1931.

Because gold is chemically inert, it survives the passage of time, the ravages of nature, the vagaries of the weather, and the machinations of humans. When Rome fell, nearly every ounce of gold ever mined or ever drawn from the mountain streams since the beginning of time was still sitting somewhere, residing in some form and designed for some use, except for what might have been lost in storms at sea.* Even that lost gold was still shining in its watery burial grounds and was available

*Gold is so soft and malleable that some of it disappears, especially when in the form of coins, simply from constant rubbing as it passes from hand to hand.

for reclamation some day. Much of the world's supply of gold had gone through many transformations over the centuries, but all of it was still around—on fingers, toes, and necks, in hoards, in coins, in palaces, in the houses of worship, and in sunken galleons under the sea. When, for example, Childeric, founder of the Merovingian dynasty in Gaul, was buried in 481, many gold objects were placed with him in his tomb, including three hundred golden bees that had decorated his robe of state.[1] Here and there, in fact, Roman coins, jewelry, and religious objects must have contained fragments of gold that had come down from such distant sources as the queen of Sheba's bounteous gift to Solomon, from Hatshepsut's mighty column, from Darius's golden bathtub, and perhaps even from the golden calf at the foot of Mount Sinai. Today, most gold bars, much jewelry, and countless decorative objects share the same pedigree.

The events that followed the fall of Rome were so diverse in both place and time that they fail to fit into neat segments. The so-called Dark Ages had many intermittent gleams of light. Furthermore, even though the history of the eastern Roman Empire based in Constantinople was strikingly different from what happened in Europe, the interaction between East and West persisted to such an extent that an effort to sharply distinguish the two chronicles would be more confusing than illuminating.

The preoccupation with gold was one of the primary forces that tied the two areas together. Gold as both money and adornment played a central role in Byzantium. In Europe, brand-new kingdoms whose leaders had never heard of Croesus or Crassus launched their gold coinage as soon as they could; the jeweler's art flourished as well, even under the most primitive political conditions; and the traditional marriage between golden ornamentation and religion—though bumpy, like many marriages—never quite came to a state of divorce.

We look first at Constantinople, in part because its history is less familiar than Europe's. More important, gold was a dominant factor in the Byzantine Empire long before it became such a preoccupation in the West.

The Byzantine emperors ruled from Constantinople for over one thousand years. By and large, they were a decadent, corrupt, conspiratorial, cruel bunch of people. The grisly story of Irene was typical. In 780, Irene became guardian of her ten-year-old son, Constantine VI, but the degree of power that guardianship provided her was both insufficient and too transitory for her taste. She organized a conspiracy against young Constantine in 792, had him arrested, and then blinded him to be sure he would remain out of action. Irene reigned for ten years not as empress but as emperor. In 802, it was her turn to be thrown out: she was overthrown by Nicephorus, her minister of finance, and exiled to Lesbos.[2] Nicephorus managed to hold the throne for nine years before he was trapped and killed in a mountain defile while campaigning against the Bulgars. Krum, the Bulgar leader, had Nicephorus's skull lined with silver and used it as a drinking cup.[3]

My favorite in the sequence of emperors was Basil II (also known as Basil Bulgaroctonus, or "Slayer of the Bulgars"), who ruled from 976 to 1025. Basil was a role model for the villain in early Hollywood movies. He is described as "mean, austere, and irascible," with full, bushy whiskers that he liked to twirl with his fingers at moments of wrath or even while just giving an audience.[4] Basil was at least as murderous as he looked. After a great victory against the Bulgarians, he blinded the entire enemy force that survived his onslaught, sparing only each 100th man so that there would be someone to lead the poor survivors back to their tsar. Upon the arrival of his mutilated troops, the tsar promptly died of a heart attack from the shock.[5]

The Byzantine emperors may have debased their regimes morally and politically, but the integrity, purity, fame, and acceptability of Constantine's golden bezant was an overriding preoccupation with all of them. The entire history of the Byzantine Empire is marked by its obsessive focus on gold, not only as money but also as an advertisement of unrivaled opulence. Gold served as the key instrument that the emperors used along with cruelty and repression to bind together their sprawling, disparate territorial domains. The golden bezant financed the empire's imports, its armies, and its alliances with other nations.

Justinian's effort to surpass Solomon in the building of the church of Saint Sophia out of an inherited hoard of some three hundred thousand pounds of gold was just one instance of the lavish use of golden displays to shout power. All the labyrinthine palaces that the emperors maintained on the banks of the Bosporus were overlaid with copious decorations of gold and precious jewels; understatement was not their style. Emperor Theophilus deserves the prize for ostentation for the tree of gold he created to shade the gold throne. The tree and the throne were flanked by golden birds, lions, and griffins; at the arrival of a visitor, the lions would swish their tails and roar as the birds warbled a welcome.[6]

The uses of gold were so varied and so extensive that Constantinople's skilled goldsmiths were in demand throughout Europe, especially in Italy. The goldsmiths were the principal artists of the Dark Ages, during the centuries before painting, sculpture, and architecture became the predominant forms of art. They worked on the mosaics that cover the portals of Saint Mark's in Venice, on the breathtaking mosaics to the south of Venice on the Church of San Vitale in Ravenna, and as far off as Monreale outside of Palermo. When the European goldsmiths saw the beautiful and delicate work of their counterparts in Byzantium, the Byzantine style became the high fashion of the early Middle Ages. In fact, the patron saint of goldsmiths, Saint Eloi (641–660, also known as Saint Eligius), was a monk and mintmaster from seventh-century Gaul who learned his skills in Constantinople.[7] His frequent appearance in paintings right through to the fifteenth century testifies to his importance and prominence. The English goldsmiths had their own patron saint, Saint Dunstan, a Benedictine monk and skilled artist who was Archbishop of Canterbury from 960 to 988. He must have been quite a man: a golden embroidery of 1470 shows him in his workshop tweaking the nose of the devil.[8]

The gold for display was just on the surface, however. Behind the scenes, the emperors amassed huge hoards of gold coins and gold bars. Basil Bulgaroctonus had over two hundred thousand pounds of gold, much of it hidden away in subterranean chambers. Around 530, Emperor Anastasius owned a store of some three hundred thousand pounds. And Empress Theodora, who ruled about forty years after Irene, died with one hundred thousand pounds in her possession. These were huge sums for their time but make a dramatic contrast with our own era in which gold stocks are measured in thousands of tons rather than in thousands of pounds.

The gold was a security blanket. The Byzantine rulers frequently went to war, when troops had to be paid in gold, but the emperors never reached a point where their enemies ceased to threaten. The empire was constantly menaced by Bulgarians and Germanic hordes to the west and, after the seventh century, to the east and south by militant Muslims attacking every infidel in sight. Since the Byzantines could not fight on all fronts simultaneously, they paid out a never-ending stream of gold tribute to keep their enemies at bay by buying off potential aggressors directly and by bribing European allies to provide protection. Today, we would call it outsourcing security.

That approach was especially important in the case of the Lombards, with whom the Byzantine emperors carried on a long but unstable relationship. The Lombards, originally known as the Langobards (longbeards), came from what is now modern Hungary. During 568–569, with the aid of Saxons and Slavs, they invaded Italy one hundred thousand strong under the leadership of their king, Alboin—which is why northern Italy is still known as Lombardy.* Poor Alboin came to a bad end in 572. During a carousal, he attempted to ape the ghoulishness of the Bulgar Krum by trying to persuade his wife Rosamund to drink from the skull of her father, king of an enemy tribe whom Alboin had murdered. Rosamund would have none of it: she did Alboin in on the spot.[9]

The imposing Lombard invasion of northern Italy threatened the priceless Byzantine possessions of Venice and Ravenna. Without gold, all would have been lost. First, the emperors bribed some Lombard factions to fight with other Lombard factions. Then they paid out gold to recruit as allies the Franks, another Germanic tribe that had established itself in Gaul, or modern France. Gold continued to move from Byzantines to Franks, from Byzantines to Lombards, and even back and forth between Lombards and Franks, as each group used the gold to buy off or bribe the others.

Internecine warfare among the Lombards continued at a high level until the middle of the eighth century, at which point they finally got

*Readers with a fondness for colorful names should note that the name of Alboin's predecessor was Wachho.

their act together. The monarchy the Lombards established was so firm and threatening that the Byzantines were not alone in deciding the job had to be finished, once and for all—even the pope for once took the side of the Byzantines. In 754 and 756, they joined in supporting a major invasion of Lombardy by the Franks, greased along by a bribe of fifty thousand gold *solidi*.[10] Having beaten back the Lombards, the Franks then proceeded to collect gold tribute from both their allies and their defeated enemies—at one point they were collecting an annual tribute of twelve thousand *solidi*.[11] The accumulation of all that gold in what would one day be France explains why it was the Merovingian monarchs who led the way back to gold coinage in Europe after the fall of Rome. In 773–774, Charlemagne, Merovingian king of the Franks, conquered the Lombard kingdom outright and annexed it to his own empire. In return, the pope crowned him emperor of the Holy Roman Empire in the year 800. For centuries thereafter, the French coveted Lombardy as part of their natural realm, until Francis I reclaimed it for France in 1515. On this occasion, however, Francis was given only a gala meal by the pope—and not long afterward he lost Lombardy again to the current emperor of the Holy Roman Empire.

Where did all this gold come from? The towering position of the bezant in the medieval world did not depend on domestic sources of gold. The gold supplies from the Pactolus River that seemed like a bottomless well to Croesus had long since been exhausted, and no other important sources were known to exist in Byzantine territory. Although some gold came in from beyond the eastern borders from as far as Russia, the richest source of mined gold came from the old Nubian mines in southern Egypt and Sudan.

Unfortunately, Nubia was a source for the Byzantines for only a short time. The Arabian Muslims conquered those territories in the seventh century, formed lasting relationships with the Nubians,* and, in one fell swoop, cut off this seemingly bottomless source that Byzantium had enjoyed for so long.

*Those relationships have indeed lasted: during the late 1990s, the Sudan was a favorite hiding place for well-known Muslim terrorists.

The shock was profound. As one historian, Robert Sabatino Lopez, a distinguished scholar of monetary history, has described it, "The empire that amazed the world by the profusion of its riches and by the abundance of its gold coinage was constantly threatened with exhaustion of its stock of precious metals."[12] Now trade, military campaigns, taxation, and raw plunder were the only means of sustaining the golden passions of the emperors that were essential to the illusion on which so much of their power depended. Military victories brought more than booty from defeated enemies (when Nicephorus captured the Bulgarian royal treasury, he planted the imperial seal upon every object).[13] Not unlike modern privatization schemes, confiscated lands could be distributed to officials, soldiers, and sailors, a move that created new income from taxation. Nevertheless, triumphs on the field of battle were an uncertain and interruptible source. Taxation was more predictable, and the ruthless, cold-blooded, and pitiless efforts of the emperors' agents on this score would be the envy of an IRS agent in our own time. But even taxation has limits.

Consequently, after the loss of Nubia, trade and commerce became the prime means of bringing gold into the coffers of the emperors as well as to the merchants and manufacturers on whom the stream of tax revenue was so heavily dependent. Byzantine trade followed an essentially triangular pattern involving Europe in one direction and the Muslims to the south in the other. Byzantium imported hardly anything from the Europeans but sold them luxury items including the finest of textile products and the arts of the goldsmiths. The silken fabrics woven in Constantinople were as highly prized in Europe as the jewelry and adornments of the goldsmiths and were so much in demand that the Byzantines finally started to grow their own raw silk. These net exports earned sufficient gold to balance Byzantium's chronic import surplus with the Muslim countries. The Muslims also maintained a positive trade balance with Europe, selling luxuries, olive oil, and horses in exchange for timber, iron, and slaves.[14]

Immediately after the loss of Nubia, the emperors established a wide variety of arrangements to facilitate commercial activity with other countries, including a significant improvement in port facilities where officials could protect the merchandise from thieves. The emperors also imposed restraints on trade, such as severe restrictions on the export of gold and essential foodstuffs, and made a sustained effort to limit imports to food and raw materials not produced in the empire. All of this kept customs officials busy inspecting the luggage of travelers, making surprise raids on shops, checking on movements of gold bars and gold bezants, and preventing forged coins from entering into circulation.

Nevertheless, the Byzantine government failed to develop any systematic plan to encourage industry or even to keep book on the balance between imports and exports. Keeping track would have been virtually impossible in any case, without a central bank or other institution through which all the money flow could ultimately pass. Each merchant and trader settled up his own balances with his counterparts in other countries, so the gross flows of coinage in both directions were large but the net inflow or outflow was obscured.

The whole process would have been a failure without the bezant. In both military affairs and in trade and commerce, the foundation of Byzantine wealth and financial clout was this wondrous golden coin. The emperors used every means to pursue the Lydian tradition of using gold coinage not just as money but also as public relations and advertising to emphasize their power and wealth. As a contemporary of Justinian described it, the gold money of the empire "is accepted everywhere from end to end of the earth. It is admired by all men and in all kingdoms, because no kingdom has a currency that can be compared to it." Another contemporary proclaimed, "It is not right for the Persian king or for any other sovereign in the whole barbarian world to imprint his own likeness on a gold stater, and that, too, though he has gold in his own kingdom; for they are unable to tender such a coin to those with whom they transact business." One hundred years later, Justinian II (685–711) went to war against the Arabs because the Caliph had struck gold coins with his own portrait. Justinian lost, but defeat did not discourage the Byzantine chronicler, who insisted, "It is not permissible to impress any other mark on gold coins but that of the Emperor of the Romans."[15] Furthermore, Justinian won a moral victory in that struggle, for the Muslims later replaced the portraits and religious figures of the bezants with quotations from the Koran, thus distinguishing the Arab dinars for hundreds of years.[16]

The fame of the bezant has not faded with the passage of centuries: as recently as 1951, Lopez characterized the bezant as "the Dollar of the Middle Ages." Maybe even better than the dollar: "The bezant outstripped the dollar in stability and intrinsic value. Indeed, its record has never been equaled or even approached by any other currency."[17] Lopez goes on to assert that "The bezant was more than a lump of gold. It was a symbol and a faith, the messenger of the divine emperor to his people and the ambassador of the chosen people to the other nations of the world."[18]

The early issues of bezant coins portrayed the image of the emperors, occasionally their spouses, and frequently their sons. Then Justinian II decided to proclaim not only his importance but his piety. He took the revolutionary step of exhibiting the haloed bust of Christ on his coinage. For its time, this was too much. Justinian's presumption helped ignite the Age of Iconoclasm, when populace and emperors rose up to eradicate all image-venerating doctrines and practices in the churches. The coinage was incidental. The primary focus of the movement was on the golden-haloed icons that decorated the walls of the churches and that had become objects of a cult-like veneration as channels from which superhuman power descended to mankind. The result for the emperors was far from a total loss: they filled their coffers with the gold torn from the places of religious worship by the iconoclasts. Thus, the gold from the Byzantine icons did not disappear any more than the gold in the Roman coinage had disappeared; it merely showed up in a new location and form.

Iconoclasm became official policy in 730 under the reign of Leo III (717–741), leading to more than one hundred years of savage persecution of reluctant clergy, accompanied by military battles with all who dared to harbor the old ideas. Leo, as it happens, had been a favored protégé of Justinian II, the ill-behaved coin-maker. In an echo of the story of Jason and the Golden Fleece, Justinian grew suspicious of Leo and sent him off on a highly risky assignment to the far reaches of the eastern frontier. Leo surprised Justinian by accomplishing his mission and returning to Constantinople in one piece. Two emperors later, in 717, Leo marched on the capital with his troops and seized the throne for himself.

Leo was a powerful military leader who won many victories in addition to those against the opponents of iconoclasm. He ruled over an empire that included all of modern Turkey and an additional three hundred miles beyond the eastern end of the Black Sea, the islands of Cyprus and Crete, everything on the west side of the Adriatic, and all of southern Italy to about one hundred miles north of Naples. He defended his territory against repeated attacks on both land and sea by the Arabs, who were eager to establish a bridgehead in southeastern

Europe. When he was not fighting the good fight of the iconoclasts on the religious front, Leo forced the Jews under his domain to submit to baptism.[19]

The first effort to restore image worship took place at the instigation of Emperor Irene, who organized a general church council in Constantinople in 786. For this, the Orthodox Church promoted Irene to sainthood, despite her failures of character and virtue.[20] The Age of Iconoclasm finally came to an official end in 843, by order of Theodora, who had more modestly assumed the title of empress. The icons were returned to their previous locations and their veneration was restored to orthodox dogma. Coinage design rapidly followed suit. Busts of helmeted emperors now appeared holding a cross; occasionally Christ showed up on the opposite side from the emperor's portrait. Emperor John I Tzimisces went so far as to issue coins showing him being crowned by the Virgin herself, with the hand of God above.[21]

All of this was wonderful in its own way, as long as it lasted, but no hegemony in history has lasted forever. After Constantinople fell to the Crusaders in 1204, the bezant began to lose its purity to debasement and, as a result, its wide acceptability. Fifty years later, the rising Italian trading powers of Florence, Genoa, and Venice began issuing gold coins that gained as much repute in their own time as the bezant had enjoyed in its heyday. Indeed, by the middle of the fourteenth century, citizens of Byzantium were paying their taxes in Venetian gold ducats. Constantine XI, the unfortunate man who was reigning when Constantinople finally fell to the Turks in 1453, was the only emperor who appears never to have issued any coins at all. There is a saying that "The empire disappeared when it had spent its last sou."[22]

Lopez's article on the dollar of the Middle Ages raises an interesting question about the true nature of the Byzantine society, with its single-minded focus on garish displays of gold and its vaunted bezant: "Were the advantages of a stable and valuable currency worth the sacrifices that were made to keep it stable?"[23] In other words, what did the Byzantines gain in the end by pushing so hard to stimulate exports of their own goods and restrain imports of foreign goods? Just more gold.

Yes, the gold did give their currency value and acceptability in other nations. But what does it avail a nation to accumulate gold if the gold is never spent? King Midas could provide the answer to that question. In the end, the citizens of any nation have to eat, clothe themselves, transport themselves, and enjoy the good things in life.

Although Lopez was looking at events of one thousand years ago, the same question has been confronted repeatedly throughout history, especially over the last two hundred years of capitalist development. In later chapters, we shall see that the issue shook Spain after the Conquistadores started shipping gold back from Mexico and Peru, and it consumed Britain at the end of the seventeenth century and again in the course of the Napoleonic Wars when the great economist David Ricardo was deeply engaged in the debate. The issue was at the heart of the controversy between Andrew Jackson and the Bank of the United States, in the valiant but losing battle of William Jennings Bryan against "crucifying mankind on a cross of gold," in the frightful struggles to restore a functioning currency system after World War I and in the course of the Great Depression, in General de Gaulle's fanatic attack on the U.S. dollar in the 1960s, and in the virtual deification of Alan Greenspan in the 1990s.

Lopez admits that the Byzantines probably enjoyed a higher standard of living than the Europeans or the Arabs until at least around 1200, although he also suggests that the Byzantines were not necessarily winners when measured in terms of progress and growth. They appeared to have stalled at a relatively high level while other areas gained on them. Although economic progress was uneven in Western Europe and in the Arab countries, their weaker and debased currencies and their accompanying moderate inflations were generally positive influences. For example, the initial stages of the inflation of the dinar commenced while the splendor of Iraq was at a peak.[24] In addition, debasement of the coinage and inflation in both Europe and the Near East led to the rapid development of money-lending and banking, especially in Italy, which greatly facilitated economic growth in both areas. Inflation frequently takes the form of a gradually rising price level rather than a runaway explosion of economic chaos.

This process tends to uproot conservatives, make change imperative, and reward the daring. Indeed, Lopez points out, "The only Western country that resisted stubbornly and successfully the inflationary trend was England, at that period an economically retarded nation."[25] The British image of themselves as the keeper of the flame in monetary integrity persisted for hundreds of years, and not always with beneficial outcomes. Financial rectitude, though much admired, has never been a sure road to prosperity. After the surge in paper money and bank deposits produced by the enormous financing requirements of the Napoleonic conflict and World War I forced Britain to suspend convertibility of sterling into gold, the obsession with "superior-quality money" drove the British back to gold at the earliest possible moment. In both cases, drastic deflations followed, with serious social disturbances.

The decision to go back on gold in 1925, in particular, led to a sequence of decisions that smothered the economy until the policy was finally reversed six years later. The contemporary pain and suffering was bad enough, but Britain was never again able to establish the superiority of sterling that had been such a source of prosperity and pride over the centuries. In more recent times, however, when England opted out of the European Monetary Union in 1992 and left the pound free to depreciate in value, exports improved immediately and economic growth jumped ahead while England's former and more correct partners on the Continent languished in economic stagnation.

Lopez hypothesizes that the deeper reasons for the contrasts he cites may have developed from significant differences in national structure. "England and the Byzantine empire were centralized monarchies with powerful landed aristocracies," he writes, "whereas merchants and other businessmen were at the helm in the Italian communes, and bankers and . . . businessmen were influential in the . . . Caliphate when inflation began." Kings associate the purity of their coinage with their own dignity, he declares; surely this was the case with the emperors reigning in Constantinople. Merchants, in contrast, have greater flexibility in the scope of their decisions, are more loosely attached to the past, and face an inescapable necessity to seek opportunity wherever it may lie.

Lopez's explanation is appealing, but too many exceptions make it a dubious rule. An obsession with sound money has not been unique to centralized monarchies, nor have inflationary policies been limited to business-dominated societies. Henry VIII was one of the great currency debasers of all time, along with the Roman emperors, but he was also a highly successful king. One of the worst inflations in history occurred in the early 1920s, immediately after the Germans had overthrown the kaiser. But sound money was a goal that motivated the English long after Parliament had taken power away from the monarchy, sound money was a paramount consideration to Alexander Hamilton at the birth of American democracy, and sound money has been the driving force of economic policy in the German and Swiss republics since World War II.

Whatever the reason, the Byzantine Empire, with all its power and wealth, lacked the dynamic to sustain itself in the face of Europe's vigorous recovery from the barbarian invasions. Perhaps success simply made the Byzantines less lean and mean than the Europeans, who were still finding their way back from the ruins of the Roman Empire.

But the threats to Byzantine power did not come only from the west. We have already noted the impact on Byzantium of the Muslim Arabs who erupted in the seventh and eighth centuries and set out to conquer the planet in the name of Islam. The Arabs deserve a closer look: the entire world as it then existed, from the Atlantic to the Pacific, would feel the reverberations of this mighty effort to spread the Word and to grow rich from trade at the same time. As it had for the Byzantines, gold played a central role in the enterprise.

5

Gold, Salt, and the Blessed Town

The rulers of the Arab domains may have been deeply religious, but they still took the Byzantine emperors as their role models when it came to the good things in life. One has only to read *A Thousand and One Nights* to capture the flavor of this society. Despite Mohammed's admonition that "He who drinks from gold or silver drinks the fire of Hell," the Caliphs had an immense appetite for gold and the romantic and bizarre types of display that gold could provide.[1] At the wedding of the son of Harun al-Rashid, who was the protagonist of the Arabian nights, the groom's father-in-law threw gold balls around for the pleasure and possession of the wedding guests. He bestowed five thousand gold pieces on a poet and paid four hundred thousand pieces for a robe of honor for a courtier.[2] Golden trees and singing golden birds in the palace at Baghdad were the inspiration for Theophilus's extravagant throne in Constantinople. One king's sister left 2.7 million dinars and twelve thousand robes woven in gold thread and jewelry. Cairo in the eleventh century had thousands of shops selling gold, jewelry, and luxurious textiles.[3]

The Arabs had no difficulty accumulating a massive golden treasure. Their creativity at the task was impressive. They ravaged their defeated enemies, outsmarted their competitors at trade, and opened up a major source of gold that had contributed a mere trickle over the centuries before their efforts came into play.

The piles of gold collected as the prize of warfare were enormous. The booty came from Persia, Syria, Egypt, Palestine, the great westward sweep across North Africa, Spain, and from as far away as Poitiers in France before the Arab armies were finally halted there by Charles Martel in 732. The Arab invaders of Egypt in particular amassed a huge heap of treasure from ravaging the agglomeration of gold that had lain for thousands of years in the tombs of the pharaohs. They also reopened old gold mines in Egypt, Nubia, and Ethiopia while they carried out exhaustive searches for new alluvial supplies in the mountain streams of those areas.[4]

The economic consequences of these conquests were profound. It was not just the booty and the reopened mines. The Arabs soon succeeded in eating deeply into the heart of Byzantine economic power by setting themselves up as traders of extraordinary acumen and persistence. In time, they dominated the major commercial contacts that had served the Byzantines so well for so long, throughout all of the Byzantine sphere of influence, even as they built new commercial relationships all along the southern Mediterranean. The Arab ships plied the seas down the east coast of Africa and across the oceans to India and China in search of profit. They even traveled northward, through the river highways of Russia, to the Scandinavian countries, trading merchandise acquired from across the seas for furs, amber, honey, and slaves.

Trade requires money. Money conveys power. Gold serves more purposes than conspicuous consumption. Less than fifty years after the death of Mohammed, the Arabs emulated the great rulers of the past with the debut of their own gold coinage—the dinar—issued by the Caliph Abd el-Melik at Damascus. These coins, 97 percent pure gold and minted in great quantity, gradually displaced the bezant as the major international currency, circulating throughout the Arab domains and everywhere in Christian Europe as well.

The first dinars were imitations of the Byzantine coins, which gave them immediate acceptance: people are always hesitant to accept money that looks funny, regardless of whatever other attributes it may have. As we have seen, however, the portraits and religious figures of the bezants were replaced by quotations from the Koran.[5]

The appetite of the Arabs for gold was so voracious that by the ninth century even the fruits of conquest, even the revitalization of the East African sources, and even the gains from trade were insufficient to meet their needs. There never seemed to be enough gold for the elaborate forms of luxury that the Arabs devised or to maintain the hectic pace of the mints that poured out the dinars in such volume.

Luck was with the Arabs. As a result of their conquest and settlement of the northern coast of Africa, they made contact with a source of gold that had fed the fortunes of Carthage more than one thousand years earlier. The Arabs never actually possessed the West African gold mines, but their genius for trade did the job for them. For several hundred years, they enjoyed a virtual buyers' monopoly over the gold that lay hidden far to the south, below the farthest reaches of the Sahara, in an area of approximately six hundred square miles, with its southern border defined by the east–west coastline that stretches from the Ivory Coast to Nigeria. This area has also been known as the Gold Coast, although the wealth it gained later from exporting slaves may have exceeded the gold that thousands of camels had hauled so faithfully over the vast Sahara for so many years.

Although the Romans and the Byzantines had both held sway on the Mediterranean coast of Africa at one time or another, their primary purpose in occupying the area was military. They hugged the coast and its seaports, ignoring the riches that lay to the south across great unmapped wastes of pure desert. The Arabs, however, meant business when they occupied North Africa. They set up trading posts such as Tunis on the sea; they also opened up centers such as Fez and Marrakesh at significant distances inland.[6] Ultimately, their traders would appear in the heart of the Sahara itself.

Sijilmesa, where the road to Morocco crossed the main north–south route to the gold country, was the place where all the caravans met. It was described by one Arab trader as "the gateway to the Sahara. . . . One of the greatest cities of North Africa and the most famous of the whole universe . . . whither traders take goods of no value and return with their camels laden with coarse gold."[7] The city grew rich simply by taxing the huge volume of traffic that passed across its borders. Deeper into the interior were towns with exotic names, for example, Taghaza, Taodeni, and Gadames, and, most famous, the major commercial center of Timbuktu. Timbuktu was located well over one thousand miles south of the Straits of Gibraltar, on the banks of the Niger River, which, together with the Senegal to the east, enclosed much of the gold mining area.

The great abundance of West African gold had been known to people around the Mediterranean for centuries. Around 500 BC, Herodotus himself provided a lively description of the territory, which subsequent visitors over the years never failed to confirm. Reaching the gold supplies across the great unmarked and arid wastes of the desert involved a risky, complicated, and lengthy voyage, in which navigation by the stars was every bit as essential as for ships at sea. E. W. Bovill, the most authoritative contemporary historian of the Sahara, has observed that "Outside the polar regions there are few parts of the world less encouraging to human occupation."[8] Nevertheless, Herodotus provides sufficient information to tell us that active communication between the coasts and the interior Sahara existed even in his day. Ancient rock drawings reveal that the bullock was the primary means of transportation.

The camel first appeared in the Sahara some time around AD 100, perhaps introduced by the Roman legions involved in military campaigns that demanded speed. The camels probably came from Egypt, where the Persians had brought them about five hundred years earlier. This remarkable innovation in the art of transportation—equivalent in some ways to the introduction of the automobile or even the airplane in modern times—greatly shortened the time spent moving between watering points, thereby permitting a much wider range of travel. Bullocks can come close to matching camels in their ability to do without water—a maximum of about ten days—but most camels can carry two to three times as much load as a bullock. Furthermore, the best camels can cover twice as much mileage in a day as the typical bullock, which is no minor consideration when the time needed to reach the next watering hole is the difference between life and death.[9] The innovation of the camel was remarkable in another sense. The introduction of the camel, according to one authority, "contradicts the most basic Western metaphor of technological progress: here the wheel—present in North Africa and the Sahara from Phoenician times—had to be 'disinvented' to make possible the linking of the Sudan and the Mediterranean."[10]

The impact of the camel on the potential volume of trade was revolutionary. As Bovill describes this development,

> [The introduction of the camel] marked the dawn of a new era for the northern half of the continent. . . . The camel gave man freedom of movement he had never known before and brought within his reach the remotest pastures. The caravan routes lost half their terrors and new roads were opened for the flow of trade and culture.[11]

The landscape that led to the gold fields was not the only feature of the region that people from Europe and the Near East would find strange. Herodotus cites the Carthaginians as the source for the following story. The Carthaginians described to him a place on the west coast where they would neatly arrange the merchandise they wanted to trade, return to their ships, and "raise a great smoke." At that point, the natives would come down to the shore carrying gold, would leave as much gold as they believed the Carthaginian merchandise was worth, and then would withdraw from the scene. The Carthaginians, in turn, would come ashore and look the situation over. If they were satisfied, they would take the gold and sail away; if not, they would return to their ships and wait patiently. The process would continue until both sides were satisfied—but they would never see each other face-to-face or exchange a word. This "dumb barter" was characteristic of how business was transacted throughout much of the gold-bearing areas. It continues to exist in some parts of Africa to this day.

We can only speculate on why dumb barter as a method of doing business should have persisted for so long. Perhaps the natives insisted on these arrangements in order to protect themselves from traders tempted to capture them as slaves. Traders sufficiently eager to acquire what the Africans had to offer had no choice but to choose this curious arrangement.

Around 750, ravenous at the thought of all that gold down south, the Arabs launched an expedition from Morocco to conquer the gold-bearing territories. This was one occasion when matters turned out badly for the Arabs. They failed completely in their objective, suffered serious casualties, and even failed to discover where the gold was coming from. Thereafter, they obtained their gold by means of trade instead of conquest.[12]

Although the Arab and European traders in the Middle Ages occasionally offered the Africans merchandise or even the silver and copper coins that the Africans considered better money than gold, salt was the product most desperately in demand. Humans can never do without salt, but the people in the territories that produced the gold must have had an unusually intense and insatiable need for it. They were so unfortunate as to live in one of the few spots in the world where the nearest sources of salt were far distant in a land where nobody could travel faster than ten miles a day.

Substantial sources of salt did exist about one thousand miles to the north, where the salt miners, many of them black-skinned slaves, worked under extremely harsh conditions. They were nearly a twenty-day journey from the nearest towns, were often blinded by desert winds, and on occasion even starved to death because of delays in the arrival of the traders who would bring them food and fresh water to swap for the salt.[13]

Most of the salt was transported south in camel-driven caravans. At many points, however, where pasturage was so scarce that the camels could proceed no further, the great slabs of salt had to be broken into small pieces that were then placed on men's heads for the rest of the trip. One fifteenth-century traveler from Portugal described what happened next.

> Each man carries one piece, and thus they form a great army of men on foot, who transport it a great distance . . . until they reach certain waters. . . . All those who have the salt pile it in rows, each marking his own. Having made these piles, the whole caravan retires half a day's journey. Then there come another race of blacks who do not wish to be seen or to speak. . . . Seeking the salt, they place a quantity of gold opposite each pile, and then turn back, leaving salt and gold.[14]

This story is not just a matter of curiosity. It has a deeper meaning. Salt was so precious to the gold diggers that many of them would trade their gold only in return for salt. In many transactions, an ounce of gold exchanged for an ounce of salt. Bovill asserts that "Salt was so infinitely the more important [compared to gold], that it is no overstatement to say that gold was valued by the Sudanese almost entirely for its purchasing power in salt. . . . It was the basis of their domestic, as it was of their foreign, trade, neither of which can be comprehended without an understanding of how starved they were of this essential to the well-being of man."[15] Look at it the other way, however. If an ounce of salt could acquire an ounce or more of gold, fetching the gold must have been an enormously profitable operation.

Thanks to the practice of dumb barter, the uncongenial geography of the gold fields, and the natural reticence of the natives, Europeans and Arabs were frustrated for centuries in their search for the source of the African gold. The whole area acquired a kind of mysterious glow among the peoples to the north.

During the fifteenth century, Europeans developed the custom of calling the gold-bearing areas Guinea (which the British persisted for a long time in spelling "Ginney"). Indeed, the Portuguese, who were the first to explore the territory, received permission from the pope in 1481 to call their king Lord of Guinea, a title that survived until the twentieth century. In 1662, the English began to use gold imported from West Africa by the African Company to mint a coin that they called the guinea, an interesting innovation in coinage that will soon occupy our attention.

Controversy persists over the source of the name of Guinea, because no such place existed in Africa at that time. No doubt the word is a corruption of something that sounded like Guinea. A likely candidate is Ghana, but Bovill insists, convincingly, that Guinea is derived from the name of the trading post of Jenne, situated on a tributary of the Niger River about three hundred miles southwest of Timbuktu, toward the gold-mining areas.[16]

Although not well known, Jenne must have been a remarkable city. Founded in the thirteenth century, it was located in a populous region with a set of waterways that were rare for the African continent but that made Jenne easily accessible. The city was not only a commercial center of importance but a major attraction for men of letters as well. Unlike

Timbuktu, where political tensions and turnover were frequent, Jenne was a peaceful place that spread the culture of the Mediterranean throughout western Africa. According to Es-Sadi, a distinguished seventeenth-century author who was born and raised in rival Timbuktu, Jenne was "a blessed town."[17] Let us hope that Bovill had it right: such a place deserves to lend its name to a country.*

As our story has wound its way from golden palaces and religious icons, from bezants to dinars, from golden balls to golden tribute, and finally to the dumb barter of gold for slabs of salt in darkest Africa, a disturbing question comes to the surface: Where is value? For the Europeans, the Byzantines, and the Arabs, gold was the magical focal point of their material desires. Not so for the Africans.

To the Africans toiling for gold but starving for salt, the salt standard was a force far more powerful and durable than anything that the gold standard stood for in the sophisticated civilizations everywhere else on the globe. What must those poor diggers have thought of the funny people from the north country who swapped inestimable salt for stuff whose only role on earth was to give men pride and pleasure by letting them see its lustre?

The question reverberates into our own time.

*There is a functioning kingdom today in southern Ghana, known as Asante. The king sits on a golden stool instead of a throne; ceremonial appearances are marked by large quantities of golden ornaments. When the British arrived as colonizers in the late nineteenth century, the natives hid the golden stool. In 1896, the British governor general of the Gold Coast colony wanted to sit on the stool as the representative of Queen Victoria, but the tribal elders refused permission and kept it in hiding (*New York Times*, March 4, 1999).

6

The Legacy of Eoba, Babba, and Udd

As the long stagnation that followed the fall of Rome yielded to a meaningful pace of economic development after the first millennium, the search for the meaning of value became a focus of increasing study and debate in Europe. A great debate developed among the scholastics and the monks in the universities over the definition of a "just price." Saint Thomas Aquinas himself, in the thirteenth century, acknowledged that "It is true that money is subordinated to something else as its end; still, to the extent that it is useful in the quest for all material goods by its power, it somehow contains them all. . . . This is how it has some likeness to beatitude."[1] Gold is a fountain of beatitude.

Commercialization and trade cannot take place without money. Creating new monetary systems from the ground up is no simple matter, for nothing can function as money unless it comes in a format that will be acceptable to everyone who uses it. No decree establishing a system can work unless the arrangements match the values, traditions, and needs of the community. The history of money—and much else affected by money—is a long and tortuous tale of how people have tried to deal with these difficulties under widely varying circumstances.

When all money is hard—when all payments are in bullion and coin—the process is especially intricate, because supplies of gold and silver are determined by nature rather than by the humans who use them. Mines can be exhausted, countries can gain or lose from plunder, and supplies can move across borders when trade is unbalanced. But human decisions matter, too. People can hoard rather than spend their coins, which was a common practice in the political and economic turbulence of the Middle Ages.[2] Gold is a hedge against the risks of chaos, and persuading people to bring their treasure back into circulation as money is no simple matter in a world where money in transit is often plundered by robbers or lost in shipwrecks, and the insatiable demands of the state are a constant threat.

The impact of frequent changes in the relative supplies of gold and silver complicated matters throughout the Middle Ages, and would continue to mess up monetary systems in both Europe and America until well into the second half of the nineteenth century. When the amount of available gold began to exceed the supply of silver, or vice versa, the prices that determined coinage rates of each metal at the mint would vary from the prices at which people could buy or sell the precious metals in the marketplace. Under those circumstances, one or the other of the metals was likely to disappear from circulation or to be exported to countries where the opposite state of affairs happened to exist.

Nevertheless, in spite of these obstacles, and without any theoretical or even much historical background to guide them, monarchs and their citizens during the Middle Ages, and even at certain moments before 1000, succeeded in evolving—indeed, inventing—monetary systems that have developed over time into the financial world around us today. None of these systems worked without disruption for very long, but reversion to the moneyless and tradeless society of the early days after the fall of Rome was never an issue.

One of the most striking features of the great sweep of European history up to World War I was how the Europeans managed to integrate gold into their monetary systems even though Europe's indigenous supply of gold was always minimal. As a French economist writing in the early 1930s described it, "There is something strange to see these countries, which, from the end of the Middle Ages to our own time, would become the most vital forces of the world economy, while barely privileged by nature with the material that a great tradition—today more imperious than ever—obliges us to accept as the sign and receptacle of all wealth."[3] To an increasing extent, as our story moves forward, the issues in Europe shift away from a focus on the supply of gold as such and toward which nation would manage to accumulate the gold that was available and employ it to enhance their power and wealth.

The wonderful thing about gold is that its achievements in its critical role as the prototype of wealth and money did nothing to diminish its equally vital role as adornment and a radiant form of beauty. Unlike other forms of money, gold has never lost its poetic quality. It has always been both sacred and profane.

During the first one thousand years after the fall of Rome, gold's role in Europe was much less important than it had been in Byzantium or in the domains of the Muslims. That difference was not a matter of choice for the Europeans. They simply had less gold available to them. Europe had no mines that could match the copious natural supplies that were available to the Byzantines and the Muslims. The Europeans also had an insatiable desire for the spices, silks, and—in the absence of central heating—furs and rugs that the peoples to the east were only too happy to sell them. As an unfortunate result, human slaves became one of Europe's primary exports, especially to the Muslims.*

The Europeans left themselves with no choice but to reject the Byzantine fashion of covering everything in sight with gold. On many occasions, gold was in such short supply that religious ornamental objects such as crucifixes and chalices were sacrificed to the melting pots at the mints to be transformed into coins. David Hackett Fischer, in *The Great Wave*, cites a theologian, Fulbert of Chartres, who justified the practice of melting religious objects into coinage "with the causuistry that it was

*Charles Kindleberger points out the countries to the east of the Europeans—all the way to China and Japan—were what economists call "low absorbers." That is, the incomes earned from their export activities failed to generate a commensurate demand for imports.

better to sell sacred vessels to Christians than to pawn them in the hands of the Jews."[4]

You will not find the gold mosaics of the Byzantine churches on Romanesque and Gothic churches, which have austere interiors and only stone carvings on the exterior. Their color comes instead from stained glass and small work by goldsmiths on reliquaries, the chalices on the altar, and the cloaks and mitres of the higher-ranking priests. When, for example, the Benedictine Abbé Suger, the great architect and regent of France, began building the first Gothic cathedral at Saint Denis in 1137 as the resting place of France's patron saint, there was no way he could emulate Justinian's extravagance at Saint Sophia. Even the fragile work of the goldsmiths scandalized Saint Bernard. Suger was not about to back down: "If the ancient law ordained that cups of gold should be used for libations and to receive the blood of rams," he retorted, "how much rather should we devote gold . . . to vessels designed to hold the blood of our Lord?"[5] How, one wonders, would Saint Bernard have reacted if it had been he rather than Moses who descended from Mount Sinai to find his people worshipping the golden calf?

The Europeans did follow the Byzantines in the delicate use of gold known as chrysography, in which a small amount of powdered gold was suspended either in egg white or gum. In this form, the gold was then applied in the illustration of books as calligraphy, which the Europeans developed into art of exceptional beauty. The technique itself had first come into use as far back as the second century AD via Egypt and Greece to satisfy the Roman demand for luxurious articles, but it was Charlemagne who launched the European art that has come down to us as the illuminated manuscript.

Charlemagne insisted on the highest standard for books produced during his reign and gave primary responsibility for that task to an English cleric, Alcuin of York. The most famous of the books produced under Alcuin's supervision were the Godescalc Gospels, which were written in 783 for Charlemagne, and the Saint-Méthard Gospel Books, both of which now reside at the Bibliothèque Nationale in Paris. The Saint-Méthard books were written entirely in gold calligraphy, illuminated with full miniatures in gold and silver on purple ground. The lettering was designed with great care, much of it adapted from Roman writing at the time of Virgil, with the letters formed deliberately and always taking the identical form. The cursive writing that we learn in school today is a direct descendant of Alcuin's golden script of twelve hundred years ago. We write faster in modern times, however: just one initial letter in chrysography took more than a full day to execute, which made carrying out these tasks a full-time job for the monk artists assigned to them.

The most significant development in the story of post-Roman money in Europe took place in Britain, which was at that time divided into a number of small kingdoms. Credit for this innovation goes to Offa (757–796), king of Mercia, a powerful ruler, and a contemporary of Charlemagne. Offa's domain extended through central England as far north as the Ouse and Trent Rivers around today's York and Manchester and as far south as Kent, Essex, and Sussex. This territory was large enough, and sufficiently integrated into one large community by Offa, for some modest amount of trade to start. In addition, Offa had large armies to maintain, and armies in those days were made up of mercenaries who would not fight unless they had received in advance the money payments due them.

When Offa took over Kent, he found three outstanding designers and producers of silver coins, known as moneyers, who had the delightful names of Eoba, Babba, and Udd. They sound like part of a Victorian poem for children, but the combination would also have made a fine name for an eighth-century London law firm. Eoba, Babba, and Udd were master moneyers in silver and they inaugurated the longstanding leadership of Englishmen in that role.[6] England has minimal local sources of gold, but Cornwall was rich in silver deposits whose output was now fashioned into a growing quantity of coins. The English did issue gold coins for about seventy years around AD 700, but they soon began to add silver alloy and then converted all their high-denomination coins into silver, with copper or brass for subsidiary coins.

The purity of the silver pennies produced by Eoba, Babba, and Udd was so well maintained that the coins were soon circulating throughout Europe, even out to the Volga and the Don. Smaller denominations were created when people cut the pennies into halves or quarters. Later on, shillings would come into being; the word means "a piece cut off."[7]

An abundant flow of Offa's pennies was soon coming out of the mints. Offa was so busy issuing pennies that he had to add eighteen additional moneyers to his original three-man staff. The production of Offa's fine silver pennies ran into the millions—a powerful commentary on how rapidly the demand for money would increase as countries groped their way out of the Dark Ages. An even greater demand for coins lay just ahead, as the English had to arm themselves against Viking invasions and, from time to time, had to offer huge sums to these Scandinavian invaders in an effort to buy them off.[8] By the year 1000, England's coinage was the most advanced in Europe, produced by a network of more than seventy local mints spread around the country.[9]

In the year 800, not long after Offa had started minting his pennies, Charlemagne, king of the Franks and victor over the Lombards, traveled to Rome so that the pope could crown him emperor of the Holy Roman Empire as a reward. A short while earlier, in 798, Charlemagne and Emperor Irene of Byzantium had opened diplomatic relations; Charlemagne contemplated marriage with her, undeterred by Irene's lust for power. In view of Charlemagne's impending coronation, this would have been the greatest merger and acquisition in history. One of Irene's favorites frustrated the match, and two years later she was on her way to exile as a widow.

Charlemagne took the Byzantine emperors as his model by focusing on gold rather than silver. It was probably Irene who stimulated his interest in coinage, although he was also a friend and admirer of Offa. Charlemagne must have had much more gold available to him than other European rulers who either preceded or followed him for a long time afterward. He reopened the old gold mines in Saxony and Silesia and attracted goldsmiths from Byzantium to his capital at Aix. He worked on a golden desk with a map of the universe etched on its top. He had many villas, each of which had its local goldsmith. When he died, he was embalmed and buried sitting on a great gold and ivory throne that he had imported from Constantinople, together with a gold scepter, shield, and sword. Plundering gold from beaten enemies, as always, was important as a source of gold for these luxuries. For example, when Charlemagne defeated the Avars in 796, an Asian tribe who had founded the first Mongol empire in AD 407,[10] he needed fifteen wagons, each pulled by four oxen, to carry the captured booty of gold and jewels.[11]

All that splendor would have been incomplete without a gold coinage. Charlemagne set his pound equal to twenty shillings and 240 pence and a pound weight of twelve ounces—like the Romans before him and like the system the English were later to follow. Charlemagne's coinage was to enjoy only a brief life span, however, despite the longevity of his system of denominations and weights.[12] His progeny spent as much time fighting among themselves as they spent in defending their domains, and his kingdom broke apart. Yet the difficulty was due only in part to his failure to establish a line of succession that would sustain the integrity of his domains. The evidence suggests that the process of recycling old gold for monetary purposes had reached a limit that could not be breached without the introduction of new gold supplies from some source beyond Europe.

Offa's silver coinage fared better than Charlemagne's gold coins, even though Offa's English kingdom also fragmented after his death. Offa's coins situated the penny as the core of the English monetary system: until about the end of the thirteenth century, five hundred years after Offa's innovation, pennies were the primary means of payment. Offa's penny was so well established when the Normans arrived on the scene in 1066 that William the Conqueror rejected a policy of debasement for the English money.

When Richard I—Richard the Lion-Hearted—was captured by Leopold, duke of Austria, in 1192 on his way back from the Crusades, and subsequently "sold" to the Holy Roman Emperor, the ransom of 150,000 marks (the equivalent of £100,000) levied on the English people was transferred from England to the continent in the form of silver pennies. This was a pile of small change that would warrant a place in the *Guinness Book of Records:* £100,000 added up to 24 million pennies, enough money to employ over forty thousand skilled carpenters for a year.*[13] It is remarkable that the English were willing to make such a

*The *Wall Street Journal* for May 6, 1999, page A24, reports that "legend has it" that F. W. Woolworth paid in nickels and dimes the $13 million bill for the construction of the Woolworth Building in New York City.

heavy sacrifice at such an early stage of national awareness and for a king who spent so little time in England during his reign.

It is also difficult to imagine the sheer mechanics of transferring 24 million pennies. When, in 1529, Francis I of France paid over 1.2 million escudos to Charles V of Spain to ransom his two sons, the process of counting and testing the coins took four months, during which time the Spaniards rejected forty thousand coins as below standard.[14] In a later time, 1662, one hundred chests were required to handle the physical transfer of five hundred thousand large-denomination French coins.*[15]

Gold coins were so valuable in the Middle Ages that they did not circulate much among the common people.† For the most part, gold coins were used in transactions by merchants and traders involved in foreign trade, by tax collectors, by the retinue of the monarch himself, and, as we have already seen, by monarchs as a means of buying off enemies and ransoming friends and family members. All these people exercised great caution to avoid accepting gold coins whose weight or composition was below required levels of purity, thereby rendering a public service for everyone else.

A favorite method of testing quality was the touchstone, which functioned in these times in precisely the same way as it had functioned more than fifteen hundred years earlier under the Lydian kings in Asia Minor—a stone rubbed by gold objects and then compared against a set of needles containing varying proportions of gold and silver, gold and copper, and all three metals. Many merchants kept touchstones for this kind of rough-and-ready test. In cases of controversy, coins were taken to goldsmiths,

*This episode may pale in relation to the contemporary problem of the Europeans in eliminating all national currencies in favor of the euro. Destroying paper money is simple, but what of the millions of coins? The Dutch—one of the smaller economies involved—are reported to have sought space equivalent to over two football fields as an interim solution! (Personal correspondence from James Howell of Atherton, California. Probably from the *Financial Times* of November or December 1998.)

†Gold coins never circulated in the same way as conventional small change. When my grandfather in the 1920s gave me a $5 gold piece for Christmas, I waited a couple of years before I could bring myself to spend the money.

who were skilled at the use of touchstones and their companion touch-needles; for over seven hundred years, the Goldsmiths Company of London has been the official arbiter of the purity of the British coinage.[16]

The most important and reliable tests of purity were held at the Trials of the Pyx, in which a public jury of "twelve discreet and lawful citizens of London with twelve skillful Goldsmiths" presided over public examinations of coins freshly or recently issued by the Royal Mint. This ceremonial procedure probably began under the reign of Edward I in 1282; on the occasion of its seven hundredth anniversary in 1982, the trial was attended by Queen Elizabeth II and the Chancellor of the Exchequer.

Pyx derives from the Greek word for "box" and refers to the container in which the officials stored the coins selected for testing at the trial. These coins were chosen on some kind of random basis from the output of the mint—a practice still in use today in factories that check their output for uniform quality—after which they were meticulously compared with a special trial plate of the king's gold that was stored in a treasury room called the Chapel of the Pyx in Westminster Abbey. Some coins were melted down in an additional test of the purity of the gold.*[17]

These uniquely English Trials of the Pyx were serious affairs. The trials served a real purpose, because the goldsmiths and their jurymen had no conflicts of interest, performing their task in the open before the public, not in secret, for no reason except to assure the integrity of the currency. Today, we would refer to this as transparency. The whole process discouraged the monarch from debasement and encouraged people all over Europe to accept and execute transactions with English coinage.

The Trials of the Pyx are not the only evidence of the English intolerance for low-quality coins. Punishments were swift and unpleasant for moneyers and other employees of the mints who crafted poor coins or who were suspected of activities in the mints for their own benefit.

*For a more detailed description of the Trials of the Pyx and their place in the history of statistical sampling, see Stigler, 1977.

In 1124, with public confidence in English money having been destroyed by deterioration of the coinage, Henry I called before him all the mint-masters in the kingdom, about two hundred men, and punished almost half of them by chopping off their right hand. This was a punishment that fitted a crime for which higher authorities had the ultimate responsibility. As Glyn Davies, a distinguished British economist and historian, observes, "At least they were spared the stiffer penalties of being blinded or castrated or both, which were occasionally administered."[18] Similar types of punishment were by no means unusual until well into the seventeenth century. Moneyers seem to have been an unruly lot for most of history. Gibbon's *The History of the Decline and Fall of the Roman Empire* reports that Emperor Aurelian, about AD 175, complained that the workmen at the mint "adulterated the coin" and then rose in rebellion, requiring the emperor to recall seven thousand soldiers from Dacia before the uprising could be suppressed.[19]

This English tradition of "sound" currency stood in sharp contrast with the irregularity of continental currencies. The resistance to going off gold that haunted the British from 1925 to 1931 had deep roots. In 1344, for example, when the weight of the English penny had been almost unchanged for two hundred years, Edward III attempted to finance the great war against France with a small reduction in weight and followed with a deeper cut in 1351. The Statute of Purveyors enacted by Parliament in 1352 "expressed the hope that the king would no more tamper with the coinage than with the standards of weights and measures."[20]

Contrary to popular myths about the eagerness of the state to debase the currency whenever possible, the monarch had a strong vested interest in maintaining the purity of the coinage when coins were almost the sole medium for effecting transactions and for paying taxes and debts. Good coins with royal authentication stamped on them tended to exchange at a significant premium over their intrinsic value as metal, because they were so much more convenient than any other means of payment. This difference provided a source of profit, known as *seignorage*, to the kings who maintained a monopoly on the process of minting coins; anyone else engaging in that activity would live to regret it. The monarch's eagerness to earn seignorage in the Middle Ages explains why wholesale recalls of outstanding coins occurred in many countries in three- to five-year intervals, to be replaced with new coins of different design. The process was often a welcome one, as old coins constantly deteriorated from handling or were clipped by those who hoped to sell the odd pieces in the black market for money.

Offa's pennies and the Trials of the Pyx reflect the growing importance of money and commerce as Europe emerged from the darkest days of the Dark Ages. Significant as these developments may have been, they were just a beginning in which gold played only a minor role. Far more exciting developments lay just ahead. Gold was about to combine with growing economic and financial sophistication to rival political and military power in shaping the course of events around the world.

7

The Great Chain Reaction

The coming of the year 1000 was cause for great celebrations throughout the Christian world, and not just because of the arrival of the millennium. For some five hundred years, barbarians beyond the eastern and the northern borders of the old Roman Empire had repeatedly carried out violent raids on a helpless local population. In time, however, raiding lost its novelty and the former barbarians transformed themselves from outside predators into part of the scene. Like the industrious Lombards of northern Italy, they settled down, married, and raised families. Warfare of one kind or another within Europe continued through the ages, but at least the terrifying toll of the barbarian invasions ultimately came to an end. The Normans who invaded England in 1066 were far more civilized than their rough ancestors, the Norsemen, who had earlier descended into France from Scandinavia.

These developments set the scene for major advances in the uses of gold, especially in the promotion of trade, commerce, and finance. In the process, gold would become the preeminent tool in the management of economic power. Gold's strategic role became so dominant over time that the struggle to obtain adequate sources of it would motivate monarchs and nations to great deeds and tragic treachery in the years ahead.

The proliferation of great cathedrals built throughout Europe during the first three hundred years after the celebration of 1000 is dramatic evidence of how life was brightening up in Europe. Between 1100 and 1200 alone, France built more than eighty cathedrals, including Notre Dame and Chartres, to say nothing of five hundred abbeys and ten thousand parish churches. Durham, Canterbury, and Ely rose in England; Spain built Burgos, Toledo, and Santiago de Compostela; in Italy and Sicily, cathedrals were completed in Venice, Florence, Siena, and Palermo. The universities of Paris, Oxford, Bologna, and Salerno were founded. Some of literature's most famous works appeared, including *The Cid*, the *Nibenlungenlied*, the *Chansons de Geste*, and the legend of King Arthur. And great kings governed—men such as Henry II in England, Frederick Barbarossa in the Holy Roman Empire, and Philip Augustus in France.[1] The most popular role models were knights skilled in the arts of chivalry, and Saint Louis, who was known for his passionate religious and moral leadership.

The increase in population was the most important development. It was not just that fewer people were being killed. In a more peaceful environment, larger numbers of babies were born and survived. In Paris, for example, the population expanded from a little town clustered on the Ile Saint Louis in 1100 into a full-fledged city of some fifty thousand people by 1215.[2] Higher rates of population growth do not have to mean falling standards of living. In the twelfth century, larger populations made greater specialization possible, permitted more people to spend time in study, the arts, and research, and stimulated all the networking benefits that cities with a diversified population create.[3]

The optimism and vitality of this period culminated in the Crusades, the great adventure of the Middle Ages. From 1095 to around 1450, waves of Europeans—often women as well as men, and, in one instance, children—walked or sailed to Constantinople and to Asia

Minor, professing to regain the Holy Land for Christendom. These expeditions were on occasion a powerful positive expression of faith, but more often they were an escape from the tedium of small-town or rural existence, inspired by dreams of glory and even more vivid dreams of riches and treasures to be captured and carried back home.

During the 1300s, massacring infidels became a much less compelling objective as trade, commerce, and the interchange of intellectual ideas with the Arabs flourished, along with a flood of medical, scientific, mathematical, and philosophical innovations—including the windmill and the compass—provided by the Arabs. In addition, Arab shipping and transportation routes opened up access to the silks and damasks, spices and lemons, and finely woven tapestries of the countries to the east. Princes and churchmen whose predecessors had been content with bare walls and floors covered with filthy rushes now insisted on having palaces with gilded vaults, with such furnishings as curtains, cushions, embroideries, and floors covered with oriental carpets.[4] Not everything learned from the Arabs had been developed by the Arabs themselves, but the Arabs had accumulated and put to good use a substantial pool of knowledge from the Indians and the Chinese. It was this set of influences that provoked Marco Polo to take off in 1271 on his famous quest in that direction.

The Crusades imposed massive financial requirements on an unsophisticated financial structure. Quite aside from the costs of supplies and equipment, soldiers had to be fed, clothed, housed, and paid in coin acceptable in the occupied territories, where gold was the basis of all the currencies and where the armies consisted less of men motivated by religious zeal and knightly chivalry and more of adventurers and mercenaries. In addition, ransoms payable in gold were often demanded for captured prisoners. Ships that traveled full of soldiers and supplies in an eastward direction were willing to take on freight at very low rates for the trip back to Europe, rather than traveling empty, and this pattern encouraged large-scale importations of the attractive merchandise of Arabia, which in turn required payments, most often in gold.

Much of the gold used by the crusaders came from the Holy Land itself, which relieved the need to import gold from Europe. Professor Andrew Watson, in a 1967 paper for the Economic History Society, lists a wide variety of local sources, such as "subsidies paid by the Emperor of Constantinople to the Franks; tribute exacted from Arab potentates who bought off the Christians . . . booty, such as the twenty golden lamps weighing 20,000 mithqals, removed by Tancred from the temple of Jerusalem . . . taxes raised in conquered areas where the basis of the currency had long been gold." Watson asserts that these sums were "truly enormous, though they were often quickly spent." In 1191, for example, the Templars bought the island of Cyprus for one hundred thousand golden bezants and then sold it at the same price to Guy de Lusignan. Raymond of Tripoli was ransomed at a cost of 150,000 bezants and the entire army of Saint Louis was redeemed from captivity for the sum of eight hundred thousand dinars.[5]

The Christian governments in the Levant were striking gold coins as early as 1124, using captured dies so that the money looked just like the local coinage, including the usual Arabic inscriptions praising Mohammed. The Christians continued to produce such coins for another 125 years, although in time a growing proportion of the coins was counterfeit, usually base metal such as copper plated with gold.

In 1250, Pope Innocent IV, scandalized less by the counterfeiting than by Christian mints issuing coins that honored the enemy, finally took action by excommunicating all those involved.[6] Such drastic action was essential, because the Christian princes, more businesslike than spiritually inclined, had insisted on continuing to issue coins that had ready acceptance by the Muslims. In response to the pope's demands, the princes took the modest step of stamping Christian sayings while retaining the Arabic script.

Innocent appears to have been an appropriate name for this pope. One can only wonder why the Vatican was so slow on the uptake—or whether it had chosen to look the other way. Indeed, the identical sequence of events had occurred in Spain during the eleventh and twelfth centuries, and, in both gold and silver, throughout Europe.[7]

Innocent's effort was insufficient to satisfy Saint Louis, who was in the Holy Land on a crusade and added his authority to the pope's. An entire new coin appeared, the *Agnus Dei* (Lamb of God), which reflected both Louis's religious humility and his French pride: *Christus vincit, Christus regnat, Christus imperat* (Christ conquers, Christ reigns, Christ commands), the ritual acclamation of the French kings.[8]

We now move westward across the Mediterranean to the Kingdom of Sicily, which was ruled from 1211 to 1250 by the Holy Roman Emperor Frederick II, grandson of the great Frederick Barbarossa and one of the towering figures of the Middle Ages. Frederick was an enthusiastic producer of gold coins that he employed to project his economic power.

Frederick was born in Sicily in 1194, the same year his father had been crowned king of Sicily. Although a hypochondriac,[9] Frederick was a valiant crusader, established an expert bureaucracy, opened Sicily to free trade, surrounded himself with the greatest intellectuals of the age, levied heavy taxes on the clergy and prohibited them from holding civil office, built handsome castles throughout Sicily, and founded a university at Palermo to train public servants—the first European university with a royal charter. Not incidentally, he also left his mark on the gold currency of his time.

Frederick did an extraordinary amount of traveling and was almost constantly at war with the papacy. He launched the Sixth Crusade in 1227, returned to Sicily to do battle with Pope Gregory IX—who excommunicated him—and then went once more to the Holy Land, where he reclaimed Jerusalem for the Christian forces. Jerusalem fell to Muslim mercenaries later on, and despite another two hundred years of crusading, was never again in Christian hands until the British General Allenby captured it in 1917. After declaring himself king of Jerusalem, Frederick traveled back to Sicily to defend his lands against another papal attack and survived a second excommunication (as a heretic, rake, and anti-Christ).

When, to Frederick's relief, Gregory gave up the ghost in 1241, the new pope was Sinobaldo Fiesco, who adopted the title of Innocent IV. This was the Innocent (innocent?) who had so belatedly prohibited the Christians in the Holy Land from issuing coins with Arab inscriptions praising Mohammed. Frederick had expected this pope to be a friend, but that may have been innocent on his part, because Fiesco came from Genoa, Sicily's mortal enemy and determined competitor for economic dominance. Frederick and Innocent were soon involved in a vicious war with each other that included an assassination attempt on Frederick and the capture of his son, who spent the last 23 years of his life in prison. Frederick suffered a final defeat at Parma in 1248 and died suddenly two years later. Frederick's son-in-law was reduced to pawning the Sicilian throne to some enterprising Genoese businessmen in return for gold.

At the time of Frederick's death, Sicily was operating with two concurrent gold standards. One was the *tarì*, which had Arabic roots and had been in use since the ninth century. Although the *tarì* had gone through some debasement over the years, from the early twelfth century onward it was stabilized at 16⅓ carats of gold. This was better than the purity of the Byzantine *solidus* at that time and established it as one of the most stable in Europe. The coins were stamped out in a variety of sizes and tended to circulate on the basis of their weight rather than their face value. The *tarì* enjoyed such wide circulation that it became a kind of unit of account by which many items were priced.

Frederick II considered the *tarì* unimpressive and too irregular for the homeland of a Holy Roman Emperor of his exalted status. After a military victory against the Tunisians in 1231, he was assured of a substantial annual tribute in both gold coin and gold dust from the West African gold sources. Now Frederick's imperial mints began to strike a new gold coin called the *augustalis*. Robert Sabatino Lopez describes the *augustalis*, with its classical eagle imprinted on one side and the emperor's laureate head on the other, as "a startling advertising medium" and a dramatic contrast to the formless *tarì*.[10] The *augustalis* was minted in 20½ carats and weighed 5.28 grams, which gave it greater value than the Arab dinar. This impressive coin soon eclipsed the *tarì* and was in strong demand throughout western Europe and the Near East.

Genoa had long considered Frederick II and the Sicilians their arch-enemies. The Genoese nursed dreams of attaching Sicily to their own domains and had been intermittently at war with Frederick ever since 1238. Genoa derived immediate and significant benefits from the election of Pope Innocent IV in 1241, Frederick's defeat in 1248, and his death in 1250. In particular, Innocent showered privileges on his hometown and proceeded to claim the Kingdom of Sicily for the Holy See.

Genoa compensated for lack of military power with aggressive economic policies. By 1250, the Genoese were enjoying a prosperous textile industry and widespread construction of new buildings. Genoa's huge shipyards produced most of the eighteen hundred ships that sailed for Saint Louis's crusade in 1248 under the command of Genoese admirals. Commercial enterprises of all kinds were making their appearance, and bankers and merchants from the major city-states of northern Italy were there to do business. Lopez states, "The very technique of credit operations, which had constantly progressed during the last hundred years, displayed at this period a maturity not to be surpassed for many years to come."[11] The Genoese had lent large sums to both Saint Louis and Innocent IV and had been bankers to just about every important crusader. And then there was the opportunity opening up in the Holy Land for new gold coins as the Christian princes finally yielded to Innocent's insistence that they reform their coinage.

Meanwhile, increasing supplies of gold were becoming available to the Genoese. New gold mines opened up in Bohemia, but the primary source was the African gold that flowed mainly toward Genoa as a result of the favorable balance of trade that the Italians maintained with North Africa. Genoese records suggest that trade with the Levant was also turning favorable, bringing Islamic and Byzantine coins to the Italian shores for remelting into Genovese coins. Indeed, even China was complaining at that time of a loss of gold through foreign trade. Finally, a period of sustained prosperity probably led to the dehoarding of gold as well. We know that the Italians were supplying the English Treasury with gold in the middle of the thirteenth century.[12]

As Englishmen in their time knew well and as Americans have learned in the years since World War II, good money adds its luster to the world's image of a nation. A high-value gold coin, sustained in purity, was an ideal vehicle for Genoa to extend the reach of its economic prestige. In 1252, two years after the death of Frederick in Sicily, when the price of gold in Europe happened to be unusually low compared with the price of silver, Genoa began to issue a 24-carat gold coin called the *genovino* (or genoin). Oddly enough, their sour relationship led the Genoese to take the Sicilian coinage system as their model. They adopted the weight systems of the *tarì* and then stepped up the quality of the coin from Frederick's by minting it in 24-carat gold. Both features would enhance the acceptability of the Genoese money in the Sicily that the Genoans so avidly coveted.

These coins weighed about 3.5 grams, a full gram less than Constantine's original bezants, but the 24-carat purity was a big attraction.

A 3.5-gram solid gold coin would be the equivalent of about $33 of 1999 purchasing power, but the purchasing power of gold in terms of goods and services was many times greater in the Middle Ages than it is today. The high contemporary value of these coins had more than economic significance: their high value reflected prestige and glory upon their issuers. This aura was further enhanced because such coins were not meant for the use of *hoi polloi*; they circulated among the upper classes and most active merchants.[13]

We can develop a sense of the nature of the genoin by comparing it to a $2.50 gold coin in my possession (the coin is stamped "$2½" rather than "$2.50"), about the size of a dime and minted in 1865. My coin is equal to 12 percent of an ounce, or nearly the same weight as the thirteenth-century gold genoins. This little piece of arithmetic reveals three important facts. First, genoins were about the size of a contemporary ten-cent coin in the United States. Second, as a dollar in 1865 bought about seventeen times as much as a dollar buys today, $2.50 when it was minted in 1865 bought as much as $42.50 would buy today. Third, and perhaps most interesting, the tradition of the 3.5-gram coin persisted for more than six hundred years.

The chief motive of the Genoese in issuing the genoin was commercial, but they also understood that economic power and political power mutually enhance each other. Indeed, within ten years of the introduction of their golden currency, Genoese power had persuaded the Latin rulers of Constantinople that the proprietary trading privileges held by the Venetians should be transferred to Genoa. The Genoese then used their base in Constantinople to extend their trade and influence into northern Persia, the Crimea, and the farthest shores of the Black and Caspian Seas. Soon they were venturing into the upper Nile and exploring the Sudan and the Niger River basin.

The needs of commerce explain why the first steps toward minting gold coins in the Middle Ages took place in such cities as Genoa and Florence that were centers of economic and financial activity instead of in the capitals of the nation-states, such as London or Paris or even Rome. Lopez asserts that the events of 1252 touched off one of the greatest chain reactions in monetary history. . . . The return to gold did more than provide symbols and tokens: it relieved the strain which economic growth was placing on a chronically inadequate currency. . . . It was the most spectacular token of the economic gains accumulated by the Catholic world during the preceding two or three centuries, and a tangible symbol of the initial superiority of the West over the East—for the Islamic world and Byzantium, which minted gold when Europe was content with silver, now debased their gold or ceased to strike it.[14]

Lopez was accurate in using the metaphor of a chain reaction to describe what happened with the use of gold as money following the innovation of the genoin. Only a few months after Genoa had acted, the Florentines issued their *fiorino d'oro*, or florin, so called because it had a fleur-de-lys on one side. Perugia and Milan followed with gold coinages shortly afterward, and Lucca around 1273. In 1284, the Venetian ducat appeared, the most famous and successful of all the gold coins born in the course of the thirteenth century. When Shylock hears that his runaway daughter Jessica has "in one night spent fourscore ducats," he cries, "Thou stick'st a dagger in me! I shall never see my gold again! Fourscore ducats at a sitting! Fourscore ducats!"[15] The ducat served as a standard of value throughout Europe and maintained its gold content until the Venetian Republic fell to Napoleon in 1797.[16] All these coins weighed 3.5 grams and were 24-carat gold.

The issuance of new gold coins was by no means limited to Italy. Both Alfonso X in Castile and Henry III in England issued gold coins in 1257, and Saint Louis joined in at just about the same moment. Sad to relate, Henry of England's gold penny was set at an inappropriate value relative to silver and ended up a total failure. Henry began with his coin equal to twenty pence in silver, later raised to 24 pence, but the same quantity of goods that the gold could buy could be purchased more cheaply just by paying with silver. Within three months, complaints rose within the City that no one wanted to exchange the new coins for silver. Merchants had no use for them, and poor people would never spend that much in a single transaction, or perhaps in a year of transactions. No trace of these coins has been found since about 1280.

Nevertheless, the English merchants complained that they had to use foreign gold coins in their international transactions at values in terms of sterling that were unfavorable to them. In 1343, King Edward III tried issuing an English gold florin whose face value was above the market value for the gold it contained, but this, too, met with resistance everywhere, including among many of England's best customers abroad. When the Florentines refused to accept these coins, they used the quaint excuse that the coins lacked an image of Saint John the Baptist. These difficulties led Edward to issue a new gold coin the following year with a more appropriate weight, called the noble, whose sides celebrated Edward's great victories in the Hundred Years' War against the French: Crécy on land and Sluys at sea. The noble also had a checkered career in its early years, but in time it became the basic gold coin of England until well into the seventeenth century.[17]

This laggard performance by the English in large part reflected their slow pace of economic and financial development compared to developments on the Continent. In dramatic contrast to its role in the world in the nineteenth and twentieth centuries, thirteenth-century London was far less cosmopolitan than Paris or Augsburg or the Italian city-states. With a population of about fifty thousand and the only city in England except York with more than ten thousand inhabitants, London was about half the size of Paris, Florence, Venice, and Genoa and no larger than Bruges, Bologna, or Palermo.[18] The English, still feudal and rural, had not yet been consumed by the hard-headed, business-oriented calculations that led to the genoin, the florin, and the ducat, in large part because the typical English transaction was far smaller than transactions on the Continent. Even as late as the middle of the fifteenth century, aliens still controlled about 40 percent of English overseas trade; Florentine bankers financed the wars of Henry's son Edward I and bought the wool crop from Edward III. According to one authority, the Italian merchants "achieved a financial despotism which London has never had, for during a considerable period [these merchants] seem to have been able to fix quite arbitrarily their own exchange rates."[19] The arrival of the "nation of shopkeepers" still lay in the future.

Silver's convenience for small-scale transactions and relatively plentiful supplies preserved its role as the primary monetary metal for another five hundred years, but silver would never again be the sole form of precious-metal coinage in Europe. Nevertheless, the tangled interaction between the two metals escalated with the passage of time and became the source of endless disputes and complications. The tangle would by no means be limited to the two metals. As we shall see, once bank deposits and paper money in their various manifestations came into use as convenient substitutes for coins, the appropriate relationship between these powerful innovations and the precious metals became so controversial that it has never been settled even up to this very moment.

The expansion of commerce and finance caused a growing emphasis on money, but more than the give-and-take of supply and demand was at work. Money is a natural source of fascination. Money's arithmetic involves complexities of fractions and ratios, its ownership conveys power, and it is the key to the doors of foreign nations. The risk of losing it is simultaneously exciting and terrifying, and the power it conveys is irresistible. The development of commerce and banking in the Middle Ages nurtured all these interests and compulsions.

Just over the horizon, a ghastly interruption to this process was about to descend over Europe, a sequence of events so awful that for a moment money would almost cease to matter. Yet nothing with a likeness to beatitude can be suppressed for long. The glint of gold would soon shine through the terrors.

8

The Disintegrating Age and the Kings' Ransoms

The fourteenth century stands unmatched in history for its unrelenting sequence of famine, pestilence, social chaos, and warfare. It was a terrible contrast to the progress and achievements of the twelfth and thirteenth centuries in Europe. Barbara Tuchman, who wrote an entire book on the horrors of the fourteenth century, described it as "a violent, tormented, bewildered, suffering and disintegrating age, a time, as many thought, of Satan triumphant."[1] The twentieth century has witnessed its own grotesque terrors, but at least there was peace among the major powers in Europe from 1900 to 1914, from 1918 to 1939, and again after 1945. The fourteenth century enjoyed no such relief.

How could the glow of gold possibly shine through the gloom of such an age? We shall find that gold gleamed on occasion too brightly during the fourteenth century. Gold even saved lives that might otherwise have been lost. This was not a time when innovations in coinage or other financial instruments made comparable progress to what had been achieved in the preceding two hundred years, but gold did not sink back into the shadows. And then, when the horrors of the fourteenth century finally gave way in the fifteenth century to substantial progress in living standards and economic development, the available supply of gold appeared to be far below the expanding demand for it, setting great movements under way to seek for new sources of gold in other parts of the world.

The summer of 1314 was uncommonly cold and wet in Europe. Crops rotted, harvests were late, and alarmed authorities placed price controls on farm products and firewood. All these were routine disasters that had happened many times before.

The awful weather of 1314, however, was just the beginning of a succession of catastrophes. Bad crops seldom happen two years in a row, but the weather in 1315 was even worse than during the previous year. Heavy and incessant rains caused flooding that smashed dikes. Rising rivers destroyed villages. Violent storms crashed onto the coasts. The tragedy stretched from Scotland to Italy and from the Pyrenees to the homes of the Slavs. Food prices rose over fivefold and starvation was widespread. Even that was not the end. The weather wreaked havoc once again in 1316, causing the worst famine in European history. People ate cats, rats, insects, and animal droppings, and then, lacking anything better, dug up the corpses in the burying grounds. Epidemics and violent crime were widespread. Bloody and public self-flagellation was common. Scapegoats Jews, lepers, noblemen—were murdered without hesitation.*

The Great Famine, as it came to be known, was only the introductory chapter to this appalling story. In 1347, the Genoese were defending their Crimean colony of Kaffa (known as Feodosia in modern times) against a besieging Tartar army that had recently swept in from the Far East and across the great expanses of Russia. The siege was not going well for the Tartars, so they decided to use a unique projectile to catapult over the walls and into the center of Kaffa: dead bodies of their own

*Even that was not the last of the bad weather: the Baltic Sea froze over in 1316, Florence suffered one of the worst floods in its history in 1333, ferocious North Sea storms assaulted the coasts four times between 1316 and 1404, and a Norwegian priest in Greenland reported in 1350 that "the breakup of advancing glaciers made it impossible to follow the ancient sea lanes" (see Day, 1978, p. 187).

men who had just died from a particularly vicious form of the plague. Stricken with terror—and soon sickened—the Genoese abandoned Kaffa, fleeing in their galleys through the Black Sea and the Aegean toward Italy. When one of the Genoese ships arrived at Palermo in Sicily, its fleas and rats and dying humans launched what has come to be known as the Black Death.[2]

This frightful affliction spread like wildfire throughout Europe over the next two years. Population estimates are fragmentary and unreliable, but it is likely that the Black Death killed about a third of the people from India to Iceland, at least twenty million deaths. The population of Europe would not regain the levels of 1300 until the middle of the sixteenth century.[3]

Men, and an even higher proportion of women, died so fast that there was no time or inclination for last rites, nor was proper burial an option. In some big cities, the death rate exceeded 50 percent and was highest in the close quarters of monasteries. The plague had no respect for status: it took the king of Castile; the queen of Aragon and her daughter; the son of the emperor of Byzantium; the queen of France, as well as her daughter; the queen of Navarre; the wife of the Dauphin; Petrarch's beloved Laura; the Sienese painters Ambrogio and Pietro Lorenzetti; Andrea Pisano of Florence; the great historian Giovanni Villani (who died in the middle of a sentence: "in the midst of pestilence there came an end"); the second daughter of King Edward III of England; the archbishop of Canterbury, his appointed successor, and the successor's appointed successor.[4] If all this were not bad enough, in 1348—just as the Black Death was gathering momentum—a calamitous earthquake spread havoc and destruction from Naples to Venice, with aftershocks that smashed buildings and killed humans as far away as Germany and Greece.

Nature was by no means the only force to deliver violence and death in the fourteenth century. Brutal political disruptions became endemic.

In 1303, the pope was taken prisoner by a Roman mob and died shortly afterward under mysterious circumstances; one historian refers to his dying "of humiliation."[5] His successor was murdered. The next in line, a Frenchman by the name of Clement V, took the prudent step of removing the papacy to the papal enclave in his native land at Avignon in 1305, where the popes lived in high style for the next 73 years. Petrarch complained that even the papal horses were "dressed in gold, fed on gold, and soon to be shod in gold if God does not stop this slavish luxury."[6] What was the source of all that gold? It was from the bunching of bequests from the wealthy who had died from the Black Death. It was at this time that the king of France, Philip IV, prohibited any exportation of gold from France. One writer suggested that this ruling, rather than fear of physical violence, was the real motivation for the pope to move to Avignon. He argued that the papacy would have faced bankruptcy if it had remained in Rome and that it transferred itself to France in order to sustain its ample revenues from French sources.[7]

In 1327, Edward II of England, an avowed homosexual, was slaughtered with a hot iron poker shoved up his rectum. Louis X of France, known as Louis the Quarrelsome, was deposed in 1316 after only two years on the throne. In 1332, even the melancholy Danes dissolved into anarchy. In the Holy Roman Empire, Guelfs went to war against Ghibbelines. In 1338, the Hundred Years' War between England and France broke out, piling organized state-sponsored killings on top of widespread mayhem on a private level. Workers' uprisings in Italy broke out in 1346–1347. Shortly afterward, Rome was thrown into chaos by Cola di Rienzi's brutal uprising motivated by the dream of restoring the Roman republic of Cicero. In 1358, the Jacquerie produced a violent peasant revolt in France against war taxes, the burden of paying huge ransoms for captured royalty, and the pillage perpetrated by wandering mercenary veterans of the wars. In 1379, a year after insurrection in Florence, the weavers and merchants of Ghent mounted their own insurgency, going so far as to try to divert the river Lys and leading the contemporary historian Froissart to ask, "What shall they say that readeth this or heareth it read, but that it was the work of the Devil?"[8] In 1381, following a succession of new poll taxes, the English got their version of a fierce uprising by the peasants, led by Watt Tyler. Seventeen years later, Henry Bolingbroke deposed his cousin, King Richard II.

The economic consequences of all these deaths and disruptions were strange, to say the least, especially the massacre of the Black Death. As the masses of human bodies disappeared, their physical possessions and monetary wealth remained behind. This grisly process left most Europeans far richer than they had been before tragedy struck. To turn a phrase, as the poor got fewer, the rest got richer. They would soon act accordingly.

According to one historian, the citizens in Albi, in southern France, with fortunes greater than one hundred *livres* grew from 11 percent to 20 percent of the population between 1343 and 1357, while those with less than ten *livres* declined from 31 percent to 18 percent.[9] Many people died without the opportunity to write wills, leaving their wealth with no readily identifiable ownership. This led to a great demand for lawyers to settle the quarrels over questions of inheritance and succession, but it also led to opportunities for the enterprising to pick up unclaimed assets. In addition, as the supply of labor had shrunk dramatically, a scarcity of labor joined with the plethora of money to produce a sharp rise in wages and the incomes of working people.

Contrary to what one would expect under the circumstances, with so many workers leaving the farms to enjoy the temptations of the city, the price of food was remarkably stable. The loss in population was so enormous that it had an even greater impact on the demand for food than the reduced supply of food caused by the decline in the number of people engaged in agriculture.[10] With necessities taking a smaller proportion of total spending, the consumption of meat, butter, fish, wine, and exotic spices began to expand even among people at the lowest end of the scale.[11]

In the uncertain and turbulent environment, the incentive to save was minimal while the incentive to spend was irresistible. As late as 1375, a Florentine chronicler was indignant "at the spectacle of the *popolo minuto* who refused to practice their old trades, dressed themselves in a manner unbefitting their station and insisted on the finest delicacies at their table."[12] In Britain, a petition from the House of Commons in 1362 blames rising prices on "laborers [who] use the apparel of craftsmen, and craftsmen the apparel of valets, and valets the apparel of squires, and squires the apparel of knights."[13] William Langland, in *Piers Plowman*, attacked the worker "who refuses to bear the burden of poverty patiently, but blames God and murmers against Reason and curses the king and his council for making statutes [legalized ceilings on wages] to plague the workmen."[14]

The clergy were no exception. In 1351, Pope Clement VI asked his prelates, "What can you preach to the people? . . . If on poverty, you are so covetous that all the benefices in the world are not enough for you. If on chastity—but we will be silent on this, for God knoweth what each man does and how many of you satisfy your lusts."[15]

While the cost of ordinary domestically produced agricultural products was relatively stable, exotic foods came increasingly into fashion, with predictable consequences for prices. According to one authority, the price index of foreign goods such as herring, pepper, oil, sugar, almonds, and saffron rose from 100 in the period 1261–1350 to 162 during the period 1351–1400. He also calculates that per capita expenditures on wine approximately doubled at the same time.[16]

The swollen appetite for imported luxuries such as fancy foods and the increasingly popular clothing frills combined with a heavy burden of military expenditures to send the demand for both gold and silver surging. The supply of precious metals, however, failed to respond to the expanding demand. Metal shortages left the mints inactive for extended periods of time. From 1373 to 1411, the production of gold coins in England averaged only £9500 a year, about a tenth of the output prior to the Black Death.[17] Mining sources also dried up as even record high pay was insufficient to attract men to the discomforts of working the gold mines. Ordinances against exporting "good money" or precious metals accomplished no more than the regulations that required importers to use the revenues they earned to purchase domestically produced goods for export. The repetitive sequence of such orders suggests that they were difficult to enforce and frequently ignored.[18]

Controls over both wages and jobs did not fare any better. For example, Edward III's Statute of Labourers, enacted in 1351, set maximum rates of pay at preplague levels, required all able-bodied men to work, and limited the mobility of workers between jobs and even their freedom of movement between villages. Repeated attempts to enforce these restrictions would ultimately lead to Watt Tyler's hotheaded rebellion in 1381.[19]

One of the more curious—and equally fruitless—efforts to economize on gold included a multiplication of regulations with the odd name of sumptuary laws. The word derives from the Latin *sumptuarius*—to take or to spend—and has the same roots as *sumptuous*. Sumptuary also shares roots with *consume*, which breaks down into "con" and "sume." "Sume," in turn, derives from the French *sumere,* which means to take or to spend.

The purpose of these laws was to economize on scarce gold by prohibiting people from using it lavishly as personal adornment—a dubious objective in the wake of the Black Death. This was a time, as Tuchman described it, of "frenetic gaiety, wild expenditure, luxury, [and] debauchery."[20]

A statute of Edward III enacted in 1363 was typical of the fourteenth-century sumptuary laws. Edward set upper limits for the permissible extravagance of each class. Rustics were limited to blanket cloth and the coarse reddish-brown homespun called russet; grooms and servants were not allowed to wear gold in any form; gentlemen below the rank of knight were prohibited from dressing with any cloth of gold; knights were forbidden to wear gold rings. In 1380, the king of Castile went further by prohibiting all Spaniards except queens and princesses from wearing cloth of gold or gold jewelry.[21]

Like the prohibitions against the export of gold, and doubtless for the same reason, the sumptuary laws were enacted over and over again. Gold, like liquor, satisfies too many needs to survive prohibition.

The Byzantine emperors used gold to persuade others to fight and kill on their behalf. The almost constant warfare of the fourteenth century put gold to the opposite use: for the payment of ransoms that would save lives. Most of the ransoms in the fourteenth century called for the movement of gold within Europe, but the risks of military defeat in all countries meant that monarchs had no choice but to hoard massive reserves of gold as insurance against the evil day when prisoners would have to be redeemed. In the ugly environment of the fourteenth century, ransoms were especially onerous.

Should we deplore the heavy price of redeeming prisoners? The higher the price that the victors could expect, the greater the incentive to constrain the bloody slaughter on the battlefields. The ransom business—and in many ways it *was* a business—must have saved many lives, especially among the upper classes of society.

The most spectacular example of capture and ransom involved the king of France himself, Jean II, who was known as Jean le Bon. Jean loved luxury to the extreme of having the court painter decorate his toilets. In a remarkable step for his time, he commissioned French translations of the Bible so that he could read it more easily. He spent so much money on himself and on trying to fight the English that he soon became an expert at debasing the currency: eighteen alterations in the first year of his reign and seventy more over the next ten years. One churchman, who found monetary affairs in his time even more baffling than the Black Death, wrote a few immortal words on the subject:

> Money and currency are very strange things.
> They keep on going up and down and no one knows why;
> If you want to win, you lose, however hard you try.[22]

Jean le Bon's son, the Dauphin (who was also duke of Normandy), was shifty in his loyalty to his father. In April 1356, he hosted a dinner party in his castle in Rouen for his cousin and neighbor Charles le Mauvais, king of Navarre, hoping to organize a conspiracy to capture the throne of France. Charles le Mauvais was such a bad man that almost anybody compared to him, like Jean, would have been characterized as "le Bon." Jean, who had advance notice of the meeting between Charles and the Dauphin, burst in on the gathering in full armored regalia. He thereupon had some of Charles's entourage butchered, threw Charles into prison, and confiscated Charles's Norman estates.

Charles's brother and surviving associates appealed for English help to recover their estates. The English responded without delay and, under the command of the Duke of Lancaster, were soon on their way into France from Cherbourg. In July, the Prince of Wales, known as the Black Prince and one of the greatest fighters and commanders of his age (the "black" referred to his armor), landed at Bordeaux with eight thousand troops and launched a series of devastating raids as he traveled northward through western France. Jean decided that he had no choice but to face his enemies in pitched battle. Confidently leading his army of sixteen thousand men, the largest army of the century, Jean marched toward the Loire to block the Black Prince's northward approach.[23]

On September 19, 1356, the French army was overpowered by the Black Prince's forces at the Battle of Poitiers, despite superior strategic positions in the field and twice the number of soldiers. Seven hours into the battle, the English discovered Jean's unit and charged at high speed against it, "like the wild boar of Cornwall."[24] Jean fought valiantly with one of his loyal sons beside him, but he lost his helmet and began to bleed from two wounds on his face. When voices cried, "Yield, yield, or you are a dead man,"[25] Jean handed over his glove to an enemy soldier and thus the king of France became a prisoner of war.

The king was by no means the only distinguished prisoner to be taken that day. The list included the highest-ranking French military commanders and over two thousand members of the nobility. The number of prisoners was greater than the English could handle. Most of the prisoners were instructed on their honor to come to Bordeaux with their ransoms by Christmas—in the days of chivalry, such a request was a matter of routine. And still many of the English soldiers complained that their archers' aim had been too good, because the arrows that hit the French forces with such accuracy had deprived the victors of an even larger number of prisoners to hold for ransom.[26]

The Black Prince took the French king to England seven months after the battle and installed him in high style at the Savoy Palace until the ransom was paid. But how big was the ransom to be? When the French rejected a preliminary settlement in 1358, the English responded by raising their demands. Meanwhile, the clock was ticking.

In March 1359, with just six months left before the truce negotiated at Poitiers was scheduled to expire, Jean signed the Treaty of London. His desperation is apparent in the conditions to which he agreed: in exchange for his release from captivity, he yielded all of western France from Calais to the Pyrenees plus a ransom of four million gold *écus* (gold crowns, the equivalent of more than £600,000), the ransom to be collateralized by forty noble and royal hostages. If the French blocked the execution of this treaty in any fashion, Edward had the right to send his armies back to France—at the expense of the French king. Edward knew what he was doing by putting the financial burden on the enemy, for his wars in France were terribly costly. In one year alone, he borrowed two hundred thousand gold florins from his Italian bankers (on which he subsequently defaulted).[27]

When the Dauphin, serving as regent in his father's absence, received word of this total capitulation, he summoned the estates general to help him make the fearful choice between peace and renewal of the war. The response was immediate and unanimous: the treaty was intolerable, and war was to be declared on England.

The English promptly launched another protracted campaign in northern France, but this time the French resisted a pitched battle, resorting to a scorched-earth strategy instead. On April 13, when the depleted and now ragged English army was camped near Chartres, an extraordinarily powerful hailstorm hit them, accompanied by cyclone-force winds and cloudbursts of freezing rain. According to Tuchman, "In half an hour Edward's army took a beating that human hands could not have inflicted and that could hardly be taken as other than a celestial warning."[28]

It is the rare military commander who at one time or another has not heeded messages from supernatural sources. Edward III, tough though he was in many ways, decided at this point that discretion was the better part of valor. In any case, he retained plenty of bargaining power, because Jean was still his prisoner. He agreed to reopen negotiations, which were finally completed on May 8, 1360, at the nearby village of Brétigny. Jean's ransom was scaled back to three million gold crowns. The territorial concessions were also reduced, but they still amounted to about a third of France, a prize unmatched until Hitler invaded France 580 years later.

The treaty was explicit about the terms for the forty hostages to be held as security against the payment of the king's ransom. The stipulations included the king's two younger sons, his brother, the brother-in-law of the Dauphin, and nine great counts. The English agreed to return Jean from London to Calais, upon payment of the first installment of six hundred thousand gold crowns on the ransom. At that point, ten of his fellow noble prisoners would also be liberated, but they were to be replaced by forty wealthy members of the Third Estate—the bourgeoisie; like Willy Sutton, Edward III knew where the money was. The remainder of Jean's ransom was due in six semiannual installments of four hundred thousand gold crowns, with one-fifth of the hostages to be released after each payment.

The ransom would have been a terrible burden on the French under any circumstances, but especially following the depredations of the Black Death and the havoc and destruction of war. The going was so difficult at one point that the French invited back the Jews whom they had ejected from France in 1306, offering them twenty years' residence subject to payment of twenty florins per head entrance fee and seven florins annually thereafter.[29] Jean himself contributed the handsome golden dowry he earned from marrying off his eleven-year-old daughter to the rich tyrant of Milan, Galeazzo Visconti, a step that the chronicler Matteo Villani described as the king "selling his own flesh at auction."[30]

The first installment of the ransom was made in October 1360. Edward then met with Jean in Calais, and the two monarchs swore together to keep the peace into perpetuity. After four years in captivity, the king of France was finally a free man. The moment was hardly one for rejoicing. Jean returned to a country that Petrarch, on hand as an ambassador from Visconti, described as "a heap of ruins. . . . Everywhere was solitude, desolation, and misery."[31]

Nor is this the end of the story of Jean's ransom payments. Plague, which continued to reappear periodically, killed off some of the hostages in England. Other members of the group were attempting to use their own resources to buy their freedom. The ransom payments were soon in arrears. Ceded territories resisted the change in sovereignty. In 1363, convinced that his honor was in disrepute, Jean sailed back across the Channel the week after Christmas and restored himself to captivity in London, disregarding the urgent advice of his Council, his prelates, and his barons. He was received by the English with great ceremony and celebration, but he soon fell ill and died in April 1364. He was only 45 years old. A million gold crowns were still payable on his ransom.

In the end, less than half the ransom was paid, but even 1.5 million gold crowns was a colossal amount of money. It was equivalent to a full year's pay for approximately six thousand agricultural laborers, three hundred thousand sheep, or 1.6 million gallons of ale, or to more than four times the total of all the poll taxes that would stir up a vicious rebellion almost twenty years later.[32]

One other golden ransom payment is worth comment, even though it was paid in the following century. This fifteenth-century ransom was once again a consequence of the English wars with the French, which were still fitfully occupying both countries as late as the 1470s.

In 1478, King Edward IV of England abandoned an intended invasion of France in return for a down payment by the French of 75,000 crowns and an annual pension of fifty thousand additional crowns. The following year, the French also agreed to ransom Henry VI's widow, Margaret of Anjou, for fifty thousand crowns, to be paid in five annual installments. Christopher Challis's authoritative history of the English

Mint calculates that if all this money had actually been paid up to the time of the death of Edward IV in 1483—and the evidence suggests that it *was* paid—the total would have come to 517,000 crowns or £103,400. This sum compares with the Mint's total gold output of £185,684 from 1474 to 1482.

The English got a better deal than the raw figures indicate. In 1471, during the Wars of the Roses, the Yorkist leaders Edward and his brother Richard Duke of Gloucester—the future Edward IV and Richard III, respectively—had captured, deposed, and murdered the Lancastrian King Henry VI as well as his son, the prince of Wales. This event put the ex-queen, Margaret of Anjou, into the ranks of the involuntarily unemployed. One can only wonder why the French had to offer such a generous sum in order to persuade the English to part with Margaret. She must have been a terrible harridan, hanging around with nothing to do but bemoan the terrible fate that the victorious Yorkists had visited upon her husband and son.

Edward and Richard should have considered her worth disposing of at any price. In Act I, Scene 3 of Shakespeare's *Richard III*, Richard describes her to her face as "thou hateful withered hag." Perhaps that was only fair, because Margaret tells Richard off by calling him, among other things, "Thou elvish-marked, abortive, rooting hog . . . the son of hell/Thou loathed issue of thy father's loins!" Yet we must admit the possibility that Shakespeare was taking poetic license in his choice of words. Margaret was reputed to be a great beauty. After her return to France, however, she succumbed to a skin ailment, described by one more scholarly historian than Shakespeare as "a dry scaly withering of her once-golden beauty. Overnight, she became hideous. Only her eyes remained, ravaged and terrible."[33] Nevertheless, one can only speculate what the Yorkists might have done to Margaret had not her king so generously offered those fifty thousand golden crowns for the dubious pleasure of repatriating her.

Those people who survived the endless agonies of the fourteenth century must have been convinced that the darkness of their age would never lift. Yet as this terrible century finally drew to an end and the new century dawned, conditions in Europe began to improve. Peace provided opportunity to put abandoned farmlands back into use, and the lower prices for food that resulted led to an expanding population. After losing six million people from 1350 to 1400, the population of Europe grew by fifteen million—about a third—during the next fifty years and gained another nine million between 1450 and 1500. Improving food supplies also facilitated a return to urbanization, which in turn enabled commerce and industry to revive.[34]

Progress was not uniform across Europe. Italy fared best among the major European countries, and there the greatest glory of the fifteenth century was in Venice, although Florence also became a great center of commerce, industry, finance—and art—during this period. Venice remained the most important station for the great volume of trade with the lands to the east, but the city was not just a group of charming islands in the Adriatic. By the end of the century, Venice controlled most of the cities within a radius of around one hundred miles from Saint Mark's Square—including such centers as Verona, Vicenza, Ferrara, and Bologna—as well as the Mediterranean islands of Corfu, Cyprus, and Crete.

That kind of power gains gold. The territories remitted a million gold ducats a year to the Venetians, which paid for many of the palaces that are now so familiar on the Grand Canal, including the Ca d'Oro or House of Gold, whose exterior ornamentation was once generously covered with gold. This lovely edifice is familiar to millions of modern tourists, who deposit their own good money there for the pleasure of the visit.

Probably the most revolutionary developments in the course of the fifteenth century took place in an area that had been a sideshow to the Middle Ages in Europe: Iberia. The marriage of Ferdinand of Aragon to Isabella of Castile in 1469 united Spain. Under their leadership, the Spaniards finally expelled the Moors and, while they were at it, the Jews. Ferdinand and Isabella also launched a commanding dynasty that would deploy Spanish power across the entire European landscape and, in time, in the Americas as well. One daughter was married to the king of England, the other, Joanna the Mad, to the oldest son of the Holy Roman Emperor. Poor Joanna earned her name because she carted her husband's cadaver around with her for many years after his death. The contribution of Ferdinand and Isabella and the Spanish to the history of the Americas needs no elaboration.

Meanwhile, the little country of Portugal was also stirring. The Portuguese had always been great sailors; as early as 1300, they had established a navy trained by Genoese and Venetians. King John I, crowned in 1385, was an enlightened ruler who found ways to transform a third-rate nation of only one million people (one-sixth the population of Morocco) into a world power.[35] John signed an alliance with the English that was to last into perpetuity and is still in effect; he then cemented the deal by marrying a granddaughter of Edward III, whose brother, Henry Bolingbroke, would soon usurp the English throne from Richard II.* John's third son, Henry the Navigator, an ascetic who never married, was encouraged by his father to motivate the great explorations of his century. These explorations would lead to the discovery of the sea route to the Far East around the Cape of Good Hope, the discovery of America, and Magellan's triumphant discovery of the sea passage from the Atlantic to the Pacific during his ships' circumnavigation of the globe. The Portuguese were so turned on by their successes in exploration that the country was significantly depopulated of men of working age, unable to resist the temptation to join in. Many of these men either settled in far-off lands or disappeared in shipwrecks.

European output of gold during the fifteenth century was smaller than ever relative to the needs of the times. According to one authoritative estimate, domestic gold production in Europe in 1400 was no more than four tons.[36] In money, that works out to about one million ducats.[37] It is estimated that the Venetians alone exported the equivalent of a ton of gold a year in the form of ducats during the fifteenth century, significantly reducing the available supply of gold.[38] Economic historian Charles Kindleberger cites estimates that as much as 5 percent

*The Treaty of Methuen in 1703 admitted Portuguese wines to Britain at duties one-third less than on French wines, while Portugal agreed to import from Britain a variety of goods that the Portuguese were unable to supply to Brazil. Brazilian gold sailed to Britain to pay for what the sales of Portuguese wines could not cover; Brazilian gold coins were common currency in England at the time. Some scholars believe that this treaty converted Portugal into an English colony (see Kindleberger, 1996c, p. 71).

a year of the coinage also disappeared due to ordinary wear, hoarding, shipwreck, and movement into plating for decorative purposes.*[39]

After some three thousand years of developing civilization, the total amount of gold in Europe in 1500 in all forms—coins, hoards, and every manner of adornment and decoration—could have been fashioned into a cube only two meters in each dimension. This modest supply meant that even small discoveries or transfers had a magnified effect on the gold market.[40]

The economic historian John Day, in an essay titled "The Great Bullion Famine of the Fifteenth Century," cites striking examples of the shortage of gold coins that developed during the fifteenth century as well as the fruitless efforts by governmental authorities to do something about it. "In 1409, the Paris money-changers protested in chorus that they had no bullion for the mint at any price. The civil war years (1411–35) witnessed the rapid decline of the influential goldsmiths' guild of Paris for lack of metal, lack of clients, and because of new restrictions on the manufacture of gold and silver artifacts, which were intended 'to prevent the destruction of the king's coinage.' "[41] An ordinance issued at the port of Bruges in 1401 required merchants to settle all foreign exchange transactions entirely in gold; the ordinance was repealed eight months later because so few paid attention to it.[42] The mints of the Estates of Flanders were shut down from 1402 to 1410.[43] The output of the Tower Mint in London, which averaged around £5000 in gold coins in the 1460s, fell to £2000 from 1476 to 1485 and then virtually came to a halt over the next ten years. Silver coinage shows similar trends.[44] Day estimates that total bullion reserves in Europe shrank by 50 percent between about 1340 and 1460.[45]

The dearth of both silver and gold provoked a reversion to barter in many communities, especially for local payments. Pepper, worth more than its weight in gold, was the most popular commodity enlisted for this purpose; German princes even called their bankers "peppermen."[46] Although this kind of improvised money served a purpose, the import flow of such commodities as pepper was uneven, which made their prices uncomfortably volatile. A few bags of pepper unloaded in Amsterdam or London could quickly depress its price. Not so a few bags of gold or silver. As a result, paper currencies—essentially promissory

*Even this could be an understatement. See Day 3, footnote 8.

notes issued by high-quality borrowers—began to circulate, but Day argues that "The circulation remained overwhelmingly metallic. Even in mid-eighteenth-century England, on the threshold of the industrial revolution, it was estimated that minted coin accounted for 90 percent of all the money in circulation. . . . As late as 1861, Italian circulation consisted of 75 percent coin."[47]

When money is in short supply, people try to economize on the amount they spend for goods and services. The usual result is a declining price level. That is precisely what happened during the fifteenth century. Reliable estimates indicate that prices for commodities throughout western Europe fell by anywhere from 20 percent to 50 percent between 1400 and 1500. In Aragon, for example, the index of prices fell about 20 percent.[48] The price of English wheat fell by half between 1360 and 1500, while the price of rye in Frankfurt dropped even faster.[49] Similar trends in the Low Countries and Italy demonstrate that this was a universal phenomenon in fifteenth-century Europe.

At the same time, however, the demand for gold was so great that its price moved in the opposite direction. In England, where developments were typical of trends throughout Europe, the price of gold climbed slowly but almost without interruption from 23 shillings an ounce in 1345 to 40 shillings by 1492.[50] The resulting increase in the purchasing power of gold meant that the volume of commodities that an ounce of gold could buy doubled, at the very least, between the beginning and the end of the fifteenth century. As a consequence, this was one of the few periods in history when gold was spent instead of hoarded.

Gold has always been a valuable prize, but the alluring combination of falling commodity prices and rising gold prices promised tempting rewards for those who could find new sources. In that setting, the great explorations of the fifteenth century appear to have been an inevitable response.

Or was it inevitable? One might argue that the forces of raw economics were only an incidental cause of the passion for exploration across the seas in the 1400s. Perhaps these enterprising voyages to reach the ends of the earth were just one more manifestation of the spirit of the Renaissance, a new age that broke with the more rigid mindsets that religion had imposed on the Dark Ages and the Middle Ages, a time that encouraged bold experimentation in art, culture, and science. Progress in navigation and the expansion of geographical knowledge were natural by-products of the important innovations during the Renaissance in mathematics, in measurement, and in perspective. The discovery of the world was what the Renaissance was all about. Between 1492 and 1500, the size of the world known to Europeans more than doubled; 25 years later, it had more than tripled.[51]

At first glance, this explanation appears to make sense, but the contention that the great explorations could not have happened in an earlier age leads to two strange and counterintuitive conclusions. First, if the surge in the purchasing power of gold had occurred during a less innovative era, there would have been no one like Henry the Navigator, Columbus, or Magellan—explorers who were unable to resist the temptation of extraordinarily profitable rewards from hunting for gold across the seas. Sailors would have gone along traveling the traditional routes as though nothing had happened to the market for gold. Second, if the great explorations were purely a consequence of the adventurous spirit of the Renaissance, these voyages would have taken place even if the price of gold was falling while the price of commodities was rising. Neither of these possibilities makes much sense.

The argument need not end there, however. The search for gold was not the only motivation for these remarkable adventures. Dreams of glory and, perhaps even more important, the zeal to convert heathens to Christianity were also part of the inspiration. However, dreams of glory and the enthusiasm for turning heathens into Christians were surely not unique to the Renaissance. Men have always fantasized great deeds, and Christians have always been eager proselytizers.

The burning hunger for gold remains as the critical stimulant. The hunger for gold is always "burning," but it burned especially bright in the fifteenth century. The Spaniards and the Portuguese, and, later on, the English, the Dutch, and the French, conveniently managed to blur the distinction between the desire to do good works in the name of God and the desire to fatten their purses. The effort to become rich and powerful and to bring the blessings of Christianity to the great unwashed are characteristically presented with a blended rationale that must have been a source of great self-satisfaction.

Columbus summed it up well when he wrote to Ferdinand and Isabella about his early encounters with the natives of the lands he discovered:

> So your highness should resolve to make them Christians, for I believe that . . . you will achieve the conversion to our holy faith of a great number of peoples, with the acquisition of great lordships and riches and all their inhabitants for Spain. For without doubt there is in these lands a very great amount of gold.[52]

9

The Sacred Thirst

Before railroads crossed the United States, you could reach San Francisco faster and cheaper by water from China than by land from Saint Louis.[1] This simple fact explains why the greatest challenge to western Europeans seeking gold and expanded trade in the fifteenth century was to find a direct sea route to India and the Far East. Success in that venture would replace the strenuous and hazardous overland paths that for hundreds of years had carried cargo and humans on horseback or mule or on foot.

The Portuguese were the first to step out and lead the way to the Discovery of the World. This was no coincidence. Portugal is such a narrow country that, relative to its small population, it ranks first in Europe in coastline facing the sea. Portugal was also one of the poorest countries in Europe at the end of the Middle Ages, which meant that even small, profitable discoveries could make a big difference. Political disturbances and monetary depreciation in the dark days of the fourteenth century had ruined the gentry and galvanized them to seek new fortunes in foreign undertakings. The whole environment provided the perfect setting for Prince Henry the Navigator's single-minded zeal for using the seas to expand Portugal's power and influence.

Gold was the primary objective of the Portuguese explorations, but that was not all. All the fifteenth-century explorers claimed that they were on a new crusade to smite the infidels and convert them to Christianity. When the inhabitants of distant lands turned out to have dark skins, the Portuguese soon convinced themselves that taking these poor souls as slaves was a great convenience that facilitated the process of religious conversion while incidentally satisfying the pressing demand for low-cost labor. Slavery was thus an afterthought, a by-product of the search for metallic treasures, but it became increasingly important.

Prince Henry's immediate goal was to contain the threat to Portugal itself from the Moorish pirates who preyed on shipping in the western Mediterranean. These pirates, later known as the Barbary Pirates, would still be a danger to trade and travel when John Paul Jones pursued them nearly four hundred years later. Henry opened his campaign in 1415 by capturing the Moorish city of Ceuta, just east of the Straits of Gibraltar on the north coast of Africa. Ceuta was an immensely wealthy city that served as the main Mediterranean port for the goods that Arab traders brought from Africa and Asia. In particular, Ceuta was the primary port for the caravans that brought African gold across the desert for shipment to Europe. As the Portuguese troops ravaged every corner of Ceuta, they found plenty of evidence of the golden resources of West Africa.

The capture of Ceuta opened up a compelling strategy to Henry and his men: if they could transport the output of the African mines by sea to their own shores, they could outflank the rest of Europe by circumventing the tedious and expensive voyage by camel across the Sahara desert to the northern Mediterranean trading posts. The arithmetic involved is worth setting forth in detail.

Depending upon its quality and endurance, a camel can carry between 120 and 200 kilograms of cargo across the desert for eight to twelve hours a day at 2.5 to 5.0 miles an hour. Let us take the average camel—carrying 160 kilograms for ten hours at, say, 3.5 miles an hour. That camel would cover 35 miles a day. The distance from the Mediterranean coast at Morocco to the gold country is nearly two thousand miles—roughly the distance from New York to Las Vegas, or from one end of the Mediterranean to the other—which means that the camel would have to spend about 55 days in travel (although there was a wide range around this average as well). Upon completing the trip, we should note, the camel had to be given an extended rest period to recover from his labors. A man could usually manage four camels at a time. As the caravans numbered from as low as three hundred camels to as many as 3500, the crews would vary from 75 to nearly nine hundred men; even the smaller caravans wending their way across the sands must have been quite a sight. A caravan of one thousand camels, each carrying 160 kilograms, would have transported a total of 160 metric tons of cargo.

A ship at sea moves more slowly than a camel, at approximately 60 percent of the camel's speed. However, a ship travels 24 hours a day; the camel caravans had to travel at the pace of the slowest camel and for only a third to one-half of a 24-hour day. Consequently, a ship can readily cover more than twice as much distance as a camel in one day. As the distance by sea from Gibraltar to the gold country is at most twice the distance across the desert, the ship has a modest advantage in travel time—even though, like the camel, it needs refitting after long voyages. The big advantage is manpower. The arithmetic above indicates that, at four camels per man and 160 kilograms per camel, a man was responsible for about 0.7 tons of cargo. On a ship, depending on the size of the vessel and the crew required, a man could be responsible for anywhere from three tons to fourteen tons.[2] The ship is vulnerable to loss in storms or to piracy, but camels could fall ill and entire caravans could be attacked by Berbers and other nomads.

These fifteenth-century ships incorporated the lateen sail, a remarkable technological innovation that had been developed in the eastern Mediterranean as early as the second century AD but came into wide use only in the Middle Ages. Unlike conventional square sails, which were positioned horizontally and limited the movement of a ship almost entirely to running ahead of the wind, the lateen sail was triangular and positioned vertically to the length of the ship. It could swing from port to starboard and back again, which for the first time made tacking possible for larger ships, so they could take the wind on either side. This innovation significantly extended the range of the sailing ships—without it, Columbus could never have discovered America.

Prince Henry and his men began by launching a systematic policy of aggression against Moroccan cities, first on the Mediterranean side and then on the western, Atlantic side. The payoff came in short order, in the form of a rapidly growing traffic in slaves, indigo, and sugar between Africa and Portugal. Gold began to flow as well, but the volume appeared to the Portuguese to be no more than a trickle compared with their grandiose expectations. They were convinced that somewhere down the western coast of Africa they would discover the *rio d'oro*, a river of gold in both a literal and figurative sense. They had to keep pushing farther.

It was not just a matter of sailing down the coast until they found the *rio d'oro*. Although the Phoenicians and a few later explorers had made some short voyages in that direction, no one had ever thoroughly explored the west coast of Africa by sea. The few reports that existed were unanimously scary. Arab sailors, who were used to plying the east coast of Africa, fed the Mediterranean folklore of boiling hot seas on the western side, swarming with serpents waiting to grab human flesh from the decks of the ships. The lucky survivors of such a voyage would suffer the terrible fate of seeing their skin transformed from white to black.[3] The winds were dangerous, the natives unfriendly, and the actual source of the gold an unsolved mystery.

Despite the perils, the prize was too seductive to be frightened away. Bit by bit, in successive voyages, the Portuguese navigators crept down the coast, braving poisoned arrows, building fortresses, and capturing slaves (Moors would do when blacks failed to appear, or Moors cooperated by supplying the blacks). Even though progress was slow, the Portuguese mariners never lost faith that they would ultimately discover the elusive river of gold. Finally, around the middle of the century, the Portuguese caravels succeeded in rounding the thick western part of Africa where the coast faces southward. There was the area of Guinea, where the population was predominantly black rather than Moorish.

The participants in these adventures were colorful characters. One in particular stands out, a merchant of Venice by the name of Alvise da Cadamosto. Cadamosto arrived in Portugal in 1454 and approached Prince Henry for permission to participate in the African trade. Convinced that Venetians knew more about maritime trading than anybody else, Henry hastened to agree to Cadamosto's request. Cadamosto fully lived up to Henry's expectations: he was an expert in evaluating commercial prospects.

We are grateful to Cadamosto for having left a journal of his voyages that is invaluable for its information and irresistible for its charm. It was he, for example, who first reported back to Europe on the silent bartering of salt for gold along the Niger River. Yet, with all his travels into the interior—at one point he was 250 miles inland—and his ability to get along with suspicious natives, he was unable to unlock the secret of the source of West African gold.

One of Cadamosto's unforgettable encounters was with King Budomel, a petty tyrant who ruled over a group of villages composed of grass huts. Budomel had countless wives, each of whom was waited on by five or six young girls. Cadamosto noted, "It is customary for the King to sleep with these attendants as with his wives, to whom this does not appear an injury." That was hard work: "Budomel demanded of me importunately, having been given to understand that Christians knew how to do many things, whether by chance I could give him the means by which he could satisfy many women, for which he offered me a great reward." Cadamosto did not reveal his response to this request.[4]

By the early 1470s, the Portuguese had established a major trading post on the south-facing coast of West Africa, which they named San Jorge de Mina. Although they erected an imposing capital at San Jorge and carried on an active business with the natives to the north and to the west, the Portuguese never managed to become owners or even to participate in the operation of any of the African gold fields. The gold that returned to Portugal by way of San Jorge de Mina was acquired in a set of barter arrangements in which the Portuguese paid for it by trading salt, capes and robes, red and blue cloth, canvas, copper and brass pots and pans, coral, red shells, and white wine.[5] Business was good. By the early 1500s, approximately seven hundred kilograms of gold a year was moving from Africa to Portugal, a meaningful sum when all of Europe's total annual output was no more than about four tons and Portugal's was no more than zero.[6]

In August 1487, Bartholomeu Dias, an experienced Portuguese explorer of African waters, sailed from Lisbon in command of two caravels and a supply ship with orders to go around Africa to India. Six months later, Dias was the first European to moor his ship on the southeast coast of Africa. He continued on some way, with every intention of continuing on to India, but his men were impatient to go home, especially as the supply ship had fallen far behind. Dias had no choice but to turn back, which meant that Vasco da Gama would be the first to reach India in 1497 and start the process of establishing major Portuguese posts throughout Asian waters. Turning his ships around, Dias sailed once again past the cape at the bottom of Africa, which his king would later name the Cape of Good Hope, because it leads on to the passage to India.[7]

In December 1488, Dias returned to Lisbon, sixteen months after his departure. One of the people in the audience who came to hear him report in detail on his voyage was a Genoese seaman named Christopher Columbus, who took copious notes as he listened to Dias's presentation.

Columbus was the son of a weaver; like many other Genoese, he had gone to sea at an early age. He had been on a ship sunk in battle, had sailed to the eastern Mediterranean and possibly to Turkey, had been on a voyage to Iceland that had stopped at Ireland, and had sailed through many of the known waters on the African coast. Samuel Eliot Morison, his most distinguished biographer, emphasizes that Columbus was one of the best navigators and seamen of his day. He had no doubts that the sea route he envisaged straight out into the Atlantic would not only replace the overland routes to Asia but by heading straight west would make much more sense than the tortuous eastward routes that the Portuguese were attempting to establish. Columbus was confident that he would find gold, but by shortening the time involved he would also significantly reduce the cost of the voyage to India and the rest of Asia, making possible the shipment of a substantially larger variety of goods. He was also deeply religious and dreamed of spending the gold he would earn from his pathfinding voyage on a crusade to win back the Holy Sepulcher from the Muslims.[8]

Columbus lived for a long time in Lisbon, where he married a local girl and worked on occasion as a mapmaker. Convinced that Portugal would be the obvious country to back him, Columbus approached the throne in 1484, offering the first chance to sponsor and finance his voyage. Yet King John II, the nephew of Prince Henry and grandson of John I, turned Columbus down flat. The Portuguese, growing fat on their African arrangements and their newfound linkages to the Indies via the Cape of Good Hope, saw no need to take on another big risk. John was in any case put off by Columbus's insistent demand that the king make him a knight, admiral of the Ocean Seas, and viceroy and governor of all lands discovered, in addition to turning over 10 percent of all profits from these lands—which specifically included gold. These were precisely the terms that Columbus would later manage to squeeze out of Ferdinand and Isabella.

Still hopeful, Columbus turned to the Spanish monarchs in 1486. The commission they appointed to study his proposal took until late 1489 to decide that his idea was without merit: the trip would take too long, and they doubted whether any lands remained to be discovered. After that, Columbus was rejected by Henry VII of England, whose advisors ridiculed the whole idea as fantastic. Charles VIII of France also said no.

At that point, Columbus saw no choice but to give up the whole thing. Four European monarchies had turned him down, scorning his conviction that he was offering them the most direct, the most economical, and the fastest route to the Indies. He decided to return to mapmaking.

Queen Isabella, however, had never lost interest in Columbus's ingenious plan. The risks were obvious, but the rewards could be tremendous: Columbus's shorter route would give Spain the means to take the leadership in the Indies away from the Portuguese, while the gold that he promised would finance and support the dynasty that she dreamed of creating. So Isabella summoned Columbus back, even providing him with money for a new suit and a mule to carry him to her. At first the news was excellent, as Isabella's new commission did approve his proposal. Then came the bad news: the Grand Council rejected what they considered to be Columbus's exorbitant demands for titles and financial rewards.

Defeated and dejected, Columbus mounted his mule and headed back home. He had just begun the trip along the mule path when a horseman caught up with him and told him to return to the queen. An influential advisor had prevailed upon her to change her mind. That was in April 1492. Four months later, just before sunrise on August 3, Columbus and his crew made confession, took communion, and boarded their ships. Columbus's command to weigh the anchors ended with the words, "in the name of Jesus." The rest is history.[9]

Two days after touching land on San Salvador, which Columbus was certain was offshore from Japan, or Cipangu as the Spaniards called it, he sailed onward in search of his goal. He was confident that he would soon be able to confirm Marco Polo's observation that the palaces in Japan were roofed with gold—he carried a copy of Marco Polo's writings with him as a guidebook to the lands he expected to visit.[10] The bits of gold that the natives wore as nose plugs only increased the sense of anticipation. As soon as he noticed that the Indians did not put much value on their gold, he hastened to offer them beads and caps in exchange. That was a profitable trade-off!

The natives Columbus encountered on San Salvador told him about a large island nearby named Cuba, which sounded enough like Cipangu to convince Columbus and his crew that their goal was now within reach. They landed on Cuba on October 28, but they found no gold. Although they did discover tobacco, it held no interest for them; nothing except huge quantities of gold would satisfy them. From October 12, 1492, to January 17, 1493, when Columbus headed back to Spain, his diary mentions gold more than 65 times.[11] Indeed, his entry of October 13, 1492, the day after the first landing, reports, "I was attentive and took trouble to ascertain if there was gold."[12] He was encouraged by the dark skins of the natives, for Europeans had long believed that dark skins would be a sure sign of the presence of gold. While sailing along the Cuban coast, he noted in his diary, "From the great heat which I suffer, the country must be rich in gold."[13]

Columbus was euphoric over his discoveries, but he as well as his early followers faced painful disappointments. The lands they had discovered were not the Indies after all, although Columbus still thought he was in Asia even during his third voyage six years after the first. Worse, the continental landmass they encountered appeared to be such an endless barrier that nobody could figure out how to get around it to reach the Indies, the only objective that made the whole dangerous business worthwhile. If the amount of gold on these lands had at least met their expectations, that would have been some compensation for the frustration of missing out on their ultimate objective. Gold there was, but surely no bonanza.

The marching orders were nevertheless certain. As King Ferdinand had commanded, "Get gold, humanely if possible, but at all hazards—get gold."[14]

In 1510, a debt-ridden, disgruntled Spanish farmer from Estramadura named Vasco Núñez de Balboa decided to leave Hispaniola (now Santo Domingo) and join an expedition to Darien, the area where the Isthmus of Panama connects to the northern shores of Colombia. There was gold in central Hispaniola, where the Spaniards worked both the mines and the Indians so hard that by 1519 only two thousand of an original population of more than one hundred thousand remained and slaves were already being imported from Africa to do the mining.[15] Nevertheless, rumors were rife in Darien about vast supplies of gold somewhere to the south, perhaps near a sea whose uncertain existence might lead to the gold. When Balboa arrived in Darien, he became close friends with an illiterate swordsman, also from Estramadura, whose name was Francisco Pizarro. Pizarro, like Balboa, was a man who did not flinch at danger if a venture promised a commensurate reward.

The move to Darien did nothing to solve Balboa's financial problems. One day in September 1513, still frustrated and in trouble with the law, Balboa was weighing some gold when a barbarian chieftain came up, scattered the glittering metal around the room, and cried, "I can tell you of a land where they eat and drink out of golden vessels, and gold is as cheap as iron is with you."[16] This was all Balboa needed to prompt him to lead a great enterprise he expected would bring him to King Ferdinand's attention. He proceeded to gather together a group of 190 Spaniards, aiming to track down the rumored gold sources once and for all and also to resolve the mystery of the incomplete search for an ocean route to Asia. Despite three weeks of attacks by hostile Indians, insects, and snakes, Balboa's men hacked their way westward until they came to an abrupt escarpment. The Indians told them that the slope on the other side of the crest led down to a great sea. John Keats had the wrong man but the right ocean—and the full sense of this great moment—when he wrote,

Then I felt like some watcher of the skies
When a new planet swims into his ken;
Or like stout Cortez when with eagle eyes
He stared at the Pacific and all his men
Look'd at each other with a wild surmise
Silent, upon a peak in Darien.
[*On First Looking into Chapman's Homer*]

A couple of days later, Balboa waded into the surf of the Pacific with drawn sword and claimed "the great South Sea . . . with all that it contained," for the king of Spain.[17] And then, setting a standard for cruelty to the Indians that many other Spaniards would emulate, Balboa and his men mercilessly plundered the copious treasure of gold objects that they found in the Indian villages. The elegance and dazzling sophistication of these semiabstract objects evidently held no meaning for them.[18] They were far more fascinated by the traces of gold ore they uncovered on the sandy shores of their South Sea.

This glittering achievement failed to solve Balboa's problems, and he seems to have been in chronic trouble with authority. Some time after the discovery of the Pacific, at a moment when Balboa was making plans to sail southward on his newly discovered sea toward Peru in search of more gold, the governor of Darien accused him of treason and ordered him to be beheaded. The governor, who had been sent out with fifteen hundred men by the king of Spain after receiving the electrifying news of Balboa's discoveries, happened to be Balboa's father-in-law; the executioner assigned by the governor to this task was none other than Francisco Pizarro.

Pizarro was an illegitimate child, abandoned by his mother on the church steps of the town where he was born. He grew up tough, a man of great endurance and strong leadership skills. At a time when most men rationalized their mistreatment of the Indians as motivated in some way to improve their lot and bring them the blessings of Christianity, Pizarro refused to mask his goals. After the victory in Peru, when a priest asked him to do more to convert the natives, Pizarro's response was, "I have not come for any such reasons. I have come to take away from them their gold."[19]

He was a man of iron will and unshakable confidence in his own abilities, regardless of the obstacles placed in his way. Consider this astonishing fact: Pizarro's first decisive contact with the Incas did not occur until 1532, which was eight long years after the first exploratory expedition down the Pacific coast from Panama with one ship and one hundred men. He even made two trips back to Spain during those eight years to firm up royal support and sufficient resources for the campaign in Peru.

William H. Prescott's *The Conquest of Peru*, first published in May 1847, is one of the great works of nineteenth-century American literature, vividly written with exceptional grace and impeccable historical scholarship.* Prescott takes a dim view of the hypocrisy of the Spaniards in justifying their terrible deeds in the name of Christ, yet he cannot help but admire their courage, ingenuity, and audacity in the face of the staggering odds against them.

After scaling the wild passes of the Andes, often on paths scarcely wide enough for a horse and flanked by sheer drops of thousands of feet into the abyss, two hundred Spaniards managed to subdue an empire of at least 3.5 million people[20] that included large portions of the modern states of Ecuador, Peru, Bolivia, Chile, and Argentina.[21] At the turning point in the campaign, Pizarro's little army overcame the resistance of thirty thousand Inca soldiers trained to fight at altitudes of over ten thousand feet.

The Spaniards were hardened, brave, and ruthless fighters, but, as with Cortez's men in Mexico, they were surprised at the advantage they achieved by appearing godlike to the Indians. The pale faces, cannons and muskets, trumpets, horses, shining armor, and wagons were awesome and frightening to the Indians. Despite a society that was in many ways more highly structured, agriculturally productive, and artistically sophisticated than the Spanish, these Indians had never invented the wheel and their ubiquitous llamas could hardly match the speed, ridability, and intelligence of the horse. Their only technological advantage was an extraordinarily effective relay system of highly trained runners who carried news and information up and down the majestic Andes on roads as good as Roman roads, functioning with such remarkable efficiency that they even delivered live fish from the coast to the nobility living high in the mountain valleys.

The decisive climax to what is a long story occurred in November 1532, when Pizarro and his men reached a watering place high up in the mountains called Caxamalca, where the Emperor Atahualpa, "the Inca,"

*The edition in my possession was published by the Heritage Press, New York, in 1957. It contains a fascinating biography of Prescott by the great naval scholar Samuel Eliot Morison.

or Child of the Sun, had taken up temporary residence.* Atahualpa was well aware of the approach of the Spaniards and, in fact, had sent emissaries to bid them welcome. The Spaniards had been especially interested in one of those emissaries because he came drinking *chicha*—the fermented juice of the maize—from golden goblets that his attendants carried for him.

As the Spaniards looked down on the verdant valley and the little city of Caxamalca with its ten thousand inhabitants, they spotted the hot baths where the emperor and the princes came to take the cure. They also observed a less attractive feature: a mass of white covering several miles. These were the tents of the Inca's army, a spectacle that startled the Spaniards by their immense numbers. But it was too late to turn back.

The Conquerors, as Prescott calls them, found only empty streets as they entered Caxamalca. After a short distance, they came to an immense open plaza surrounded by low buildings containing capacious halls, presumably barracks for the Inca's soldiers. Pizarro was determined to occupy this area.

Pizarro immediately dispatched a small force toward the Indian encampment, commanded by his brother Hernando Pizarro and his senior colleague Hernando de Soto. De Soto would later make his mark exploring in Florida for the Fountain of Youth; he died in 1542 on the shores of the Mississippi, having found neither the Fountain of Youth nor any North American gold, but he would have a Chrysler car model of the 1930s named after him. In addition, there was one Indian member of this detachment, who had been taught enough Spanish to act as interpreter. The Spaniards called him Felipillo.

The Spaniards found the Inca seated in a spacious courtyard with attractive structures around it and a fountain in the center, surrounded by nobles and women of the royal household. He was about thirty years old, handsome, more robust than many of his countrymen, with a large head and bloodshot eyes that made him look fierce. Hernando Pizarro greeted Atahualpa and informed him that the Spanish commander and his men were "the subjects of a mighty prince across the waters . . . come . . . to offer their services, and to impart to him the doctrines of the true faith which they professed." De Soto then invited the Inca to visit the Spaniards

*Prescott spells the name of this city and other Inca cities with an *x*, whereas modern writers tend to use a *j* instead. I have adhered to his spelling system.

in their quarters on the following day; the Inca bluntly accepted the invitation. As a defensive measure, the Spaniards never dismounted from their horses, but this still left them in a position to respond eagerly to invitations to drink the sparkling *chicha* from golden vases of extraordinary size handed up to them by the dark-eyed beauties of the harem.

Hernando and his contingent returned to their comrades in a state of high anxiety over the evident strength and discipline of the military forces of the Inca. In addition, the level of civilization was much more impressive than anything they had observed in the lower regions of the country. Pizarro, however, was undaunted. He gave a rousing speech to his men, reminding them that "If numbers, however great, were on the side of their enemy, it mattered little when the arm of Heaven was on theirs."[22]

Pizarro had concocted an audacious scheme that—if it worked—would give his side an overwhelming advantage despite the enormous differences in military strength: he would take the Inca prisoner in the face of his own army. This was a high-risk strategy, but he had no doubt that the huge disparity in manpower had put him in a situation so desperate that a more modest effort would have been doomed.

The next morning, Pizarro hid his troops throughout the buildings on the plaza, with his artillery of two small cannon in the fortress. He made certain that all the arms were in good order, that the armor was shining, and that the horses were garnished with bells to make maximum noise at the crucial instant of attack. Then mass was said. "One might have considered them a company of martyrs," Prescott observed, "about to lay down their lives in defence of their faith, instead of a licentious band of adventurers, meditating one of the most atrocious acts of perfidy on the record of history!"[23]

The Inca's royal procession appeared a few hours later but halted about half a mile from Caxamalca and began to pitch their tents. Pizarro sent a messenger to ask Atahualpa to join the Spaniards as soon as possible, as both dinner and entertainment had been provided for him.

Atahualpa swallowed the bait—whole. He arrived with only a few warriors, and without arms. Was Atahualpa so absolute in his own empire that he had no fear of entrapment? Or did he simply figure that a small troop of only two hundred men would never even contemplate such a brazen deed? Whichever it was, his lighthearted decision would seal his doom.

Atahualpa may not have brought his army with him, but he did not spare the numbers of the rest of his retinue; five thousand or six thousand people filled the square in Caxamalca. There were hundreds of menials, singing as they cleared the path the Inca would follow. Nobles came in costumes of checkered red and white squares, while the guards and the Inca's immediate attendants wore a rich blue livery and a profusion of bright ornaments. The Inca himself was carried high on an open litter of gold and seated on a massive throne, also of gold. He wore a collar of enormous, brilliant emeralds and his hair was decorated with a variety of golden ornaments.

When he and all his people had gathered in the square, without a Spaniard in sight, Atahualpa wondered aloud where they had all gone. At that moment, the chaplain appeared, holding a Bible in one hand and a crucifix in the other. He was accompanied by Felipillo, the Indian interpreter. The chaplain announced that he had come to set forth to the Inca the articles of true faith, which he proceeded to do at great length. He finished by explaining the role of the pope, who had commissioned the Spanish emperor, "the most mighty monarch in the world, to conquer and convert the natives in this western hemisphere. . . . [His] general, Francisco Pizarro, had now come to execute this important mission."[24]

Atahualpa exploded. "I will be no man's tributary," he announced. "I am greater than any prince on earth. . . . For my faith, I will not change it. Your God, as you say, was put to death by the very men whom he created." He halted to point to the sun, then just beginning to set behind the mountains, and added, "But my God still lives in the heavens and looks down on his children." He took the Bible from the shocked friar's hands, looked at it briefly, and then threw it on the ground, declaring, "I will not go from here until your comrades have made me full satisfaction for all the wrongs they have committed."[25]

The priest ran to Pizarro and commanded him, "Set on at once; I absolve you."[26] Pizarro waved a white scarf, a cannon boomed from the fortress, and his men, some mounted and some on foot, dashed into the plaza shouting their battle cry: "St. Iago and at them!"[27] The Indians panicked. Stunned by the thunder of the artillery and muskets and blinded by the sulfurous smoke, they made no resistance as the Spaniards trampled them down with the horses and slashed into their defenseless bodies. Meanwhile, the Inca, still up on his heaving litter, saw his faithful nobles falling in a desperate attempt to protect him. Indeed, Pizarro himself ran to protect the Inca from excessively eager Spaniards and received a wound on his hand for his efforts—the only wound the Spaniards suffered that day. The massacre of the Indians continued for a long time until thousands of them had fallen. The precise number of dead is a matter of dispute, while the crowd of prisoners was beyond counting.

Some of Pizarro's troops wanted to put the prisoners to death, or at least to disable them by cutting off their hands. Pizarro refused and liberated all the prisoners except for a sufficient number to tend to the needs of the Spaniards. "In this respect," Prescott comments, "the most common soldier was attended by a retinue of menials that would have better suited the establishment of a noble."[28] Shades of the fourteenth-century Florentine chronicler in the previous chapter, who had complained "at the spectacle of the *popolo minuto* who . . . dressed themselves in a manner unbefitting their station and insisted on the finest delicacies at their table."[29]

As the Spaniards settled down to await reinforcements from the Spanish base on the coast, Pizarro used the time to become better acquainted with his captive. Atahualpa, on his side, closely observed the Spaniards. He soon discovered that they had an appetite even more potent than their repeated efforts to convert him to Christianity: the love of gold.

One day Atahualpa proposed a deal. If Pizarro would set him free, the Inca would arrange to have the room he occupied filled with gold as high as he could reach, all within two months; the gold would come from the royal palaces, temples, and public buildings. The area of the room was about 17 feet by 22 feet, with a height of nine feet. Pizarro eagerly accepted the proposition. As Atahualpa stood on tiptoe, a red line was drawn at the height he indicated, a notary recorded the details of the agreement, and Atahualpa dispatched couriers to execute the task.

Pizarro also sent emissaries to the capital city of Cuzco, a difficult journey of over six hundred miles across the mountains, where they found the great temple of the Sun covered with plates of gold and royal mummies within, each seated on a gold throne. The Spaniards ripped seven hundred plates from the temple walls, each about the size of the lid of a chest and weighing around 4½ pounds. Before the Spaniards were through, they had packed two hundred loads of gold to be carried back to Caxamalca on the backs of the humbled Indians. This was just a preliminary foray: a larger and more rapacious trip to Cuzco would take place later on.

Meanwhile, gold was arriving from all over Peru, from the Inca's temples, palaces, and other public edifices, to satisfy his contract with Pizarro. The gold came in many forms—goblets, ewers, salvers, vases in great variety, ornaments and utensils, tiles and plates, curious imitations of different plants and animals, and a fountain that sent up a sparkling jet of gold. Pizarro selected a small sample of these objects to ship back to the emperor, Isabella's grandson Charles V, who was known as Charles Quint. He inherited the throne of Spain via his mother, Joanna the Mad, and had also been elected emperor of the Holy Roman Empire—a position his father's father had occupied. Only Napoleon and Hitler at their zenith have ruled over a larger area of Europe. We shall encounter Charles again in a later chapter.

Except for the tiny lot that Pizarro sent to Spain, not a single piece of that heap of gold in Atahualpa's room has survived in its original form, but the small quantity of Peruvian gold work that escaped the clutch of the Spaniards and has come down to us is breathtaking.* Gold was so easily obtained at high purity from the river deposits in Peru that the art of working gold began there at an early time. By 500 BC, golden diadems, earrings, bracelets, and plaques were being created. There are even earlier objects with clear Chinese and Vietnamese influences, which suggests that Asian sailors were finding their way across the Pacific at a time when Europeans were barely managing to paddle themselves around the Mediterranean.[30] Admittedly, we do not know whether the Asian sailors ever found their way back.

The Peruvians at the time of the conquest were beating out thin gold into vessels and masks of great variety, complexity, and opulence. Among the more spectacular achievements were enormous beakers in the form of a human effigy, a difficult technical task with startling impact on the viewer. Some of these beakers show the head in an inverted position; one thereby drank out of the neck, indicating that these beakers probably represented the head of a defeated enemy with the user symbolically drinking from the enemy's skull—just like the Lombards. A woolen tunic has been found that contained thirty thousand miniscule plaques of sheet gold.

*A visit to the Jan Mirchell collection at the Metropolitan Museum of Art in New York is an unforgettable experience.

At the other end of the scale, the goldsmiths created sheets of gold with repoussé relief designs to cover walls, such as those that the Spaniards ripped from the temple walls in Cuzco.[31]

Except for the small exhibit reserved for Charles V, all the accumulated treasure was transformed from adornment to money, as one article after another disappeared into the melting pots to be recast into gold bars of a uniform standard. Pizarro assigned this task to the Indian goldsmiths, the same men who had created many of these beautiful objects. The work consumed a full month, but it produced 1,326,539 *pesos d'oro*, which Prescott calculated as the equivalent of $15 million when he was writing his book in the 1840s.[32] That would set the value in today's money as $270 million, a handsome return for one's efforts under any circumstances, but that sum cannot convey the importance of this treasure in the far smaller economies of the sixteenth century. This calculation does not include the throne on which the Inca had made his tumultuous arrival—190 pounds of 16-carat gold, or the equivalent of one year's output of the Peruvian gold mines.[33] That prize Pizarro reserved for himself. If we convert the *pesos d'oro* into weight and express the result in tons, the Indians must have filled Atahualpa's chamber with nearly five tons of gold, which is more than the total annual output of gold within Europe at that time, or, even more impressive, the equivalent of twenty years of production by the Peruvian gold mines.[34] In contrast, it is worth recalling that Justinian poured twice as much gold into Saint Sophia and that Jean II's ransom, at three million crowns, was more than double the mass of gold in Atahualpa's chamber. No wonder Justinian believed that he had surpassed Solomon and the French people rose up in revolt at the burdens imposed on them!

The account of the Inca has a hideous ending. Newly arrived Spanish troops saw little point in continuing to shelter Atahualpa and were strongly opposed to liberating him. Pizarro resisted the pressure at first but ultimately yielded. He put the Inca up for trial under charges of having usurped the throne, squandering public revenues, practicing adultery and idolatry, and attempting to instigate an insurrection against the Spaniards. The kangaroo court lost little time in finding Atahualpa guilty.

After the sentence was pronounced, Atahualpa turned with tears in his eyes to Pizarro and asked, "What have I done, or my children, that I should meet such a fate? And from your hands, too, you, who have met with friendship and kindness from my people, with whom I have shared my treasures, who have received nothing but benefits from my hands!"[35] Pizarro turned away without reply.

On August 29, 1533, two hours after sunset, they lit the torchlights on the plaza and tied Atahualpa, chained hand and foot, to a stake surrounded by the fagots of his funeral pyre. The friar who had first lectured him on the blessings of Christianity appeared once again to hold up the crucifix before him and warn him of eternal damnation if he did not renounce his pagan religion and accept Christ. Atahualpa refused to yield. Finally, the priest promised Atahualpa that if he converted they would provide him with a quick death by garroting him rather than subjecting him to the extended agonies of the stake. Desperate, the Inca complied, accepting baptism with the name Juan de Atahualpa in honor of Saint John the Baptist, on whose day this unhappy event happened to fall. Then the executioner performed his gruesome task while the Spaniards muttered prayers for the salvation of the Inca's soul.

The end of the story of the Conquerors reads like a morality tale. Adam Smith decried "the sacred thirst of gold" that drove the explorers and Conquerors into the New World, and he was right.[36] The quenching of that thirst led most of these men to a bad end, beginning with Balboa himself.

Pizarro's original company broke into factions that drowned the spirit of their great adventure in bloody internecine quarrels over leadership and spoils. After the enormous efforts they had invested in the conquest of Peru and the terrifying risks they had faced, many of the men never realized their dreams of returning to Spain with their golden wealth to live the easy life. Some lost their lives in battles with the Indians or in civil wars among themselves. Others lost their gold, because it was too heavy to carry in the constant fighting—like Ruskin's man on the sinking ship. And many lost it in betting for high stakes in gambling games with friends.

The history of the Pizarros ends in the most bizarre tragedy.

Hernando Pizarro returned to Spain with his treasure in 1540, where he was imprisoned at the behest of his enemies for twenty years and emerged an old and infirm shadow of the great soldier he had once been. Francisco Pizarro was assassinated in 1541, while having dinner in his own home in Lima, by conspirators from a group of dissidents. As the swords were plunged into his body, he cried, "Jesu!" and kissed the cross he had traced with his finger on the bloody floor.

In time, after the Spaniards had grabbed every loose piece of gold and golden object they could find, the joy of plunder had been exhausted. Mining, which was serious business, had to take over. The Peruvian mines were great river gorges, shaped like caves and often reaching as far as sixty feet into the earth. Totally dark, these passages had room for only one man at a time, who crouched his way in, scraped out as much gold as he could from the rocks, crouched his way out, and was followed by another man to perform the same task.[37]

Under the Incas, this hard work was supervised and carefully modulated to prevent exhaustion and to sustain the lives of the miners. Under the Spaniards, the merciless labor of the mines was devastating to the natives, as it was in every other golden venture of the Europeans in the New World. What an irony! Gibbon's *The History of the Decline and Fall of the Roman Empire*, emphasizing the importance of Spanish gold to the Roman Empire fifteen centuries earlier, tells us that "Spain, by a very singular fatality, was the Peru or Mexico of the old world. . . . The oppression of the simple natives [of Spain], who were compelled to work in their own mines for the benefit of strangers, form an exact type of the more recent history of Spanish America."[38]

Later on, when the Portuguese began to exploit the huge gold resources of Brazil, the death rate of the Indians was so high that the native population was decimated and great numbers of African slaves had to be imported to take their place. The descendants of these black slaves account for a significant part of today's population in Brazil. There was also the usual story of the transmittal of the white men's diseases, but the conditions of virtual slavery at the mines threw human life away as though it mattered not at all.

Most ironic, the deluge of gold from the New World did not even bring Spain the wealth and power that the Conquerors had originally promised and that the king anticipated. But that is the topic for our next chapter.

THE PATH TO TRIUMPH

10

The Fatal Poison and Private Money

A monumental mass of gold and silver sailed across the Atlantic from the New World to Spain during the 1500s.* According to one authority, the total European stock of gold and silver at the end of the century was nearly five times its size in 1492.[1] The volume was so enormous that the armed convoys that transported the treasure to Europe averaged about sixty ships; on occasion, the convoys included as many as one hundred ships. Each of these vessels carried over two hundred tons of cargo in the 1500s and around four hundred tons on larger ships in the 1600s.[2] In 1564 alone, 154 ships arrived at Seville to debark their cargo of treasure.[3] At the end of the sixteenth century, the precious metals accounted for the bulk of the value of everything shipped from America to Spain.

As we trace the impact of all that gold on the European economy in the course of the sixteenth century, we shall see that the story has an

*Estimates of the production and shipment volumes of precious metals vary widely. Good data are available on how much actually crossed the ocean; discussions of the differences in the estimates revolve primarily around how much gold and silver was smuggled and escaped from official routes. Suffice it to say that the volume was enormous relative to the amount of gold and silver treasure in Europe at the end of the fifteenth century. Most studies either accept or take as their starting point the meticulous and comprehensive work of Earl Hamilton (see Hamilton, 1934), subsequently updated by Morineau, 1985, and Attman, 1962. Readers wishing to pursue this subject in detail should surely consult those works.

ironic twist at the end. Gold had to face silver as a rival for most of history, but a serious rival to both precious metals was blossoming by the end of the sixteenth century—forms of paper money as debt instruments issued by private parties instead of by governments. All the excitement about gold in the 1500s was in essence a celebration of the past. While no one was paying much attention, the future was beginning to emerge.

The Spanish government was extraordinarily effective and efficient in accomplishing the complex task of moving the treasure across perilous and hostile seas. The gold and silver were loaded on ships at Vera Cruz in Mexico, Trujillo in Honduras, Nombre de Dios on the Atlantic side of Panama, and Cartagena in Colombia. The area of the Caribbean enclosed by these ports came to be known as the Spanish Main, a name that has lingered on in romances ever since. From there, the ships traveled to Cuban waters to join together in convoys, or *flotas*, for the long voyage to their home port of Seville. Two to eight armed galleons accompanied the *flotas* as protection against the pirates and buccaneers who roamed the seas waiting to pounce on treasure-filled vessels.* The *flotas* also provided at least a hope of rescue, of cargo if not men, when heavy storms threatened to sink one or another of the galleons.

When vessels were forced by storms or fear of attack to put in at any port other than Seville, passengers were forbidden to land or to make any offer to trade in treasure. Once the cargo reached Seville, everything was transported under the tightest security to the House of Trade, where it was weighed and placed in special chests in a treasure chamber; both chests and chamber were provided with triple locks, with each of the three keys carried by three different officials of the House. The metal was smelted and refined right there. Some of it was then minted, but significant amounts of bullion were delivered to the creditors of the Crown, most of whom resided in other lands.

It staggers the imagination to consider the skill required to gather together, organize, control, and maintain contact with that many sailing

*These warships were also authorized to carry cargo. On one occasion, a galleon was so heavily loaded that her lower gun ports were under water (Parry, 1967, p. 202).

ships on a voyage of over three thousand miles of open ocean, with no handy means of communication such as the wireless systems or radar used on the convoys sent out four hundred years later from America to Britain in World War II.* By comparison, piloting one thousand camels across the wastes of the Sahara must have been a cinch. There was another big difference between the convoys of the 1500s and the convoys of the early 1940s. In World War II, the ships carried black gold—oil—plus food and armaments to defeat the Nazis; in the 1500s, the freight amounted to nothing more useful than shiny metal ingots. People knew what to do with the precious cargoes carried through the submarine-infested seas of the North Atlantic, but the Spaniards had a far more open-ended set of options for the precious metals. More often than not, they made the wrong choices.

Although losses to the Spanish *flotas* from pirates were a lot smaller than losses from storms at sea—or from German submarines in World War II—the danger of attack was a constant worry. There was a rumor around Spain that Charles V cried with joy every time word came in of the safe arrival of a *flota*.[4] Charles V, the reader should be reminded, was King Charles I of Spain through his mother, the daughter of Ferdinand and Isabella; he was also Charles V, emperor of the Holy Roman Empire (Charlemagne having been Charles I in that role). Generally known as Charles Quint at the time, he is most often referred to today as Charles V, the nomenclature that I follow here. He plays an active role in the later pages of this chapter.

As the historian Kenneth Andrews describes the times, piracy was elevated to a preferred branch of policy by Britain, France, and Holland, each of which was seeking a piece of the action in America that the Spaniards and Portuguese had claimed exclusively for themselves. Spain was also at war at one point or another with each of these countries during the sixteenth century. There were thirteen organized English expeditions to the Caribbean, and doubtless many free-lance junkets, just during 1570 to 1577.[5] Nevertheless, despite all the romance about the pirates and their occasional dramatic successes, the records of the House of Trade contain many accounts of failed attacks and safe arrivals.[6] Whole fleets were intercepted and defeated only three times,

*For a detailed and fully documented study of the Spanish Navy and the entire process of Spanish shipping from the New World, from construction to sailing, see Phillips, 1986.

twice by the English and once by the legendary Dutch admiral Piet Heyn in 1628.[7] More often, stragglers ran into difficulty. In March 1569, for example, 22 Spanish and Portuguese ships were brought into Plymouth, where the English happily relieved them of their precious cargoes.[8]

The most serious and sustained threat to Spanish shipping came from Sir Francis Drake, who made a specialty of plundering gold from the Catholics of Iberia. His efforts made his crew rich, quite aside from the fortune he kept for himself and the even bigger sum that he turned over to the English Crown. His hatred of the Spaniards was reciprocated: they referred to him as "the master-thief of the unknown world."[9]

Drake kept at the task, off and on, for nearly 25 years. He even landed in Panama in 1572, aiming to capture the Atlantic-side port of Nombre de Dios and thereby interdict the north–south route of Spanish gold. A wound in his leg forced him to abandon that project, but he and his men succeeded in seizing a pack train loaded with gold en route to Nombre de Dios from Panama City on the Pacific, with £20,000 worth of coins to show for their efforts.

Drake's famous voyage on the *Golden Hind* during 1577–1579 snared more than ten tons of gold, silver, and jewels from Spanish ships, first on the Atlantic side, and later, after sailing through the Straits of Magellan, on the Pacific side.[10] Drake then sailed up the coast of California before crossing the Pacific. He landed at Point Reyes on the shores of Marin County on San Francisco Bay and claimed the territory in the name of Queen Elizabeth of England. In 1586, the Venetian ambassador to Madrid reported that Drake had landed on Santo Domingo, Puerto Rico, and Cuba and had "returned to England with 38 ships laden with much booty."[11] In 1595, the queen sent Drake back to Panama to capture Nombre de Dios and Panama City and hold them for ransom. This time he succeeded in taking Nombre de Dios, but he in turn was conquered by a fatal case of dysentery, along with many of his shipmates, and was buried at sea.

One might think that Spain in the middle of the sixteenth century should have been the richest nation in Europe by a wide margin. It was not. The impact of this immense and sudden addition to monetary wealth was felt throughout the rest of Europe and even out to the Far East, but in Spain no lasting payoff remained from the spectacular exploits of the Conquerors and the fountains of blood that flowed from white men and Indians. The gold came in one end and went out the other like a dose of salts.

How was it that the Spaniards were able to mismanage one of the greatest windfalls of all time? Why did so much of the fruits of history's first gold rush end up in the hands of others? Part of the answer to these questions was local, indigenous to the character of sixteenth-century Spain. Part, and perhaps a larger part, was the result of the dynamic and restless environment of the era, in which the rigid structure of Spanish society was ill-fitted to participate.

Once the gold began arriving in quantity, the Spanish were far more proficient at spending than at producing. The massive imports of gold and silver stimulated the spending skills at the same time that they stifled Spain's incentive to produce. Spain acted like a poor man who makes a great windfall at the gambling tables but comes to believe that the money is his destiny rather than a nonrecurring event. This event was indeed nonrecurring: copious as the shipments of gold to Spain may have been during the 1500s, they peaked in midcentury and dropped off sharply after 1610; silver shipments peaked around 1600 and fell into a steep decline after about 1630.*[12]

During the sixteenth century, five-sixths of outgoing cargoes from Spain, primarily to the colonies, consisted of goods grown or manufactured in other countries.[13] Late in the century, the Cortes, or Parliament, declared, "The more of [gold] that comes in, the less the Kingdom has. . . . Though our kingdoms should be the richest in the world . . . they are the poorest, for they are only a bridge for [the gold and silver] to go to the Kingdoms of our enemies." Another Spanish observer, Pedro de Valencia, wrote in 1608, "So much silver and money . . . always has been fatal poison to republics and cities. They believe money will keep them and it is not true: plowed fields, pastures, and fisheries are what give sustenance." Still another complained, "Agriculture laid down the plough, clothed herself in silk, and softened her work-calloused hands. Trade

*As the best estimates depend only on official data, differences of opinion exist as to precisely how much seventeenth-century imports fell below shipments during the 1500s. The surging growth, however, did come to an end by 1600 (see Kindleberger, 1989, p. 28).

put on a noble air . . . went out to parade up and down the streets."[14] Instead of transforming the gold and silver into new productive wealth, the Spaniards paid the precious metals out to other countries and spent so much that debts to foreigners soared. As early as the 1550s, there was a popular saying that "Spain is the foreigners' Indies," because so much good Spanish money was being paid over to foreigners for "puerilities"—baubles like bangles, cheap glassware, and playing cards.[15]

Spain had also committed a costly economic blunder in the Columbus-year of 1492, even though the decision had brought joy and pride at the time it was made. The Jews and the Muslims were both expelled in 1492. Some Jews remained by converting to Christianity, but the vibrant intellectual community that had contributed so much to Spain for hundreds of years rapidly disintegrated. Most Christian Spaniards at that time were peasants or soldiers, illiterate and without any knowledge of the simplest kind of arithmetic. The nobility were either idle or romantic warriors.

The Jews and the Muslims, in contrast, were highly educated, leaders in mathematical and scientific developments, and immune from the Christian strictures against usury. They were the skilled governmental administrators and men of business. The Muslims in particular had a long heritage of trading, importing, and exporting. With their departure, Spain lost almost all of the native merchant class that was essential in a time of dynamic economic development throughout Europe. Instead, Cadiz and Seville, the primary economic centers of sixteenth-century Spain, were filled with foreigners—Genoese merchants and bankers, German moneylenders, Dutch manufacturers, and purveyors of every kind of goods, services, and finance from all over Europe, even Bretons and people from as far away as the North Sea area.[16] Almost all of the massive borrowing by Spain in the sixteenth century was financed by foreigners.

The departure of the Jews and the Muslims was a loss in another sense. Because of its geographical location, Spain is not on the route that traders and travelers would take in going from one place to another. The line of countries from France eastward, and the projection of Italy and Greece down into the Mediterranean, were on the east–west crossroads of travel and trade through Europe. There was no need to cross Spain, unless you were coming from Africa, and even then Spain was not the only possibility. As a result, Spain tended to be more provincial and ingrown than the countries to the north and east; only Seville, Barcelona, and Bilbao had any significant connections with the rest of Europe. The cosmopolitan flavor came from the Jews and the Muslims, who had many contacts in other lands dating back for centuries. Their departure cut that link to the outside world, leaving Spain dependent on foreigners whose allegiance was elsewhere.

One authoritative study has summarized Spain's situation as a dreadful paradox:

> Gold and silver merely acquired their international status in Spain, without being in any way connected with the Spanish economy. . . . There was an abundance of metals without any productive development, a rise in prices without any monetary alterations. In short, sixteenth century Spain was characterized by a separation between money and merchandise.[17]

The greatest waste inspired by Spain's gold was not in the baubles or in the loss of commercial and financial sophistication. It was in the dreams of glory of the Spanish monarchs. Gold has always been associated with power. Once the kings of Spain realized how much new wealth the discoveries of gold in the American colonies would bring them, they convinced themselves that their wealth was great enough to bend the world to their will, especially in the fiery matter of Catholicism versus Protestantism. In the middle of the century, half of all business conducted in Spain was for the account of the king.[18]

Charles V, who ascended the throne in 1516 at the death of his grandfather, Ferdinand, was determined to make Spain the dominant power in Europe. But Spanish power was not sufficient for Charles. He also wanted to follow in his other grandfather's footsteps and become emperor of the Holy Roman Empire. That job did not pass by inheritance; you could become emperor only through election by a group of Germans appointed by the pope and called electors. Francis I of France had identical ambitions. An intense bidding war to buy the votes broke out, in a no-holds bribery contest, with Francis backed by Genoese bankers and Charles by the Fuggers, the great Augsburg banking family. Charles won, but at a cost of 850,000 florins, which pushed him in debt to his ears. He proceeded to engage in 27 years of warfare with Francis I, with intermittent truces that were invariably violated and at one point that almost led to a personal duel between the two monarchs. Charles also claimed the Netherlands as part of his empire, and left his son, Philip II, to deal with the fruitless eighty-year struggle to tame the Dutch and the Belgians, during which most of the fighters on the Spanish side were mercenaries who would fight only for payment in "good money"—that is, gold or silver. Philip, in turn, was so bold as to try to topple Queen Elizabeth of England in 1588 with his ill-fated venture known as the Spanish Armada, to say nothing of his sporadic campaigns against the Turks, who had launched an aggressive move into the Balkans and eastern Mediterranean.

These adventures had to be financed. The 37 million ducats of external debt accumulated by Charles V during the forty years he was king of Spain exceeded by two million ducats the total value of the precious metals assigned to the crown that reached Seville from America in those years.[19] In 1572, the cost of the war in the Netherlands was running at an annual rate of 14.4 million florins, but the Spanish were able to come up with only 7.2 million florins in all of 1572 and 1573. By July 1576, King Philip owed the troops 17.5 million florins. Stretched beyond his means, Philip ordered payments to his creditors stopped, confiscated two shipments of silver that he owed them, and forced the creditors to convert most of his debts into long-term loans—nearly wiping out the Fugger banking house in the process. Philip's bankruptcy led his army of mercenaries to break apart in mutiny and desertion. It was said that at one point the captain general did not have enough money for lunch.[20] Philip thereby introduced the Western world to the relatively rare but shattering phenomenon of default by a sovereign or, in today's parlance, by a sovereign state. Spain would go on to repeated financial crises in 1596, 1607, 1627, and 1647.[21]

Meanwhile, a lot was going on throughout Europe, not just in Spain. In spite of the continuous depredations of warfare and religious turmoil, these unpleasant developments played themselves against the background of the High Renaissance, when artistic and scientific achievements reached extraordinary levels. Leonardo, Tintoretto, Raphael, Palladio, Cellini, Michelangelo, Titian, Dürer, Cervantes, and El Greco were all active during the 1500s. The great cathedral of Saint Peter's rose up on the banks of the Tiber, well splashed with gold in its interior. Copernicus and Galileo were exploring the solar system, while businessmen for the first time took the giant step of using double-entry bookkeeping.[22] This was also a period when Latin was being replaced by vernacular languages, which facilitated communication among the great mass of individuals, including some very rich ones, who had neither been to universities nor joined the clergy.

The single most important event of the century occurred in 1517 when Martin Luther posted his 95 theses on the door of the church in Wittenberg. The Reformation tore through Europe like a hot poker, transforming beliefs and revolutionizing artistic styles while ripping across political and dynastic relationships. The Reformation was in some instances the cause of wars, but war was in any case an almost constant way of life in the 1500s.

England was at war for a total of fourteen years. In 1545, at war with Francis I and simultaneously threatened by an invasion from Scotland, Henry VIII had 120,000 men under arms—and drawing pay from his treasury. Henry was forced to borrow money at interest rates as high as 16 percent and even seized all the lead in the kingdom to be sold for export. In a vast privatization plan that bears some resemblance to those carried out in many countries during the 1990s, Henry sold off valuable properties that he had grabbed from the monasteries and the churches when he veered into Protestantism after his divorce in 1533.[23] As a final step, Henry resorted to debasement of his currency.

No matter how painful and expensive the wars were, the English spent much less time at war than the Spanish and the French, and the difference probably explains the relatively rapid economic development in England during the reign of the Tudors. The Spaniards fought with France for nearly thirty years. The major struggle was over who would dominate Italy, but that contest was in addition to Spain's ill-fated Armada against England and their brutal campaign to subdue the Netherlands. Religious wars were also fought within nations, many continuing at an unrelenting pace well into the seventeenth century. The result was repeated repudiation of debts by both the Spanish and the French.

The Europeans did not fight only among themselves. Just beyond the eastern Mediterranean, the Turks launched a sequence of campaigns against Europe that would continue with only brief interruptions for over one hundred years. In 1529, the Turks were at the gates of Vienna for the first time. They ravaged Italy and Sicily in the 1530s. They were at war with Venice from 1537 to 1540 and again from 1545 to 1564, but suffered a major naval defeat at Lepanto in Greek waters in 1571.

Most of the military activity within Europe resulted from the ambitions of the great dynasts of the age—Charles V in Spain and Francis I in France. Henry VIII (1509–1547), who was eager to establish and maintain the legitimacy of his own dynasty in England, acted as a kibitzer and occasional participant in the struggles between Charles and Francis, continuously playing one against the other. Henry's choices were limited in the early years, as Charles was the nephew of his first wife, Catherine of Aragon, but Henry also played at making alliances with Francis.

France was not among the lucky countries to discover gold in the New World, but France did gain gold from trade and from picking off Spanish galleons on the way to Seville from America. Francis I (1494–1547) was a great believer in the tradition that gold was essential for public relations, for ostentatious display, and for messages of power. His tastes were by no means unusual for an age in which Flemish and Burgundian embroidery was lavished with gold thread, when gold was becoming increasingly visible in church adornment, when nobles' ranks were distinguished by the weight of the gold chains they wore around their necks (Henry VIII had a "masseye gold cheyne" of 98 ounces), and when knights went into battle wearing doublets strewn with gold and gems.[24]

Francis was an enthusiastic patron of the arts, and when he arranged for Benvenuto Cellini to be released from a Roman prison to come work at the French court, he declared to Cellini, "I will choke you with gold!"[25] Cellini proceeded to produce a salt cellar so sumptuously decorated with gold and jewels that Francis cried out with astonishment when he saw it.[26] Francis was a connoisseur of more than the arts: he was also famous for his many amours, and observed that "A court without women is a year without spring and a spring without roses."[27] In 1515, Francis followed in Charlemagne's footsteps in fighting the Lombards: he conquered northern Italy and was feasted by the pope.

Francis now considered himself the most powerful monarch in Europe. Nevertheless, in order to cover himself against Charles V's increasing threats to capture Italy for the Holy Roman Empire, Francis decided to make an alliance with Henry VIII. It is worth mentioning that Charles succeeded in his goal of throwing the French out of Italy. The battle of Pavia in 1525 was a total defeat for Francis, who ended up Charles's prisoner, marking the second occasion on which a king of France became a prisoner of war. Charles was no model of chivalry, as Edward III had been when he captured Jean II: Francis languished for a year in a dank cell in Madrid, where he passed the time writing songs and poems. Charles proceeded to take complete control of Italy and allowed his troops to sack Rome with a violence that was barbarous even for those times. The control of Italy included the control of the papacy, which is why Pope Clement VII found himself unable to authorize Henry's divorce from Queen Catherine of Aragon, Charles's aunt. Henry had every reason to be shocked at the pope's rejection: the pope had earlier named him "Defender of the Faith," in return for Henry's zeal in condemning Martin Luther as a mortal enemy of all good Christians.

Henry and Francis encountered each other face-to-face in 1520 at Guynes, in the neighborhood of Calais, at a summit meeting that accomplished even less than most summit meetings. Francis was unaware that Charles V had traveled to London for a secret meeting with Henry just prior to Henry's departure for France, which is one reason that the meeting at Guynes ended up as more pomp than circumstance, with the lavish overlay of ceremony and display obscuring empty confrontations on matters of substance.

Henry crossed the Channel aboard the *Henri Grace-de-Dieu*, the Royal Navy's largest ship, accompanied by enough smaller vessels to transport a retinue of 4500 for himself and twelve hundred for Queen Catherine, to say nothing of three thousand horses and a wide variety of associated equipment. Upon his arrival at Calais, Henry's chancellor, Cardinal Wolsey, rode on a mule with golden stirrups to the French camp to proclaim the arrival of the English.

The encounter between the two posturing monarchs has come to be known as the Meeting on the Field of Cloth of Gold. The title is apt. The ground was not literally covered with cloth of gold, but the participants lavished gold all over their costumes, and the 2800 tents that Francis supplied for the occasion were covered with so much cloth of gold shimmering in the sunshine that the observer sensed himself immersed in gold.[28]

Five days after Henry's arrival, at the precise moment announced by a gun firing a salute, the two kings and their elaborate entourages began to move toward each other to meet at the appointed spot at Guynes. The

French archers rode with weapons sheathed in gold, followed by the marshals of France all shining in cloth of gold. Then came two hundred nobles clad in uniforms of gold and crimson. Francis himself wore a cassock of cloth of gold, while his horse was decked out with gold filigree.

The English were not to be outdone in gaudy golden display. Wolsey was accompanied in the procession by fifty giant men carrying gold maces with knobs as big as a man's head.[29] Shakespeare, in his play about Henry VIII, described the sequence of events this way:

> Today the French
> All clinquant, all in gold, like heathen gods,
> Shone down the English; and to-morrow they
> Made Britain India; every man that stood
> Show'd like a mine. (Act I, Scene 2, 18–22)

The reference to India was to the Indies, which at that time still referred to all of the New World. Shakespeare's hyperbole that every man "Show'd like a mine" suggests that the English were so covered with gold that they looked like a gold mine.[30] Gold was so much in everyone's consciousness that one of Henry's aides commented that the beard Henry grew for the occasion "looks like gold."[31]

The entire setting was marked by fluttering flags and faux palaces, and included two fountains that spouted red wine the whole time (they say that 1520 was a pretty good year). Henry even prompted a spontaneous wrestling match with Francis, a twisting tussle in which Henry ended up on the grass, purple with rage. Elaborate jousts on horseback and archery contests alternated with meals of "cygnets [swans], venison, pike, heron, pies of pears, custard and fruit . . . kid, sturgeon, peacock, quails, pheasant, egrets."[32] No wonder the chef was called Merryman.

Withal, Henry and Francis were at war with each other only three years later. Had all the gold flaunted at their summit blinded them from reality? Now they had to use their gold for grimmer purposes.

While all this was going on, and to some extent *because* all this was going on, profound economic changes were at work in Europe and, in a secondhand kind of way, in Asia as well. The behavior of prices and the demand for money in Europe changed so dramatically in the course of the 1500s that economists refer to this period as the Price Revolution of the Sixteenth Century. The Price Revolution, the ceaseless warfare, the rapid growth in international trade, and expanding economic relations with trading partners thousands of miles away in the Far East galvanized methods of doing business and transformed the character of financial transactions. Regardless of the difficulties that monarchs may have had with their finances in the sixteenth century, affairs in the private sector reached a far more sophisticated level than at any time in the past.

The Price Revolution defined the tone of the entire century. A pattern of rising prices was first visible in Italy and Germany from about 1470, the low point for the decline in prices that had set in following the Black Death in 1349. Then, like another kind of plague, inflation infected Europe in a series of steps. It took hold in England and France during the 1480s, extended to Iberia in the next decade, and appeared in eastern Europe in the early 1500s. Although prices did not rise in every single year, for agricultural prices in particular are characteristically volatile because of weather variations, the low point reached in each decline tended to be higher than the previous low, while each high point tended to set a record on the upside.[33]

Anyone who has lived through an inflationary period can testify that inflation is always unsettling because it clouds the future with uncertainty, but the shock of sustained inflation to the inhabitants of Europe in the sixteenth century was shattering. They had no prior experience with it, no good economic theory to explain it, and no established rules of behavior or policy with which to manage it. There had always been brief episodes of inflation in response to crop failures, but the Price Revolution of the Sixteenth Century persisted for more than one hundred years before it tapered off at long last. No other inflation in history has been so stubborn.

The price increases were most rapid in raw materials, especially food. In England, wood, livestock, and grain rose fivefold to sevenfold from 1480 to 1650; manufactured goods merely tripled.[34] A 700 percent increase over 170 years compounds at only 1.2 percent a year, but, with wages rising less than half as fast as the prices of necessities, it was the tenacity and the duration of the inflationary pressures that shook people. The purchasing power of money and of labor incomes deteriorated at what appeared at the time to be an alarming rate.

What caused this deterioration? A weighty literature has accumulated to record the debates on this matter. The bottom line of the controversy is that no one cause can be held responsible for the long duration of the Price Revolution. The economic historian Glyn Davies describes it as "strange and profound."[35] Contemporary observers in the sixteenth century engaged in plenty of dispute. Just a few of the causes mentioned in the literature of the time include the decline of agriculture, ruinous taxation, depopulation, market manipulation, high labor costs, vagrancy, luxury, and the machinations of businessmen like the Genoese.[36]

Some modern authorities argue that the combination of rapid increases in population and a much slower rate of growth in food supplies was responsible for igniting the inflationary fires. The European population numbers had begun to recover from the Black Death and the Hundred Years' War some time early in the fifteenth century. The largest advance was from 45 million in 1400 to sixty million in 1450, but the population increased by another nine million to ten million people during each fifty-year period up to 1600. By that time, the population had doubled from the level of 1400. In 1550, the number of people in Europe finally exceeded the 73 million mark set way back in 1300, a short while before the catastrophes of the Black Death.[37]

Food supplies, which had been ample up to the early part of the fifteenth century, could no longer keep up with the increase in the number of mouths to feed. Agricultural output would probably have lagged population growth in any case, but two other factors contributed to the shortage of food. The first was the shift, particularly in England, from arable to pastoral farming, as the profitability of sheep farming overtook the profitability of growing food; the second was the continuing drift of labor into the cities. In 1538, a German writer commented that "There are so many people everywhere, no one can move."[38] Perhaps he had paid a recent visit to Florence, where by 1561 the average size of households was 7.8 people, which was double what it had been 120 years earlier.[39]

Inflation has always appeared during wartime, when spending leaps ahead and production of peacetime goods and services tends to fall. Tacitus wrote that "*Pecunia nervus belli*" (Money is the sinew of war),[40] and there was not a single year of complete peace on the European continent during the one hundred years from 1551 to 1651. The fiscal problems of financing these wars were intensified by the character of the sixteenth-century tax systems, which put almost all the burden on the lower classes. As it was the lower classes who fell furthest behind in the inflationary process, government revenues lagged even as inflation-cum-warfare was constantly driving government expenditures higher. Jumbo fiscal deficits and exploding government indebtedness were the inevitable consequences. Two resulting financial innovations were Spain's *asientos* and France's *Grand Parti*, both of which were forms of borrowing in the capital markets—the modern convention—which supplemented the traditional method of privately negotiated debts that piled up on the accounts of the bankers in Italy, Germany, and Holland.

There was another method of royal finance that was by now an old trick: increasing the supply of money through devaluation of the currency. In 1523, the Spanish Cortez urged Charles V to reduce the gold content of Spanish coins in order to curtail the distressing outflow of their highly valued coins to other countries. That way, they could mint a larger number of coins with the same amount of gold. Charles waited until 1537 to take the step; the magnitude of his needs is apparent from his decision to make this move even after Cortez and Pizarro had provided him with what looked at the time like a bottomless pit of gold bullion. Other rulers followed suit. Henry VIII's policy from 1542 to 1547 was so blatant that his move became known, with the uppercase letters, as The Great Debasement. Henry's debasement was a direct result of the war with France in the 1540s, when, as described by one historian, he "worked the Mint for all it was worth."[41]

Monarchies were not the only urgent spenders in this environment. Inflation generates its own self-sustaining urgency. As goods become more valuable to people than money, inflation encourages hoarding by consumers and especially by businessmen and farmers. More elaborately, hoarding takes the form of speculation, in which people buy in advance of their needs or try to corner the market, either to beat anticipated price increases or to resell the goods at a higher price later on. All of this intensifies the upward pressure on prices and then encourages even more hoarding and speculation.

But what about the impact of American treasure on the Price Revolution? Adam Smith had no doubt about that: "The discovery of the abundant mines of America seems to have been the sole cause. . . . there has never been any dispute about the fact or the cause of it."[42] At first glance, it appears obvious that the flood of new money coined from the treasure of the New World must have been the driving force that supported inflation for so long. Population may have outstripped the supply of food, but babies do not normally come into the world with silver spoons in their mouths. If overpopulation were an automatic cause of inflation, countries like India and Bangladesh would have led the world in inflation while countries with slower-growing populations would have steady or declining prices. The facts fail to fit that hypothesis by a wide margin. In some instances, population growth in excess of food supplies may be a necessary cause of inflation, but it is hardly sufficient. Where does the increased population get the wherewithal to pay the higher prices?

The question suggests an answer: money supplies must increase. That reasoning supported Adam Smith's didactic conclusion that the abundant mines of America were responsible for the price inflation. Smith's view stemmed from a remarkable piece of economic research in 1568 by a French observer named Jean Bodin, who went all the way back into ancient history to demonstrate how rising amounts of gold and silver were associated with higher prices. He pointed out that the prodigious inflow of precious metals from America had landed in Spain and that prices in Spain were higher than in France and Italy: "Spain is rich, haughty, indolent. . . . It is . . . the abundance of gold and silver that causes, in part, the dearness of things."[43]

Bodin is the spiritual father of monetarism, an important branch of economic theory spelled out most authoritatively by Nobel Laureate Milton Friedman, who has asserted that inflation is always and everywhere a monetary phenomenon. When prices in general are rising, the buyer has to spend more money for the same basket of goods and services. That is, inflation cannot continue unless it is financed in some fashion. If buyers cannot find the extra money they need to maintain the same level of purchasing, they will have to cut back and buy fewer things, thereby limiting the ability of sellers to keep raising prices. Monetarists therefore contend that the Price Revolution of the Sixteenth Century would never have endured for such a long period of time had it not been nourished by the increased money supply produced from the New World's gold and silver bullion.

Yet fitting the facts to that monetarist theory is not as easy as Bodin made it appear. Not all the treasure remained in Europe as money. Hoarding, as always, kept some of it out of circulation. Gorgeous ornamentation in the churches took a share. And, as we shall see in the next chapter, a significant amount was shipped off to Asia, never to return.

Furthermore, although prices started rising around 1470 and were climbing throughout Europe by 1500, American gold did not arrive in Spain in any significant quantity until 1520; the Peruvian discoveries took place after 1530, and the big silver discoveries did not begin to bear fruit until about twenty years after that. The relationship continues to be confusing after 1600. The imports of gold and silver to Seville appear to have peaked about 1590, to have remained at a high level for another thirty years or so, and then to have fallen off precipitously from around 1620 to the end of the century. Yet prices kept on climbing, at rates that seemed to bear no relation to the arrivals of fresh supplies of the precious metals. In England, for example, prices doubled between 1600 and 1650.[44]

However, the Seville data are questionable, because an increasing supply was unloaded downstream at Cadiz or in Lisbon, and illegal diversions from official routes were also growing. Gold is too easy to smuggle for official statistics to be trustworthy. Analysis of informal kinds of information concludes that the flow of precious metals to Spain actually increased after 1600.[45] The huge Brazilian gold mines began shipping to Portugal after 1700, but by that time the Price Revolution had played itself out. Even so eminent an authority on monetarism as Anna Schwartz, one of Friedman's principal colleagues, has described the experience of the Price Revolution as a "contradiction of the basic hypothesis" of monetarism.[46]

Other economists take issue with monetarism's focus on just one economic variable. They prefer to turn the argument upside down. The Price Revolution of the Sixteenth Century, viewed from this vantage point, was not the result of an increased *supply* of money in the form of the precious metals; rather, the rising price level magnified the *demand* for money, arousing the Spaniards to redouble their efforts to bring in gold and silver from America. Seen from this perspective, expanding money supplies are not the cause of inflation but the result of it.

Whichever and whatever was the cause of the Price Revolution, the inflow of treasure must have contributed to its persistence. A dramatic example of this phenomenon appeared in the course of the long struggle between Francis I and Charles V.

After Charles captured Francis at Pavia and imprisoned him in Madrid, he forced Francis to sign a ruinous treaty that was to be secured by Francis's two oldest sons, seven and eight years old, as hostages. Goodbye to the French claim to Lombardy! The children remained prisoners for four years, until they were ransomed by Francis's promise to pay two million gold crowns to liberate them. Payment began with 1.2 million crowns sent in a boat that crossed the river at the French–Spanish border at the precise moment as the boat carrying the princes headed in the other direction. The exchange was delayed (as mentioned in Chapter 6) until four months had been spent counting the coins.[47]

This enormous transfer of gold put a painful squeeze on the French nobility, clergy, and taxpayers while stimulating a wave of spending in the Spanish economy. As a result, prices in Spain were soon higher than prices in France. The resulting disparity in prices produced such a surge in French exports to Spain—everything from wheat, wine, and brandy to hammocks, candles, and canvas—that the transfusion of gold and silver was soon running in reverse as monies returned to the French side of the border.[48]

The most curious aspect of this whole sequence of events was what happened to the value of gold itself, and silver along with it. The precious metals were no more immune than anything else to the inexorable influences of the law of supply and demand. The European supply of gold in the sixteenth century expanded rapidly, as the deluge of gold imports from America joined with the flow of gold from new mines and improved mining technology in eastern Europe and especially in Hungary.

Consequently, although the price of gold rose along with everything else in the course of the Price Revolution, the gold price changes were much more subdued. For example, the price of gold in England, reported in shillings, climbed from forty to sixty shillings an ounce between 1492 and 1547, a rise of 50 percent, then was stable for the next fifty years, and then had a further modest increase to 74 shillings by 1611.[49] That was a total advance of 85 percent—way below the increases in wages, clothing, or food. Although the English had no gold resources of their own in the Americas or anywhere else to draw upon, there is reason to believe that the supply of gold in England increased at a rapid pace nevertheless, thanks to huge gains of treasure through piracy and war.[50]

Adam Smith provides ingenious insights into this phenomenon. The quantity of any commodity, he asserts, regulates itself in every country according to the demand of those who are willing to pay enough to bring it to market. No commodity regulates itself "more easily or more exactly" by this rule than gold or silver, because their high value and small bulk make it so easy to transport them from the places where they are cheap to the places where they are expensive. This physical relationship explains why gold prices are so much more stable than the prices of commodities "that are hindered by their bulk from shifting their situation." Therefore, "When the quantity of gold and silver imported into any country exceeds the effectual demand, no vigilance of government can prevent their exportation. All the sanguinary laws of Spain and Portugal are not able to keep their gold and silver at home. The continual importations from Peru and Brazil . . . sink the price of those metals there below those in neighboring countries."[51] Therewith, Smith provides an additional insight into the inability of the Spaniards to hold on to their precious gold.

The Price Revolution and the discovery of the copious gold resources of America were abrupt shifts from the past, but additional significant economic innovations were at work during the sixteenth century. Indeed, the trade fair, a traditional institution, now began to play a more important role in the economic scene, initiating a mutation in the role of gold that has continued to the present day. The expansion of this institution is notable for its civilized character, which made a dramatic contrast to the warfare, religious controversy, pillage, and plunder that persisted throughout these centuries.

Beginning in the Middle Ages, the trade fair developed into an essential institution for doing business—displaying wares, buying them, and selling them in a world where most towns were tiny places, without a bank on every street corner and without a supermarket just a five-minute automobile drive from the house. It was also a world without telephones, Federal Express, the Internet, or news services that could quote or advertise the prices of goods, financial instruments, and foreign exchange. Without central gathering places, merchants could not supply themselves or were limited to only one or perhaps two local sources; large customers could not locate the merchandise—and, more often, the bankers—they needed; the multiplicity of monies and of credit instruments could not be settled to pay the obligations that accumulated in the course of thousands of transactions. In today's world, the annual Frankfurt book fair, the colorful expos in Las Vegas for the high-tech industry, and the longstanding Leipzig fair for industrial machinery are pale shadows of this vital and essential institution of earlier times. Furthermore, most of these modern fairs meet annually, whereas the fairs that concern us here met at least twice a year; Lyons, one of the major locations, held its fair four times a year.

Unlike local situations, where merchants exchanged wares with their neighbors, transactions at trade fairs would permit a merchant to buy without necessarily having something to sell, or vice versa. One-sided purchases often require financing, because the buyer is not making an offsetting sale. The format of the fairs thus became increasingly elaborate, and during the sixteenth century, financing the purchases at the fairs became as important as merchandise itself. In many instances, the transactions were financial without regard to any movements of goods.[52] Although fairs took place in many centers in Europe, both geographical and political factors determined the locations of the key towns where the major players met and where kings provided special protection and facilities for foreigners; at Lyons, the great preponderance of foreigners were from Florence, Milan, Lucca, and Genoa.[53] At the great fairs, the merchants and financiers were dominant, with representatives of municipal or royal institutions playing a subordinate role. The popularity of the fairs rose and fell as trade patterns and political hegemonies varied over time—the Champagne area, Antwerp in the fifteenth century, then Geneva, from which a French king lured the fair to Lyons, and then to the eastern French town of Besançon and finally Piacenza. In Piacenza, the fairs were known as Bisenzone, an Italianization of Besançon.

Many booths at the fairs were occupied by the money changers; in the fair of Medina del Campo in Spain, trading in promissory notes drawn in different nations' currencies, called bills of exchange, was the only activity. The money changers must have had a busy time indeed. One authority lists 48 different kinds of gold coins circulating in Europe in the sixteenth century, including eleven from Italian cities, nine from the Netherlands, six from England, and smaller numbers from Spain, France, Portugal, and Hungary.[54]

Merchants struggling to deal with this multiplicity of monies were the targets of many popular jokes. In Chaucer's "Shipman's Tale," the merchant is so involved with his counting board that he leaves word not to be disturbed, no matter what. A young monk takes advantage of this situation to make advances on the merchant's lusty wife, who bangs on her husband's door crying,

> How longe tyme wol ye rekene and caste
> Youre sommes, and youre bookes, and youre thynges?
> The devel have part on all swiche rekenynges![55]

Nevertheless, the money changers were much less involved with developments in coinage than with the increasing substitution of paper-money instruments for the inconvenience and complications of payment in coin. The principal vehicle for these kinds of payment was the bill of exchange, an instrument developed by the Italians in the thirteenth century, perhaps earlier. This was a remarkable financial innovation that lent itself to a wide variety of uses and formats.[56]

Here is a simple example of how a bill of exchange worked.* Two transactions take place: Franco in Italy buys wool from Berthold in Flanders, while David in Flanders buys wine from Carlo in Italy. Franco, however, does not pay Berthold directly, and David does not pay Carlo directly. Instead, Carlo "draws" a bill of exchange on David, a sheet of paper declaring that David owes him such-and-such an amount of Italian money for the wine. Carlo sells this bill to Franco, which means that Franco's purchase of the bill has satisfied Carlo. In order to pay Berthold for the wool, Franco now sends that bill to Berthold, who turns around and sells it to David, which means that David's purchase of the bill has satisfied Berthold. Thus, both shippers, Berthold and Carlo, have been paid, but by the other fellow's customer rather than by their own: Franco has paid Carlo instead of Berthold, while David has paid Berthold instead of Carlo. The wine, the wool, and the bill that Carlo has drawn

*This is a simplified version of the example in Kindleberger, 1993, p. 41.

on David move across the borders, but no money goes from Italy to Flanders or vice versa.

This is an oversimplified explanation, but it indicates the essence of the process. In reality, there is no reason to believe that each transaction will precisely equal the other, or even that Franco and Carlo or Berthold and David will readily find each other. In order to settle up these differences, a lively market built up in the trading of bills of exchange. In 1585, for example, bills drawn on merchants and bankers in Amsterdam were trading in Antwerp, Cologne, Danzig, Hamburg, Lisbon, Lübeck, Rouen, and Seville.[57]

In these markets, dealers rather than principals would buy the bills and then would settle up the balances among themselves; dealers often acted as bankers by advancing payments to suppliers of merchandise and collecting later from the buyers of the merchandise. By settling differences rather than gross amounts and by making the business one in which a large number of dealers participated, these bill markets significantly reduced the need for coins to settle bilateral differences. On one occasion, a million *livres tournois* changed hands without a single penny being disbursed.[58] That entire process, however, could not have functioned as well without the institution of the trade fairs, where the dealers and money changers could meet with one another, buying and selling bills back and forth, and working out their payments in foreign exchange as Italians settled with Flemish dealers, the Flemish settled with the English, and so on.

Remarkable changes developed from these arrangements. Merchants no longer had to travel to settle up their accounts, and when they did travel they went to centers with trading posts where transactions could be settled most efficiently. Consequently, the centralized operations of the fairs attracted an increasing volume of financial transactions. Merchant firms became more diversified as a result and in time turned into the great family firms that grew up in this age, such as the Fuggers in the Holy Roman Empire, the Medici of Florence, and later the Rothschilds and Baring Brothers.

The whole concept of money was being transformed. The traditional public money of the prince in the form of coins stamped or engraved as official government issue now shared the money circulation with private money in the form of credit instruments that served as means of payment in transactions involving both merchants and bankers. When an individual in the modern world engages in the dominant form of doing business by writing a check instead of paying with paper currency, that is private money at work. That arrangement first developed during the fifteenth and sixteenth centuries with the growing use of the bill of exchange and the trade fairs where transactions were cleared and settled and where foreign exchange trading became a major activity.[59]

The private money had to be expressed in some kind of denomination, just as people keep money in bank deposits or write checks today denominated in dollars or sterling or euros. Nobody issues a check denominated in a given number of specified gold coins or weight of gold bullion, any more than someone in the sixteenth century who drew a bill of exchange would denominate it in a number of coins or weight of bullion. Money in the private world had to be expressed in terms of a unit of account, such as dollars or euros, which was a convenient *numéraire* for defining the size of the transaction and the local money used by the parties to settle up. A unit of account is an abstract concept—you cannot see the dollars that a check transfers, nor can you feel them, bite into them, or weigh them. The only concern of the owner of private money is that the prince so regulate the supply of public money that the integrity of the unit of account is stable instead of withering away in the fires of inflation.

If we extrapolate these developments through the centuries, they define much of the subsequent history of gold as money in Europe and the United States. Over time, gold coins circulated less frequently and gold bullion served only to settle up very large transactions or to cover the unfavorable balance of trade between Europe and the Far East. This does not mean that gold became less of a fixation or less valuable—we have only to think of the drama of the gold rushes of the nineteenth century to understand that—but the nature of its role in the system did begin to change.

Furthermore, India and the nations of the Pacific looked on gold in a fashion quite different from how it was perceived by people in the West. The view from China, Japan, and India is interesting in its own right, but, as we shall see in the next chapter, the attitudes of those nations raise profound questions about the nature of money and the role of wealth.

11

The Asian Necropolis and Hien Tsung's Inadvertent Innovation

After all the convoys, piracy, and plunder had brought the gold and silver from the New World to Europe, almost none of that massive movement of precious metals ended up where the Europeans expected it to end up. The entire flow lingered only briefly in Europe and then continued eastward to Asia. There is even some evidence that the outflow of gold and silver to the Far East may have exceeded the total imports from America between 1600 and 1730.[1] During the first 25 years after the establishment of the East India Company in 1600, bullion accounted for 75 percent of all the cargo shipped eastward.

Asia turned out to be a sponge for gold and silver. Only a tiny quantity ever came back to Europe. The reasons for this one-way movement are not obvious, and one is tempted to agree with Kipling that east is east and west is west and let it go at that. But what happened is not that trivial.

The Europeans may have grumbled about the loss of their beloved gold and silver to the East, but their desire for the spices, tea, silk, and other luxuries of Asia was so insatiable that they had no alternative. The people in Asia clearly considered gold and silver to be more desirable than the tin, lead, mercury, woolens, and furs that the Europeans offered for sale. That the one-way trade continued for so long is perhaps evidence enough of how satisfactory it was to the Asians, but another revealing piece of evidence is available: the prices of goods in China, Japan, and India varied very little relative to the precious metals.[2] If the process had been an unstable one, the Asians would have refused to continue selling their products to Europe or would have demanded a far larger quantity of gold and silver relative to the physical volume of tea, silks, and spices shipped out.

If you believe that the Asians had a peculiar set of priorities, you will have to concede that the priorities of the Europeans were just as strange. Europeans also put the highest value on the precious metals. They would have considered themselves much wealthier if they could have retained the gold and silver and shipped out the useful stuff like iron, tin, and furs. Even as wise an observer as the Scotch philosopher and historian David Hume fell into this trap when he wrote in 1752 that "The skill and ingenuity of EUROPE in general surpasses perhaps that of CHINA, with regard to the manual arts and manufactures; yet we are never able to trade thither without grave disadvantage."[3]

More than one hundred years before Hume, Thomas Mun, son of a moneyer, master merchant, and key executive of the East India Company, had a keener sense of the reality of this trade: "If those nations which send out their monies do it because they have few wares of their own, how come they have so much Treasure. . . . I answer, Even by trading with their money; for by what other means can they get it, having no mines of Gold or Silver?"[4] Mun was responding to criticism of the East India Company for shipping so much in precious metals eastward, but in fact the transactions proved to be highly favorable to the Europeans. We have already noted that, in contrast to Asia, the price of gold in Europe fell relative to the prices of other commodities. Hence, it was an illusion that the Europeans were getting the worst of the bargain. With the Asians so accommodating by accepting gold and silver, the discovery of America now enabled Europe to satisfy, to a much greater extent than in the past, the longstanding hunger for the products of Asia. Spices cannot be grown anywhere but in Asia, because their development depends on the monsoon rains, while silkworms and tea plants also require a particular kind of climate. The Europeans did learn to convert their earth into fine white china and to execute beautiful designs on it, but the products of the Far East were still esteemed for the mark of status they provided and for the adventure implicit in having obtained them.

Even the Europeans far away in the American colonies were infected with the import virus. The Peruvian silver city of Potosì and the port city of Lima were famous for their displays of silk, porcelain, lacquer ware, precious stones, and pearls from China, while Mexicans paraded around in cottons from the Philippines, silks from China, and calicos from India.[5]

With all that gold and silver pouring in from the New World, the Europeans were behaving precisely as classical economic theory would have predicted. It was the Asian sponge that was in defiance of theory. The patterns of predictable responses to fresh inflows of money were first set forth in systematic fashion by early economists such as Thomas Mun and William Petty in the first part of the seventeenth century. In 1752, however, David Hume developed the theory more fully in an essay titled "Of the Balance of Trade." According to Hume, the movement of money from one area to another is inherently unsustainable and destined to reverse itself. The money piling up in the pockets of the citizens of the gaining country will encourage them to go out and buy things, while the loss of purchasing power in the losing country will lead its citizens to tighten their belts and buy less; prices will rise in the gaining country and fall in the losing country. This shift in demand will in time reverse the flow of money back to the country that first suffered the outflow. As a result, Hume argued, "It is impossible to heap up money, more than any other fluid, beyond its proper level."[6]

The sequence of events related to the ransoming of the sons of Francis I was a perfect illustration of Hume's theory—the gold moved from France to Spain in payment of the ransom, squeezing French citizens in the process but simultaneously encouraging the Spanish to spend more money abroad. No wonder, then, that Spain's newly acquired treasure found its way back to France.

Hume used his theory to explain why Spain and Portugal failed to hold on to the gold and silver they imported from their colonies overseas. "Can one imagine," he asked, with his own peculiar use of uppercase lettering, "that it had ever been possible by any laws, or even any art of industry, to have kept all the money in SPAIN, which the galleons had brought from the INDIES? Or that all the commodities would be sold in FRANCE for a tenth of the price they would yield on the other side of the PYRENEES, without finding their way thither and draining from that immense treasure?"[7] Hume's theory would also explain why the countries that accumulated gold by exporting to Spain would in turn display a voracious appetite for imports from the East (they were under no obligation to import from Spain), especially as Europeans were able to keep replenishing their supply of precious metals after 1500 from both New World sources and increased domestic production. Thus, the Europeans played according to Hume's rules.

Not so in Asia. Contrary to Hume's hypothesis, the precious metals did "heap up" in China, India, and Japan. Hume may have been correct that fluid cannot accumulate beyond its proper level *when the fluid is contained*, but what about when the fluid flows into a vessel so enormous that the inflow is meaningless? A seventeenth-century English merchant, echoing a metaphor in Ecclesiastes, made an appropriate observation when he lamented that "Many streams run thither (India), as all rivers to the sea, and there stay."[8] The economic historian Earl Hamilton has noted that "The East [was] a necropolis of European treasure even in Roman days."[9] Even today, India is the largest buyer of gold in the world, where gold continues to be the most popular form of portable wealth; the Indians spend more on gold than on cars, two-wheeled transport, refrigerators, and color televisions combined.[10]

An identical replay of this phenomenon has occurred in our own times. From 1986 to 1998, Japan exported nearly 60 percent more merchandise than it imported; in 1998 alone, the excess was almost 70 percent. Even though the Japanese spent more on foreign services than foreigners spent on Japanese services, and even though the Japanese made capital investments abroad, Japan's holdings of foreign exchange—the equivalent of the gold absorbed in the 1600s—"heaped up" from less than $30 billion in 1986 to around $200 billion at the end of 1998. This put Japanese foreign exchange reserves above the total combined foreign exchange reserves of France, Germany, Italy, and the United Kingdom in late 1998. Like the Asians of yesteryear, the Japanese prefer to save their money and accumulate treasure instead of going out and spending it on imports from abroad.

Consider what would have happened in Europe if Asia had been less happy about accumulating the precious metals in exchange for their spices and silks, and then consider what would happen today in the United States if the Japanese abruptly decided that adding to their dollar treasure no longer made sense for them. In either case, Asian goods would cease to be available to the West—no more silks, spices, Toyotas, or Sonys—unless the Asians were to reverse their habits and decide that perhaps they *would* like to acquire goods and services other than monetary assets from the West. That choice was just as critical in earlier centuries as it is today: without the gold and silver to ship out, Europeans would have been denied the pepper and curry, the luxurious textiles, and the magnificent china dishes on which they placed such high values.

Why did the immense quantities of gold and silver that were shipped to China, Japan, and India accumulate instead of provoking a reverse flow of demand for goods from Europe? Did the Asians of the 1500s and 1600s have a natural predilection for the Protestant Ethic, with its focus on the virtue of saving, a set of beliefs that most of them back then had probably never heard of? Were Asians so innocent, or so neurotic, about gold and silver that the sheer joy of ownership was enough to keep them importing useless precious metals in exchange for valuable commodities that they could themselves have eaten and worn? Or was a different set of forces acting upon the Asian scene?

One thing is certain: Asians derived much pleasure from their ownership of gold. Gold's natural attributes of malleability, indestructibility, and dazzling beauty appeal to people in any part of the world. The Asian rulers were just as convinced as Hatshepsut, Croesus, Justinian, Abbé Suger, Atahualpa, and Francis I that gold conveyed both a sense of power and a sense of magical beauty.

Marco Polo is a revealing authority for this view. In 1271, he traveled from Venice to China, remaining in the area for twenty years. Although he did not reach Japan, he obtained descriptions of it from his Chinese contacts. Even allowing for the obvious exaggeration in his many colorful tales, the frequency with which Marco Polo refers to gold is notable.

The index of my edition of his *Travels* contains 26 separate items in which he discusses gold, and nearly as many for silver. The amount of space Marco Polo gives to gold and silver together is much greater than the attention he gives to any of the other Asian products in greatest demand in the West, such as spices and silk.

Most of the time, Marco Polo was in the service of the great Mongol leader Kublai Khan, a man who sent emissaries every two years to the Tartars to select between four hundred and five hundred of the most beautiful girls to join his already overflowing inventory of concubines; the Great Khan made do with thirty or forty girls whom he selected from each biennial group. These served the Khan in rotating groups of six "in his chamber and his bed, ministering to all his needs."[11] Those women were in addition to his four official wives, each of whom had three hundred ladies in waiting, and each one of those—according to Marco Polo—"has in her court ten thousand persons."[12] This may be a huge embellishment of the truth, but it contains an important hint about puzzling patterns of Asian foreign trade.

A man supporting a household like Kublai Khan's is clearly not a penny-pinching believer in the principles of the Protestant Ethic. On the contrary, Marco Polo's descriptions of the Khan's palaces are breathtaking. He contends that the palace in the capital city of Cathay was the largest palace ever built, where "there is nothing to be seen anywhere but gold and pictures."[13] He also describes the magnificence of another ruler, who built a tower in his palace grounds that was covered with gold a full finger's breadth in thickness, and was so completely covered that the structure appeared to be made entirely of gold.

The most amusing employment of gold was in a province under the rule of Kublai Khan called Zar-dandan. In its capital city of Vochan, the men —not the women—made casts of their teeth and used these casts to cover their entire mouthful of lower and upper teeth with gold. In Vochan, money talked!

Marco Polo also reported on Japan, "a very big island [where] the people are fair-complexioned, good-looking, and well-mannered." Gold is found there "in measureless quantities," and one reason they possess so much of it is that "no trader, nor indeed anyone else, goes there from the mainland." He then describes a palace of the island's ruler, "that is in truth a veritable marvel. Just as we roof our houses and churches with lead, so this palace is roofed with fine gold. And the value of it is almost beyond computation. Moreover, all the chambers, of which there are many, are likewise paved with fine gold to a depth of more than two fingers' breadth. And the halls and the windows and every other part of the palace are likewise adorned with gold."[14] Shades of the tabernacle ordered from Moses on Mount Sinai! This is the passage from Marco Polo's *Travels* that spurred Columbus on when he reached Cuba and thought he was in Cipangu (Japan).

Gold seems to have been almost everywhere Marco Polo visited. In Vochan, the town of the lovely teeth, gold was so plentiful that one ounce of it exchanged for only five ounces of silver at a time when one ounce of gold in Europe fetched upward of ten ounces of silver and the gold/silver ratio would approach 1:14 after the big American silver mines brought about a radical increase in the European supply of silver relative to gold.[15] In Tibet, where the natives used salt for money and were "very poorly clad, in skins, canvas, and buckram . . . there are rivers and lakes and mountains in which gold-dust is found in great quantity. . . . The province produces plenty of . . . cloth of gold."[16] Marco Polo also mentions gold in India, where he claims it was so plentiful that it exchanged on a ratio of 1:6 for silver.[17] In addition to modest indigenous supplies of gold, India imported large amounts of both gold and silver in the 1500s and 1600s in exchange for cotton, most of it coming in via the major trading post of Malacca in Malaysia.[18]

Everything that we have seen so far reveals that Asians did not perceive gold as money in the same way that Westerners viewed it. Even before Croesus, people in Europe and the Near East were using gold as money, first in bars and then in coins. For at least two thousand years before Columbus discovered America, Europeans had viewed gold coins as the ultimate expression of financial might and sophistication. Coinage, however, democratized gold, because it circulated among members of the public. Asian rulers held no such notions. They shared the Western delight in gold's beauty and what it signified in terms of power, but they considered gold too important to be used as money that would be passed around from one dirty and ignoble hand to another. Releasing gold to public circulation would dilute the power of the state.

As a result, most Chinese money over the centuries has been fabricated out of materials of little value.* Small amounts of gold coins were minted after the sixteenth century, but they were used primarily for ceremonial purposes, such as being thrown on occasion at professors when the students approved of their lecture.[19] China did not issue any coins of precious metals in meaningful amounts until 1890, and then in silver, although Mexican silver pesos—of all things!—circulated in some quantity in China between 1700 and 1826.[20]

This conception of a monetary system had a long tradition in China. In 255 BC, when the many feudal Chinese states were united by a great general named Qin Shu Huangdi into a single political entity, Qin promptly declared himself the emperor and built the Great Wall to protect his domain (*Qin* is pronounced "Chin" and is the derivation of the word China). It was his tomb that was guarded by the famous terracotta army discovered by archeologists at Xian in 1974. At that time, the longstanding Chinese coinage system—which probably predated the use of coins in the West—consisted of awkward cast-bronze pieces that looked like hoes, knives, and cowrie-shaped shells. Qin replaced these forms with cast-bronze round coins punctured in the middle with a square hole. These small base-metal coins came to be known as *cash*, the Tamil word for money that is now the common expression reserved for ready, liquid money. Although the denominations and weights of the coins changed over the centuries, the familiar characteristic design of round Chinese coins with the square holes remained unchanged for over eight hundred years.[21]

The holes in the coins made it possible to string together a large quantity for carrying or for trading: the coins were made out of such low-value material that a trader or his customer had to handle many coins even for transactions of modest size. If some of the coins had been minted from metals of more value—at least in the eyes of the beholders—to provide for larger transactions, fewer coins would have been needed and carrying them around would have been less burdensome. As in the West, the coins could have been carried in pockets or purses.

Some things are never learned, as the frantic coin counting for ransoming Richard I and the sons of Francis I reminds us. The following

*During the go-go days of the 1960s, some of the dubious debt issued by highly leveraged conglomerates was referred to facetiously as "Chinese paper."

story about Chinese money in World War II shows that even in modern times people have failed to understand simple principles about how to denominate whatever is in use as the means of payment.

Chiang Kai-shek's embattled government in World War II was based in Chongqing (spelled Chungking in the 1940s), far in the interior of China with no access to the seas in any direction. All aid from the Allies, from food to tanks, had to be flown in over long distances, often passing through Japanese anti-aircraft fire or attacks by Japanese fighter planes. As Chungking had no facilities to print currency, all the Chinese paper money was printed in the United States, which meant that the critical materiel of warfare had to share space with currency in the cargo aircraft. China was also suffering from a vicious inflationary spiral caused by a severe shortage of the necessities of life and massive amounts of currency being paid out to troops and workers. With prices rising so rapidly, stacks of paper money were absorbing more and more precious cargo space.

The American economic advisors to Chiang urged him to order currency in larger denominations, because what had once cost $1 was now costing $10 or more. It made no sense to keep shipping one-dollar bills when ten-dollar bills would buy what one-dollar bills had once bought, and the ten-dollar bills would take up one-tenth the cargo space—and in time one-hundred-dollar notes could replace ten-dollar notes. Yet the currency orders never kept pace with the inflation. The planes continued to be crammed with excessive amounts of low-denomination notes occupying cargo space desperately needed for food, oil, weapons, and ammunition. Similar myopia in adjusting denominations to price increases explains the stories about people running around with wheelbarrows full of currency in the German hyperinflation of the 1920s.

About one thousand years after Qin, during the reign of Hien Tsung (806–821), a severe shortage of copper induced the emperor to use sheets of paper for money in place of bronze coins. If there was no point in making payments with useful stuff, the emperor reasoned, why not go all the way and adopt paper? This newfangled idea appears to have been more of a historical accident than a stroke of financial genius, but the long perspective of history suggests that Hien Tsung's inadvertent innovation should join printing, gunpowder, and the compass among China's most enduring contributions to the civilization of the world. Hien Tsung not only passed on his invention to posterity; his successors also paved the way for the inevitable route that most paper money systems have followed: overissue and uncontrollable inflation.[22]

The lessons were learned in China early on. In a book called *A Treatise on Coinage*, published in 1149, a historian named Ma Twan-lin warned in strikingly modern terms that "Paper should never be *money* [but] only employed as a representative sign of value existing in metals or produce. . . . The government . . . wished to make a real money of paper, and thus the original contrivance was perverted."[23] We shall see that this argument reappears almost verbatim in Britain in the course of the Napoleonic Wars, dressed in different clothes but containing the same substance. About six hundred years had to pass, until 1455, before the Chinese decided that they could control their money supply more effectively with metallic coins than with paper money, but they were still so far ahead of the West that another three hundred years would pass before printed banknotes became common in Europe.

Marco Polo was so impressed with the paper money of China that he considered it a kind of magic. As he characterized it, Kublai Khan's "mint . . . is so organized that you might well say that he has mastered the art of alchemy."[24] The paper for the money was manufactured out of mulberry tree bark and cut up into various sizes to reflect the differing denominations; a note representing one thousand coins measured nine by thirteen inches—an awkward size but light as a feather, while one thousand coins weighed eight pounds. The proper officials then wrote their names on the papers and stamped them with the seal of the Great Khan. At that point, according to Marco Polo, "The procedure of issue is as formal and authoritative as if they were made of pure gold or silver. . . . The money is authentic. . . . Of this money the Khan has such a quantity made that with it he could buy all the treasure of the world."[25]

Marco Polo reported that the Khan ordered every payment, everywhere in his empire, to be made in paper currency. Then Marco Polo delivered the punchline that exposed why this money worked as well as it did and why he thought that the Khan could buy all the treasure of the world with it: "*And no one dares refuse it on pain of losing his life.*"[26] There's legal tender for you! But no force was involved, according to Marco Polo. Everyone was "perfectly willing" to accept these papers in payment, "since wherever they go they pay in the same currency."[27] The system provided a neat system for the government to finance itself.

The Khan did not restrict his expenditure of the paper money merely to current operating expenses of his government. He deployed his power to greater advantage. Whenever traders arrived in his domain with pearls, precious stones, gold, silver, or other valuables, or when any town possessed gems or precious metals, they were required to surrender all their treasure to the Great Khan. These people accepted the paper money in exchange for their valuables "willingly," because they could use it to pay for the goods they bought throughout the Great Khan's dominions. By this means, Marco Polo concluded, "The Great Khan acquires all the gold and silver and pearls and precious stones of his territory," and this is how the Khan "has more treasure than anyone else in the world."[28] This "willingness" may have had to do with more than the Great Khan's raw power, although surely that was a necessary condition for the success of the paper money. China's huge landmass may have made its economy more self-sufficient than any individual country or city-state in Europe. Thus, concerns about acceptability of the paper money abroad, if any, were at least secondary.

What Marco Polo failed to point out was that the Khan thereby accumulated assets that were accepted as assets anywhere in the world, while the people who held paper money in exchange held assets that were accepted only in the Great Khan's dominions. Seen from that perspective, Marco Polo was correct that the Khan had mastered the art of alchemy. His paper money turned into gold—at least at his palaces.

Was the exchange unfair? In 1933, the U.S. government prohibited the ownership of monetary gold by any individual, company, or political entity except the federal government itself (jewelry and works of art were excluded from this prohibition). All monetary gold within the borders of the United States or imported into the United States had to be turned over to the government and converted into dollar-denominated bank deposits or everyday coin and currency. This law was still less restrictive than Kublai Khan's, because foreign governments and central banks such as the Bank of France or the Bank of England were free to convert their dollar balances back into gold—until August 15, 1971. At that moment, President Nixon joined up with the Great Khan. As the expression of the time put it, the gold window was shut down. Even foreign governments and central banks could no longer exchange dollars for gold. In his own fashion, Richard Nixon had mastered the art of alchemy.

Meanwhile, the story in Japan was much the same as in China. The Japanese used gold for adornment, not money. Unlike many other forms of art, the work of the goldsmith in Japan developed late and was never as notable as Japanese pottery, sculpture, or painting. When it came to money, the Japanese just copied the Chinese practice, as they had already copied art and the alphabet from China, except that the Japanese clung to metallic money rather than converting to paper.

Copper was the first metallic money, followed by bronze, which economized on the copper. When the Chinese changed over to paper money in the ninth century, they had no more use for their metal coins, so the Japanese obliged them by importing the superfluous coins. For the next few centuries, the Chinese would continue to supply the Japanese with all the bronze coins they needed. As trade was considered demeaning in Japan, and the economy was in any case less developed than in China, the demand for money was correspondingly smaller. Marco Polo himself had observed that no traders ventured from Japan to the mainland, which meant that foreign trade played no role in the Japanese economy until much later on.

Around 1600, a rising price for gold provoked a minor mining rush in Japan, to satisfy increased demand in China as well as the Japanese emperor's desire to advertise his power. Portuguese shipping was then just beginning to reach the Japanese seas, and so a modest amount of foreign trade was developing. The Portuguese exchanged Chinese silks for Japanese silver, which they then sold in Macao, Malacca, and India in exchange for spices until the Japanese spoiled a profitable triangular line of trade by cutting off the Portuguese. Why? The Portuguese had tried to convert the Japanese to Christianity.[29]

The Japanese finally began issuing their own coins around this time, but these home-grown specimens were still copies of the Chinese money and were even inscribed with the appropriate Chinese characters. Japan also started issuing a limited amount of gold and silver coins in oval or rectangular shapes to suggest the ingots that had circulated for a short time as money in the Middle Ages, but these had such high value—one was worth about a ton of the copper coins in daily circulation—that they were used for the most part in ceremonial transactions among the nobility.[30] The stones of Yap would have functioned more efficiently! Even in the latter half of the nineteenth century, after Admiral Perry's arrival, the Japanese coinage continued to copy foreign coins, this time of American and British money; *yen*, which means "round coin" in Japanese, was also the word they used for dollar, with *sen*, the word for a copper coin, standing for cent.[31]

To return to the main question: Why did the gold and silver of the West move in only one direction toward the East? What was going on in Asia that led people to value precious metals more than the food, clothing, and home decoration that they shipped in such volume to Europeans?

One answer has already been suggested. From the viewpoint of the Asians, the supplies of gold and silver they were importing were money only in a very indistinct sense. They did not perceive the precious metals as something that people use to exchange for something else, either now or at some point in the future. Rather, the Chinese, Japanese, and Indians considered the precious metals to be commodities—that is, goods with a genuine use value that rendered these goods worth keeping for their own sake rather than as a means of payment. Gold was for decorating a bride, for baubles, for ornaments, and, most important, for hoarding. Indeed, burying treasure in the East was akin to conspicuous consumption, similar to the insatiable demand for fancy gold watches in our own time.[32] This view of gold explains why Asia was a sponge for precious metals rather than one of Hume's nations where "it is impossible to heap up money, more than any other fluid, beyond its proper level." *The Asians were not playing the money game.*

What, then, was the utility of gold and silver in the eyes of the Asians? As with everyone else, beauty and resistance to rust were important elements. Adam Smith charmingly observes, "A silver boiler is more cleanly than a lead, copper, or tin one; and the same quality would render a gold boiler still better than a silver one. The principal merit [of the precious metals], however, arises from their beauty, which renders them peculiarly fit for the ornaments of dress and furniture. No paint or dye can give so splendid a color as gilding."[33]

That is not all: scarcity matters, too. Smith refers to rich people who never appear to themselves so rich "as when they appear to possess those decisive marks of opulence which nobody can possess but themselves. . . . Such objects they are willing to purchase at a higher price than things much more beautiful and useful, but more common."[34] Wealthy Asians were no exception to this general rule.

The strangest feature of gold is that there has never been a moment when it has ceased to be scarce. There have been moments when the supply of gold increased faster than the supply of silver, and gold's price fell relative to the price of silver (to say nothing of the dramatic drop in the price of gold after disinflation took hold in the world economy of the 1980s), but the price nevertheless has always remained high enough to indicate that gold was far from a glut on the market. Steel sells for 2¢ an ounce; gold sells for more than ten thousand times as much.

Gold remains a definitive mark of opulence. Thus, the mystique of gold as a store of wealth, which is critically dependent on its scarcity, has added lustre to gold as a symbol of power, whether it accents the halo of a saint or covers the roof of a palace, whether it dangles from the ear or surrounds the neck, and whether it fills the room of a captive emperor or the storage cells of the Federal Reserve Bank of New York. Darius must have had great fun in his bathtub.

In the long run, the cupidity and stupidity of human beings are what motivate the drama, although nature contributes by distributing gold arbitrarily and unevenly around the globe. There was never a time when gold was not in constant demand for ostentation or for hoarding.

Hoarding is similar to buying an insurance policy. Like an insurance policy, hoarding gold has a cost, for the idle metal earns nothing. However, you sleep better knowing that you hold some kind of a hedge against the chance that the catastrophes you fear may actually occur. This motive is as powerful among poor peasants and laborers as among kings and princes. But the insurance policy can work only as long as everyone else continues to consider gold an item of highest value. For that essential condition to be met, people must continue to agree with one another that gold is scarce.

The distribution of income in Asia provides a second answer to our question about the strange equilibrium that kept gold moving in the eastern direction and useful commodities such as spices and silk moving to the west. Evidence developed by modern economists indicates that average per capita wealth in Asia in the sixteenth and seventeenth centuries was close to average per capita wealth in Europe.[35] Adam Smith himself pointed out that China was one of the richest and most fertile countries in the world.[36]

Averages can be dangerously deceptive when the dispersion around them is wide. The per capita figure for Europe is of some value as at least suggestive, but the per capita measure for China, or any part of Asia at that time, obscures the reality that a tiny number of people lived in an environment of luxury and indulgence while the masses existed at levels that were horrible even by the standards of the poorest people in Europe. Adam Smith was eloquent on the subject. In describing conditions in Canton to illustrate his point that the poverty in China far surpassed that of "the most beggarly nations in Europe," he wrote:

> The subsistence which they find there is so scanty that they are eager to fish up the nastiest garbage thrown overboard from any European ship. Any carrion, the carcase [*sic*] of a dead dog or cat, for example, although half putrid and stinking, is as welcome to them as the most wholesome food to the peoples of other countries.[37]

Under conditions like this, the gold-consuming nobility of China were aware of no loss to themselves in shipping the products of their land out to Europe, because the privileged class was so small and wielded so much power that their consumption could be, and usually was, as conspicuous as they wanted it to be without any sense of prodigality on their part. Gold and silver, on the other hand, had a limitless market in Asia, for both ostentation and insurance against uprisings and war. What looked like an irrational exchange with the Europeans at first glance thus becomes an understandable set of transactions when viewed from the perspective of class structure and tastes. Similar observations apply, with only minor variations, to Japan, India, and the island kingdoms of the Pacific.

As Marco Polo did not have a graduate degree in economics, we can pardon his hyperbole when he says that stamping the paper money of the Great Khan made the process "as formal and authoritative as if [the notes] were made of pure gold or silver. . . . The money is authentic." Nevertheless, his evaluation of the paper currency of thirteenth-century China was keen enough to touch on matters that will concern us repeatedly in later pages, topics such as the interaction between specie—money in metallic form—and money in its more ephemeral forms such as paper, bookkeeping entries, and computer blips. Marco Polo's respect for Kublai Khan's stamp on the mulberry currency also raises important questions about money issued by the state and its relationship to the private money that enters today into the huge volume of transferring funds, either by check or electronically, from one private bank account to another.

Kublai Khan's stamp bestowed authenticity and the attributes of gold and silver on his paper money only because Kublai Khan's state was all-powerful—in China. Marco Polo missed that essential point. No one in England would have been able to use the Chinese notes to pay for a pint of beer at the local tavern, and no French king could have paid ransoms with it. Hence, this money did not have the true attributes of gold and silver. In fact, no one outside China would even have known what to do with the mulberry notes unless they were planning to go to China to buy some silk or vases. Otherwise, the Khan's currency was valueless outside China.

People demand that their money must have *value*. In fact, valueless money is not even money, because it would not serve as a means of payment and would be nothing that anybody would want to accumulate or consider as wealth. Metallic money, or paper money convertible into metal, is usually considered to have more value than a system that uses paper only. As Ma Twan-lin reminded us, "Paper should never be *money* [but] only employed as a representative sign of value existing in metals or produce." The presumption here is that metals are more limited in supply than paper, which means that metallic systems should prevent money from becoming valueless.

Yet there is a strong superficial resemblance between Croesus's turning out great supplies of gold coins by mining the Pactolus and a Chinese emperor who turns on the printing press. Croesus and the emperor both produce an expansion in the supply of money. The difference is in the international consequences. A gold coin would buy a pint of beer anywhere when foreign paper notes would not. Nevertheless, from a domestic viewpoint, the similarities between Croesus and the emperor are much closer than they appear at first glance. The world just thinks about them differently.

The policies of the Great Khan demonstrated that the power of the state is a strategic element in establishing and sustaining value. The "continentals" printed by the government of the American colonies during the Revolutionary War became a metaphor for worthlessness, but the dollars of the federal government, authorized by the Constitution, have been acceptable for over two hundred years and throughout all our wars. Lydia, Genoa, Florence, and Venice were not just economic powerhouses but also had strong local governments before they issued their famous gold coins, but who ever heard of a gold coin issued by Manchester or Liverpool? The French have changed their monetary system on many occasions over the centuries, which is probably why French peasants have earned the reputation of being congenital hoarders of gold. The pound sterling has the longest uninterrupted history of all, just like the English monarchy. After the breakup of the Soviet Union, the Russians had a hard time establishing the international acceptability of the ruble, while after German unification the East Germans had the great advantage of exchanging their currency for the firmly established deutschmark.

Since we left Offa and his silver coins way back around 800, the English have played a subordinate role in our story. It is now time to move England to center stage, for developments there during the years from 1700 to 1810 materially expanded the role of gold in the financial system, formalized it, and shaped the broad structure of the world economy as we know it today. In the course of recounting these events, we shall hear an echo of Hien Tsung's inadvertent innovation of paper money, because the key incident was just as unplanned and just as historic in its consequences.

12

The Great Recoinage and the Last of the Magicians

In 1661, King Charles II of England issued an Order-in-Council mandating the adoption of a revolutionary innovation in the manufacture of coins—the use of machinery in place of hammering out the coins by hand. The innovation in question was not a gadget that someone invented one day and that went into effect the next. Technological change is often disruptive to established habits. The workers and officials in the national mints who earned their living by doing things the old-fashioned way fiercely resisted the introduction of any modification in the manufacture of coins. Even with a King's Order-in-Council to force its introduction, a full installation of the new method had to wait more than thirty years, and then came about only because a financial crisis had forced the issue.

It was in the aftermath of that crisis that, quite without warning, the markets for the precious metals in Britain suddenly decided that silver was out and gold was in as the standard for the value of the pound sterling. Without anyone having planned this sequence of events, we shall see that they led, step-by-step, from Charles's Order of 1661 to the establishment of a set of hallowed institutions based on a central role for gold. These institutions would rule the world economy throughout most of the nineteenth and twentieth centuries. Thus, although the story here begins by focusing on silver, the golden threads are laced through it from start to finish.

The Lydians and ancient Greeks who first introduced coins into general use hammered their coins out by hand, one at a time. In view of the millions of coins produced over the next one thousand years all over Europe and in the East, it is astonishing that nobody succeeded in developing a faster method. But no one did. Indeed, more than speed of production should have motivated a change. From the very beginning of coinage, the smooth edges of hammered coins had encouraged people to clip or file off tiny pieces of metal that could be accumulated until the quantity was sufficient to be melted down into bullion, which the clippers then resold to the mint for a fresh supply of coins. The process was too profitable to be stifled by the severe punishments dealt to the clippers who were caught at their work. In the thirteenth century, Jews were often accused of clipping even when they were innocent. In 1270 alone, 280 Jews were beheaded for the crime.[1]

Despite the impact of clipping on the currency, the traditional methods of minting coins continued without any semblance of change until early in the reign of Queen Elizabeth of England, when a man named Eloy Mestrell experimented with using horses to power the coin-stamping machines and using this machinery to redesign the edge of the coins so that clipping would be immediately visible. Ingenious as he may have been, Mestrell generated little enthusiasm for his efforts and was fired in 1572. That was not the last to be heard of Mestrell, for he was hanged in 1578 for counterfeiting![2]

Nevertheless, Mestrell's efforts encouraged others to keep trying. In the 1620s, the chief engraver at the Paris Mint, Nicholas Briot, succeeded in introducing a workable technique for frustrating the coin-clipper. Briot's approach was to edge the coin with either a kind of graining or with inscriptions that would make the clipper's efforts immediately visible, no matter how tiny the piece he clipped. No luck:

the traditionalists in the Paris Mint refused to go along, leaving Briot instead of the coin-clippers in a state of frustration.[3]

Briot was not ready to give up. In 1625 he went to England, where he started producing what came to be known as milled coins at the Tower Mint in London. Again there was resistance from the hierarchy at the Mint. As the moneyers were paid by the number of pounds of coins they struck, they were not lightly going to relinquish much of their metal to a Frenchman and his new-fangled devices.[4] Briot's total output in 1631–1632 amounted to around 26 pounds of gold coins and 211 pounds of silver coins, compared with more than four thousand pounds of gold and fifty thousand pounds of silver turned out by conventional methods; by 1638–1639, Briot's silver coin production was approaching one thousand pounds, but this was still a minor effort.[5] The evidence also suggests that Briot's coins were turned out by hand rather than by machine.[6] Briot temporarily faded from view from about 1640 to the 1660s.

In 1645, the French, thinking better of the matter, finally eliminated the hammer at the Paris Mint and replaced it with horse-drawn machines that performed the entire job from rolling out the metal to stamping out the designs on the faces and milling the edges to foil the clippers. That success led the English Commonwealth to invite Pierre Blondeau, the chief engineer at Paris, to follow in Briot's path to London.* The authorities at the Mint permitted Blondeau to produce milled coins, but from just a small portion of a huge silver treasure that the English had plundered from a captured Spanish galleon; the rest of the silver was transformed into coinage by way of the hammer.[7]

This story has a happy ending. With the restoration of Charles II to the throne of England in 1660, the process of change accelerated. Briot was recalled to London, Blondeau was given a 21-year contract, and Charles's Order-in-Council of 1661 declared that "All coin [was] to be struck as soon as possible by machinery, with grained or lettered edges."[8] Blondeau died in 1672, before he could complete his contract, but during his employment at the Mint he had the moneyers fully subordinate to him and sworn to secrecy about what they learned from him.[9]

*The English Commonwealth was the government headed by Oliver Cromwell that assumed the rule of Britain after Charles I was beheaded at Whitehall on January 30, 1649. The monarchy, under Charles's son Charles II, was restored in 1660.

In addition, Charles II issued a warrant on Christmas Eve 1663 to create a new gold coin that would be produced entirely by the mechanized methods. This coin soon became identified as the guinea, because it was fabricated from gold imported from West Africa by the newly established Africa Company. Charles's warrant defined the new coin as equal to £1 (twenty shillings of silver). This was a substantial piece of gold—at about eight grams, or a quarter of an ounce, it weighed more than twice as much as a genoin or florin of the thirteenth century. Appropriately enough, the guinea was stamped with a little elephant, the sign of the Africa Company.[10] The edges were inscribed with a motto that read *Decus et Tutamen*, or Ornament and Safeguard, which is believed to have come from a clasp on the purse of Cardinal Richelieu, Blondeau's former patron. New issues of silver coins manufactured by these methods soon followed after the appearance of the guinea.[11]

The handsome new coins, with their elegant designs and milled edges, were a vivid contrast to the coins that had been circulating in England for sixty years since the previous recoinage in 1601. Those were a tattered lot, repeatedly clipped and sadly worn from constant movement from hand to hand. Nevertheless, people continued to use the worn coins because anyone who brought them back to the mint to exchange for new full-weight coins would have received much less in face value than the face value that was stamped on them.

Although clippers were hanged "by the half-dozen," according to one contemporary authority, the gallows seem to have been an inadequate deterrent for such a simple and profitable means of getting rich. The clipping continued at a merry pace, especially on half-crowns (two shillings sixpence) and shilling coins that were larger and thicker than the smaller denominations.[12] In 1652, Blondeau estimated that the weight of the average old coin was 20 to 30 percent below its original weight. Hopton Haynes, who served as Assay Master of the Mint, calculated that a bag of coins with a total face value of £100 in 1695 had half the weight that the same bag would have had in 1686.[13]

In a way, the clippers performed a public service, for the coins over time had become unequal in weight and thickness as well as less than perfectly round. Haynes observed that the clippers would file with such skill that the coins became "as flat and as smooth as the blanks at the Mint are before they have been in the press."[14] Samuel Pepys recounts an anecdote about a workman from the Mint who made a profit by stamping out counterfeit small-change groats that were as good or better than the true groats then circulating. Groats were small coins equal to four pennies; three groats made one shilling. The workman was caught, but "He was neither hanged nor burned [because] the cheat was so ingenious . . . and so little hurt to any man in it, the money being as good as commonly goes."[15]

In addition to the difficulties over the quality of the coinage, problems had also developed in the ratio of gold prices to silver prices. The great silver mines of Mexico and Peru poured their output into Europe in such volume during the first half of the 1600s that the price of silver in Europe began to fall. Thus, a man who wanted to exchange silver for gold would have to offer increasing amounts of silver to obtain an unchanged quantity of gold—or, to put it the other way, an ounce of gold commanded increasing quantities of silver. Meanwhile, the price of silver in India during the first half of the 1600s was so high that only nine or ten ounces of it were needed to buy an ounce of gold, compared with fifteen ounces in England. The price of an ounce of silver in India, in fact, was far higher than the amount of coinage that an Englishman could obtain by bringing an ounce of silver to the Mint.

The economics of the business was irresistible. There was a great rise in exports of silver, with most of it shipped out by the East India Company. English merchants and manufacturers complained bitterly that the company was shortchanging English goods, especially woolen cloth, which had been called "the flower of the king's crown, the dowry of the kingdom, the chief revenue of the king . . . the gold of our Ophir, the milk and honey of our Canaan, the Indies of England."[16] The Indians, unfortunately, had no use for the woolens, but they certainly had a steady demand for silver.

Pressure built up to raise the price of silver at the Mint in order to keep more of it at home and to provide for a larger supply of silver coins. From January 1690 to December 1695, the coinage of silver had amounted to only £19,383.[17] Money was so scarce that the government by proclamation raised the face values of foreign silver coins in order to discourage people from exporting them. Meanwhile, the demand for gold was surging, because it was so profitable to exchange gold for silver that would be exported to Asia. This was one of the forces that would push the price of guinea coins in the market above the officially declared value of twenty shillings.

The result was that Charles II's impressive revolution in minting methods and associated innovations in currency administration ended up by serving little purpose. Most of the new silver coins disappeared into hoards or were shipped to Asia for fancy prices instead of functioning as English money. Meanwhile, the currency was further reduced by the continued prevalence of clipping, so an increasing number of coins was becoming unacceptable in trade or in payment of debts. If England were to have a proper currency for daily use as well as for accumulated wealth, a major reform would be unavoidable.

The big obstacle to a total recoinage was the uncertainty as to who would bear the cost of the difference between the face value on the coins and their true value based on their shrunken weight. Blondeau had warned that the longer the authorities waited, the more the coins would be clipped and the more costly the ultimate outcome would be. Nevertheless, the government diddled with the problem for so long that the Stuarts had been overthrown and William and Mary were occupying the throne by the time the monarchy finally got around to the task in 1696.

Important events immediately preceded the decision to inaugurate a recoinage. As usual, those events revolved around a war, this time a mighty effort to defeat or at least contain Louis XIV of France, the most aggressive European leader since the Romans and up to the time of Napoleon. Hostilities had broken out in 1689 and immediately took their toll on the Exchequer. By 1697, William III was over £20 million in debt. Taxation, personal loans, and lotteries helped to raise revenue, but not enough. The result of the shortfall was the establishment of the Bank of England, an unusual deal between the government and the men of "quality" who were shareholders of the Bank (that uppercase letter B forever after identified that bank as *the* Bank). Under this arrangement, the Bank would lend the government £1.2 million at the moderate interest rate of 8 percent, in return for which the institution would be established as the first private company to do business as a limited-liability corporation, or so-called joint stock company—in the rapidly growing field of banking—just like the institutions of our own time.*[18]

The founding of the Bank would turn out to be a momentous step in the history of Britain, as the institution over time would steadily increase its influence—even its power—over the banking system and the general economy, the gold stock, and Britain's financial relations with the rest of the world. In later years, the Bank came to be known familiarly as the Old Lady of Threadneedle Street, an expression whose meaning varied from a friendly nickname to a bitter expression of disdain, depending upon the circumstances.

This was, however, just one step in a broad advance in economic growth and increasing financial sophistication in England, unleashed after the Glorious Revolution of 1688 had resolved, once and for all, the religious uncertainties surrounding the monarchy and permitting the country finally to get down to business.† As credit throughout the English economy expanded at a rapid rate, the inevitable price inflation soon took over, affecting all commodities, then the precious metals, and finally a wave of speculation in the youthful stock market. As always happens in such environments, countless fraudulent issues were uncritically gobbled up by a greedy public in a market where losing money appeared to be an impossible outcome. The economic historian Charles Kindleberger cites "a proposal by several ladies . . . to make, print and paint and stain callicoes."[19] (Subscribers must be women dressed in calico.) Daniel Defoe, the author of *Robinson Crusoe*, issued a tract that described the "Scandalous Trade" as one in which "There is not a man but will own 'tis a compleat System of Knavery . . . founded in Fraud, born of Deceit, and nourished by Trick, Cheat, Wheedle, Forgeris,

*The Dutch East India Company, founded in 1602, was the first permanent joint stock company. Commercial banking firms with limited liability developed much more rapidly in the United States than in Britain during the first half of the nineteenth century.

†See Bernstein (1996), Chapter 5, for an extended discussion of English economic and financial development in the 1600s, including the establishment of Lloyd's insurance.

Falsehoods, and Delusions . . . preying on the Weakness of those whose Imaginations they have ever elevated or depres'd."[20]

Circumstances were ripe for the speculative fever to spread to the guinea, originally coined with gold that was worth twenty silver shillings. With the silver currency continuing to deteriorate, the rumor mills were busy churning out the news that the recoinage was finally about to happen—but under terms that were still uncertain. Just as in our own times, the uncertainty led to a "flight to quality"; people began to shift from silver coins into guineas, even if they had to pay a premium to protect the value of their assets.

In March 1694, guineas were trading at 22 shillings, but a year later they were trading at over 25 shillings. The guinea hit thirty shillings in June 1695, creating a rush to bring gold to the Mint for coining into guineas, which in turn drove the price of gold from eighty shillings up to 109 shillings. At that point, the swollen supply of guineas was tempering the rise in their price—£750,000 of gold was coined in 1695, compared with only £65,000 the year before—at the same time that the leap in the price of gold made the other side of the transaction too expensive to justify its continuance.[21] The government had another weapon to throw at the speculators: the tax collectors announced that they would not accept guineas as payment of taxes at a value as high as thirty shillings.

The speculation in the guinea finally persuaded the authorities that they could no longer postpone the recoinage. Matters had progressed to a point where no old silver coins were coming into the Mint for coining, because they weighed so little that the quantity of new silver coins given out in exchange would be too far below the face value of the old coins to make the exchange practicable. As Sir Dudley North, a contemporary expert, saw the matter, "There is a great fear that if clipped money be not taken there will be no money at all."[22]

Although recoinage occupied the attention of the politicians for most of the 1690s, a long series of parliamentary reports and committees had managed to produce a large volume of words but no legislation. The shift from words to deeds finally began in September 1695 following the publication of *An Essay for the Amendment of the Silver Coins* by

William Lowndes, a veteran civil servant and Secretary of the Treasury.* The *Essay* was a remarkable document in which Lowndes traced in great detail the entire history of English coinage over the 629 years since the Norman Conquest.

On the basis of this analysis, Lowndes recommended replacing the clipped money with new milled silver coins. These new coins would reflect the diminished value of the silver in the clipped money handed in: the new silver shilling coins would have only 80 percent as much silver as the old shilling coins they were replacing. This step was the equivalent of raising the price of silver at the Mint, because anyone bringing a given amount of silver to the Mint for coinage would now receive 25 percent more shilling coins than formerly.

The harm was already done, Lowndes argued, and this step would simply confirm what everyone recognized.[23] Why not acknowledge the reality of the situation? Indeed, without this change, no silver would be brought to the mint for coining. If there was to be a shortage of coins to pay for merchandise or to repay debts, business would be depressed and production would be curtailed. There was no dishonor in this process: the great Queen Elizabeth herself had taken essentially the same step in the 43rd year of her reign. Lowndes was also emphatic that the recoinage should not wait until the end of the war, because such a step "does but postpone the Cure of a Disease which may destroy us before such remedy can take effect."[24]

Lowndes's recommendations immediately ran into the opposition of Charles Montagu, the Chancellor of the Exchequer, the cabinet member under whom Lowndes worked. Montagu enjoyed the vigorous support of the distinguished philosopher John Locke. Locke had been deeply involved in political activities for many years and was one of the original subscribers to the Bank of England, but he also became one of the most articulate proponents of the Age of Reason; his reputation in this area was launched when he was 58 years old, by his essay of 1690, *Essay Concerning Human Understanding*. His position in the controversy over the recoinage, however, though cloaked in what appeared to be cold logic, was heavily colored by emotion.

*The discussion that follows is necessarily compressed. Much of the controversy focused on what to do about the official price of silver, which is largely omitted below. For an authoritative and lively account of the disputes and the decisions in these matters, see Li (1963), pp. 83–107.

Locke presented himself as a so-called hard-money man who would tolerate no tinkering with the traditional official weights and standards of the English coinage, regardless of the physical damage that the coinage might have suffered in the interim. To Locke, a coin that read "one shilling" on it was a one-shilling coin; that the coin had been clipped down to a shadow of its former self was irrelevant. One shilling stood for a specific weight of silver and should continue to stand for that same specific weight to eternity. To require the holder to exchange old shilling coins for new coins equal to less than one shilling was the equivalent of government appropriation of private property; Locke satirically referred to this possibility as "public clipping."[25] In 1844, Prime Minister Robert Peel would draw directly on Locke's position, when he defined a pound as "a certain definite quantity of gold, with a mark upon it to determine its weight and fineness . . . the engagement to pay a pound means nothing else than the promise to pay to the holder . . . that definite quantity of gold."[26]

Locke argued further that if Britain was losing silver to foreign countries, the proper solution should be to reduce the demand for imports, even though the country was at war. He personified the issue with a "Country Farmer who lives within Compass, increases his Stock by diligence and frugality, is never in debt at the year's end but has a balance always to receive at the foot of his accounts."[27]

Here, once again, Locke was anticipating future disputes in these matters. His view that austerity is the preferred cure for an outflow of precious metals would be invoked in the course of the Napoleonic Wars and was destined to become the standard response under the nineteenth-century gold standard. Indeed, this doctrine motivated both British and American policy decisions at the depths of the Great Depression in 1931 and was one of the dominant causes of the shattering worldwide deflation of the 1930s. Finally, Locke felt most strongly that accepting a devaluation of the currency in the form advocated by Lowndes would simply provide justification for committing this dreaded deed over and over again in the years ahead, or even "next week."[28] Locke's view echoed an earlier seventeenth-century statement against devaluation, in a marvelous metaphor by Sir Robert Cotton: "That the enfeebling of coin is but a shift for a while, as drink to one in a dropsy, to make him swell the more."[29]

Locke's logic for his case was weaker than his zeal, but the zeal was eloquent and persuasive.* Montagu and Locke won the day. The battered shillings would be exchanged at their original face value for the new shillings, with the loss to be borne by the Treasury—and ultimately by the taxpayer. The stage was now set for the recoinage to begin.[30]

The English of the sixteenth and seventeenth centuries were inordinately fond of calling major events the Great "Whatever." Henry VIII's attack on the integrity of the currency came to be known as the Great Debasement. When the members of Parliament in 1641 decided to tell King Charles I what they thought of his reign, they called their resolution the Grand Remonstrance; the battle to overthrow him that began the following year was known at the time as the Great Rebellion (today as the Civil War). The plague that hit England in 1665 and killed one hundred thousand people, just before the beginning of this chapter in our story, was dubbed the Great Plague. The terrible fire that destroyed most of London in the following year is referred to as the Great Fire. And the recoinage that began at the end of 1695 has come to be known as the Great Recoinage.†

Carrying out a great recoinage of the currency is an extremely complicated process, but in this instance it turned out to be extremely messy as well. The king's first proclamation appeared on December 19, 1695, citing that "The Lords Spiritual and Temporal, and the Knights, Citizens, and Burgesses in Parliament assembled, having taken into consideration the great Mischiefs which this our Kingdom lies under, by reason that the Coin, which Passes in Payment is generally clipped. . . . the most Effectual Way to put a stop to this Evil, is to prevent the currency thereof."[31] The proclamation then proceeds to specify a series of dates after which no clipped coins could be offered in payment to anybody except in payment

*The issues involved are complex and go to the very roots of what we mean by money and the "standard." For a full discussion of both sides of the matter, see the passages in Li (1963) cited above, pp. 83–107.

†The English continue to refer to World War I as the Great War.

of taxes or loans to the king. By April 2, 1696, "No such Money Clipped . . . shall Pass in any Payment whatsoever."[32]

The immediate result was panic. Nobody wanted to take clipped coins in payment, so business ground to a halt, and in any case most people did not pay all their taxes during the short span of time before the stated dates. On January 21, 1696, a month after the original proclamation, Parliament relented by passing "An Act For Remedying The Ill State Of The Coin," which extended the process into the latter part of June and restored a semblance of order.

Nevertheless, turbulence bubbled up from time to time over the details of the arrangements. Although £4.7 million (containing no more than £2.5 million in silver by weight) had been received at the Exchequer by the final cutoff date of June 24, well over £2 million more remained in the hands of the public, especially among the little people who had been unable to get to the Exchequer in time.[33] The government losses between what they received and what they had committed to pay out were to be covered by a tax on windows, but the losses had been underestimated by a wide margin, forcing the government to borrow to cover the deficit. The Mint, meanwhile, was so overwhelmed by receipts of clipped money that people who brought coins in for exchange had to depart empty-handed with only a promissory document. The resulting shortage of metallic money disrupted retail trade. At the same time, the market price for silver remained above the face value of the silver in the coins, so many of the new coins disappeared from circulation. It was November before the job was complete, by which time the horses that powered the presses of the Mint had been so busy that £700 had to be paid out just to haul away their manure.[34]

There were riots, petitions, and instructions to justices to "administer the poor law, but above all to keep the peace."[35] Edward Bohun wrote from Ipswich on July 31, 1696, that "Our tenants can pay no rent. Our corn factors can pay nothing for what they have had and will trade no more. . . . Many self murders happen in small families for want, and all things look very black, and should the least accident put the mob in motion no man can tell where it would end."[36]

In November, "An Act For *Further* Remedying The Ill State Of The Coin" (my italics) established July 1, 1697, as the *final* cutoff, after which no more old coins could be brought in for exchange. By the time the long process had come to an end, three years after its commencement, £6.8 million pounds of new milled silver coins had been issued, almost all of them in exchange for clipped money and relatively little in exchange for bullion or plate. The experts estimate that another million of clipped coins owned by poor people never came in for exchange.[37]

When it was all over, the Great Recoinage had restored the weight of English money to what it had been before the Great Debasement, some 150 years in the past (Haynes's analysis of the coinage data indicates that the clipped coins amounted to only half of their original weights and face values).[38] The achievement is impressive despite all the blunders and botches, because the English carried it out while the country was involved in a major war against a powerful enemy, the kind of environment in which preserving the sanctity of the currency is usually among the lowest of national priorities. In the more distant past, sound money had been almost a religion with the English: "the ancient right standard of England" had been respected with few alterations from the Conquest to the onset of the Hundred Years' War. From Edward III to Henry VIII, however, most people believed it was the king's currency to do with as he preferred.

Even so, the depreciation in the pound over the centuries was much more limited than in all other countries—indeed, the uninterrupted history of the pound sterling from the end of the eighth century, when 240 of Offa's pennies were called a pound, to modern times is unique among the currencies of the world. The position that Locke took in 1695 was an effort to restore the older tradition of the sanctity of the weight of the currency. He caught the spirit of the occasion when he took issue with Lowndes's proposed method of recoinage, declaring, "It will weaken, if not totally destroy, the public faith when all that have trusted the public and assisted our present necessities upon Acts of Parliament . . . shall be defrauded of 20 per cent of what those Acts of Parliament were security for."[39]

Lowndes was hardly out to defraud the public or use the government to rob their pocketbooks. Rather, he was reluctant to accept the notion that any particular metallic weight was sacred. Greater flexibility in managing the currency, he maintained, might cause less damage in the long run than clinging to some arbitrary number established in the distant past. The Great Recoinage ultimately cost the taxpayers a lot of money, because the new coinage required so much more silver than the silver the Exchequer received from the old coins that were turned in for exchange. Furthermore, the immediate impact of the recoinage on the English economy was deflationary, which may have helped the bankers and the rich who had applauded Locke's position but was painful indeed to anyone who owed money.

Locke's arguments had the great attraction of being cloaked in virtue, prudence, stability, and tradition. Resisting them took more sophistication than his opponents could muster in that day and age. The dispute, however, was a basic one with broad social and political implications beyond the purely economic. It would still be resonating in 1821, when Britain officially established the gold standard; it was at the root of William Jennings Bryan's famous cry of defiance about crucifying labor on a cross of gold; it would come back to haunt Winston Churchill as Chancellor of the Exchequer in the 1920s; and it would continue to stir controversy over expansionary versus contractionary economic policies throughout the rest of the twentieth century. Nor can we expect these kinds of disputes to vanish in the twenty-first century.

At this point, an unexpected character appears on center stage: the most distinguished scientist of his age, and surely among the most influential scientists who ever lived, Sir Isaac Newton. In March 1696, just a few months into the turbulence of the Great Recoinage, Newton took on the post of Warden of the Mint at the invitation of his good friend Charles Montagu, Chancellor of the Exchequer.

What could possibly have been the Chancellor's motivation in choosing Newton for such a task? Newton had spent most of his life as a total nerd, uncommunicative, introverted, unapproachable, and far removed from the chaotic realities of politics and finance. Yet he was also a passionate believer in the pseudo-science of alchemy, to which he ascribed profound religious as well as chemical significance. Consider this description of him by the famous English economist John Maynard Keynes in 1942—exactly three hundred years after Newton's birth:

> In the eighteenth century and since, Newton came to be thought of as the first and greatest of the modern age of scientists . . . one who taught us to think on the lines of cold and untinctured reason. I do not see him in this light. . . . Newton was not the first of the age of reason. He was the last of the magicians, the last of the Babylonians and Sumerians, the last great mind which looked out on the visible and intellectual world with the same eyes as those who began to build our intellectual inheritance rather less than 10,000 years ago. . . . [He was] the last wonder-child to whom the Magi could do sincere and appropriate homage.[40]

Newton's progress from nerd to active politician and prominent civil servant was roundabout, to say the least, but when Newton broke out of his shell and joined the world at the age of 55, the new man was as different from the old as a butterfly is to the caterpillar from which it originates.[41]

An only child, Newton was born on Christmas Day 1642 to the wife of a farmer who had died soon after Mrs. Newton had become pregnant. The baby was so small that neighbors commented he would have fitted into a quart pot. Three years later, Newton's mother remarried and left him in the care of her parents for most of his boyhood—a rift that scarred his personality for life.

His talents, however, were visible early. The headmaster of the local school was convinced that Newton should go to Cambridge immediately after graduating, but his mother kept him working on the family farm for two years before she relented. Consequently, when he entered Cambridge in 1661, he was older than most of his classmates, which only added to his sense of loneliness and isolation. He also entered on the lowest social rung as a *subsizar*, which meant that he paid his way by cleaning the rooms and emptying the bedpans of his wealthier classmates.

Somewhere along the line, Newton had become deeply religious, Puritan in orientation, violently anti-Catholic, obsessed with sin, and meticulous about religious observance. There is little doubt that his beliefs contributed to his egocentric personality, but they also inspired his unflagging dedication to hard work and his passion for discovering nature's truths as a reflection of the greater glory of God. However, his poverty dominated his religious motivations when it came to money. He earned extra cash by becoming a moneylender—scruples kept him from ever lending more than £1 to any individual at a time—which did nothing to overcome his lack of popularity among the other students. One confession in his notebooks echoed Job when he wrote that he had been "Setting my heart on money more than God."[42]

During his second year at Cambridge, Newton encountered a classmate named John Wickens, an equally solitary and high-minded young man. They became roommates and shared quarters for twenty years. Newton had no relationships with women or any intimate friendships with anyone other than Wickens until much later in his life. Wickens did most of Newton's dirty work in all his many experiments but especially in the frenetically conducted, elaborate, and ecologically perilous experiments in alchemy that they carried out for many years in Newton's apartment. Nevertheless, at the end of those twenty years, the two men separated and never had any further contact with each other. The cause of this abrupt and permanent rupture remains a mystery.

When Newton graduated from Cambridge, he had already determined that his life's work would be to unravel the laws that governed God's universe. He saw no conflict between his immediate scientific ambitions and his intense concentration on the arts of alchemy. According to the fascinating intellectual biography of Newton, *The Janus Faces of Genius: The Role of Alchemy in Newton's Thought*, by the late Newtonian scholar Betty Jo Dobbs Teeter, Newton believed that the whole truth is made up of many parts. The parts can be found everywhere, not just in mathematics and physics but in alchemy, light, and even in ancient theology and prophecy. He was an ardent explorer of many such areas, but always with the discipline and rigor of the theoretical scientist. He never did produce gold from his alchemical experiments, but he learned a great deal of value about chemistry in the process.

Newton progressed rapidly up the academic ladder at Cambridge and received a full professorship in 1669 at the young age of 27 in recognition of achievements that had already earned him the reputation as the most advanced mathematician of his age. His first lecture to students, in 1670, was a pathbreaking exploration into optics. It must have been hard going for students, for no one showed up at his second lecture. In fact, no one showed up for just about all of the lectures Newton gave at Cambridge over the next seventeen years. In time, he cut the length of his talks from half an hour to fifteen minutes, but he was punctilious about appearing for each scheduled class.

The circumstances that changed Newton's career were totally unexpected. He had moved out into the real world to some degree by becoming involved with the Royal Society, a group organized for the exchange of scientific ideas and research, but his spiritual residence was in the ivory tower until 1685. In that year, James II, the new king and a Catholic, determined that he would attack the rigidly Protestant Cambridge Establishment by forcing them to admit Father Alban Francis, a Benedictine monk, to Magdelene College "without requiring him to perform the exercises requisite thereunto . . . and without administering unto him any oath or oaths whatsoever."[43] The master of Magdelene, John Peachell, was a weak man, an alcoholic, and ill-equipped to deal with a situation that was distasteful to the entire university, especially when the king warned him, "Disobey at your peril."[44]

This was just the moment when Newton's *Principia* was about to be published and he was approaching the peak of his scientific achievements. But when he heard of the affair of Father Alban, Newton's anti-Catholic sentiments boiled over and he became deeply involved in the struggle. Despite his efforts, he was little help: the king's intimidation of the scholars at Cambridge was merciless, Peachell was dismissed from his post, Newton's own position hung by a thread, and Father Alban took up residence at Cambridge. The victory was short-lived, however. Before the monk had received his degree, James had been overthrown by William and Mary, who were Protestants. The traditional anti-Catholic religious barriers at Cambridge remained unchanged, while Father Alban departed the premises.

Newton was never quite the same again. The episode suddenly whetted his appetite for public life at a time when he was already world-famous for his scientific discoveries. He ran for Parliament and won. He began to function as a man about town, for the first time including a lot of female companionship. He renewed his acquaintance with Montagu, whom he had met when the latter was a Fellow at Trinity College in Cambridge. Then he met John Locke, who refers to Newton as "the incomparable Mr. Newton." Newton instructed Locke in mathematics and physics, while Locke exposed Newton to political theories and practice. Newton was an apt pupil, for Locke even consulted with him prior to presenting his original report on the recoinage to Montagu in 1695.

Although he brushed off the rumors that were beginning to circulate around Cambridge about his imminent departure, by the end of the 1680s Newton was eager to obtain a post in government. The opportunity finally came along in March 1696, when Montagu informed him that the position of Warden of the Mint, at five hundred or six hundred pounds per annum, "has not too much business to require more attendance than you can spare."[45] In addition to the salary, the post received a royalty on every ounce of gold and silver issued by the Mint. Most Wardens of the Mint before Newton looked upon the job much as Montagu described it.

Four days later, Newton broke abruptly with his past studies and experiments, packed up his belongings in Cambridge, and moved to London. On May 2, he started work at the Tower, the home of the Mint since 1300. In a single moment, he ceased his career as an introverted, secretive, mysterious scientist—the last of the magicians—and transformed himself into the first of the policy wonks. The break was astonishing in itself, but the choice of new career appears even stranger: imagine Albert Einstein leaving Princeton to become second-in-command at the Bureau of Printing and Engraving in Washington—or even as an Assistant Secretary in the Treasury Department.

When Newton took up his responsibilities at the Mint, the Master, or chief of the organization, at that time was Thomas Neale, a lazy man with a strong taste for drink. Neale and the Mint staff hardly knew what hit them upon Newton's arrival. Even Montagu himself had no idea that this theoretical academic would turn out to be a motivated, skillful, energetic, and demanding administrator who would devote himself not just full-time, but overtime, to the task at hand.

For the first few weeks on the job, Newton took up residence in a tiny dank room that was right next door to the clanking presses being worked by three hundred men and scores of horses (remember the £700-worth of manure produced there). He was on the scene when work began at 4 AM and when the night shift took over, six days a week. He studied the entire process in great detail and continuously discovered methods to accelerate the output of coins. Later on, he bought himself a nice house in London and began to live like a gentleman, but his fiendish attachment to his work at the Mint persisted.

Despite sixteen-hour days, Newton was also educating himself into an economist. He spent as much time as he could with such people as Locke, Montagu, and Lowndes and read everything he could find on the subject. Then he started writing—voluminously—on the history of economics, commerce, and currency systems. Lacking a photocopying machine, he even employed young men to make duplicate copies of everything he wrote. Through it all, he was maneuvering to displace Neale and become the Master of the Mint. He made himself as visible as possible, clashing with government contractors over the prices they charged the Mint and then lustily entering into conflict with the Governor of the Tower, where the Mint was located. He was tireless in overcoming bureaucratic inertia (a physical principle that was integral to his scientific work) and went so far as to use secret agents around the countryside to root out the villains who continued to clip the coinage. This once puritanical introvert began to frequent the lowest public houses in the city to arrange secret meetings with informants from the brothels and gin houses. He carried out interrogations and attended hangings, always keeping detailed accounts of everything.

In December 1699, Thomas Neale died and Newton at long last achieved the promotion he had desired for so long. He became Master of the Mint.

We must now briefly retrace our steps. During the Great Recoinage of 1695–1696, the government attempted to bring down the bloated price of the guinea by refusing to accept guineas in payment for taxes at a price higher than 22 shillings. Nevertheless, at 22 shillings it was still profitable to import gold to be coined into guineas, exchange them for silver coins, and melt the silver into bullion for export to the East. As the basic day-to-day coinage of England was silver, and as silver was the standard that defined the pound sterling, this process could not be allowed to continue indefinitely. The difference between the two metals as coins and as bullion was unsustainable.

Something had to give. There was no doubt that it was the price of gold that was going to have to back down. As a special Report by the Council of Trade put it on September 22, 1698, "For it be impossible, that more than one Metal should be the true Measure of Commerce; and the world by common Consent and Convenience [has] settled that Measure in Silver; Gold, as well as other Metals, is to be looked upon as a Commodity . . . its value will always be changeable."[46]

In February 1699, the Treasury reduced the acceptable price of guineas to 21*s* 6*d*, hoping thereby to halt the process.* The gold imports fell off slightly, but then a record import of £1.5 million came into England in 1701, and silver continued sailing off toward Asia. Newton in his position of Master of the Mint issued reports on the problem in both 1701 and 1702, pointing out that, at current rates of exchange, a guinea's weight of gold was worth from nine pence to a full shilling (twelve pence) higher than in the other countries of Europe. His strong recommendation was to reduce the guinea further to 21 shillings. Renewed fighting with France cut off the imports of gold for a while and made any further changes in the coinage unnecessary until the Treaty of Utrecht was signed in 1713. At that point, the flood of gold imports gathered renewed strength. Over £4 million came in over the next three years. When the East India Company exported three million ounces of silver in 1717, the authorities once again turned hopefully to the wisdoms of Sir Isaac Newton.

Newton's "Representation to the Right Honourable the *Lords Commissioners* of His Majesty's Revenue" has become a famous document in the history of money. The reading of it is a tedious business, and the essence of the content is no more than simple arithmetic reciting the values of various weights of gold and silver in different countries. A great scientist's mind was hardly necessary for this particular task. Nevertheless, his words have earned their immortality from the timing of their appearance and the recommendations with which Newton finishes his essay.

As an example of the literary tone of the "Representation," here are the opening phrases of the substance of the document:

> *I humbly represent,* That a Pound Weight Troy of Gold, 11 Ounces fine, and 1 Ounce Allay, is cut into 44 Guineas and Half, and a Pound Weight of Silver, 11 Ounces, 2 Penny Weight fine, and 18 Penny Weight Allay, is cut into 62 Shillings; and according to this Rate, a Pound Weight of fine Gold is worth 15 Pounds Weight 6 Ounces, 17 Penny Weight and 5 Grains of fine Silver, reckoning a Guinea at 1*l.* 1*s.* 6*d.* in Silver Money.[47]

Newton then proceeds to carry out similar kinds of calculations for Spanish pistoles, French lewidors (Louis d'Or), and Dutch and

*From this point forward, I use the convention for expressing prices in English style, with *s* for shillings and *d* for pence.

Hungarian ducats, as well as examining the situation in Italy, Germany, Poland, Denmark, Sweden, China, and Japan. He confirms that the demand for silver for export "hath raised the Price of exportable Silver about 2*d.* or 3*d.* above that of Silver in Coin, and hath thereby created a *Temptation to export or Melt down the Silver Coin, rather than give 2d. or 3d. more for foreign silver.*"[48]

Newton's argument ends up with the observation that "There seems nothing more requisite, than to take off about 10*d.* or 12*d.* from the Guinea, so that Gold may bear the same Proportion to the Silver Money in *England* which it ought to do by the *Course of Trade and Exchange in Europe.*"[49] On the basis of Newton's advice, the Treasury issued a proclamation on December 22, 1717, prohibiting anyone to pay or receive the gold guinea coins at a value different from precisely 21 shillings. The outcome was not the expected outcome. Newton had it wrong on two scores.

First, as matters turned out, 21 shillings was still too high a value for the guinea: defying Newton's predictions, the imports of gold and exports of silver continued, even though at a reduced rate. The process persisted, in fact, for about thirty years, beyond 1717, by which time full-weight silver coins had disappeared from circulation.

Second, Newton was confident that the laws of supply and demand would solve the matter so that the problem would simply go away with the passage of time. He was confident that the continued increase in the supply of gold would bring down the price of guineas as denominated by silver shillings. "If things be let alone," he wrote, "till silver money be a little scarcer, the gold will fall of it self. . . . And so the Question is, Whether Gold shall be lowered by the Government, or let alone 'till it falls of it self, by the Want of Silver Money?"[50]

That is not what occurred at all. Newton's forecast turned out to be wrong on a more fundamental level than merely expecting the laws of supply and demand to bring everything to rights. He was correct that in the end gold would have to decline in value relative to silver. But, like many economists since then, he went astray in assuming that the future would look like the past. Economics is evidently a lot more difficult than physics, even for a genius like Newton.

The unexpected happened: the price of gold did not "fall of itself." In fact, it did not fall at all. Instead, the guinea held steady at 21 shillings, while silver coins began to exchange at more than face value. Gold still lost value relative to silver, but the price that moved to accomplish that shift was the price of silver, not the price of gold. Although the ultimate outcome was the same either way, *the markets themselves, without any Acts or Orders-in-Council or Representations, had silently but decisively established gold in place of silver as the standard for the pound.*

As so often happens, the markets were way ahead of the officials. As late as 1730, John Conduitt, Newton's successor at the Mint, was still reciting the old story that "Gold is only looked on as a commodity, and so should rise or fall as occasion requires. An ounce of fine silver is, and always has been, *and ought to be,* the standing and invariable measure between nation and nation"[51] (italics added). Reality, however, had moved strongly and decisively in the opposite direction since 1717. For more than two hundred years, the price of gold in Britain would remain set at £3 17*s* 10½*d* while the price of silver would succumb to violent fluctuations.* Until the official devaluation of the pound in the terrible crisis of 1931, £3 17*s* 10½*d* became a kind of magic and worshipful combination of numbers that governed English monetary policy.

This unanticipated outcome was a direct reflection of the increasing popularity of the guinea. The guinea's consistent weight and fineness made such a vivid contrast with the rotten state of the silver coinage up to the Great Recoinage that people preferred to accept the guinea wherever possible. Bankers held it as reserves, tax collectors welcomed it in order to avoid the arguments about what a worn silver piece might be worth, and economic activity in England at that time had developed to a point where a large-denomination coin such as the guinea was no longer just an inconvenient curiosity.

From the moment when Elizabeth I ascended to the throne in 1558 to the foundation of the Bank of England in 1694, a period of 136 years, the Mint had issued no more than £15 million in gold coinage, of which half was in guineas that appeared after 1663. During the 45 years from 1695 to 1740, the Mint produced £17 million gold coins. The story on

*The figure £3 17*s* 10½*d* was derived by translating the 129.4 grains of gold in the guinea into its money price of 21 shillings.

silver is precisely the opposite: £20 million in the earlier period versus £1 million in the latter.[52]

Isaac Newton is the anti-hero of this chapter of our story. Quite aside from his scientific achievements, he deserves heroic status as the first civil servant in history bold enough to employ the laws of supply and demand to make an economic forecast that would determine public policy. He is the anti-hero, nevertheless, because he inaugurated a tradition that will haunt future chapters of this history: economic forecasts by policymakers that turn out to be wrong! Newton did a lot better predicting the future movement of an apple than of the price of gold.

The real hero of this chapter, the guinea, came to a strange end. A direct descendant of Croesus's stater, Constantine's bezant, the ducat, the genoin, and the florin, the guinea remained the basic gold coin of England for another one hundred years after the events just described. In 1821, under George IV, the guinea came to an official demise when it was replaced by the sovereign, which was set equal to precisely £1 instead of the awkward 21 shillings of the guinea.

The guinea lingered on not as a coin but as a denomination or offbeat unit of account. Prices quoted in guineas had snob appeal and served as reminders of a great past. Doctors on Harley Street quoted their fees in guineas, and fine jewelry and clothing were priced in the same fashion. But 21 shillings no longer made sense as a denomination when Britain joined the rest of the world and abandoned their historic shillings and pence for the metric system in 1969. The guinea finally vanished, remaining as a romantic memory or, on occasion, as a precious Christmas gift to children from doting grandparents who still owned a few of the beautiful coins stamped with the little elephant.

Nevertheless, the process that the guinea began would stretch far into the future. From the moment that the markets established the supremacy of gold as the standard in 1717, the English never looked back. Over the next two hundred years, most of the rest of the world followed in their footsteps, though not always willingly. Silver never quite lost its charm and gold never quite performed its task without difficulty. The next chapter tells about one of the biggest bumps that the English encountered in trying to manage their currency with gold as the standard.

13

The True Doctrine and the Great Evil

On February 22, 1797, three frigates from the French navy sailed into the harbor of the tiny fishing village of Fishguard on the southwest coast of Wales and proceeded to land about twelve hundred armed soldiers. This little foray was confronted almost immediately by the local militia under the command of Lord Cawdor.* The French also caught sight of an approaching troop whose red cloaks and tall black hats convinced them that they were facing a contingent of the crack British unit, the Grenadier Guards—an even more serious danger.

This fearsome band was nothing of the sort. The French soon discovered that it was nothing more than a gathering of Welsh women in traditional festival costumes.† The costumes did not inhibit the women from beating up the bewildered French soldiers. One of these women, Jemima Nicholas, was so adept at wielding her pitchfork that she was

*Thane of Cawdor was the title to which King Duncan raised Macbeth—as the three witches had predicted—on the very evening that Macbeth and his wife were to murder the king. There is still a Lord Cawdor at the present time.

†My source for the details of this adventure, Yahoo.com, "Wales on Britannia: History Timeline 1793–," adds that the French troops were drunk, which made overcoming them all the easier. There is also evidence that the French troops were merely convicts put into uniform. The Welsh name for Fishguard is *Abergwaun*, and the local Royal Oak Inn has a copy of the treaty that ended the French invasion.

credited with the capture of fourteen French soldiers.[1] The French commander, an Irish-American general, was compelled to submit to an ignominious surrender.

Rumors of an impending French invasion had been circulating for several months, with a series of reports from Paris referring to that danger. French warships had gathered at Brest at the end of 1796 and had headed off toward northern Ireland around Christmas, evidently hoping that the Irish would join in their invasion. On February 21, there was a false rumor of French ships off Beachy Head on the southeast coast, which provoked English warships to head out to sea from Portsmouth. The next day, the battle of Fishguard took place.

Just what the French had in mind with this expedition remains obscure. Napoleon was off invading Italy, and Fishguard was about as far away from British power centers as anyone could get. The most reasonable explanation is that the French were making a low-cost but deliberate effort to create a panic in England. Seen from this viewpoint, their project was a smashing success.

Like so many other events in this history, the foolish French effort had profound unintended consequences. Its ultimate impact reached far beyond the village of Fishguard or the nationwide panic that this comic opera episode ignited. The sequence of events that got under way as a result of Fishguard would lead in time to a great debate about gold, the causes of inflation, the international position of the pound sterling, and the proper function in all this of the Bank of England. The views of the highest political leaders and the most respected economists and bankers on these matters would command front-page attention. The debate would reach all the way back to the controversies between Locke and Lowndes at the time of the Great Recoinage about one hundred years earlier, and it would reverberate once again 125 years later in the wake of the terrible war of 1914–1918. It would guide British policy all the way up to the outbreak of World War II, when the farce of Fishguard had long since been forgotten.

The excitement provoked by the French invasion launched a rush to withdraw gold from the banking system as frightened citizens stormed

banking offices to cash in their paper money, almost all of which consisted of banknotes issued by the Bank of England as well as notes issued by smaller banks. While the Bank of England notes were the most widely accepted form of paper money in circulation—and traditionally referred to as Bank notes—the greatest fear was over what would happen to those small banks and the acceptability of their banknotes as means of payment in the event of an invasion.

In contrast to the paper currency, gold was perceived as the ultimate money, indestructible in value and forever acceptable no matter who would be running the government, even if it were the French. The very idea that the Bank's gold reserve was rapidly diminishing therefore served as a self-fulfilling prophecy as people dashed to the banks to convert the paper notes into gold while there was still some gold left to withdraw.

On Saturday, the 18th of February, even before the incident at Fishguard, fears of a French invasion had provoked a run on the banks in Newcastle (some 350 miles from Fishguard), forcing the local banks to shut their windows on the 20th. The panic soon spread to London and other major centers. The withdrawals were draining the Bank of England's gold stock at the rate of £100,000 a day, out of a gold reserve that had already shrunk under wartime conditions from £7 million at the end of 1794 to £5 million at the end of 1795 and then to only about £2 million at the end of 1796.[2]

Word of the "invasion" at Fishguard reached London on the morning of Saturday the 25th, three days after the fact, forcing the management of the Bank to face the unprecedented and unpleasant prospect of refusing to redeem Bank notes in gold. The Directors informed Prime Minister Pitt, who sent an urgent message to King George III at Windsor on Saturday evening to join a council to be held at the Bank on Sunday. In addition to the King, the Sunday meeting included Pitt, the Lord Chancellor, the Governor and Deputy Governor of the Bank, and two of the Directors. At the conclusion of the meeting, the government issued an Order-in-Council whose most important passage read as follows:

> It is indispensably necessary for the public service that the Directors of the Bank of England should forbear issuing any cash [i.e., gold] in payment until the sense of the Parliament can be taken on that subject and the proper measures adopted thereupon for maintaining the means of circulation.[3]

On March 9, the House of Commons transformed the Order-in-Council into a full-fledged act, the so-called Restriction Bill, which indemnified the Bank against the legal consequences of refusing to pay out gold in exchange for the Bank notes. The bill also made it official that all payments in Bank notes were to be "deemed payments in cash."

A public relations campaign swung into action at once to reassure the public and to prevent the gold crisis from turning into an even more intense panic. On Monday, February 27, in words that sounded like the exhortations of the darkest days of the Battle of Britain in 1940, the *Times* of London published a lead editorial invoking the spirit of the embattled English at the time of the Spanish Armada, when the danger to life and property was much greater. At noon that day, the leading bankers and merchants of London met at the Mansion House, home of the Lord Mayor, where they passed a unanimous resolution declaring that it was their intention to receive without hesitation notes of the Bank up to any sum of money that would be owed to them and that they would make their own payments in Bank notes as well. This resolution, which received four thousand additional signatures, was published in newspapers throughout the country. The Directors of the Bank then issued a notice declaring that the Bank was in a "most affluent and prosperous situation, and such as to preclude every doubt as to the security of its notes," with assets (primarily claims on borrowers) some £4 million in excess of liabilities, not even counting the debt owed by the government of close to £12 million.[4] This reassurance about the financial condition of the Bank was critically important, as many smaller banks had either failed or suffered a dangerous deterioration in their condition during the excitement provoked by the original declaration of war against the French Revolution in 1793.[5]

Despite the soothing words about the Bank, the Order-in-Council of February 26 and the Restriction Bill that followed were shockers. The crisis was unique up to that point in history. Governments had often devalued and debased their coinages in other wars, but then only coins were involved. The Chinese had made a mess with their paper currency, but then no coins were involved. This was the first time that the markets had attacked a paper currency freely convertible into gold coins or bullion, a right that had existed for over a century. The Bank of England itself had been established as the paradigm of financial soundness and responsibility. The Bank's notes had been "as good as gold." Indeed,

Bank of England currency, decorated with the corporation's seal and engraved with Britannia seated on a bank of money, was deemed more acceptable than obligations of the government itself.

Suddenly, all that changed. With the vaults almost bare of gold, the Bank notes were now no more than pieces of paper. The claims on borrowers may have exceeded the Bank's liabilities, but those claims were far from the same thing as gold; even if the borrowers repaid all their loans, the Bank would still have only Bank notes on hand to pay out.

The impact of this unexpected rupture can be gathered from the memoirs of a Scotch banker, Sir William Forbes, who recalled the experience in his *Memoirs of a Banking House*, published in 1803. Forbes describes how he felt on the morning of March 1 when the first word of "this interesting event" reached Edinburgh:

> Now it was that I certainly did think the nation was ruined beyond redemption, when so novel and alarming a circumstance had taken place at the Bank of England, which had ever been considered the bulwark of public and private credit. . . . All ceremony or etiquette. . . was now out of the question when we had to think of what was to be done for our joint preservation on such an emergency. . . . The instant this resolution of paying no more specie was known in the street, a scene of confusion and uproar took place of which it is utterly impossible for those who did not witness it to form an idea. Our counting house . . . was instantly crowded to the door with people clamorously demanding payment in gold of their interest-receipts . . . they were mostly of the most ignorant classes . . . all bawling out at once for change. . . . Both gold and silver specie was hoarded up and instantly disappeared.[6]

Nevertheless, the way the English dealt with these matters, once the crisis had passed, was as extraordinary as the decisiveness of the authorities at the moment of a crisis that none of them had ever faced before. As Forbes continued his account, "It was a matter of agreeable surprise to see in how short a time after the suspension of paying in specie, the run on us ceased [and] how quietly the country submitted . . . to transact all business by bank notes for which issuers give no specie as formerly."

There was no argument against the principle that gold must continue to be the central foundation of the monetary system, and that some day redemption in specie would be restored. The language of the long sequence of government orders that was to follow gives every indication that most people believed that the arrangements were temporary, with normal conditions soon to be restored. The entire objective was to reach a point where notes could once again be converted into gold on demand. The embargo would endure for 24 years, until 1821, a length of time that even the most pessimistic observers never anticipated. But widespread confidence in an ultimately happy ending to the tragedy meant that acceptability of the Bank notes was at no point brought into question anywhere. The notes continued to function as though nothing had happened to the gold reserves. When Winston Churchill observed during World War II that "England loses every battle but the last one," he was reflecting a spirit that had long been typical of English perceptions of themselves and their state.

Let us step back for a moment, in order to gain better perspective on these dramatic events. Some brief history and overview of the mechanics of the English monetary system might be helpful.

It is important to recognize that the English monetary system—like the English political system—had evolved by trial and error, without the rigidities of legal stipulations and regulations that characterized the French system of government and that Napoleon and his successors did nothing to diminish. Public and private money circulated together and reinforced each other. The government's money was the coinage, most of which consisted of the golden guinea, although silver coins and token coins of smaller denominations also circulated.* More than one hundred years before the crisis of 1797, however, private paper money had begun to substitute for coins in large transactions. Bills of exchange, as we have already seen, were often endorsed over from one holder to another and thereby became a kind of paper money. In addition, many people who owned gold coins would deposit them with a goldsmith for safekeeping, accepting in exchange a receipt for the gold that could then be used as a means of payment because it was redeemable in gold

*In 1816, Parliament ruled that silver coins henceforth were tokens that would be acceptable based only on their face value, not their metallic content.

on demand. Indeed, the total output of gold during the century as a whole averaged only twenty tons a year.[7]

More important, banking grew at a rapid rate throughout the eighteenth century, and it was customary for banks to pay out the proceeds of their loans in the form of promissory notes to customers; these notes, in a variety of denominations and engraved and watermarked to defy forgers, would then circulate from hand to hand as money. When the Bank of England was established in 1694 and made the original loan of £1.2 million to the government, part of the proceeds paid out to the government was in the form of Bank notes, which the government used to purchase supplies for its campaign against Louis XIV. Those notes circulated among businesses and the public as money but were also held by other banks as a reserve to cover withdrawals of deposits.

The consequences of this unplanned structure were profound. As the volume of banknotes replaced the coinage of government in daily circulation, the supply of money in daily use was now joined directly to the volume of credit provided by the privately owned banking system. In essence, the private sector overtook the public sector as the primary engine of money creation. Although most money in use today is in the form of checking accounts rather than paper currency, the basic eighteenth-century relationship between bank credit and money supply remains intact. By the end of the eighteenth century, in fact, a rising share of money was already being held in the form of checks and deposits much as we know them today.

These developments do not mean that gold coins or bullion ceased to be important because their hand-to-hand circulation declined. English money was clearly defined by its weight in gold—the 129.4 grains of gold in the guinea that worked out to an ounce of gold being equal to £3 17*s* 10½*d*. Even though guineas resided for the most part in the safes of goldsmiths or the faithfully guarded vaults of the Bank, the assurance that they were there was what appeared to make the system work. The various forms of private paper—bills of exchange, goldsmiths' receipts, and banknotes issued by commercial banks throughout the country—could always be exchanged for the notes of the Bank of England, and Bank notes could always be exchanged for gold, or specie as it was often called in those days. For example, before February 26, 1797, anyone with £210 in notes could go to the Bank at any time and receive two hundred golden guineas in exchange.

Most of the time, nobody bothered. Yet when business was booming and the price of gold in the marketplace was rising, or when sterling was losing value in the foreign exchange markets, two hundred golden guineas could command more than £210 in the City markets or the equivalent of more than £210 in foreign financial markets. At that point, it would be profitable to convert £210 in notes into two hundred guineas and then exchange the guineas for some larger amount in the financial markets.

In 1783, after the end of the American Revolution, the Bank had made an energetic effort to halt such a process before it had much opportunity to begin. Private business activity was expanding rapidly, with prices about 10 percent higher than they had been four years earlier, and the Bank's stock of gold coins began to shrink.[8] In response, the Directors of the Bank of England refused additional credits to merchants and other borrowers, who had to turn elsewhere for credit. The result was a sharp rise in interest rates, a cooling of speculative fevers, an immediate improvement in the exchange rate between sterling and continental currencies, and a return flow of guineas to the vaults of the Bank.[9] Thus, the staunch faith in gold had transformed the shiny metal that most people viewed as the ultimate form of wealth into a powerful vehicle of checks and balances (a role that gold would continue to play, in one form or another, and not just in Britain, for the next 174 years). What everyone considered to be the riskless asset seemed to subdue the risks in the entire economy.

The crisis of 1797 and the Restriction Bill that sundered the linkage between Bank notes and gold tore apart this unofficial but powerful system of controls. With the golden counterweight no longer operative, the economy was now operating completely on paper currency.* Hien Tsung's inadvertent innovation, which, with "continentals" and *assignats*, had caused disasters in financing the American and the French revolutions just a short time back, was now about to make its debut on the more conservative shores of Great Britain. In the words of Lord Lansdown, contemplating the consequences of the Restriction Bill, "A fever is as

*Shifts in the relative price of gold and silver might have led to the establishment of a silver standard in Britain, but the attachment to gold was so strong that coinage of silver was suspended in 1798, and silver never again became legal tender except for payments not exceeding £25 (see Jevons, 1875, p. 69).

much a fever in London as in Paris or Amsterdam; the fall will be slow perhaps, and gradual for a time; but it will be certain."[10]

The original issue of the *assignats* in December 1790 had amounted to eight hundred million *livres;* on October 23, 1795, over twenty billion were outstanding. The Paris riots that ensued paved the way for Napoleon's rise to power and forced the government to abandon the worthless *assignats* for a metallic-based system based on gold and silver.

Where did the French gold come from? Much of it was a return of capital that had fled the country during the *assignat* regime. In fact, the events in France were the main reason that the Bank of England's gold reserves were so low when the Fishguard adventure occurred: gold that had earlier been transferred to England by frightened Frenchmen now began to return to France, driving the Bank of England's gold reserve from £6 million in early 1795 to only £2 million in early 1797. Napoleon had inadvertently laid the groundwork for the panic that ensued from the Battle of Fishguard.[11]

In addition, however, acting in the tradition of the great conquerors of the past, Napoleon lost no time in launching his career as a ruthless accumulator of monetary treasure (among other things) from vanquished nations. In a note to the *Directoire Executif* on June 1, 1796, he informed his colleagues that "Two millions of gold are en route [from Italy]. They leave tomorrow with a hundred carriage horses, the most beautiful one can find in Lombardy. They will replace the mediocre horses that pull our carriages."[12]

Napoleon remained steadfast as a "hard-money" man throughout his reign. He had no choice. If he had even whispered the possibility of issuing an inconvertible paper currency, the nightmare of the *assignat* experience would have provoked an immediate flight of all the gold in France to safer havens abroad. Thus, Napoleon's keen monetary management skills enabled him to succeed where every other leader had failed. This was probably the only major war in history to be conducted without currency depreciation in one form or another.[13]

Lord Lansdown was right: the fall was slow and gradual, but inflation ultimately took hold in Britain. Prices in 1802 were lower than they had been in 1800, but they climbed 30 percent between 1802 and 1807 and by another 15 percent over the next three years. Prices had doubled from their 1797 level when Napoleon succumbed at Waterloo in 1815.[14]

The inflation was associated with a substantial increase in money and credit. No longer constrained by the gold supply, the Bank's loans to business—so-called commercial bills under discount—more than quadrupled between 1797 and 1810. The Bank has never supplied the financial markets with such an explosion of credit except during the extraordinary conditions of the two World Wars of the twentieth century. By no coincidence, the Bank's note issue expanded from approximately £10 million to £25 million over the same period of time, with half the increase having occurred just since 1807, while deposits at the Bank were increasing at about the same pace. The Bank's holdings of coin and bullion fluctuated with the fortunes of war but were at no point equal to as much as 50 percent of the Bank notes outstanding; in 1794, before all these troubles began, the gold reserve had been equal to 70 percent of the outstanding notes.[15]

Beginning in 1808, the price of gold began a rapid ascent. By 1809, the gold in a guinea was fetching £4 10*s* an ounce in the marketplace, well above the price of £3 17*s* 10½*d* that had defined the value of gold when Isaac Newton was pondering the matter back in 1717. Sterling was also losing value relative to the currencies of other nations—toward the end of 1809, the pound was exchanging in Hamburg, Amsterdam, and Paris from 16 percent to more than 20 percent below its official par values.[16] The result was a 50 percent decline in the Bank's holdings of gold coins and bullion between February 1808 and August 1809, even though these holdings had been replenished since the low point at the enactment of the Bank Restriction Act in 1797. The restoration of convertibility appeared further off than ever.

The financial community was outraged.[17] On August 29, a 38-year-old stockbroker as spokesman for this community submitted the first of three letters on this matter to the *Morning Chronicle*, complaining that the public "do not seem to be sufficiently impressed with the importance of the subject, nor of the disastrous consequences which may attend the further depreciation of the paper."[18] His name was David Ricardo, and this was the first time his name had appeared in print. The letters and additional commentary subsequently appeared as a tract titled "The High Price of Bullion."

Ricardo was born in 1772, when Adam Smith was fifty years old and Thomas Malthus, Ricardo's beloved friend and unremitting intellectual opponent, was six years old; Ricardo first met Malthus in 1809 at the very moment he was sending in his letters to the *Morning Chronicle*.[19] Ricardo's father was a Jewish merchant banker and stockbroker—jobber, as the English call it—who took his son in as an employee when the boy was only fourteen. The firm prospered, even though it had to limit its trading activity to a section of the Royal Exchange known as Jews Walk. Ricardo remained in business with his father for seven years, until he fell in love with a Quaker girl. At the age of 21, he broke with his family, married Miss Wilkinson, adopted the Quaker religion, went into business at the Exchange on his own, and, more than most people, lived happily until he died suddenly at the age of 51.

Ricardo scored an enormous success as a stock jobber, years before he had any idea that he would become one of the most famous theoretical economists of all time with the publication of *The Principles of Political Economy and Taxation* in 1817. His brother once observed that "Perhaps in nothing did Mr. R. more evince his extraordinary powers than he did in business. His complete knowledge of all its intricacies . . . his capability of getting through, without any apparent exertion, the immense transactions in which he was concerned—his coolness and judgment—enabled him to leave all his contemporaries at the Stock Exchange far behind."[20]

As the English government debt climbed ever higher during the course of the Napoleonic conflict, Ricardo became one of the major underwriters of those government securities each time they were issued to the public. Like investment bankers today who like to take care of their friends, Ricardo would occasionally allot a small cut of these deals to his chum Malthus, a parson and academic of modest means whose fame as an economist would in time rival Ricardo's. In 1815—at the moment when the battle of Waterloo was approaching—Malthus could not stand the strain of being exposed to what might happen to his little nest egg if Wellington were to lose. He pleaded with Ricardo "to take an early opportunity of realizing a small profit on the share you have been good enough to promise me."[21] Ricardo obliged but held on to his own much more substantial position. For Malthus, Napoleon's defeat at Waterloo was good news and bad news: good news as it was for all Englishmen but bad news for the enormous opportunity missed. For Ricardo, it was 100 percent stupendous news. Just two years later, he published his magisterial work, *The Principles of Political Economy and Taxation.* The remarkable friendship with Malthus survived these events unscathed. After Ricardo's death, Malthus declared that "I never loved anybody out of my own family so much."[22]

Ricardo's letters to the *Morning Chronicle* about Britain's shrinking gold reserve and the depreciation of the pound in the foreign exchange markets attracted much attention. About six months after the publication of Ricardo's letters, and after extended debate in Parliament and the press, a little-known member of Parliament named Francis Horner moved for the establishment of a parliamentary committee to look into the whole matter in detail, to examine expert witnesses, and to prepare a report and recommendations for the House of Commons upon the completion of their task. Eighteen days later, the House announced the appointment of "The SELECT COMMITTEE to enquire into the Cause of the High Price of GOLD BULLION, and to take into consideration the State of the CIRCULATING MEDIUM, and of the EXCHANGES between Great Britain and Foreign Parts."[23]

What came to be known as the Bullion Committee numbered 22 members, most of whom were experts from the world of finance; some, such as the Joint Paymaster of the Forces, were civil servants. The hearings ran for a total of 31 days between February 22 and May 25, 1810, during which the Committee took testimony from 29 witnesses from business, finance, academia, and government. The Committee's report provides the full identity of all the witnesses, except on page 19, where it refers to a "very eminent Continental Merchant," who, according to further commentary on page 25, was "intimately acquainted with the trade between this Country and the Continent"; Ricardo's testimony refers to this gentleman simply as "Mr. —." Edward Cannan, who wrote an authoritative commentary on the whole matter in 1919, concludes that "An obvious conjecture is that this modest Mr. Blank was the great N. M. Rothschild."[24]

The report never indicates which members asked the questions of the witnesses, on the theory that the questions were being raised by the committee "as a body."[25] The most active members, and the primary authors of the Committee's final report, were Francis Horner, Henry Thornton, and William Huskisson. A barrister, Horner was one of the founders of the *Edinburgh Review*, to which he had contributed several articles on banking. Like Adam Smith before him, he had been born and educated in Edinburgh but had spent two years in England "to rid himself of the disadvantages of a provincial dialect."[26] Thornton, a banker; had written an early textbook on banking theory that had issued dire warnings about the abuses of paper credit. Huskisson had earlier been associated with some of the leaders of revolutionary France and had publicly expressed his disapproval of their plan to issue the *assignats*. He subsequently became President of the Board of Trade (equivalent to Secretary of Commerce in the United States) and, as the economist Glyn Davies phrased it, "suffered the final dubious distinction of being killed by a train at the ceremonial opening of the Liverpool to Manchester Railway in 1830."[27]

In June, while the report was still in the hands of the printer, Horner wrote the following to a friend:

> The Report is in truth very clumsily and prolixly drawn; stating nothing but very old doctrines on the subject it treats of, and stating them in a more imperfect form than they have frequently appeared before. . . . One great merit the Report, however, possesses; that it declares in very plain and pointed terms, both the true doctrine and the existence of a great evil growing out of the neglect of that doctrine. . . . We shall in time (I trust) effect the restoration of the old and only safe system.[28]

Despite Horner's demurrer about its literary quality, the report was a best-seller for its time; it was out of print three months after its appearance in August. For someone who encounters it nearly two hundred years after its publication, the report is an extraordinary document. Horner's letter indicates that there was nothing wishy-washy about the effort: the conclusions and recommendations are indeed plain and pointed. A reader could disagree with the hard line taken by the authors and still be startled by the sophistication of the economic analysis. At its best, the report accurately reflects the most important economic ideas developed by David Hume and Adam Smith even while anticipating concepts that would appear in theory books only years in the future, especially in relation to the theory and practice of the gold standard system that would develop over the course of the nineteenth century. Indeed, the clarity and thoroughness of the presentation of monetary theory matches Milton Friedman at his best. A document of equivalent quality written by today's members of Parliament or the U.S. Congress would be inconceivable.

The issues confronted by the Bullion Committee were essentially the same as the arguments between Lowndes and Locke in the period before the Great Recoinage of 1695. The Committee's report builds on the basis of an overarching assumption that was never open to question at any point—that gold is the paramount asset. The authors refer at the outset to "the sound and natural state of the British currency, the foundation of which is gold."[29] A few pages later, echoing Ricardo's affirmation in his third letter to the *Morning Chronicle* that "Gold Coins are now become, in the practice and opinion of the people, the principal measure of property,"[30] the report asserts, "In this Country, Gold is itself the measure of all exchangeable value, the scale to which all money prices are referred."[31] And, finally, "Gold in Bullion is the standard to which the Legislature has intended that the coin should be conformed and with which it should be identified as much as possible. . . . It is most desirable for the public that our circulating medium should again be conformed, as speedily as circumstances will permit, to its real and legal standard, Gold Bullion."[32]

Gold is not only the standard for the domestic currency: "Bullion is the true regulator both of the value of a local currency and of the rate of Foreign Exchange."[33] This statement is the core of the "true doctrine" to which Horner's letter refers. The "great evil growing out of the neglect of that doctrine" was the price inflation that was cutting so deeply into the purchasing power of money.

To the Committee, following upon the analysis in Ricardo's letters to the *Morning Chronicle*, the whole problem was obvious and its solution was simple. The problem arose because "A general rise of all prices, a rise in the market price of Gold, and a fall of the Foreign Exchanges, will be the effect of an excessive quantity of circulating medium in a country which has adopted a currency not exportable to other countries, or not convertible at will into a Coin which is exportable."[34] The "great evil" had developed from what Horner had characterized as "the neglect of that doctrine." The solution, therefore, was to restore convertibility of the currency into gold at the earliest possible moment.

Meanwhile, the Committee took the position that the Directors of the Bank of England should act *as though* gold were still functioning as the true regulator despite the embargo on the free convertibility of paper currency into gold. That is, the Bank should ignore the reality of the pure paper currency system that had been forced upon the nation and respond instead to the unambiguous signals provided by increases in the price of gold and the weakness of the pound in the foreign exchanges. Upon the appearance of those signals, the Bank should curtail its credit activities, thereby restraining the growth in the money supply, just as it had done under identical conditions in 1783, 1793, and 1797. The Bank should manage its affairs under the restraints of a *virtual* gold standard, to put it in today's lingo. Ricardo would emphatically endorse this view in his 1816 tract on the high price of bullion. He asserted that *"[If the Directors] had acted up to the principle which they have avowed to have been that which regulated their issues when they were obliged to pay in specie . . . we should not have been exposed to all the evils of a depreciated, and perpetually varying currency"*[35] (italics in original).

The report angrily contradicts the evidence of several witnesses that the increase in the price of gold was merely the result of a scarcity, or excess demand, for gold. If that were the case, the report asks, why was the price of gold stable in France and the other continental countries? There was no scarcity of gold: "That guineas have disappeared from the circulation, there can be no question; but that does not prove a scarcity of Bullion, any more than the high price proves that scarcity." No, no, no! The authors cite the testimony of a dealer who acknowledged that "he found no difficulty in getting any quantity [of gold] he wanted, if he was willing to pay the price for it."[36] The price of gold rose because of the "excessive quantity of circulating medium." The high price of gold was in fact proof that the supply of money was "excessive." No greater authority than that "very eminent Continental Merchant" agreed that the fall in the foreign exchange value of the pound would never have happened if paper money had been convertible into guineas: "I value everything by Bullion," he declared. He went on to inform the Committee that the whole problem had arisen simply because the Bank was "not allowing Bullion to perform those functions for which it seems to have been intended by nature."[37]

The Committee then proceeded to interview the Directors of the Bank to determine whether they "held the same opinion and derived from it a practical rule for the control of their circulation."[38] The flat-out response from the Directors was that they held no such opinion. The controversy rages back and forth, but the Bank's position was succinctly set forth in the statement of Mr. Whitmore, the former Governor, who informed the Committee that "The present unfavorable state of the [foreign] Exchange has no influence upon the amount of [the Bank's] issues, the Bank having acted precisely as they did before. . . . The amount of our paper circulation has no reference at all to the state of the Exchange."[39] The current Governor, Mr. Pease, agreed: "I cannot see how the amount of Bank notes issued can operate upon the price of Bullion, or the state of the Exchanges. . . . I never think it necessary to advert to the price of Gold, or the state of the Exchange, on the days on which we make our advances."[40]

The Directors stubbornly refused to yield, to a point where their testimony sounds almost as though they could not even comprehend what the Committee members were driving at. Ricardo, in a letter to Malthus some years later, characterized them as "indeed a very ignorant set."[41] Sixty-five years later, in reviewing these events, the great Victorian economist Stanley Jevons was just as impatient as Ricardo had been with the opponents to the Committee's arguments. Their refusal to get the point provoked him to write, "So unaccountable are the prejudices of men on the subject of currency that it is not well to leave anything to discretionary management."[42]

Nevertheless, the Directors perceived themselves as merely doing what they were retained to do—meeting the demands of creditworthy borrowers. One could hardly accuse them of forcing Bank notes into circulation. As Mr. Whitmore explained to the Committee, "There will not remain a Note in circulation more than the immediate wants of the public require. . . . The Bank Notes would revert to us if there was a redundancy in circulation, as no one would pay interest for a Bank Note he did not want to make use of."[43] Another director, Mr. Harman, declared that by acting in that manner the Bank "cannot materially err."[44]

After the Committee's report refuses to accept any of these arguments, it expresses some second thoughts about the Bank. Despite "great practical errors," the report goes on to admit that the Directors had in fact shown "a degree of forbearance" and that the Bank should continue to merit the public's confidence in "the integrity with which its affairs are directed, as well as in the unshaken stability and ample funds of that great establishment."[45] The root of the problem lay in the failure of the Bank Directors to distinguish between what appears to be a legitimate loan to a deserving merchant and the impact of the resulting increase in money supply on the economy as a whole. But one can hardly blame the Directors, for the Restriction Bill itself imposed upon them an excessive amount of responsibility that had become tangled in massive conflicts of interest between private objectives and public needs.

This line of reasoning leads to the Committee's most important conclusion. Their words here are worth quoting at some length. Echoing the principles about the role of gold originally set forth by David Hume and Adam Smith, the report provides the first and perhaps the most authoritative justification for the establishment of the gold standard as the superior system for managing an economy's money supply. The entire thrust of the statement is to throw up a sharp contrast to what can happen when money is not convertible into metal and such decisions are left to just plain human judgments.

After pointing out the power over the economy that the suspension of cash payments transferred to the Directors of the Bank, the Committee goes on to contend:

> In the judgment of the Committee, that is a trust, which it is unreasonable to expect that the Directors of the Bank of England should ever be able to discharge. The most detailed knowledge of the actual trade of the Country, combined with the profound science of all the principles of Money and Circulation, would not enable any man or set of men to adjust, and keep always adjusted, the right proportion of circulating medium in a country to the wants of trade.
>
> When the currency consists entirely of the precious metals, or of paper convertible at will into the precious metals, the natural process of commerce, by establishing Exchanges among all the different countries of the world, adjusts, in every particular country, the proportion of circulating medium to its actual occasions. . . . If the natural system of currency and circulation be abandoned, and a discretionary issue of paper money substituted in its stead, it is vain to think that any rules can be advised for the exact exercise of such a discretion.[46]

Ricardo, writing on the subject a year later, affirmed the superiority of the decisions of the markets over those of bankers with responsibility to regulate the currency: "The exportation of the specie," he wrote, "may at all times be safely left to the discretion of individuals."[47]

In short, the markets know best; their signals must determine policy. The Committee's logic leads them to a clear and unqualified recommendation: "That the system of the circulating medium of the Country ought to be brought back, with as much speed as is compatible with a wise and necessary caution, to the original principle of Cash payments at the option of the holder of Bank paper." Nothing else would provide "sufficient remedy for the present, or security for the future."[48] These words would continue to echo through the endless debates over money that lay ahead.

The House of Commons did not provide an opportunity to debate the findings of the Bullion Committee until the spring of 1811. In the meantime, pamphlets on the subject appeared in great quantity, instructing the public on the fine points of the issues involved. This was also the moment for the appearance of Ricardo's *The High Price of Bullion and the Depreciation of Bank Notes*. The topic became so hot that one newspaper bribed a clerk at the Bank to steal a confidential copy of the names of the Bank's borrowers, which appeared the next day on the paper's pages.

On May 6, 1811, by which time the note issue had risen by another £2 million and the price of gold had extended its climb, Francis Horner finally transformed words into action by submitting to the House sixteen resolutions designed to implement the proposals contained in the Bullion Committee's report. Horner begins by tracing the sequence of events in the crisis that led to the formation of the Committee, after which he carefully defines the legal definition of a pound sterling in terms of its weight in gold and declares that Bank notes are promises to pay in such money.

His resolutions end with two specific recommendations. First, that for as long as the suspension of convertibility continues, "it is the duty of the Directors of the Bank of England to advert to the state of the Foreign Exchanges, as well as to the price of Bullion, with a view to regulate the amount of their Issues."[49] The second proposal urges all possible haste in returning to convertibility by moving the end of the suspension of cash payments from "Six Months after the Ratification of a Definite Treaty of Peace," as originally stipulated in the Restriction Bill, to "Two Years from the present Time."[50]

Henry Thornton then added an extended analysis of runaway inflations in Sweden, France, Russia, and America. He went on to explain that the longer the depreciation in the value of the paper pound persisted, the more difficult it would be to reestablish the old standard. This was a point of primary importance, similar in its substance to the dispute in

1717 between Locke and Lowndes. "If the inflation provoked by the paper pound were to continue for eight, ten, or even fifteen or twenty years," Thornton declared, "then it may be deemed unfair to restore the ancient value of the circulating medium, for bargains will have been made and loans supplied under an expectation of the continuance of the existing depreciation."[51]

That is, when a rising price of gold significantly reduces the amount of gold that a pound can buy, all who owe money would be badly hurt if they were forced to pay the equivalent of the amount of gold that a pound would have bought when they had originally signed their contracts. Such misgivings reappear on every occasion when the authorities have been faced with the painful choice of snuffing out depreciation of their money or allowing it to continue.

Horner's resolutions were debated in the House for four days. The first fifteen resolutions were defeated by a vote of 150 to 75; the final resolution to change the cutoff date went down by 181 to 47.

What happened? Despite all its eloquent arguments, the Bullion Committee had simply ignored the brutal reality that Britain was engaged in the greatest war in history up to that time—a true precursor to the total wars of the first half of the twentieth century. The most important financial objective for the government was to encourage the highest possible level of production of food, coal, ships, guns and ammunition, and uniforms. Consequently, the leadership of the government was reluctant to put any brakes on the money supply as long as the war continued and the government was spending more money than it was receiving in tax revenues. Although the Bank had increased its holdings of government debt by very little up to 1810, its position in government securities would more than double between 1810 and the end of the war in 1815.[52] The Chancellor of the Exchequer was vehement on the subject, announcing that the Committee's recommendations were equivalent to "a declaration that we must submit to any terms of peace rather than continue the war."[53]

Other members of the House, concerned about precisely the problem that agitated Thornton, were reluctant to return to the old relationship between the pound and gold when prices were already so much higher than they had been when the rupture took place—the very issue that would nearly tear Britain apart in the 1920s. A third group resented the attack on the management of the Bank and rose to their defense. It is amazing that the most vocal part of the opposition came from sheer incredulity that the Bullion Committee could have figured out matters properly and that the Bank's notes were actually "depreciating."

The most dramatic response to all of the extended debate, and the defeat of Horner's sixteen resolutions, was provided by a young nobleman named Peter King. Because he was a nobleman, he was known by the delightful name of Lord King. As a member of the House of Lords, Lord King had been denied the opportunity to participate in the debate, and so he decided to drop his own private bombshell to underscore the validity of the Bullion Committee's analysis and Henry Thornton's worries about the impact of changing monetary values on contracts drawn in fixed sums.

"For the defence of his property," Lord King informed his tenants that he would no longer accept Bank notes at face value in payment of their rents. He maintained that there was no reason why he should suffer just because prices had risen so much since they signed their various leases. Consequently, he proposed to give each of his tenants a choice of two options. They could pay him their rent in an amount in gold equal to the amount of gold that could have been purchased with Bank notes at the time their lease was signed, or they could pay him a sufficient amount of Bank notes to purchase that amount of gold at its present price. He even went so far as to declare his preparedness to pay his own creditors in similar fashion and to reduce the rent payments from his tenants if prices were to decline and the purchasing power of Bank notes improved. He then published his speech in a pamphlet that incorporated tables to help his tenants and any other interested parties to figure out what the adjusted payments would be.[54] Lord King's announcement caused such a furor that Parliament passed special legislation declaring that the face value of contracts was inviolate and could not be so revised.

There were more crises, more hearings, more public debates, more inflation, and even deflation before Parliament finally restored the convertibility of Bank notes into gold in 1821. By that time, the usual period of deflation that has followed major wars had driven the price level all the way back down to its level in 1797. The distortion that bothered Lord King in 1810 had been washed out of the system. Full cash payments in gold were restored and a new coin was issued, the sovereign, equal to twenty shillings and 20/21 of the amount of gold in a guinea; in preparation for this moment, the Mint produced a total of 35 million sovereigns in 1821.[55] The gold standard was now an acknowledged reality, enshrined in official legislation. The British arrangements became the model for the rest of the world to follow for nearly one hundred years.

The system put metal above man in managing the nation's money supply. Nobody ever thought that it would be easy to figure out how much money is the right amount. Most people want more money than they happen to possess, but easy money can lead to inflation in which all the extra money loses value. Consequently, managing a money system is a task mired in ambiguity, which is why today's central bankers are better at double-talk than plain English. Baron Rothschild is rumored to have said on one occasion that he knew of only three people who understood money, and none of them had very much of it.

The act of faith underlying the gold standard was in the ability of free markets, expressed by changes in the price of gold, to do a better job than policymakers at this complex task. In this structure, gold was expected to support a system of checks and balances so that the supply of money—like Goldilocks's chair—would never be too large or too small.

But what happens when the quantity of the ultimate standard of value itself begins to grow? What, in essence, is the difference between the Bank of England creating paper money by generously accommodating their commercial customers in the early 1800s and the cornucopia of gold that the rash and daring prospectors of the nineteenth-century gold rushes contributed to the supply of cash in the United States, Australia, and South Africa? If Francis Horner had been alive when Francis Drake poured a flood of gold into the English economy in the late 1500s, would he have complained?

Gold is a product of the earth, not some construct dreamed up by economists and financiers. Although the sober members of the Bullion Committee acknowledged that new supplies of gold might be discovered, they never contemplated anything to match the enormous gold strikes around the world between 1848 and the end of the century. The golden nuggets in the stream at Sutter's Mill in California made Croesus look like a piker, and Australia, the Klondike, and South Africa were yet to come.

The excitement generated by the gold rushes was a vivid reminder of the central role that gold has played in our civilization. It is time to take a closer look at precisely how that happened.

14

The New Mistress and the Cursed Discovery

The yarns of the nineteenth-century gold rushes in California, Australia, the Klondike, and South Africa have been told over and over, in books, movies, and on television. Every library devotes yards of its shelves to the subject. All these accounts of adventure and personal drama are gripping, but they reduce a great story to too small a scale. The scope of the nineteenth-century discoveries dwarfed everything that had happened up to that point in the history of gold. Gold production in the United States surpassed both iron ore and petroleum in value until after World War I. Seen from that perspective, the gold of Croesus, Pizarro, and the caravans of the Sahara shrinks to tiny pinpoints. Furthermore, although the huge increase in gold supplies made possible the establishment of the international gold standard, the economic impact of the discoveries was radically different from the Price Revolution of the Sixteenth Century and quite the opposite of what most experts confidently expected to happen.

True, the Spanish discoveries of gold in the New World lifted world output of precious metals—gold plus silver—in the course of the 1600s to over seven tons a year, about double what it had been before those discoveries. By 1700, the total world stock of precious metals was five times as large as it had been in 1492. Then, thanks to Portuguese discoveries in Brazil, production doubled again in the eighteenth century.[1]

By 1859, with California, Australia, and Siberia all going strong, total world output of gold alone was 275 tons a year, which was more than ten times the average annual output during the eighteenth century. At that rate, the amount of gold produced in ten years matched the production from all sources over the entire 356 years from Columbus to 1848.[2] And that was before the Klondike, Colorado, and South Africa opened up at the turn of the century. World gold production by 1908 was over one hundred times what it had been in 1848 and 4.5 times the levels of just twenty years earlier.[3] By 1908, the total amount of gold in all forms—coinage, hoards, adornment, and decoration—could have been fashioned into a cube ten meters in each direction—an enormous expansion from the two-meter cube of 1500 that represented three thousand years of developing civilization (see page 110).[4]

Quite aside from the contrast in supplies, the character of the entire affair bore little resemblance to the gold strikes of the 1600s. The gold of the New World was found by adventurers who led the king's armies and employed military power to lay claim to entire nations in the name of the newfound wealth and plunder. The gold in California and Australia was discovered by independent prospectors panning in the rivers and working for themselves in a full expression of pioneering spirit, followed by businessmen who replaced the individual prospector with heavy capital equipment such as dredges and drills. The gold then traveled to banks and national treasuries on railroads and steamships whose high speeds and black smoke obliterated the memories of the romance and perils of the Spanish Main or the camels of the Sahara. Little of the nineteenth-century gold production ended up in Asia, although silver continued to move eastward.

In the 1500s, the gold discoveries were accompanied by even more important new supplies of silver in both Peru and Mexico, so silver continued to be the primary form of money in Europe and America until well into the nineteenth century. The influence of all the imports of gold from America did not even begin to dislodge silver in England until 1717, in Isaac Newton's time, and another one hundred years had to pass before Britain's Parliament established the official gold standard. But the deluge of new gold supplies in the 1800s finally established gold's dominance over silver in the world's monetary system. By 1900, the gold standard had been adopted almost everywhere; in many countries, silver was demonetized (ceased to be acceptable as money) except for small-coin transactions.

Finally, although there were constant warnings about the glut of gold and the inevitability of higher prices, inflation did not take hold until the very end of the nineteenth century except for very brief periods of time. This experience was a dramatic contrast to the Price Revolution of the Sixteenth Century. Indeed, the behavior of the price level was in many ways the most startling and interesting of the consequences of the nineteenth-century discoveries of gold.

Tradition paints the nineteenth-century gold rushes as historical accidents of some kind, with unsuspecting individuals stumbling onto sudden riches and the word spreading like wildfire. That tradition contains an important element of truth, but it is incomplete. The gold rushes of the nineteenth century were something more than bursts from the blue. People had been aware of gold-bearing areas in California, Canada, Australia, Alaska, and South Africa before the excitement turned hot in those areas. But the rapidly expanding world economy and financial system made the role of gold as money and as a standard even more important than it had been up to that point. Enormous prizes were to be won by the lucky individuals who beat the odds and managed to emerge with some gold from the turmoil and struggle of daily life in the gold rushes.

Although one could hardly describe the situation in the early 1800s as a bullion famine, the copious flow of gold from Latin America had peaked out during the 1790s as Brazilian supplies began to dry up. Then in 1810—the year the Bullion Committee held its hearings—Mexico rose up in a revolution against Spain that ignited a series of wars of independence in Latin America, disrupting the production of precious metals for nearly twenty years. This turbulence in Latin America was one of the reasons that Great Britain postponed restoring convertibility of Bank notes for six years after the defeat of Napoleon in 1815.

A dire world gold shortage was postponed, however, even before gold was found in California, as a result of discoveries in the land of the first and least famous of the nineteenth-century gold rushes—Russia. Gold had first been discovered in the Urals in 1744, but output remained modest until 1823, when, sensing opportunity, Czar Alexander I mounted a major effort to develop the country's bounteous gold resources. Annual production in the Urals rose from less than two tons in 1823 to more than five tons by 1830 and kept on climbing. The explorers were even more successful when they moved eastward into Siberia; production in that area had reached eleven tons a year by 1842. By 1847, the Russians were supplying over 60 percent of world gold production. As a result of the discoveries in other countries, the Russian share of the total declined after that date, but the Russians found so much gold over the years that their output was all the way up to sixty tons when World War I broke out in 1914.[5] By the time Stalin's prisoners were working the notorious mines in the Ural mountains and in Siberia, Russia had been turning out enormous amounts of gold for over one hundred years.

The development of Russian gold production bore no resemblance to the Wild West and the entrepreneurial character of the gold rushes that would stir the imagination of adventurers in North America and Australia. Most of those prospectors went home empty-handed, but at least they had had the opportunity to hit the jackpot and enough of them succeeded to keep the crowds pouring in. Not so in Russia. Digging into the freezing tundra, the tsar's miners were essentially serfs who lived and worked for pitiful wages from 5 AM to 8 PM, six days a week, in rough and marshy terrains. None of the gold they dug up would be theirs. The whole affair was either under the direct control of the crown or of a small number of rich landlords whose gold revenues were taxed by the tsars.

The contrast was striking between the downtrodden workers and their bosses, who lived in high style despite the inclement climate and forbidding landscape. A nineteenth-century visitor to Siberia dining in the home of one of these moguls described a repast as fine as anything served in the palaces of Saint Petersburg. The dinner began with oranges from the French Riviera, served on a plate of Japanese porcelain; the sumptuous meal that followed was accompanied by wines from Spain, the Rhine, and Bordeaux, and finished off with Arabian coffee and Havana cigars.[6]

In California, the discovery of gold in 1848 took place two years before the territory was admitted to statehood and even before a peace treaty had been signed in the Mexican War. The news about Sutter's Mill spread through the neighboring communities in short order and almost emptied out San Francisco within a few weeks. With no radios, television, or Internet, however, word reached the rest of the country more slowly. The first deposit of gold from California at the U.S. Mint did not arrive until December 8, 1848, at which point it was greeted by one periodical as "the new mistress."[7]

The big rush did not begin until 1849, after President Polk mentioned it in his State of the Union address to Congress, which is why the prospectors (and the San Francisco football team) came to be known as the Forty-Niners rather than the Forty-Eighters. The long delay between the discovery and Polk's announcement was the primary impetus for the first revolution in telecom—the establishment of the Western Union Company and the wiring of the entire United States for telegraphy. By 1853, over one hundred thousand people had swarmed into California, including 25,000 Frenchmen and twenty thousand Chinese, and annual gold production approached eighty metric tons; production would peak as early as 1853 at around 95 tons.[8]

The name Sutter's Mill has always been associated with the onset of the California gold rush. Poor Johann Sutter! In essence a good man, not a greedy man, Sutter was grieved rather than thrilled to hear about the golden nuggets in the stream on his property. He was so far out of step that he ultimately landed in deep trouble and came to a sad end.

In 1876, when he was 67 years old, Sutter received a visitor named H. H. Bancroft, a historian who persuaded him to dictate his memoirs about his mill and the gold rush. Sutter had also kept a diary. Edwin Gudde, a member of the faculty at the University of California, put all this material together in 1936 and edited it for publication. The result is a charming volume, much of it in Sutter's own words, that provides a vivid picture of every aspect of life, politics, and military activity in the 1840s. The summary that follows in no way does it justice.

Sutter was born in western Switzerland in 1803 and fled his homeland in 1834, hounded by creditors and facing a term in debtor's prison.

He took himself to the United States, where, after brief sojourns in New York, Saint Louis, and Santa Fe, he set out for California by way of Oregon, Vancouver, Hawaii, and Sitka in the Aleutians, before proceeding to Yerba Buena, as San Francisco was known in the 1830s. In August 1839, about eighteen months after his departure from Santa Fe, he chose his spot in the Sacramento valley, not far from where the state capitol is located today, after firing a salute from his boats on the Sacramento River that frightened away the deer, elk, timberwolves, and coyotes in the area. Sutter named his domain New Helvetia, and he had to become a Mexican citizen in order to formalize his claim there.

Sutter managed New Helvetia as a small empire, including a bell that rang each morning like reveille at an army post, and insisted on elegant manners by all workers, white and Indian alike. By 1846, there were sixty buildings in New Helvetia, including a bakery, a barracks, a tannery, and a blanket factory, plus twelve thousand head of cattle, over ten thousand sheep, two thousand horses and mules, and fields producing over forty thousand bushels of wheat.[9] Sutter believed he had every chance of becoming the wealthiest man on the Pacific Coast. "My best days were just before the discovery of gold," he recalled.[10]

The need arose for a large sawmill. As the valley had no timber, Sutter decided to look for a site in the mountains and settled on Coloma on the south fork of the American River. He assigned the job of building the mill to his chief mechanic, James Marshall. On January 24, 1848, Marshall appeared at Sutter's office back at headquarters and asked to see Sutter alone, insisting that the door be locked. Marshall pulled a white cotton rag out of his trousers. He opened the cloth and held it before Sutter, who saw about 1½ ounces of gold dust in flakes and grains. "I believe this is gold," said Marshall, "but the people at the mill laughed at me and called me crazy."[11]

Sutter took a dim view of the consequences: "During the night the thought burst upon my mind that a curse might rest upon this discovery. . . . From the very beginning I knew what the outcome would be, and it was a very melancholy ride on which I started the next morning."[12] Sutter went up to the mill and told all the working men that they must keep the discovery a secret for six weeks until the flour mill he was building down below could be finished. "But this was not to be. Women and whiskey let the secret out."[13] Nevertheless, Sutter succeeded in keeping the discovery within a limited area around Fort Helvetia for over three months.

On May 4, everything changed when a neighbor who had visited the site ran through the streets of San Francisco with a bottle of gold dust, shouting, "Gold! Gold! Gold from the American River!"[14] Within a few weeks, the surrounding area went crazy. Even the recently opened school in San Francisco had to be closed because both teachers and pupils had gone off to the mines.

And so begins Sutter's lament: "All my plans and projects came to naught. One after another, all my people disappeared in the direction of the gold fields. . . . Only the sick and the crippled remained behind. . . . The damage which I suffered in 1848 is inestimable." Squatters settled everywhere: "My property was entirely exposed and at the mercy of the rabble. . . . I was alone and there was no law."[15] The gristmill was never finished; even the stones were stolen, along with cattle and horses, the bells from the fort, hides, and barrels.

Sutter spent years of frustrating efforts in the law courts attempting to reclaim his land from the squatters. After five years in Washington, trying without success to adjudicate his claims, he retired to the little Pennsylvania town of Lititz. In 1880, he was back in Washington, trying for the sixteenth time to have his claim confirmed by Congress, but Congress adjourned without taking action. Two days later, at the age of 77, Sutter was dead. The memory of his sawmill, however, remains very much alive.

When the news of the discovery of Sutter's Mill reached Australia at the end of 1848, a crowd of Australians took off at once across the Pacific to join in the fun. Among them was an English-born man who had scraped together a living for some years in the Wellington district of New South Wales, about 170 miles west of Sydney. His name was Edward Hammond Hargraves, described by the historian Richard Hughes as "a corpulent bull-calf of a man."[16] After two years of panning and scrambling in California, with nothing to show for his efforts, Hargraves spent his last dollars to head back to Australia. He was still hopeful, however: he took his panning equipment back home with him, because he was struck by the geological similarities between the gold area in California and the Wellington area in Australia.

On February 12, 1851, Hargraves and his guide were poking on horseback along a tributary of the Macquarie River when, as Hargraves described it, he felt "surrounded by gold." Gold came up in four of the first five pans they dipped into the river. Hargraves exclaimed to the guide, "This is a memorable day in the history of New South Wales. I shall be a baronet, you will be knighted, and my old horse will be stuffed, put in a glass case, and sent to the British Museum!"[17] None of those things happened, but it was indeed a memorable day. As the news spread, Hughes relates, "It was as though a plug had been pulled and the male population of New South Wales had emptied like a cistern, in a rush toward the diggings." One of the Sydney newspapers reported, "A complete mental madness appears to have been seized by almost every member of the community." Within six months, fifty thousand people were digging for gold.[18] It is interesting to note that ice from Thoreau's Walden Pond in Massachusetts, loaded in sawdust, was shipped fifteen thousand miles to Melbourne, unloaded onto carts, and dragged by horses several hundred miles to the goldfields so that the miners who had won out could enjoy cold drinks![19]

By November, bags of gold were pouring in a great flood to waiting ships. The first shipment to London at the end of 1851 was 253 ounces. Six months later, weekly shipments were averaging half a ton. Gold was soon turning the crudest workmen into pretentious gentlemen. "It is not what you were, but what you are that is the criterion," as one contemporary observer wrote.[20] Miners were heard to say, "We be the aristocracy now and the aristocracy be we."[21]

As newcomers poured into Australia, they transformed a minor-league penal colony of 45,000 men into what would turn out to be a flourishing and well-diversified nation. Hughes summarizes these turbulent times well: "Gold disturbed the order of Anglo-Australian society—from pastoral aristocrat to convict—with shudders of democracy."[22] Indeed, the most remarkable consequence of the Australian gold rush was the end of "transportation"—the forcible exile of English criminals to the horrors of Van Diemen's Land on the island of Tasmania. No terror clung any longer to the name of Australia when a man could find the riches of his dreams there. With a quarter of Britain's men clamoring for tickets to Australia, the Governor-General had to admit that "Few English criminals . . . would not regard a free passage to the gold-fields . . . as a great boon."[23] In medieval times, gold had saved lives by serving as ransoms; in nineteenth-century Australia, gold led to the end of the barbarous conditions on Tasmania in December 1852, less than two years after Hargraves felt "surrounded by gold."

Although the rush to the Klondike was dramatic and colorful because of its location and its hostile terrain, the Klondike was relatively unimportant in the long history of gold. In this instance, a couple of fishermen prospecting for salmon in a tributary of the Yukon called the Thron-diuck River—later transformed to Klondike—spotted gold in the waters one August afternoon in 1897. The advance guard of the rush came from Circle City, which was down the Yukon, a bustling center of gold prospectors with the usual complement of dance halls and saloons. It took until the following spring before the first shipments of Klondike gold sailed south to California. Fifteen hundred people in Seattle, including the mayor, sailed north within ten days of the first news.

Before it was all over, one hundred thousand people had set out for Dawson City, less than half of whom were able and willing to hang in during the rugged trip and actually made it to the gold-bearing areas. Four thousand found gold and about four hundred struck it rich. The most abundant areas were few in number and had been pretty much used up by 1900. For all the hoopla, all the gold mined in Alaska since 1880 has amounted to less than 10 percent of the gold mined in all the other parts of the United States over the same period of time.[24]

The South African story has a different flavor. Yes, South Africa has its counterpart of James Marshall or Edward Hargraves in the person of George Harrison, who happened upon an outcropping of gold in 1886 while digging up stone to build a house for a widowed neighbor not far from the city of Johannesburg. But South African gold does not appear in nuggets and little of it shows up in surface outcroppings. Instead, the gold lies embedded in an imposing body of ore in what are called reefs that average only about one foot thick and lie as deep as one mile underground. Depth is by no means the least of the miner's problem: the ore is so low-grade that a ton of it contains no more than an ounce of pure gold, which does not willingly separate itself from the raw rock.

Despite the rush that at its peak brought as many as two thousand immigrants a week to South Africa, gold mining there required so much capital that it was big business almost from the very start, with the diamond men from Kimberly leading the way.[25] Even so, like the Klondike, the boom in South Africa seemed to be coming to an end within three years of Harrison's discovery at Widow Oosthuizen's farm: the high hopes lay buried in the hideous heaps of slag that piled up like grotesque mountains from which just a trickle of gold—and an equally pitiful volume of profits—had been dislodged. Despite repeated efforts with different kinds of chemical processes to extract more gold from the ore, the tons of gold-bearing rock just continued to accumulate, refusing to part with their precious contents in sufficient quantity to make the business profitable.

As the ore brought to the surface of the earth appeared thinner and thinner, all the earlier excitement yielded to pessimism. The stocks of the mining companies crashed, some falling 95 percent from their previous values. One observer predicted, "Grass will grow in the streets of Johannesburg within a year."[26] That was another famous flat-out prediction that turned out to be wrong almost as soon as the words were uttered. As often happens with people who yield to panic, selling gold-mining shares at that moment would turn out to be a colossal error.

In late 1889, Allan James arrived on the scene, representing a Scottish corporation called the African Gold Extracting Company. James announced that his company had developed a process called cyanidation that would solve all of South Africa's problems. Although scientists in Britain, the United States, and New Zealand had experimented with cyanide as far back as the 1840s, without clear success, the process that James offered was one that worked. The cyanide was stirred and decanted after a few hours. These steps tended to separate the gold from the ores, and then zinc was applied to precipitate the gold.[27]

A pilot plant was erected in May 1890 that performed all the miracles that James had promised. The process made possible the profitable production of gold from newly mined ore, but that was not all: the huge piles of slag could now be attacked and profitably turned into lovely yellow metal. The African Gold Extracting Company soon negotiated a royalty with the mining firms that was the equivalent of $1.36 per ounce of pure gold, to be earned on every ton of ore that was treated with the cyanidation process; with the world price of gold at that time around $21 an ounce, this was a handsome royalty indeed.

The cyanidation process had been developed by John Stewart MacArthur, a chemist from Glasgow, who had teamed up with an unlikely pair of physicians with intense curiosity in such matters, Robert and William Forrest. MacArthur described their efforts "in a glory-hole under the consulting rooms of the Forrests. . . . We did most of our work between 8 PM and 2 AM when the Forrests had finished their day's work. . . . It was usual to have pies and pots of tea sent in from the nearest restaurant. . . . When we were more than usually sleepy, Dr. Robert brought out a bottle of a weird mixture labeled 'kid-reviver' and gave us a dose all around to keep awake."[28]

The cyanidation process was an immediate and smashing success. The sophistication of the MacArthur–Forrest achievements turned South African gold production into one of the high-tech industries of the late nineteenth century.[29] Cecil Rhodes's consulting engineer was on the right track in 1890 when he predicted that, thanks to cyanidation, the value of the annual gold output in South Africa would exceed £20 million before the turn of the century, at a time when the total world output of gold was not much more than that.[30] Gold production rose from less than a ton in 1886, when the first discovery was made at Widow Oosthuizen's farm, to fourteen tons in 1889 and then to nearly 120 tons in 1898 before the outbreak of the Boer War. The 120 tons had a market value in 1889 of about £16 million.[31]

After four years of paying those fat royalties to MacArthur and his associates, the gold-mining companies came to the conclusion that the African Gold Recovery Company (as it subsequently came to be known) was getting too much of a good thing. The Chamber of Mines entered into negotiations to reduce the royalty rate, but MacArthur and his associates stood fast. Their greed would do them in. After four months, the Chamber gave up on negotiating and brought suit in the High Court to contest the validity of the MacArthur patents. Their argument claimed that the patentees were not the true inventors, that the process was not new when it was patented, that the final specification was faulty, and that others had used the process in South Africa before MacArthur's group had done so.[32]

The result was an extraordinarily protracted and expensive lawsuit. Evidence was taken from mining experts in the United States, Canada, Australia, Hungary, Korea, Japan, South America, India, and Russia. The president of the Royal Society in England and a covey of physicists and chemists in scores of universities either testified or provided affidavits. There were two years of preparation before the hearings began, and the judges did not render their verdict until November 1896, nine months after the hearings had started. The extended arguments were highly technical—fascinating perhaps to chemists but drudgery for lay readers. The decision of the judges (two in favor and one against) ran to seventy pages.

The bottom line was loud and clear: "It was found on the facts by the majority of the Court that the processes above mentioned were not novel and had been anticipated, and consequently the Court declared the said patents void. . . . There is nothing novel in the weakening or diluting of a well-known solvent or re-agent for the purpose of winning gold from quartz."[33]

Despite this judgment, MacArthur's cyanidation process has been associated with South African gold mining ever since its introduction, with only minor modifications from the original patents. In 1988, almost one hundred years after Allan James arrived on the scene with news of the cyanidation process, C. E. Fivaz, a metallurgical consultant to the Chamber of Mines, made the following comment on the subject in the course of his presidential address to the South African Institute of Mining and Metallurgy:

> Had it not been for the invention of the MacArthur–Forrest cyanidation process, there is every likelihood that South Africa's economic development would have died before it even had a real chance to begin its true growth. I rank this invention . . . along with the great ones in the mining field such as the development of explosives and the reciprocating rock drill. . . . [It] was the most significant technological development in the extractive-metallurgical industry during the past century.[34]

So MacArthur should have ended up a wealthy and famous man. Such was not to be the case. MacArthur followed Johann Sutter into oblivion and poverty. He died a poor man in 1920. Sutter was ruined because he had too little greed at the sight of gold; MacArthur was ruined because he had too much.

In the autumn of 1857, an alarming series of articles appeared in the Parisian *Revue des Mondes* on the inevitable inflationary consequences of the burgeoning supplies of gold from the gold rushes in Russia, California, and Australia. The author, Michel Chevalier, was a man of some note, strong opinions, and bold ideas. He was the only professor of economics in France in his lifetime, economic advisor to Napoleon III, and author of *Letters from North America,* a lengthy description of his travels in the United States. Chevalier had such passionate feelings about the rights of women—that they had to be freed from the laws of fidelity in marriage if they were to achieve equality with men—that he spent a year in jail in 1832 for "outrage to morals." At various times, he advocated a trans-Andean railroad, a trans-Siberian railroad, and a tunnel under the English Channel.[35]

Chevalier also issued the warnings from his article in pamphlet form, twice the length of the newspaper series, after which his work was translated and published in London in 1859 under the imposing title of *On the Probable Fall in the Value of Gold: The Commercial and Social Consequences Which May Ensue, and the Measures Which It Invites.* The "probable fall in the value of gold" includes the possibility that the glut of new gold supplies would force down the price of gold relative to silver, but the outcome that most concerns Chevalier is a loss in gold's *real* value—namely, inflation, or an increase in the price of everything except gold.

Chevalier writes with great flair, which makes his book fun to read, but his work is above all a statistical tour de force. He is in command of a dazzling accumulation of facts about gold supplies, gold production, the banking system, the uses of gold in finance as well as in "the habits of luxury," and even crude estimates of what modern economists refer to as nominal gross domestic product, or a measure of the monetary value of a nation's total output of goods and services.

In the late 1850s, at the time Chevalier was writing his book, wholesale prices were indeed about 35 percent above the levels prevailing before the discoveries in California and Australia. The end of the decade of the 1840s, however, marked the final stage of a long decline in prices that had set in after the conclusion of the wars against Napoleon. Prices in 1857 were not much higher than the average of the preceding twenty years and were 40 percent below the peak of 1813; price performance outside the United States was even more subdued.[36] Chevalier is well aware of these facts and goes to some length to point out the transitory influence of the recent business expansion on the price level. He emphasizes at the outset that "I shall generally reason as if these new gold mines had not yet produced any appreciable effect."[37]

After a sophisticated analysis of the nature of money, the magnitude of the new supplies of gold relative to the past, and the interaction between the prices of gold and silver, Chevalier concludes that "The only way to prevent a fall in the value of gold, and a consequent rise in the price of commodities, would be the discovery of a new demand, equal in extent to the increased supply [of gold] thrown upon the markets of the Western World." And then he asks: "Is the opening of such an outlet possible or probable?"[38] His answer to his question is an unqualified no. He arrives at this conclusion after adding up his estimates of the increase in the demand for gold that might develop because some countries might wish to add to the proportion of metal in their currencies, because of the rising needs for gold currency impelled by the growth of business and population, and because of the necessity to offset the disappearance of gold from monetary circulation due to wear and tear, hoarding, and the "habits of luxury."[39]

Chevalier is at his most interesting when he reasons that "the multiplication of money which must take place in consequence of the extension of commerce" will be far too small to absorb the great glut of gold pouring into the system.[40] He defends this position by observing that the financial system "has undergone and is undergoing continually great improvements, almost as great as those of the steam engine"—the key technological innovation of his age.[41] Fifty years earlier, he informs us, a steam engine of forty horsepower would have cost £4000, but now, in 1857, as the process of manufacture has substantially reduced the necessary amount of cast or wrought iron without any loss of strength or safety, a steam engine of similar horsepower would cost only £1000. "It is the same with the instrument of exchanges," he asserts. "Formerly, [business transactions] called into requisition a large quantity of metal, gold or silver. Now for the same extent of business, a much smaller quantity suffices."[42]

Just as improved materials have reduced the cost of the steam engine, so "a number of ingenious contrivances" are reducing the amount of metal required for commercial transactions. Most transactions, in fact, are conducted without the intervention "of a single crown-piece. . . . Letters of credit, bills, cheques, and other instruments of the same kind are multiplied in proportion to the extension of commerce, but the specie required for these transactions experiences hardly any increase."[43] Even the use of banknotes had grown at a snail's pace: in the ten years from 1846 to 1856, for Great Britain—"the great seat of commerce"—the circulation of banknotes increased only from £30,925,123 to £31,001,027.[44]

On the financial side, Chevalier reports that at the Clearing House of London, where the banks settle their accounts with one another, "[with] a mass of transactions amounting to 1,500 millions or 2,000 millions sterling annually . . . not a shilling is wanted. . . . All is settled by the transfer of sums from one account to another in the books of the Bank of England."[45]

Chevalier's arguments in this connection bear a striking resemblance to conditions in the second half of the 1990s. Like the steam engine in the first half of the nineteenth century, the key technological innovation of our own age—the computer—has been continuously and dramatically reduced in price over the years, with improvements rather than deterioration in quality. At the same time, as in Chevalier's era, the breathtaking pace of financial innovations such as credit cards and other substitutes for cash have enabled the volume of business transactions to expand at a rate that has been far faster than growth in the supply of money. Exotic financial instruments such as options, futures, and swaps have revolutionized the entire world of trading financial assets by driving activity to volumes no one could have dreamed of even ten years ago.

Chevalier also explores the question of whether the demand for gold for jewelry and other forms of adornment might expand, now that such generous supplies of the metal have become available. No hope here, either, for the world appears to have changed from the days of

Francis I and Henry VIII: "The age is less pompous than it is supposed to be, or rather it does not exhibit its pomp by a display of gold ornaments."[46] In England, the manufacture of articles of jewelry "is an atom in comparison with total production."[47] The same is true for France. Taking Europe and "the civilised States of North and South America" together, and figuring everything on the generous side, the highest estimate for jewelry consumption that Chevalier can concoct is 25 tons a year.[48]

Jewelry is not the only form of adornment that involves gold, however. "Paris gilds itself not a little, and is surprisingly addicted to gold lace."[49] This observation leads him to an elaborate set of calculations to demonstrate that the great malleability of gold allows a small amount of the metal to cover a huge area. For example, a ton of gold would suffice to gild an area of about 179 acres or 144,000 salons—"at least twenty times the number which are thus embellished in one year in all those cities where the houses are of a character to require their interiors to be gilded."[50] As far as gold lace is concerned, a gold piece of twenty francs contains gold enough to gild a thread that would extend from Calais to Marseilles.

In short, "mankind is not rich enough, nor will it soon be, to pay so dearly for so large a mass [of gold]. To find an outlet, it is absolutely requisite that so vast a production should be accompanied by a great reduction in value."[51] Chevalier concludes that the only way to dispose of these masses of gold is

> by coining them and forcing them into the current of circulation. This current . . . receives and carries off all that is thrown into it; but the process of absorption and assimilation is on one condition, namely, that gold diminishes in value, so that in those transactions where heretofore ten pieces of gold had for example sufficed, eleven, twelve, fifteen, or even more, will be required. In a word, if gold is to enter into the circulation in indefinite quantities, it is by being subjected to the rigorous law of a continually increasing depreciation.*[52]

*Chevalier did concede that the process, though inevitable, would be retarded by the offset of French exports of silver to India, a "parachute" to slow the fall in the value of gold. This observation hardly does justice to a complicated and often fascinating story related, as centuries earlier, to the ability of the East to absorb huge quantities of the precious metals. See, especially, Flandreau, 1996, and Kindleberger, 1989.

The predictions conveyed by Chevalier's elegant, elaborate, and persuasive analysis turned out to be far wide of the mark. The actual sequence of events bore no resemblance to his dour prophecy or even to the long, grinding period of inflation that followed the sixteenth-century discoveries of precious metals in Mexico and South America. Prices during the last forty years of the nineteenth century never rose by more than 5 percent above the levels of the late 1850s, and they remained well below those levels from 1875 to the outbreak of World War I.[53] The contrast with the 1500s and 1600s is all the more remarkable because the magnitude of the nineteenth-century discoveries was so much greater than the new supplies that opened up after Columbus first crossed the Atlantic in 1492.

One explanation for the wide difference in economic performance between the 1500s and the 1800s is in the frequency of warfare in the 1500s. Although living standards did improve during the sixteenth century, warfare mercilessly consumed much production and mercenary manpower. The hundred years from the fall of Napoleon to the onset of World War I were also marked by wars, including the American Civil War, the Franco-Prussian War in 1870, and the British expedition to the Crimea in the 1850s, but those struggles, though bloody, were relatively brief, and both the United States and Europe enjoyed peace just about all the rest of the time.

Chevalier grossly underestimated the rate of economic growth over the next fifty years—growth so impressive that it swamped the "vast production" of gold that had provoked him to push a panic button. We cannot sit in judgment of his gaping forecast error, because what happened was so far outside the bounds of what anyone had ever experienced before. If Chevalier's forecast was wrong by such a wide margin, imagine the astonishment of the authors of the Bullion Report of 1810 at how the pace of economic activity would appear to outrun the growth in the stock of gold.

Consider just the decade of the 1870s in the United States as an example—a decade marked by persistently declining prices and a serious depression that began during 1873 and was still felt to some degree in 1879. Thanks in large part to immigration, population rose by 30 percent. The miles of railroad track in operation more than doubled (the golden spike that linked the railroad system from the Atlantic to the Pacific had been driven in place in 1869). In New York State, railroad traffic by the late 1870s was for the first time exceeding traffic on canals and rivers. The number of farms rose by 50 percent and the dollar value per acre rose even as the prices of farm products were dropping—eloquent testimony to how agricultural productivity was cutting production costs. The output of coal, pig iron, and copper more than doubled; lead multiplied sixfold.[54] Overall, industrial production grew at an annual rate of better than 5 percent a year from the end of the Civil War to 1900, which meant that output at the end of the century was 5½ times as great as it had been in 1865.

One other measure conveys the dramatic process of economic growth in the nineteenth century. In 1800, the United States consumed a total of three trillion BTU of energy—coal, wood, hydropower, and petroleum. In 1850, at the time of the gold discoveries in California and Australia, energy consumption was up to 219 trillion BTU. It tripled in the next fifteen years and then rose twelvefold over the next 35 years. At the end of the century, energy consumption was at 7322 trillion BTU, a growth rate of 7.3 percent a year from the day that James Marshall stumbled onto gold at Sutter's Mill.[55]

At a time such as the present, when technological change and leaps in productivity are accepted as a matter of course, we have difficulty conceiving of what technological innovation was like in an age when discontinuities were both immense and abrupt. Here, for example, is a letter from a nobleman who had gone from Manchester to Liverpool in 1833 to visit the grave of his old friend, William Huskisson, the poor co-author of the Bullion Committee Report who had been killed by Stephenson's famous *Rocket* at the opening ceremonies of the Liverpool and Manchester Railway in 1830:

> I arrived at Manchester last night at 11 o'c. This morning at 7 I rose, and at 8 had the carriage mounted on the Ry . . . and at ½ past 9 was at Liverpool—32 miles in 90 minutes!!!. . . . You would have laughed to have seen Thompson and James on the box of the carriage, while we were sometimes flying on the rly. a mile in 2 minutes. Thompson trying to grin with his tongue out and his fingers all on end, and James quite as usual, only losing his hat now and then.[56]

In reading these lines, we must recall that through all of human history up to that time people had never been able to travel faster than a horse could carry them, and even a horse could sustain its highest speed for only brief periods of time. My own maternal grandmother, who was born in 1860, always referred to the family automobile as "the machine," an expression she continued to use right up to her death at the age of 86 in 1946.

There was a modest degree of correlation between gold production and price inflation, especially after 1870, but nobody took notice. Year-to-year price changes were in any case so irregular and erratic that no underlying inflationary trend was able to rise to the surface until the full impact of the South African discoveries made themselves felt in the world economic system after 1900—and even then the perception of inflation was delayed or muted.* The most striking evidence of the public's relaxed view of the probability of inflation is in the behavior of interest rates, which moved up and down without any systematic linkage to what was happening in the price level for commodities and services.[57]

Chevalier's inability to comprehend what would happen to the productivity of the economic system was enough to make mincemeat of his gloomy predictions. This aspect of the matter, however, was not the only development that doomed his forecast to failure.

He devotes two pages to the practice of hoarding, which he describes as "to hide money in secret places." He denigrates this habit as "belonging to an uncivilised state of society, in which riches take refuge under ground to escape spoliation."[58] As a faithful and enthusiastic participant of an age of great physical improvement in the way of life and the democratization of the political system, Chevalier minimizes the likelihood that hoarding as he defines it would amount to very much. He even goes so far as to suggest that "In the Europe of our

*A technical statement of this point in economist-speak would be as follows: "Box-Jenkins procedures at both quarterly and annual frequencies identify the price level over 1870–1914 as a random walk with little drift, and inflation consequently as approximately zero-mean white noise, in both the United States and the United Kingdom" (see Barsky and DeLong, 1991, p. 824).

day, the quantity of the precious metals which issue from their hiding-places is, in all likelihood, greater than that which seeks refuge there."[59]

Although we have no good data to test Chevalier's hypotheses about hoarding, we do know that he failed to recognize a demand for hoarding *in a civilized state of society* that would turn out to be untold magnitudes greater than any amount of gold that individuals might hide to escape spoliation. The growing acceptance of the gold standard, following Britain's first steps in that direction in the early 1800s, created an enormous demand for gold for hoarding—not by individuals but by the central banks of the nations, such as the Bank of England and the Bank of France, or the U.S. Treasury. A hoard of gold was the major line of defense against an unexpected surge in imports or outflow of investment capital to other financial centers. With the huge expansion in economic activity and international trade and investment, those gold hoards were essential to give nations freedom of action and to attract new capital to their shores. "Sound money" and "sound banks" were defined by the accessibility of gold to be paid out on demand to anyone who came to the windows and asked for it. Countries gaining gold were held in high repute; countries on the losing side were viewed as in deep trouble.

As a consequence, little of the "vast production" of gold that troubled Chevalier moved around from hand-to-hand. The largest part of it was transferred into idle hoards in monumental buildings that looked like Greek temples, where the heaps of gold enjoyed the more polite name of "reserves." Let us turn now to see how all that worked and what kinds of trouble erupted in the wake of the international gold standard.

15

The Badge of Honor

The international gold standard shimmers from the past like the memory of a lost paradise, embodying all the nostalgia of the Victorian and Edwardian eras—stability, harmony, respectability. The glow attached to this nostalgia is not based in myth but stems from a vivid reality. From the end of the American Civil War to the outbreak of World War I—a brief period of only fifty years—the international gold standard acquired a mystique that radiated far beyond the simple discipline that it imposed on its members. The control of gold over the affairs of human beings has never been so absolute, nor the worship of gold by hard-headed financiers and statesmen so humble.

As we shall see, the gold standard developed all the trappings of a full-fledged religion: shared beliefs, high priests, strict codes of behavior, creed, and faith. The gospel had been drafted by the Bullion Committee of 1810, inspired by Ricardo. The altars at which the members of this religion worshipped were the meticulously mounted stacks of gleaming gold bricks in the vaults of the banks. The high priests were the monetary authorities, in most cases the managers of the central banks such as the Bank of England or the Bank of France, in less frequent cases the finance ministers or secretaries of the Treasury; controversy exists over whether there was a pope or the equivalent. Like many great religions, the gold standard compelled dreaded punishments for those who dared to stray from the straight-and-narrow, but it also promised absolution to those who pledged to reject apostasy by vowing to return to the fold as soon as possible. The gold standard provided its believers with comfort, community, pride, and a sense of immortality.

The group of nations that adopted the gold standard developed into a kind of fraternity—an enviable and exclusive group whose members protected one another from the hazards and uncertainties imposed on them by the world beyond their borders. The great economist and historian Joseph Schumpeter described the attraction of the gold standard as a search for national prestige, "a symbol of sound practice and badge of honor and decency," with a value that was independent of purely economic advantages.[1] A contemporary member of the Austrian parliament warned his colleagues about the loss of "esteem" that their nation suffered by being "a scrap-of-paper economy."[2] A Russian economist asserted that "Membership in worldwide civilization is unthinkable without membership in the worldwide monetary economy."[3] John Sherman, a prominent member of the U.S. Congress and of presidential cabinets, declared that a currency without redeemability into gold was a "national dishonor."[4]

Britain was the charter member of the club, even its inventor. The United States, though on a bimetallic silver/gold standard at the time, was one of the first to follow in Britain's footsteps by rejiggering the price relationship between the two metals in 1834 to establish a *de facto* gold standard; a gold standard *de jure* would wait for another 66 years, after the struggle between the silver advocates and the supporters of gold had been finally resolved in favor of gold. The Germans came aboard in 1871, financing their gold reserves with part of the indemnity paid by the French after their defeat in the Franco-Prussian War—an indemnity equal to five billion francs, which was about one-third of France's total output of goods and services.*[5] The French went with gold afterward, not in a full, immediate step but by limiting the permitted volume of silver coinage. As we shall see, the move was considered "precautionary and revocable" and was motivated by a desire to complicate the German effort to dispose of their silver stocks.[6] By 1876, Italy, Belgium, Switzerland, the Scandinavian countries, the Netherlands, and Belgium had all signed on. At the end of the decade, only India and China among major countries were still on a silver standard.

*The French did not pay the indemnity in specie. They issued a perpetual bond (a bond with no maturity), skillfully underwritten by the Rothschilds, that had many buyers outside of France. The resulting foreign exchange was transferred to Germany.

The reverence for gold in the nineteenth century was so steadfast that it led to a persistent decline in the prestige and, ultimately, the acceptability of silver as money. This view was summed up best by English Prime Minister Lord Liverpool when he pointed out that "Coins should be made of metals more or less valuable . . . in proportion to the wealth and commerce of the country in which they are to be the measure of property."[7] It was not just silver that was downgraded in this fashion. Once the gold standard was in place, paper notes and bank deposits as well as holdings of foreign exchange were considered as little more than convenient substitutes for the "real thing," assets that enjoyed acceptability purely by virtue of being convertible into gold.[8]

The most compelling feature of the gold-standard system was the ingenious manner in which it combined primitive trust in a shiny metal, reaching back to the earliest times, with a highly sophisticated dynamic that served gold's purposes so well in the years of vigorous industrial and financial development before the First World War. The primitive and sophisticated properties reinforced each other in a manner that was unique in history and that the world since 1914 has never been able to replicate.

So potent was this image after the Armistice in 1918 that few people dared to suggest—or even notice—that the gold standard had been rendered obsolete by the social, economic, and political earthquakes unleashed by the bloody struggle of the First World War. Andrew Boyle, biographer of Montagu Norman, the man who served as Governor of the Bank of England from 1920 to 1944, put it this way: "Anyone rash enough then to have advocated a different course might well have been locked up and certified as insane. No alternative plan was conceivable."[9]

Almost every country took extraordinary political risks to restore the gold standard, even if compromises in format and structure were unavoidable. For more than fifty years after the guns of World War I had fallen silent, the deferential respect for the autopilot of gold lingered on, in one form or another, while gold continued to manage—or mismanage—large areas of the world economy.

If the gold standard finally turned out to be an anachronism amid the international and economic turbulence of the twentieth century, might the twenty-first century offer a different set of circumstances? The possible answer to that question must wait until the end of our story.

The primitive notions supporting the gold standard traced their origins back to the prestige and international acceptability of Croesus's staters, when gold first started to perform as money in a systematic fashion. From this root, the religion of the international gold standard had just one absolute commandment: gold, and gold alone, is the ultimate form of money, the *standard*. A country on the gold standard defined its money—pound, franc, lira, dollar—in terms of a specified and immutable quantity of gold. Its own citizens, and the world around them, expected the authorities to maintain full and free convertibility of its banknotes and bank deposits (private money, as we saw in Chapter 10) into gold at that fixed ratio, *come what may*.

The numbers are fussy, and the convention of measuring weights in grains is annoying, but the ratios are important for they define how many units of one currency such as pounds sterling will exchange for units of another currency such as dollars or francs. For example, Britain's sovereign coin, which was the equivalent of one pound sterling, was defined in 1870 as 113.0016 grains of gold, a setting that reached all the way back to a parliamentary resolution of 1717, a familiar date. This was equal to about a quarter of an ounce, the same weight as a modern 25¢ piece. The dollar's weight in gold was set at 23.22 grains or $20.67 per ounce in 1837, after having fluctuated between 24.68 grains and 22.85 grains from 1791 to 1837.*[10]

The result of the definitive settings of 113.0016 grains to the pound and 23.22 grains to the dollar was an automatic and invariable rate of exchange between the two currencies, an act of faith that £1 would equal $4.86 (the result of dividing 113.0016 by 23.22) forever and ever. Under those conditions, fluctuations over time around this rate would be minimal and determined primarily by the costs incurred in shipping gold across the Atlantic between London and New York.

These publicly announced relationships to gold were inviolate. The international gold standard amounted to nothing more than that. As long

*As it takes almost five hundred grains to add up to one ounce, we can see that the difference between 24.68 grains and 22.85 grains is tiny indeed. The dollar was originally defined in 1795 relative to 371.25 grains of silver instead of being defined directly in gold.

as the gold parities were intact, dollars or krone were as welcome as pounds in London and marks or rubles were as welcome as francs in Paris, in an era in which globalization of capital and trade was as forceful a process as it has been over the past 25 years. Nobel Laureate Robert Mundell has succinctly described this system: "Currencies were just names for particular weights of gold."[11]

The sophisticated dynamic of the system arose from the robust tension between the good news and the bad news in the gold standard. The good news was in the many advantages of having a currency that was universally acceptable because it was backed by stuff before which humanity had been genuflecting since the beginning of time. This meant that holders of your currency would not desert you at the first sign of trouble. In rare cases such as Britain's sterling, foreigners were willing, or often even more willing, to hold sterling and make their payments in sterling in preference to their own currency, just as people around the world use dollars today. The British derived major benefits from these arrangements, because the Bank of England could function with low levels of gold reserves, which produce no income, unlike the hoards carried by the other central banks and Treasuries. Thus, in 1913, the Bank held only $165 million in gold, compared with $678 million at the Bank of France and $1.3 *billion* at the U.S. Treasury.[12] The Bank of England did come in for criticism from some conservative circles, who held that the low level of gold reserves showed that the management of the Bank was putting the interests of the shareholders above the needs of the British banking system as a whole.[13]

The bad news was the shattering loss of acceptability that would afflict a nation that mismanaged its affairs or was caught in the whirlwind of a global economic crisis. Then investors, traders, and speculators would rush to redeem their paper and bank deposits for gold, depleting the country's precious stockpile. This cataclysmic outcome was frequent among the smaller but aspiring nations, most of which were dependent on the volatile markets for raw materials. The senior members of the gold standard club went to the brink more often than the nostalgia about the gold standard might suggest, but none of them ever succumbed to apostasy despite frequent narrow escapes.

Nobody invented this remarkable system, no grand plan was ever devised, no one ever wrote a rule book on the necessary codes of behavior. The closest thing to an official guide to the gold standard was in the words of the Bullion Committee in 1810: "Gold is itself the measure of all exchangeable value, the scale to which all money prices are referred. . . . Bullion is the true regulator both of the value of a local currency and the rate of the Foreign Exchange."[14]

Luck, politics, geography, and the laws of physics had as much to do with the spread of the gold standard as any of the monetary theories then in vogue; most of the imposing theory that later supported the gold standard came along after the fact. It was 1875 before Stanley Jevons set forth the dominant philosophy underlying the gold standard that we quoted in Chapter 13: "So unaccountable are the prejudices of men on the subject of currency that it is not well to leave anything to discretionary management."[15]

Isaac Newton, traditionally stuck with the honor—or blame—for launching the gold standard, had no such idea in 1717. Rather, he made a faulty estimate of the appropriate ratio between gold prices and silver prices, leaving Britain unintentionally on the gold standard. Despite Newton's miscalculation, the British did not officially abandon a bimetallic standard of gold plus silver until 1816, when silver coins were converted to small change with limited legal tender. The British defenders of silver remained vocal for another thirty years.[16]

Until the 1870s, every movement toward a European gold standard was as unplanned as Newton's. Two metals were necessary, because gold coins are so valuable that the system could not function without a widely accepted subsidiary coinage. In most countries, convertibility of paper currency and bank deposits into gold was perceived as nothing more than a variation on the theme of a bimetallic standard that consisted of both gold and silver; elsewhere, silver was the sole standard. The only constant was that specie—metallic-based money—was imperative all the way. The world would not outlive that primitive notion for many decades to come.

Despite gold's glitter, glamour, and prominence in many aspects of life, silver was the primary form of money right up to the middle of the nineteenth century. Angela Redish, a British economist, has argued that the main reason the gold standard succeeded during the nineteenth century was that "New technology employed by the Mint was able to make [silver] coins that counterfeiters could not copy cheaply and because the Mint accepted the responsibility of guaranteeing the convertibility of [these] tokens."[17] The plentiful supply of good silver coins, in contrast to the pathetic clipped coins of the late seventeenth century, provided for payments in small transactions, while gold lorded over the system of large transactions and liquidity reserves.

Silver was always more plentiful than gold, as Offa's pennies remind us. It is no coincidence that the French word for money, *argent*, translates as silver, or that "sterling" has defined English money for centuries, even when the pound was defined only by gold.[18] Even during the disputes over gold during the days of the Bullion Committee and its immediate aftermath, silver was a major focus of attention. Both Ricardo and Locke favored one metal over two as the standard, but in 1816 Ricardo opted for silver rather than gold for this purpose. He based his argument on silver's "greater regularity of supply and demand," and its use by all foreign countries, arguing that the inconvenience of its bulk could be entirely offset by substituting paper money as the "general circulation medium."*[19]

Silver might have been number one forever, but it has two disadvantages. First, silver lacks gold's glamour because it tarnishes so much faster than gold; silver has never driven men and women to the extremes of greed that have been motivated by gold. Second, silver's bulk is much greater than gold's. In the days of Locke and Newton, one thousand guineas at £3 17*s* 10½*d* weighed about 18½ pounds, while the same amount of money—£1050—in silver coins would have come to nearly 280 pounds. The cost of transporting a given amount of money in gold coin was therefore much lower than the cost of moving the same value in silver. With commerce, industry, and international trade and finance growing with unparalleled vigor in the course of the nineteenth century, this simple physical difference against silver operated as a tax on international movements and in the end may have been as important as "honor and decency" in tipping the scales in favor of gold.[20] Another factor in favor of gold was that a given physical volume of each metal

*Ricardo changed his mind in 1819 and came out for gold, because of a concern that new mining machinery in the silver mines would result in a glut that would cause an "alteration" in silver's value, "whilst the same cause is not likely to operate upon the value of gold" (see Friedman, 1992, p. 153). He should have had an opportunity to discuss the matter with Chevalier after 1848!

at the Mint could produce a much higher value of gold coins than silver coins.

The bimetallic system did have its advantages, although any arrangement based on metal was destined to be vulnerable to shocks such as new discoveries or new mining technologies, wars, the changing tastes of the Asians, and the fruits of plunder. A convincing justification for bimetallism was made in 1791 by Alexander Hamilton in a remarkable document in which he invented the American monetary system, including its metallic standards, the decimal system, coin denominations, and many smaller details. The coins were to include three gold coins—$10, $5, and $2.50—then a dollar, half-dollar, quarters, dimes, and half-dimes in silver, plus a copper penny and a half-penny. The decimal structure of denominations was a radical break with the long tradition of Offa's pennies, with 240 to the pound, and the use of the multiple of twelve in so many other monetary systems that developed in Europe.

Although Hamilton set the pattern for economists in times to come by offering innumerable arguments "on the one hand" and then "on the other hand," he concludes after great deliberation that "The Secretary is upon the whole strongly inclined to the Opinion that a preference ought to be given to neither of the Metals for the monetary unit."[21] His document emphasizes the importance of having a money that would be acceptable in the varied systems of all countries and therefore warns against the consequences of converting one of the metals into "mere merchandize [*sic*]."[22] He goes on to make an even more important point that reveals his extraordinary foresight: "To annul the use of either of the metals, as money, is to abridge the quantity of circulating medium; and is liable to all the objections, which arise from a comparison of the benefits of a full, with the evils of a scanty circulation."[23] An insufficient supply of gold—except briefly in the 1850s—would turn out to be a recurring concern for the world economy during the entire nineteenth century.

There is a case that the great international gold standard was by no means an inevitable development. Marc Flandreau, a contemporary economist, has declared that the elimination of silver and its replacement by gold as the sole standard in the 1870s was "a blatant failure of international cooperation"—nothing more than a narrow-minded decision by the French to depress the price of silver in order to make life difficult for the Germans, who were trying to unload their stock of silver and establish a gold standard.[24] In 1911, the most prominent economist in the United States, Professor Irving Fisher of Yale, went even further, contending that the growing shortage of gold in the first half of the nineteenth century would have driven the world to desert bimetallism and transfer its allegiance to a silver standard, if gold had not been discovered in California and Australia "as though to save the day."[25]

The sequence of events leading to the final triumph of gold in Europe was indeed dramatic. As in the sixteenth and seventeenth centuries, North America and Asia continued to swing monetary developments in Europe and were the source of most of the severely protracted disturbances.

The story begins in the fledgling United States of America, which in 1791 followed Alexander Hamilton's advice to set the mint price of gold equal to \$19.3939 and the mint price of silver at \$1.2929, which works out to a ratio of 15:1. This happened to be the moment when supplies of gold from Brazil began to decline, to be followed soon afterward by the Latin American revolutions and a precipitous drop in precious metal shipments from the Western Hemisphere. Then Napoleon insisted on a specie-backed money system in France, followed by England's attempt to return to convertibility of sterling into gold. With supply falling and demand rising, the price of gold in the markets around the world soon climbed to more than fifteen times the mint price of silver. One could now bring fifteen ounces of silver to the U.S. Mint and receive one ounce of gold in return, then go into the market and use that ounce to buy more than fifteen ounces of silver, and then repeat the process.

The process was so irresistible that the United States found itself with only silver circulating and gold gradually disappearing from the monetary system. As a practical matter, the country was on a silver standard. This disparity between gold and silver persisted for over forty years. By 1834, the gold-silver price ratio in world markets had changed from 15:1 to about 15.625:1. A growing shortage of gold coin was now interfering with commercial and financial transactions. Michel Chevalier, the French economist who would be so concerned about the flood of gold from the California gold rush, spent over a year in the United States during 1833–1834 and wrote back home that "Since I have been in the United States, I have not seen there one piece of gold money, except on the scales at the Mint. Once minted, gold is embarked for Europe and remelted."[26]

In 1834, Congress finally recognized that 15:1 was no longer the appropriate ratio of the mint price of gold to the mint price of silver and that an adjustment closer to the reality of world markets could be postponed no longer. But Congress did not set the new ratio of mint prices at 15.625. Instead, it went all the way to 16:1, which worked out to the gold price of $20.67 an ounce that prevailed for another 99 years.

This step threw the prevailing flows of metal into reverse. Now it was profitable to bring an ounce of gold to the mint, obtain sixteen ounces of silver, go into the marketplace and repurchase the ounce of gold for the equivalent of only 15.625 ounces of silver, and repeat the process. The members of Congress were fully aware that they were stimulating the demand for gold in their choice of 16:1. Two factors, both strongly political, determined the decision. The first was a desire to "do something for gold," because modest amounts had been discovered in Virginia, the Carolinas, and Georgia. Second, these decisions coincided with Andrew Jackson's war against the Second Bank of the United States—known as Biddle's Bank—whose banknotes were a favored medium of exchange at the time. The politicians hoped that a rising supply of gold coins would be a ready substitute for the banknotes and would weaken Biddle's position.

The United States was now effectively on a gold standard, even though official legislation establishing the gold standard would not be enacted until 1900. Silver continued to function as subsidiary coinage, but gold was the major holding into which currency and bank deposits could be converted.[27]

These shifts were the inevitable consequence of using a commodity as a standard of value for the monetary system. The demand for gold and silver depends on more than monetary factors, for these metals have additional uses such as adornment or as hoards against uncertain futures. At the same time, nobody knows when new discoveries will occur. Thus, a variety of forces played upon world prices for gold and silver in the nineteenth century, creating constant disturbances within the monetary system as divergences developed between prices set in the marketplace and prices set at the mints. The experience of 1834 was just the first act in the drama. More violent upheavals were yet to come.

The discoveries at Sutter's Mill in California in 1848 and Hargrove's discovery in Australia in 1852 shook the world. The supply of gold coming into the markets ballooned and pushed the price of gold in the marketplace downward. Now silver appeared relatively expensive. People ceased to bring silver to the mints for coining and hoarded it by cashing in their paper money or bank deposits and even giving up gold in exchange for it. In 1850, about three times as much money circulated in silver coin as in gold coin; by 1860, the amounts were roughly even.[28]

Silver was the primary factor that kept gold from turning into a glut on the market after the discoveries in California and Australia. As it had for a long time, silver traveled to Asia during the 1850s in high volume, especially to India. Chevalier pointed out that the exports of silver acted like a "parachute" to cushion the fall in the price of gold and the expansion in the supply of money, thereby postponing the terrible inflation that he feared was inevitable. Shipments of silver into India quadrupled from the 1840s to the 1850s; French exports alone rose steadily from 82 million francs in 1850 to 458 million francs in 1857. Then came the American Civil War, which shut down American exports of cotton and led to an abrupt surge in the demand for Indian cotton; India obliged by importing even more silver in exchange.[29]

Just as suddenly, everything went into reverse after the Civil War came to an end. The demand for gold showed no signs of diminishing while the Indian demand for silver had a precipitous drop. During 1870–1875, total Indian imports of silver were smaller than in the year 1865 alone. When a huge silver deposit known as the Comstock Lode was discovered in Nevada in 1859, the glut had clearly switched over to silver.

For silver, the timing could not have been worse. In view of Britain's economic leadership in foreign trade, other countries began to give serious consideration to shifting to a pure gold standard like Britain's—but the difficulty of disposing of their stocks of silver in an oversupplied market was a major deterrent. Germany was especially eager to make the changeover to gold, for the Germans wanted to be perceived by the world as a great power. Germany also wanted to be on the same standard as Britain in order to meet the growing need for sterling to pay for raw material imports from the outposts of the British Empire. Ludwig Bamberger, a politician who played a major role in putting Germany on the gold standard, admitted as much when he declared, "We chose gold, not because gold is gold, but because Britain is Britain."[30]

Germany seized on the opportunity provided by its victory over France in 1871. The indemnity paid by the French relieved the Germans of the necessity of liquidating silver in order to finance its purchases of gold. They waited until 1873 to begin their silver sales, even expecting some to be bought by the French. The French not only refused to cooperate but took a more drastic step. On September 5, 1873, the day after the last payment on the indemnity, France limited its silver coinage to 280,000 francs a day and cut it again in November to 150,000.[31] The result was another sharp drop in the demand for silver.

The French ended up outdoing themselves. Too many other countries joined in the selling wave in an effort to avoid being caught with a stock of silver money that was worth less almost by the hour. The game became a self-fulfilling prophecy. A decision that the French perceived as a tactical rather than a strategic step provoked a steady fall in the price of silver from over sixty pence per ounce in the 1860s to only 52¾ pence in 1876 and 51 pence by the end of the 1870s.[32] By that time, an ounce of gold in the marketplace was bringing eighteen times as much as an ounce of silver; by the end of the century, the amount was up to thirty times as much as an ounce of silver. As the glut of silver drove the ratio of market prices further and further away from the ratio of prices at the mints, anyone who used gold to buy silver at such depressed prices in the market and then brought the silver into the mint for coinage enjoyed a profitable, riskless, and irresistible activity. The process rocked the gold standard to its very foundations and threatened to bring down the whole structure. The only defense was to eliminate silver as a monetary metal except for small coins.

That is precisely what happened during the course of the 1870s, beginning in 1873 in France, and also in the United States, as we shall see in the next chapter. That sequence of events explains why so many countries hastened to follow Germany into a pure gold-standard system.

Thus, the fabled international gold standard was built from the dust of the disaster to silver—by 1893, even the mints in India were closed to the coinage of silver. The gold discoveries in California and Australia and the Comstock Lode in Nevada, the appetite of Indians for silver, the American Civil War, and Germany's overwhelming ambition to be a great power in effect backed the world into a system that no one had anticipated and that many people were reluctant to accept. Once in place, however, the system displayed remarkable durability for the next half-century.

The establishment of the international gold standard during the 1870s was no guarantee of smooth sailing for the world economy, but the system did tend to limit the magnitude of the inevitable crises that developed from speculation, overinvestment, and excessive competition in a system in which governments offered no safety nets even when all hell appeared to be breaking loose. An outflow of gold served as a danger signal that soon gave rise to defensive actions by the central banks in the form of rising interest rates. If those efforts failed to stem the tide, the central banks tended to step in and come to one another's aid, frequently in partnership with the larger private banking institutions.

The very idea that a major nation would allow itself to run out of gold was unthinkable—credibility, in other words, was beyond question—which meant that these kinds of credits were forthcoming before matters flew out of control. The easing in the crisis that resulted then made possible repayment of the credits, and the repayments renewed the credibility that kept the whole system functioning. These facilities, it should be emphasized, were available among the major powers. Countries on the periphery—including the United States—often had to fend for themselves and did run out of gold or silver reserves.

Devotion to the system was so complete that countries could even take the drastic step of suspending convertibility of their currency into gold under special circumstances and continue to do business almost as though nothing had happened. On the rare occasion when a member country was forced to suspend convertibility, everyone understood that the step was taken to *protect* its gold hoard so that it would be able to avoid deserting the system when the crisis was past. Most of these special cases arose in times of war. We have already seen how Britain set the precedent during the Napoleonic Wars. Convertibility was suspended in the United States from 1862 until 1879. In both cases, convertibility was ultimately reestablished at the old parity. These precedents had a profound influence on Britain's decision in 1925 to return to gold convertibility at the old parity after going off in World War I. The French, however, took a less orthodox course in the 1920s by resetting the relation between the franc and gold at a rate that gave full recognition to the enormous rise in French prices over the years since 1915. The French lived more happily than the British for a while, but not forever after. In the case of both France and Britain, however, any course other than a return to the gold standard would have been unthinkable.

One of the most spectacular—but by no means atypical—crises in the age of the gold standard occurred in 1890, largely as a result of ill-advised and mismanaged investments in Argentina by the respected London house of Baring Brothers. Barings came perilously close to bringing the Bank of England itself to its knees.

Along with their devotion to the gold standard, the British had long led the way among the European nations in the development of financial markets and institutions. As the resources of the City expanded, the British capital market became the leading source of funds for economic growth all around the world. Britain was the largest supplier of capital for the development of the railroad system in the United States, but British capital also poured into many developing economies in Latin America and in Asia. Argentina was a special favorite. Henry Dana Noyes, one of the best informed and most articulate of American commentators on the financial scene of the late nineteenth century, observed that "Into no foreign state had English capital rushed with such reckless eagerness as into the Argentine Republic."[33] Noyes took a dim view, arguing that the Argentine climate "was precarious for production, its currency depreciated, and its government untrustworthy."[34]

Noyes's observations have the advantage of hindsight. The enthusiasm for Argentina from 1870 to 1890 was well justified by the impressive growth achieved by this nation. Immigration to Argentina in those years doubled the population, with Europeans who were very different from the "flotsam and jetsam" that headed to the United States. Many brought capital with them to acquire and develop the vast territories of land available for ranching and for agriculture. The result was a surging demand for roads, railways, waterworks, and industrial enterprises. Just during the brief period of 1882–1889, European investors poured $1 billion into Argentina.[35] As one knowledgeable observer has pointed out, there was "no well-governed country in Europe which could get so large a credit in relation to its people."[36]

This drama played itself out in classic fashion. By the end of the 1880s, credit was pouring in so rapidly that service on the outstanding debts began to outrun capacity to pay, the flood of money was clinging to the sticky fingers of the politicians, and inflation began to raise its ugly head. In just one year, money in circulation increased by $270 million.

Meanwhile, back in Europe, business activity was accelerating, stimulated in part by an enormous borrowing of £11 million by the British government to build ironclad battleships, followed by similar efforts in France, Russia, and Germany. The stock markets across Europe were roaring ahead and building speculative froth of their own; on Wall Street from 1884 to 1889, stock prices appreciated by over 50 percent.*[37] At the same time, capital was also moving to the newly discovered nitrate mines of Chile and the gold and diamond mines in South Africa.

In 1889, concerned about the swindling and greed that were sweeping the speculative manias, the Bank of England and the German Reichsbank sharply raised their key interest rates. The impact was immediate and fevers cooled—which meant that security prices fell and took an excruciating toll on those poor investors who had let themselves be lured in at the very top of the bubbles.

The timing was unfortunate. The Argentine wheat crop failed, followed by a bloody political revolution in the summer of 1890. Financial panic broke out in Buenos Aires. The repercussions on the leading banking houses in London were immediate, most notably on Baring Brothers.

*See Wirth, 1893, pp. 219–229, for a vivid description of the derrings-do. For a more scholarly and technical analysis of the events leading up to the Barings crisis, the tensions between the Bank and the Treasury, and the uncertain and uneasy development of the art of central banking, see Pressnell, 1968, especially pp. 167–193.

Baring Brothers had underwritten £42 million of Argentine securities during the 1880s—£28 million in 1888 and 1889 alone—a significant portion of which remained unsold, leaving Barings the unwilling owners. The message in the family motto that had become the company logo, *Virtus in arduis* (Fortitude under difficulty), now seemed very garbled indeed.

As the Barings were among the most respected families in Britain, the shock was devastating far beyond even the huge amounts involved. The diary of one contemporary reported, subsequent to the resolution of the crisis, that "The West End social life of Lord Revelstoke (the partner blamed for the crisis) so enraged the Stock Exchange that it was 'ready to lynch him.'"[38] Barings had been a leader in international financial markets "when the Rothschilds still bought and sold old clothes."[39] In 1792, they had played a primary role in financing the British war effort against the French Revolution and Napoleon. In 1803, they played the lead in the financing of the American purchase of the Louisiana Territory from the French. They led the European financing of U.S. foreign trade and the U.S. government up to the outbreak of the Civil War. In the early 1840s, the managing partner, Alexander Baring, later Lord Ashburton, was ambassador to the United States and negotiated the Maine–Canada border with Secretary of State Daniel Webster. Ashburton's direct descendants served as Chancellor of the Exchequer, as First Lord of the Admiralty, as Viceroy of India, and as *de facto* ruler of Egypt from 1883 to 1907.

The Barings crisis could not have hit at a worse moment. The Bank of England's gold reserve had been as low as £9 million in 1889 and was less than £11 million at the height of the crisis. Baring Brothers alone was going to require at least £4 million immediately in order to avoid closing its doors.[40] The Bank of England now anticipated withdrawals of gold by the Bank of Spain and the State Bank of Russia. Although the Bank's interest rate had just been raised to 6 percent, William Lidderdale, Governor of the Bank (as the office of chief executive was known) and no fool, was convinced that further increases in the Bank's interest rate would merely signal the intensity of the difficulties they were facing. "It would have taken a very high rate indeed to bring gold over in quantity," Lidderdale later explained to the Chancellor of the Exchequer.[41] Nevertheless, *The Economist* magazine reported on November 15 that the Bank's gold reserve was "just about sufficient for ordinary home requirements, but it was too small to meet exceptional demands."[42]

In desperation, the Bank turned to the Rothschilds, a powerful competitor of Barings. Rothschilds and the Bank together put up £15 million as a start to the complex and painful process of paying off the loans that Barings had been forced to make to finance their unwanted inventory of unsold Argentine issues. The Rothschilds were then asked to serve as intermediary for a loan of £2 million of gold from the Bank of France (on the previous occasion when the Bank had borrowed from the French, in 1839, Barings had served as the intermediary). The French agreed to the loan, at only 3 percent interest, and even shipped the gold across the Channel to British soil. Another £1.5 million in German gold coin was obtained from Russia, while the Russians also agreed to refrain from withdrawing their substantial deposits at Barings. At that point, the Bank of France offered an additional £1 million in gold. Follow-the-leader: always eager to be in good graces with the Bank of England, a consortium of domestic banks in London now stepped forward and agreed to put up most of the remaining funds required to satisfy the creditors of Baring Brothers.[43]

Perhaps the most remarkable aspect of the whole operation was the discretion and secrecy with which it was carried out. The Governor of the Bank of England had excellent sources of information on what was going on in the City, and on Friday, November 7, the first rumors reached him about some big houses that might be in danger. Three days later, Lidderdale had the Chancellor approach Rothschild; before the week was out, the Russians had come along. By the 14th, word "began to ooze out that something was up," but by that afternoon the entire deed was done.[44]

It was indeed an elegant performance. Charles Kindleberger, a leading historian of financial crises, has observed that the rescue operations in the Barings crisis were seen "as a measure of the strength of the London financial system more than the Baring failure was taken as a sign of weakness."[45] He goes on to cite a judgment expressed by another historian just 25 years after the crisis that the Bank of England is "the leader of the most colossal agglomeration of financial power which the world has so far witnessed."[46]

Without the cooperation of the French and the Russians, the story would have had a horrible ending, but the tradition of cooperation was well established by that time. The Bank of England, supposedly the keystone of the system, drew on the support of the Bank of France nine times between 1826 (also with the help of the Rothschilds) and 1920, in addition to the help rendered in the Barings crisis; in other crises, the city of Hamburg and the Reichsbank came to England's aid. In 1861, the Bank of France drew on support from the Bank of England, the Russian State Bank, and the Bank of Amsterdam.[47] The Swedish Riskbank borrowed from the Danish National Bank in 1882. In 1898, the Banks of France and England cooperated to help out the Reichsbank. The Bank of France and the Reichsbank came to the aid of the Bank of England in 1906 and 1907.

All this assistance was predicated on the assumption that preservation of convertibility into gold at fixed rates was the bedrock of economic policy, before which *all other considerations* had to give way. Without that assumption, the credits that gold-standard countries provided to one another would have been far less generous and would have come with much more onerous conditions.

The classic sequence of events when trouble developed is the opposite of what tends to happen in our own time. Who but the naive today would put such firm confidence in either credibility or cooperation? Now speculators flee a currency in trouble, putting it into ever greater trouble, destabilizing its relationships with the outside world until they become completely untenable. In the nineteenth century, a pledge to maintain gold parity was accepted at face value. At the end of the twentieth century, such a pledge was usually taken as a sign that whatever parity existed would soon go down the tube. In the contemporary scene, only grudging cooperation is forthcoming, and then with strings attached so lacerating that domestic political considerations may even necessitate rejecting the proffered aid.

Nevertheless, the magnitude of the emergency of 1890 brought home to all the central bankers the necessity of holding much larger gold reserves than they had considered adequate up to that point. Faith in the power of interest-rate policy to hold disaster at bay was not abandoned, but emphasis began to shift toward accumulating a hoard of gold big enough to build credibility to a degree beyond question. This step would reduce the heavy reliance on managing the gold reserves solely by varying interest rates. The German war reserve accumulated after 1900, and held separate from the Reichsbank's reserve, became an object of envy. Shades of the emperors of Byzantium!

Barry Eichengreen, a leading authority on the history and functioning of the gold standard, emphasizes that the critical reason for the success of the gold-standard system was the unquestioning attachment to credibility—the rejection of any possibility that a nation would allow itself to go permanently off gold or to vary its gold parity—and to the cooperation that such credibility warranted. Other writers, such as Charles Kindleberger, are convinced that it was the hegemony of the Bank of England that kept the system functioning through thick and thin, leading the way toward interest-rate changes, serving as lender of last resort, and managing international cooperation. He echoed the views of John Maynard Keynes, who referred to the Bank as the "conductor of the international orchestra."[48]

All the experts agree that the gold standard operated in a congenial economic and political environment. Despite recurrent financial turbulence, the period between the end of the American Civil War and the outbreak of World War I was marked by a mighty force of economic growth and industrialization in both America and Europe. Peace helped, too: no major wars were fought within Europe from 1870 to 1914, while the only military activity to engage the United States was the Spanish-American War of 1898.

There was an additional element of great importance, more political than economic. An economy with a fixed rate of exchange between its currency and the currency of other nations must be prepared to see its domestic economy dominated by the requirements of the gold standard. If the gold stock was flowing outward, interest rates had to rise to attract foreign funds and the domestic economy had to be suppressed to curtail imports. No safety nets of any kind were allowed. That was bad news for the workers who lost their jobs and saw their wages cut as well as for business firms whose profits were slashed. But those were the rules of the game. The system simply could not have survived if the objectives of domestic economic stability and high employment had dominated the objective of defending the gold stock. No matter how intense the pain, the political arms of the governments—parliaments or executives—never dreamed of intervening, because the pain was for the Greater Good.[40]

Remember that this was the age of Queen Victoria and King Edward VII. The type of political outcry that we would expect today was in large part absent in the nineteenth-century environment of Europe, or, to the extent that voices were raised, men in positions of power paid little heed to them. Even among economists, macroeconomic considerations and business cycle analysis did not occupy the attention of mainstream theorists; it was only in the underworld of such people as Karl Marx that those concerns were expressed. The doctrine of laissez-faire and minimal government interference in business and financial affairs was the ruling philosophy for most of the period.

This viewpoint suggests that the success of the international gold standard might have been more symptom than cause. It did operate in an environment in which growth continuously bailed out policy errors, the burdens of international debts within Europe never expanded beyond manageable levels, and international cooperation could be taken for granted rather than depending on painful and conditional support.

A famous contemporary got the point at the time, without any benefit of hindsight: Benjamin Disraeli told a group of Glasgow merchants that "It is the greatest delusion in the world to attribute the commercial preponderance and prosperity of England to our having a gold standard. Our gold standard is not the cause, but the consequence of our commercial prosperity."[50] If ever there was a time in human history when circumstances combined to make the world economic system function as people expected it to function, this was it.

The widespread failure to recognize the profound truth in Disraeli's observation is eloquent testimony to the power of the mystique that the gold standard acquired in the course of the nineteenth century, despite the choppy history from which it originated. The unquenchable conviction that the gold standard *explained* its benign environment is the dominant reason why the Europeans insisted on putting themselves through all the trials and tribulations associated with efforts to restore and then to maintain the gold standard from 1921 until its final demise in 1971.

Although much of this chapter applies equally to Europe and the United States, the differences between what happened on the opposite sides of the Atlantic Ocean may have been more profound than the similarities. The key distinctions were political in nature. All of these differences were shaped by the unique character of a brand-new country only one hundred years old when all of these events were taking place. The United States was also situated far away from Europe's two thousand years of shared history and the old-boy network that dominated its financial institutions. On top of all that, American society was more open and fluid than European society, the forces of democracy and the passion for liberty and equality were more vocal and more determined, and most of the wealth was "new wealth" rather than wealth handed down by a landed aristocracy or the ancestral fortunes like those of the Rothschilds or Barings. Until the very end of the nineteenth century, therefore, many Americans were reluctant to join in the European enthusiasm for the system, especially with the constraints it imposed on freedom of action.

The final years of the 1890s in the United States made a fitting climax to the story of the nineteenth-century gold standard. We shall now see what led up to those events and how the local variations on the theme of near-disaster played themselves out.

16

The Most Stupendous Conspiracy and the Endless Chain

The United States strides the world today as a financial colossus, but this perception is a far cry from the America of the nineteenth century. In those days, bank failures were common, foreigners were fickle in their taste for American securities, and the U.S. gold stock was all too often on the verge of pouring out to other nations. The stability of the currency and the financial bases of growth were constantly vulnerable to attack from the outside.

Indeed, as this chapter makes clear, the so-called Gay Nineties were far from gay. The era is also known as the Gilded Age. The very rich did live like kings, but these years were marked by a persistent shortage of monetary gold in the United States. The decade was a sequence of cliff-hangers with the gold stock, record-high unemployment, political tumult, social unrest, and huge bear markets on Wall Street.

The nation had no easy means to cushion these blows. Americans enjoyed none of the credibility that permitted the central banks of the major powers—governing financial institutions such as the Bank of England and the Bank of France—to carry on their clubby habits of borrowing gold from one another whenever any of them happened to be in trouble. Consequently, Americans were denied the opportunity to receive credits from the others when they needed credits and were excluded from the process even when they were in a position to extend credits. Yet the United States needed the gold if Americans were to continue to do business with a world in which the gold standard was becoming the dominant monetary system among the major powers.

It was not just that the United States was considered an upstart nation, too young to be reliable as a financial partner. The consistency of the American attachment to the gold standard was always under suspicion. Uncle Sam's behavior did nothing to change this image. The management of nineteenth-century financial policy in America appeared to Europeans like a ship with no keel, where the passengers crowded together on the bridge and shouted the captain down, so that the ship's course was set by the loudest shouts and even then its route remained uncertain.

Popular opinion among Americans held that the gold standard was a devilish concoction of foreigners, especially the hated British and British Jews in particular. One typical cartoon of the 1890s carried the title, "THE ENGLISH OCTOPUS: It feeds on nothing but gold!" A map of the world appears below this caption, with the tentacles of the octopus extending out from Britain and wrapping themselves around every continent. A second caption appears below: "'The Rothschilds own 1,600,000,000 in gold.'—*Chicago Daily News*. This is nearly one-half the gold in the Chicago wheat pit."[1]

The Europeans had an additional reason to keep Americans outside the pale: the United States had no central bank like the Bank of England. Whatever management of financial policy did exist was in the hands of the Treasury Department in Washington, whose leadership was inherently political and answerable to Congress. Yet Americans were stubborn about changing their ways. From the very beginning, a largely rural and self-centered nation displayed an instinctive suspicion of city folks, bankers, and anyone who was suspected of fooling around with foreigners. Americans clung to their atomized commercial banking structure, with its thousands of little independent banks dispersed throughout the countryside and regulated by the states rather than by Washington. Much of this rickety edifice remained in place right through to the final moments of the twentieth century.

Most political rhetoric reflected these themes over and over again. America's financial provincialism persisted even as the country became more industrialized and a rising share of the population drifted toward the cities. As late as 1913, when the United States decided at last to join the world and establish a central bank, the structure of the Federal Reserve System was braced with strong regional checks and balances that restrained the power of the governing body in Washington.

Another and perhaps even more important problem festered throughout the nineteenth century: the United States waited until 1900 before legally committing itself to a gold standard. Until then, Americans remained officially on Hamilton's bimetallic standard, in which silver had equal standing with gold. These arrangements were supported by the powerful and boisterous silver interests, and not just because silver mining was an important economic activity in the western states. Farmers and others who were characteristically debtors favored the largest possible money supply and saw inflation as a blessing rather than a curse. Silver plus gold equaled more money in the system than gold alone. But silver became something bigger than just a viable candidate to serve with gold as a monetary standard. Silver was a potent symbol for the struggle of the Little Man against the Established Powers. Propelled by universal suffrage, the rallying cries of equality and democracy rang out louder here than in the Old World.

No wonder foreigners were so skeptical of America's intentions with regard to gold.

In 1861, early in the Civil War, a shrinking gold stock led Congress to suspend convertibility of dollars into gold, a customary move under the circumstances. In another customary wartime move, the Treasury financed part of the wartime expenditures by issuing a new paper currency. This paper money, convertible into nothing at all, carried the official imprint of "U.S. Notes." They were more commonly known as greenbacks, however, a nickname that is still in use as a generic identifier of today's American dollar—which is also convertible into nothing at all. Like today's paper money, the greenbacks were legal tender, which means that a creditor could not legally refuse to receive them in payment of debts due; as a result, the greenbacks were also referred to on occasion as "legal tenders." Roughly $300 million in greenbacks were in circulation from 1863 until 1971, at which time it was decreed that they were no longer serving any function that was not already adequately provided by Federal Reserve notes.[2] From that point forward, the Treasury stopped issuing greenbacks and, in 1991, the entire remaining stock held by the Treasury was destroyed. It is worth noting that Federal Reserve notes are also green on one side—and are no more convertible into gold today than were the greenbacks of earlier days.

Gold did not disappear from the scene during the greenback era, although gold coins in circulation fell from over $200 million at the outbreak of war in 1860 to only $150 million in 1865 and continued to decline to a low point of $65 million in 1875.[3] The government lived up to its contractual promises to pay interest and principal on the national debt in gold but simultaneously required importers to obey the law to pay their customs duties in gold. Gold continued to circulate in daily payments in the West.

A dollar in greenbacks never commanded a dollar's worth of gold, because there was no certainty that the day would ever return when people could take their greenbacks to the bank and exchange them for gold coins. This condition was the same as in England during the Napoleonic Wars when sterling convertibility was suspended: if paper currency and bank deposits are not convertible into gold, gold ceases to serve as money and becomes a commodity whose price in terms of money is destined to fluctuate.

During most of the Civil War, a dollar's worth of gold cost about $1.30 in greenbacks. In an audacious experiment in 1864, when Jay Gould and Jim Fiske tried to corner the gold market, one buyer paid as much as $310,000 for approximately $100,000 in gold, but that was only a transitory event. Matters improved after the Union victory in 1865, and by 1869 the greenback notes were being valued at better than 90¢ on the dollar. In January 1875, Congress passed legislation that pledged full resumption of convertibility by January 1, 1879, and authorized the Treasury to borrow the money to acquire a gold reserve, if such a step should prove necessary.

The road to 1879, however, was marked by two notable events that are striking examples of the law of unintended consequences. One took place right after the end of the war; the other came along eight years later.

The first of these events was launched by the Secretary of the Treasury's annual report for 1865. Using the nomenclature of "legal-tenders" to refer to the greenbacks, the Secretary asserted that "The present legal-tender acts . . . ought not to remain in force one day longer than shall be necessary to enable the people to prepare for a return to the constitutional currency."[4] This expression of rectitude enjoyed wide public support. In early April 1866, the House of Representatives joined in by passing a resolution of support by a margin of 144 to 6. Appropriate legislation to start retirement of the greenbacks followed ten days later.

This overwhelming consensus was about to fall apart almost as soon as it had come together. Seldom have the public and its representatives failed so completely to foresee the consequences of their decisions. The myopia is difficult to comprehend. Throughout history, the arrival of peace had always led to an economic downturn, including persistent deflationary pressures on the price level. The end of the Civil War proved to be no exception. Prices had more than doubled in the course of the war, but by 1868 the price level had already fallen by some 15 percent. Financial rectitude was likely to make matters worse.

Second thoughts on the decisions of 1866 appeared in short order and more than a decade of public outcry lay ahead. With prices falling, reducing the supply of greenbacks to an amount equal to the available stock of gold would be certain to intensify the pain already inflicted by deflation on farmers, many business firms, and all debtors. Early resumption of convertibility, virtuous as it had appeared only three years earlier, now began to generate strong opposition.

The problem was that, to paraphrase a familiar aphorism, the $20.67 represented by an ounce of gold didn't buy what it used to buy. Resumption of convertibility would have put the country into a position where the existing gold stock would have purchased less than half what it could have bought before 1860, making the monetary noose even tighter. Even worse, the purchasing power of foreigners' gold would also have withered, and the prices of American exports of cotton and grains would have remained out of line with world markets. Not even the experts seem to have given any consideration to officially cutting the amount of gold in the dollar in half, thereby doubling the effective size of the gold stock. Legal currency debasement of that nature was just not part of the nineteenth-century view of what the gold standard was all about. Just as in Britain after the Napoleonic Wars, resumption was going to have to wait until the price level had receded to a manageable level before the currency could be locked back into gold.

The second example of the law of unintended consequences took place in 1873, seven long years after the pious expressions about the desirability of an early resumption of convertibility into gold. This one turned out to be a real blockbuster.*

By 1873, pressure was building to stop pussyfooting around about the promises for resumption. The time had come to tidy up the currency and finish the job.[5] Congress held an extended series of hearings on the subject and then passed the Coinage Act of 1873, which listed the various denominations of gold and silver coins to be minted by the Treasury from that time forward. The legislation passed through Congress by the overwhelming margins of 110 to 13 in the House and 36 to 14 in the Senate.

The Act of 1873 contained a startling omission. There is not a single word that refers to the historical standard silver dollar of 371.25 grains that dated all the way back to Alexander Hamilton's establishment of the coinage of the United States. The only mention of silver is for subsidiary small-denomination silver coins. The consequences were momentous: the Coinage Act of 1873 finished off the legal status of bimetallism in the United States.

If the Coinage Act of 1873 had included the standard silver dollar, the demand for silver in the United States to coin silver dollars would have brought huge sums of silver for coinage to American shores. Gold, in contrast, would have moved out from the United States into world markets, to be converted into silver at an irresistible rate of exchange, just as had happened from 1791 to 1834 when gold was in short supply and silver was the underpriced metal. Under those circumstances, resumption of convertibility in 1879 would in all likelihood have been to a silver standard rather than a gold standard.

*The description of events that follows relies heavily on Milton Friedman's elegant and charming discussion of this matter in Friedman, 1992, Chapter 3, especially pp. 51–61.

This event occurred at the precise moment when the price of silver was in any case under powerful downward pressure in world markets, in response to the French decision to reduce the volume of silver coinage and German efforts to replace their silver stock with gold. Even worse, the Act of 1873 occurred at a moment when the pressures of deflation in the United States began to intensify, as output was growing rapidly while the money supply failed to follow along. Wholesale prices would fall by 30 percent by 1878, and stock prices followed suit.[6]

When the silver advocates woke up to what had happened, they were in a state of shock over what had taken place under their very noses. Later on, after much of the dust had settled, Senator William Stewart referred to the demonetization of silver as the "crime of the nineteenth century." One of his fellow opponents, Senator John Reagan, carried this theme even further by declaring that these events comprised "the greatest legislative crime and the most stupendous conspiracy against the welfare of the people of the United States and of Europe which this or any other age has witnessed."[7]

Some scholars are convinced that what has come to be known as the Crime of 1873 inspired Frank Baum's immortal story, *The Wizard of Oz*, published in 1900. One could argue that the book is a parable in favor of silver coinage and against gold. Oz is the abbreviation of ounce, and the Land of Oz is the East where gold is the favorite. The cyclone that comes out of the West with such power is the movement for unlimited coinage of silver. Dorothy is the plucky, kindhearted American who represents the little people against the moguls of finance. The Emerald City is Washington, and the Wizard, who lives there, the personification of humbug. A detailed and entertaining analysis of this case appears in a delightful article by a Rutgers professor named Hugh Rockoff.[8]

Crime the Coinage Act of 1873 was not; conspiracy it might well have been. Contemporary evidence demonstrates that the consequences were clear to the major decision makers. H. R. Linderman, the director of the mint, advised the Secretary of the Treasury in 1872 that ". . . Several causes are now at work, all tending to an excess of supply over demand for silver, and its consequent depreciation." In his memoirs, published in 1877, he observed that the Act "placed the United States upon the single gold standard. . . . The weight of opinion in Europe and America was against the practicability of maintaining a double standard on any basis which might be selected, in favor of a single gold standard." John Sherman, chairman of the Senate Finance Committee, had since 1867 made little secret of his determination to demonetize silver. Sherman even went so far as to have a bill for that purpose drafted at the end of 1869. He was joined in his efforts by both Linderman and the Secretary of the Treasury.[9]

It is difficult to find a satisfactory explanation for why so few people beyond this tiny circle were aware of what lay ahead. There had been no effort to keep the contents of the Coinage Act a secret. The Act was before Congress for three years before its passage by overwhelming majorities. The chairman of the House subcommittee that considered the bill declared that it had come to him from a Senate committee that had given it "as careful attention as I have ever known a committee to bestow on any measure." Congress ordered the Act to be printed thirteen times. Its text occupied 144 columns in the *Congressional Globe*. Representative Hooper, who steered the Act through the House, was explicit in his references to the demonetization of silver. Linderman's Report of 1872 had been published by the time Congress voted the passage of the Act. If, as Lincoln had asserted, you can fool all of the people some of the time, this was clearly a case in point.[10]

The main drama of the 1870s was to occur in 1879, following the official resumption of convertibility of paper currency into gold that took place as scheduled on January 1. Some of the gold on hand to meet demands for redemptions had been accumulated from a surplus of tax revenue (largely tariff receipts) over expenditure, with the remainder purchased abroad with funds that the Treasury borrowed in the capital markets.

Yet conditions were ominous and the viability of the resumption process remained uncertain. Despite passage of the Resumption Law, the credibility of the nation's devotion to gold appeared to be every bit as questionable as it had been in the past. America's export trade was slipping and the prospect of a significant loss of gold to Europe became a general expectation. How certain could anyone be that the Treasury would be either able or willing to live up to the obligation that the Resumption Act had imposed on it?

The day was saved for the U.S. gold stock by a remarkable act of nature. In May, snow fell in France, and England suffered a destructive frost, followed by rains that persisted until late summer. The disaster to British and French crops was almost unprecedented. Bad weather also hit Austria, Germany, and Russia, where the wheat crops were the poorest and smallest in ten years. Just to help matters along, the Indian cotton crop failed. As we shall see, this lucky turn of events was only the first of several occasions on which nature would be kind enough to come to the rescue of the U.S. gold stock at the last minute.

While the catastrophic European weather set wheat prices soaring, the weather in America was perfect. U.S. crops were turning out to be enormous. In addition, an event with great future significance occurred to provide further help to the American trade balance: the tidewater pipeline from the newly discovered Pennsylvania oil wells was completed, swelling American exports of oil to the whole world.

Gold soon began to travel back from Europe toward America. By mid-autumn of 1879, $60 million had come in to the United States. The government's reserve of gold, already rising, climbed from $120 million at the close of June to $157 million in early November. The Treasury was now in a position to pay out gold not just for notes presented for redemption but for the government's ordinary disbursements for goods and services. This was just the beginning. It was almost as though Joseph were on hand making his weather forecasts to Pharaoh: for at least another three years, the extraordinary balance in America's favor in agriculture persisted and attracted even more gold from across the oceans.[11]

We now fast-forward to 1890, the year the Barings crisis hit in London. Just as the currency crisis of 1998 in Asia ricocheted onto markets for Russian and Latin American securities, the Barings crisis of 1890 had a devastating impact on the appetite of foreigners for dollar-denominated securities. The backlash from Barings would turn out to be only the first of a number of forces that shaped the first half of the 1890s into a roller-coaster of economic and financial horrors.

Even before the impact of the Barings crisis had begun to be felt in the United States, another major victory by the silver camp served to aggravate the continuing doubts about America's commitment to the gold standard. In July 1890, Congress passed the Sherman Silver Purchase Act (named after the same Sherman who had wanted to demonetize silver twenty years earlier), in essence to obtain support for higher tariffs from the eighteen senators from the nine states west of the Mississippi, where most of the silver resources of the United States were located. The Act stipulated that the Treasury would be required to make monthly purchases of silver to the tune of $50 million annually, double the amounts authorized in the legislation of 1878. Furthermore, payments for the silver were to be made in a new paper currency, the Treasury notes of 1890, which were full legal tender and were redeemable on demand in either gold or silver at the discretion of the Secretary of the Treasury.

That was not all. The Sherman Act was passed when Congress was also at the point of appropriating substantial additional sums for regular government expenditures that would significantly increase the outflow of money from the Treasury. As the Treasury was already having a difficult time making ends meet, the new legislation soon pushed the government into a deficit position. Today, the government would go into the markets and borrow to finance the deficit. In the 1890s, the first response was to cover the deficit by drawing down cash balances—legal tender paper currency or gold itself. Cruel irony was added to the situation when the silver bloc saw an early upward burst in the price of silver rapidly dissipate under the pressure of such heavy selling abroad that the new source of demand was soon overwhelmed.

The timing could not have been worse. Once the Barings crisis broke loose in London, Europeans not only liquidated their holdings of American securities; they chose to convert the proceeds into their home currencies, which ultimately meant shipping their money back in the form of gold. In the first six months of 1891, exports of gold from the United States exceeded the total of gold exports in any twelve-month period in the previous 25 years.[12] The outflow made an alarming dent in the reserve the Treasury held against redemption of the legal tender paper currency into gold. Now everything pointed to a run on the U.S. gold stock, in which the only objective of each holder was to cash out his dollars into gold before every other holder could beat him to the windows of the Treasury.

Nature came to the rescue in 1891 on short notice, just as it had saved the day in 1879. The South Russian wheat crop, the second most important European source of supply, was a total failure. The French harvest was the worst since the disasters of 1879. The farms of the United States, meanwhile, produced the largest grain crop in history, 65 percent above the previous record. Once again, the outflow of gold was stemmed.

This time the respite was brief. No sooner had 1892 rolled around than the golden hemorrhage resumed. By the end of May, the Treasury's gold reserve had fallen to $114 million, just barely above the $100 million minimum that Congress had intended the Treasury to maintain. The Treasury decided that there was no choice except to halt all government payments in gold; everything was now to be paid for in the form of legal tender paper currency. This unfortunate if unavoidable decision served only to increase the demand for gold among the public and foreigners and to raise even further doubts about the nation's commitment to the gold standard. Meanwhile, imports of merchandise had risen so rapidly in the first nine months of 1893 that they exceeded exports by the staggering sum of $447 million. In his annual report of 1892, a despondent Secretary of the Treasury confessed that a heavy deficit in revenue was impending, and warned that the whole redemption machinery of the government was in peril.[13]

The situation had by no means reached its climax. In February, the Philadelphia & Reading Railway went into bankruptcy. In April, the Treasury's reserve slipped below $100 million. In May, National Cordage, the most widely held and actively traded industrial stock on the New York Stock Exchange, followed Philadelphia & Reading into bankruptcy; its stock fell from 147 in January to less than 10 in May, pulling the whole stock market down with it in a panic collapse. Now, the solvency of the banks appeared to be in jeopardy, provoking the public to rush to withdraw their bank deposits—even paper currency seemed preferable. The run on the banks added to the hysteria and drove the interest rate on the shortest-term loans in the New York money market up to 74 percent; time loans were unobtainable.[14] Subsequent railroad failures before the end of 1893 included the Erie, the Northern Pacific, and the Atchison, Topeka, & Santa Fe, to say nothing of fifteen thousand other companies and five hundred banks. In the face of these catastrophes, the only step the government took to relieve the situation was to repeal the Sherman Silver Purchase Act of 1890.

The aftermath of all these terrible events was extremely unpleasant. Unemployment in the United States exceeded 10 percent of the labor force during every year from 1893 to 1898, by far the worst experience of any era in our history aside from the depression of the 1930s.

In April 1894, a ragtag group of several thousand unemployed men organized themselves into what came to be known as Coxey's Army. Starting eastward from the Mississippi, they overran towns and seized railroad trains before appearing at the Capitol in Washington to demand relief. Troops had to be called out to disperse them. In the following month, downward pressure on wages provoked a strike at the Pullman Company (more formally, the Pullman Palace Car Company) that lasted for over two months before being terminated by a government injunction, the first use of the anti-trust laws against labor unions; the socialist leader Eugene Debs directed the strike and spent six months in jail for his efforts. In July, labor groups took possession of the railway system, converging on Chicago while their leaders opened formal headquarters there, from which they issued proclamations "with the assurance of military conquerors."[15] The infantry had to be called out on that occasion. Nature decided to reverse her blessings and stunt crops in the United States in 1894 while providing bumper supplies to Europe. Matters were so bad that Civil Service Commissioner Theodore Roosevelt had to sell four acres at Sagamore Hill to keep his family solvent.[16]

Meanwhile, back in Washington, nothing hopeful was happening to the Treasury's financial position. The excess of expenditure over revenue only worsened. The difference had been covered in the beginning by paying out the legal tender notes, but when they were exhausted the Treasury had no choice but to start using gold to meet its current expenditures. As a result, the gold reserve was deteriorating rapidly. In February 1894, John Carlisle, the Secretary of the Treasury, decided to cover the deficit by selling a new issue of bonds that required payment in gold. His scheme failed, as the market gave the new issue a cold shoulder despite the high rate of interest that Carlisle placed on it to sweeten the deal.

Swallowing his pride, Carlisle traveled to New York himself and put intense pressure on the big banks to buy the government's bond issue, laying patriotism on the line and insisting that another panic must be averted at all costs. Reluctantly, the banks succumbed to his appeal for help. Shortly thereafter, $59 million in gold coin arrived at the Treasury in payment for the new bonds. That was the good news. The bad news was that $24 million of the gold the banks used to pay for the bonds had come from a like amount of legal-tender currency that they had redeemed at the Treasury for gold just a short time before. In actuality, nearly half of the payment for the bonds had been made in legal tenders rather than in the additional supply of gold that the Secretary so urgently required. The game had increased the gold reserve by only $35 million, not $59 million. After these shenanigans, the Treasury's reserve remained at only $107 million. The deficit for October 1894 soared to $13 million and the gold reserve sank to $52 million.

Carlisle turned once again to the New York banks. Once again, they responded to his urgent request for a loan. But once again, they redeemed legal tenders into gold to meet about half the money they had paid the Treasury for the bonds. A deeply distressed President Cleveland complained that "We have an endless chain in operation, constantly depleting the Treasury's gold and never near a final rest."[17] In January 1895, $26 million in gold was exported from the United States and $45 million in gold was withdrawn from the Treasury in redemption of legal tenders. The Treasury's gold reserve was approaching $40 million and sinking at a rate of $2 million a day.[18]

As Noyes describes the situation in the final week of January 1895, "Merchants and bankers now busied themselves putting their houses in order against the expected surrender of the Treasury. . . . [There was a] common feeling that a few days, and possibly a few hours, would settle the question finally."[19]

The five years from the passage of the Sherman Silver Act and the Barings crisis in early 1890 to the climax of January 1895 bracketed a series of gold-related disasters that slammed into the American economy with unparalleled magnitude and duration. The nature of both the causes and the effects of those events would reappear in identical form during the catastrophes and contagions that beset the emerging nations one hundred years later, from the Mexican crisis of 1994 to the Asian crisis of 1997–1998.

The difference between the two periods, however, was crucial. In the 1990s, the developed nations, and the United States in particular, joined with international organizations to extend generous credits that stemmed the tide and prepared the groundwork for recovery. In the 1890s, Europe watched while leaving the United States to suffer in isolation. Admittedly, the early 1890s were rough in Europe as well, but it was clear that the Bank of England, the Bank of France, and their counterparts across the Continent were not about to soil their coveted gold bricks by offering them in the form of credits to the untrustworthy Treasury of the United States.

Did the Europeans fail to recognize that perhaps the United States had become "too big to fail"? Indeed, the linkages between the two sides of the Atlantic were developing so rapidly, both financially and in terms of trade, that economic chaos in the United States could only have made matters in Europe far more dangerous than they already were. Or was it the opposite—were the Europeans too focused on the competitive threat from America's looming transformation into the major industrial power of the age? Whatever the motivation, we shall see in the next chapter that that particular form of short-sightedness would reappear in more than one country, with deadly consequences, in the two decades that followed the end of the First World War.

Yet the United States did not go over the brink in January 1895. Indeed, on the very last day of the month, the stock market leaped upward, the dollar suddenly started to strengthen in the foreign exchange markets, and orders to export gold were abruptly canceled. Nine million dollars of gold on ships in the harbor were unloaded overnight.[20]

What had happened? Lacking succor from the central banks of Europe and without any international organizations such as the International Monetary Fund, Americans had managed to concoct their own version of what would turn out to be the bailouts of the late twentieth century. They carried out the rescue operation with great skill by combining their genius for improvisation in the face of danger with their unabashed willingness to display raw power when required.

The power was deployed by none other than J. Pierpont Morgan, who would bring to bear all his unique authority and prestige on both sides of the Atlantic. Ron Chernow, biographer of the House of Morgan, refers to the scheme that Morgan engineered as his "most dazzling feat: he saved the gold standard." By lucky coincidence, President Grover Cleveland was a friend of the House of Morgan, having worked at a law firm right next door to the bank during the four years between his two presidential terms. The two were also neighbors in country homes in Princeton, New Jersey. Cleveland was the only Democrat for whom Pierpont Morgan had ever voted.

There was nothing easy or simple in what took place. In light of the distressed economic situation, popular hatred for New York bankers was more intense and widespread than ever, leaving Cleveland unable to turn to them as Secretary Carlisle had done only a year earlier. Even if the bankers had been more cooperative, there just was not enough gold in the United States to restore solvency to the Treasury. There was no choice but to turn to European financiers, and here the leadership continued to be with the Rothschilds. The Rothschilds agreed to attempt a European bond issue, and their first step was to approach the European branch of the Morgan bank in New York—J. S. Morgan & Co. J. S. Morgan, however, demurred, stipulating that they would participate only if Pierpont Morgan himself would handle the American side of the arrangements together with the Rothschild representative in New York, August Belmont, Jr.*

Even though the outflow of gold resumed in early February, the Cabinet in Washington was adamant in their opposition to any suggestion of a bond issue that would put the government of the United States in debt to a bunch of foreign bankers. Pierpont Morgan was apoplectic. He cabled his London partners that the United States was on "the brink of the abyss of financial chaos" and set off at once in a private railroad car for Washington, taking Belmont along with him.[21] When he was informed that there was no point in his seeing Cleveland, Morgan declared, "I have come down to see the President and I am going to

*Belmont, born Schoenberg, was the only Jew whom Morgan was willing to accept on a business basis without complaint.

stay here until I see him." He won his point. He soon joined a meeting with Cleveland, Carlisle, and the Attorney General, during the course of which a clerk came in to inform the Secretary of the Treasury that only $9 million in gold coin remained in the government's vaults.[22] Laconic as usual, Morgan stated, "It will be all over before three o'clock." Cleveland now realized he had no choices left. "What suggestions have you to make, Mr. Morgan?" he asked.[23]

Morgan presented an audacious scheme. He proposed to sell a Treasury bond issue of approximately $65 million to a European syndicate that Morgan and Rothschild would organize, payment to be made in some 3.5 million ounces of gold coin (about one hundred tons), at least half of which would be obtained in Europe. As an inducement to the European banks, the interest rate would be nearly a full percentage point higher than the New York banks had received in Carlisle's 1894 transaction.

Morgan's plan contained three critical elements. The first was in the text of the contract between the syndicate and the Treasury: "The parties of the second part, and their associates hereunder . . . as far as lies in their power, will exert all financial influence and will make all legitimate efforts to protect the Treasury of the United States against the withdrawal of gold pending complete performance of this contract."[24] In effect, the Morgan–Rothschild syndicate was going to rig the gold market. The second element was to use their own supplies of European currencies to lend to Americans who owed money to Europeans on trade or financial transactions, thereby stanching the demand for conversion of dollars into gold. Finally, the syndicate bound together in this undertaking every banking house in New York City with important European connections, cutting them in on the bond issue as part of the deal.

When news of this unorthodox transaction broke, the public clamor was deafening against what appeared to be a sellout to the foreign bankers. The *New York World* described the syndicate as "bloodsucking Jews and aliens." In Congress, William Jennings Bryan asked the clerk to read Shylock's bond from *The Merchant of Venice*.[25] The President was unmoved. In his annual message of December 2, 1895, Cleveland observed that he had "never had the slightest misgiving concerning the wisdom of this arrangement."[26]

The actual daily execution of the plan was watched with skepticism in both London and New York, but it worked. It worked in part because of the mechanics of the plan, but the market's understanding that Europe was providing that kind of support was sufficient to soothe the bankers and investors. The pound sterling, which had been commanding a price of $4.89 in New York, promptly dropped back to its par value of $4.86, facilitating the syndicate's extension of foreign exchange credits to American importers. Soon gold was arriving at the Treasury from Europe at $5 million a month; on July 8, the Treasury reserve was back up to $108 million.[27] A virtual buying panic in American securities broke loose on all the European markets. During the spring, every outbound steamer carried piles of American stocks and bonds consigned to European houses.

Although the syndicate did not succeed in holding the pieces together indefinitely, and further weakness appeared later in 1895, the worst was over. The worst was over in many ways, as 1896 would turn out to be the low point for business activity after so many years of recession. Prices would be up by more than 10 percent by the end of the decade. In February 1896, when the U.S. Treasury floated a loan issue of $100 million in the public markets, it received bids amounting to the extraordinary sum of $568 million, inspiring the New York Chamber of Commerce to pass a resolution declaring that "The success of this loan should dispel every doubt as to the ability and intention of the United States Government to redeem all its obligations in the best money in the world."[28] The Treasury's gold reserve would never again fall below $100 million.*

Despite these dramatic victories, the silver enthusiasts in 1896 mounted the most powerful of all their attacks on the gold standard. In a convention held in tents in open fields in Chicago, near the present location of the University of Chicago (and what Milton Friedman informs us was known as "Sin Corner" in the 1930s),[29] they persuaded the Democratic Party to nominate William Jennings Bryan of Nebraska,

*When the Gold Standard Act of 1900 was passed, it provided for a reserve of $150 million against redemption of paper notes, to be replenished back to $150 million any time that the reserve might fall below $100 million.

only 36 years old, to oppose the 53-year-old Republican William McKinley in the presidential election of 1896.

This was the only election in American history in which the nature of the nation's monetary system came to occupy the central focus; such an issue today would probably lead the voters' eyes to glaze over. This feature of the campaign was not apparent at the beginning. Bryan enthusiastically attacked monopoly, high prices (!), corruption in government, and governmental neglect of the mass of the people. McKinley had been a silver advocate, had voted to authorize free coinage of silver dollars in 1877, and had also voted for the Silver Purchase Act of 1890. But he was convinced that he could win the day by concentrating on the virtues of the high-tariff legislation he so enthusiastically endorsed. McKinley soon found out he would attract no votes from the Democrats on an issue that they considered anathema. He knew, however, that many Democrats were vacillating over Bryan's unqualified support for the demand in their party's platform for "free and unlimited coinage of both silver and gold at the present legal ratio of 16 to 1, without waiting for the aid or consent of any other nation." In fact, eastern Democrats had bolted the party to form the Gold Democrats.

McKinley decided to say less and less about tariffs and more and more about the superiority of gold over bimetallism; on July 30, he came out flatly in favor of the monometallic gold standard. From that moment, the issue was joined and other topics fell by the wayside. As the campaign rolled on, both parties published voluminous quantities of campaign literature on the complex matter of monetary standards, exhorting their followers to instruct themselves on the issues. The electoral contest of 1896 turned out to be unique in history for the educational process in which the voters were invited to participate.

Despite his youth, Bryan was a formidable opponent who was known as "the boy orator from the Platte," "the silver-tongued orator," and "the Great Commoner." He was a man who always knew where he stood, with no words wasted. On one occasion, when he heard that J. P. Morgan had commented that "America is good enough for me," Bryan quipped, "Whenever he doesn't like it, he can give it back."[30] His view of economic matters was equally direct: "Money is to be the servant of man, and I protest all theories that enthrone money and debase mankind."[31] As one of Bryan's most vocal supporters put it in speaking to a group of farmers, "Raise less corn and more Hell. . . . Wall Street owns the country. . . . Money rules and our Vice President is a London Banker."[32]

Bryan's famous speech at the Democratic Party convention on July 9, 1896, was in defense of the declaration for bimetallism in the party's platform. The address deserves reading in full—it must have been a marvel to hear. The simplicity of the language, the eloquence of the phrasing, the indisputable confidence in the theme, the powerful organization of the arguments, and the alternation between a soaring sense of idealism and hard-headed political analysis are rare achievements, not just for a political oration but for the poetic quality of Bryan's prose.

Bryan began by claiming to speak "in defense of a cause as holy as the cause of liberty—the cause of humanity."[33] He went on,

> Ah, my friends, we say not one word against those who live upon the Atlantic coast, but the hardy pioneers who have braved all the dangers of the wilderness, who made the desert to blossom as the rose—the pioneers away out there who rear their children near to Nature's heart, where they can mingle their voices with the voices of the birds . . . these people . . . are as deserving of the consideration of our party as any people in this country. It is for these that we speak.

Then he takes up the cudgel against the gold standard:

> If protection [protective tariffs] has slain its thousands, the gold standard has slain tens of thousands. . . . When we have restored the money of the Constitution all other necessary reforms will be possible; but until this is done there is no other reform that can be accomplished. . . . No personal popularity, however great, can protect from the avenging wrath of an indignant people a man who is . . . willing to place the legislative control of our affairs in the hands of foreign potentates and powers.

And finally, the climactic passages at the end:

> We care not upon what lines the battle is fought. If they say bimetallism is good, but that we cannot have it until other nations help us, we reply that, instead of having a gold standard because England has, we will restore bimetallism and let England have bimetallism because the United States has it. If they dare come out in the open field and defend the gold standard as a good thing, we will fight them to the

> uttermost. Having behind us the producing masses of this nation and the world, supported by the commercial interests, the laboring interests, and the toilers everywhere, we will answer their demand for a gold standard by saying to them: You shall not press down upon the brow of labor this crown of thorns, you shall not crucify mankind upon a cross of gold.

Bryan lost the election, and by a substantial margin. McKinley scored a majority of 95 in the Electoral College and a plurality of 602,000 in the popular vote—a huge advance over Cleveland's plurality of 381,000 in his "landslide" of 1892.[34]

The impact of the election results on the financial markets was extraordinary. Bryan's noisy campaign had provoked a high degree of nervousness and uncertainty during the summer, with a steep break in stock prices, a wave of selling dollars for pounds sterling, call money at one point up to 125 percent, and a queue of individuals outside the Sub-Treasury redemption windows waiting to exchange legal tenders for gold coin.[35] Within a week after the election, stock prices soared, money rates were down to 4 percent, and gold coin began to flow back into the Sub-Treasury windows for conversion back into paper currency.

Explanations for McKinley's great victory vary. Although bimetallism had been the traditional form of monetary standard for centuries, many voters in the 1890s were so unfamiliar with its operation that they perceived it as a newfangled idea that was not to be trusted. Despite the many hair-raising vicissitudes of recent history, gold had effectively been the single standard in the United States for over twenty years. Few people had any clear memory of any other set of arrangements. These instinctive views of gold's triumph were also helped along by the larger resources of the Republican Party for organizing and conducting the educational process.

Nature, however, was also at work once again. In October, news arrived of a failure of the Indian wheat crop serious enough to convert India from an exporter to an importer of wheat. Wheat prices jumped from 53¢ a bushel in August to 74⅞¢ in October, and then to 94⅜¢ in election week. Although Bryan claimed that the "money power" was manipulating the market, the raw facts demonstrated that wheat prices could rise even under a full gold standard. Whereas the Democrats had won a small plurality in Ohio, Michigan, and Minnesota in the election of 1892, the Republicans now ran a plurality of 148,000 in these three states.[36] As we like to say in our own time, "It's the economy, stupid!"

Milton Friedman takes a different view, citing "a fascinating example of the far-reaching and mostly unanticipated effects of a seemingly minor monetary development." He ascribes Bryan's defeat to the MacArthur–Forrest invention of the cyanide gold-refining process in Scotland and its subsequent introduction in the South African mines in 1890. There was no doubt that this development promised a tremendous increase in world monetary gold supplies and, in all likelihood, the inflationary turn that the farmers and other followers of Bryan had been so desperately yearning for.[37]

Bryan later wrote an account of the campaign of 1896, which he called *The First Battle*, but that campaign would turn out to be the last battle for bimetallism. Bryan did help to launch the first battle for an impressive list of radical causes in his own day that would become law over the next quarter century: government regulation of railroads, telegraph, and telephone; control of monopolies; an eight-hour day for labor; the income tax, tariff reform, woman suffrage; and temperance, among others.[38]

When Bryan died in 1925, only 65 years old, the charismatic rhetoric he had uttered in a Chicago tent in the summer of 1896 was as pertinent and appropriate as it had been 29 years earlier. Great decisions were afoot that would press down the crown of thorns on the brow of labor and crucify mankind on a cross of gold. What powerful language might Bryan have mustered had he lived to witness the outcome?

THE DESCENT FROM GLORY

17

The Norman Conquest

Although World War I changed most of the world beyond recognition, one paramount feature of the prewar era rose triumphantly from the ashes: gold. The neatly piled bricks of gold in the vaults of the central banks dominated economic policy in the 1920s and often domestic and international political strife as well, suffusing the entire scene with a yellow glow.

Despite all the gaiety associated with the Roaring Twenties, the fixation on gold during the 1920s and early 1930s makes the period resemble a horror movie. You watch helplessly as the international power struggles and the blind attachment to gold in the wake of World War I drive the whole system toward the inevitable but catastrophic ending in the Great Depression. This is an unusual horror movie, however, because it has no bad guys. The good guys do enough damage on their own. When they are not shooting one another in the foot, they take the opportunity to shoot themselves in the foot. Along the way, the decisions that seem to make best sense at the moment turn out in the end to be nonsense.

These judgments are easy to make with the hindsight of more than seven decades. Unlike the leaders responsible for putting the world back together after World War II, the statesmen and economists of the 1920s were in uncharted territory, without any guide or precedent to help them find their way through the dark wilderness before them. Not a single episode in the history of gold or money recounted so far in this book could have been of much help. Nothing like the war of 1914–1918 had ever occurred before, in terms of scope, casualties, cost, or pain. It was natural to seek a return to the structure that most people believed had held the world together during the long peace and rising living standards of the Victorian and Edwardian eras, Disraeli's warning notwithstanding. In addition, experience had shown that mistrust in the value of money can have a powerful and destructive impact on social structures, the established order of property ownership, and economic progress. Newfangled experiments in the insecure environment of the postwar world had no attraction for the authorities, and for only a tiny number of the experts, especially in the world of finance. The road to recovery had to be paved with gold.

In Britain, the shape of the future was laid out as early as January 1918 in the report of a special committee established for the specific purpose of proposing appropriate policies for the postwar transition. Known as the Cunliffe Committee after Lord Cunliffe, its Chairman and the Governor of the Bank of England, the report based its suggestions upon "the machinery which long experience has shown to be the only effective remedy for an adverse balance of trade and an undue growth of credit." The report's unequivocal recommendation was that "It is imperative that after the war the conditions necessary for the maintenance of an effective gold standard should be restored without delay." The Committee pointed out, furthermore, that they were "glad to find there was no difference of opinion among the witnesses who appeared before us as to the vital importance of these matters." The respected periodical, *The Economist,* immediately applauded with an editorial titled "Back to Sanity" and characterized the report as "an eminently sound document."

One of the few outspoken critics was the brash John Maynard Keynes, then 36 years old, but Lord Cunliffe dealt with him by observing that "Mr. Keynes . . . in commercial circles . . . [is] not considered to have any knowledge or experience in practical Exchange or business problems."[1] The passage of time would prove this accusation to be wildly wide of the mark.

The Cunliffe Committee described an appealing goal but omitted directions on how to get from here to there. No one paused to recall Disraeli's wise observation that the nineteenth-century gold standard was the symptom, not the cause, of prosperity. Most of the basic and essential conditions that had fostered the gold standard had been torn to shreds by four years of carnage. Political alliances, government finance, international debts, Britain's leading position in global banking and finance, and the state of industrial efficiency had been altered almost beyond recognition. Recovery from the dreadful toll taken by the war would have been difficult enough even if mindsets had been less rigid and economic analysis less mired in the theories of the past. Yet it was assumed that full recovery could be achieved only when the gold standard was back where it belonged.

When the slaughter of World War I finally came to an end in November 1918, over eight million men had perished in combat, with somewhat more than half from the Allied side, including 1.8 million Russians and 1.4 million Frenchmen. Over a third of the German male population aged 19 to 22 years were gone; one in ten of British soldiers had fallen. The United States, by comparison, lost 114,000 men, less than half the losses of Romania. A total of fifteen million men on both sides were wounded, many so badly hurt that they would be dependent for support on society and on their families for the rest of their lives, beyond hope of returning to a productive existence. In northeastern France, the primary battleground of the war, more than half the roads were torn up, hundreds of bridges were destroyed, nine thousand factories employing more than ten or more people were crippled or demolished, and half of France's vital textile industry was out of action.[2]

The financial consequences were just as appalling. National debts had swelled by many multiples of their 1914 values. Difficult as those burdens were to manage, each country owed most of that money to its own citizens. But the Allies also ended up in debt to the United States to the tune of nearly $2 billion, while France, Italy, and Russia each owed the United Kingdom some $500 million.[3] These sound like piddling sums in today's economy, but one must remember that the dollar value of total current output in the United States is about one hundred times as large as it was in the early 1920s and that the economies of each of the European countries were substantially smaller than the American economy and seriously impoverished by the war. Total holdings of gold by Britain, France, and Germany at the end of the war amounted to no more than about $2 billion.[4] These debts amounted to substantial sums.

Despite early hopes, the years ahead would promise only occasional relief to Europeans from anything except the warfare itself, and in some parts of Europe even that horror persisted. Mass hunger, unemployment, and uncertainty about the value of money did not have to wait until the onset of the Great Depression. That worldwide catastrophe was just an extension of the intractable difficulties that had already been haunting one part of Europe or another off and on for ten years.

Rancor, bitterness, selfishness, and envy stained almost every aspect of international relationships, corroding the congenial cooperative spirit of the earlier years. The French, having sustained most of the physical damage of the war, insisted on payment of the outlandishly harsh German reparations; until Germany came through, the French refused to repay their debts to the British, whose land was unharmed. The British, however, had also shed copious amounts of the blood of their youth and, in the process, had liquidated a substantial volume of their overseas wealth in order to pay for the war. Without payments from the French, the British were unwilling to pay down their debts to the Americans, who had come out of the war with only minor casualties and an economy that was both wealthier and as strong and vigorous as ever.

In addition, relations between the British and the French often led to serious problems that might otherwise have been avoided. Despite the high level of casualties, the British emerged from the war convinced that the English Channel still kept them separate from "Europe" and from the massive disorders on the Continent—France's war damage, Germany's revolution and impoverishment, the breakup of the Hapsburg Empire, the Russian Revolution, and upheaval from Poland on down through the Balkans. At the Versailles Peace Conference, this attitude kept Prime Minister Lloyd George from making much effort to block the French Premier, Georges Clemenceau, from imposing a peace treaty on the Germans so brutal and impossible to fulfill that it would lead to the rise of Hitler and a war even more terrible in its toll than the war of 1914–1918. As we shall soon see, this attitude also interfered with British–French cooperation on the matter of gold at crucial steps along the way.

Meanwhile, the Americans took the position that "They hired the money, didn't they?" Standing on the indisputable evidence that the doughboys had come to the rescue of the Allies in the nick of time, the United States made concessions only when crisis conditions pushed matters in that direction or when others made proportionate sacrifices. Many Americans disapproved of the peace treaty and Wilson's helplessness to influence the outcome in the more noble directions he had promised. Consequently, there was persistent pressure to cling to traditional prejudices against "foreign entanglements." That the United States sat in comfort on by far the largest pile of gold reserves of any country only fortified the reluctance of Americans to become involved in the economic turmoil in Europe.

A small number of officials recognized how essential American cooperation was to the recovery of Europe, but they were only putting their fingers in a dike that the flood would overwhelm in spite of their efforts. Before the structure collapsed, even they managed to shoot everybody else in the foot as they were taking aim at their own.

In 1920, when the pound was trading in the foreign exchange markets at around $4.00—it would touch $3.40 at its lowest—Parliament mandated a full return to the gold standard in Britain by the end of 1925. Britain had managed this step in four years after the end of the wars against Napoleon; this time the process would consume seven years. As in the earlier episode, the primary obstacle to going back on gold was the inflated price level, but this time the hurdle was far higher. Four years after the defeat of Napoleon, prices were already back to the levels of 1799, but prices at the end of World War I were roughly three times their prewar level and in 1925 were still close to double their 1914 levels. Meanwhile, prices in the wartime United States had only about doubled, then fell back in 1921 to where they were just about 40 percent above prewar, and remained trendless up to 1929.[5]

Two additional hurdles made the task even more difficult. First, the national debt had risen by £5.5 billion during the war to well over £7 billion, but the government's budget deficit was still bulging, and the usual political haggling over who would bear the burden of rectitude seemed beyond resolution.[6] Perhaps even more serious, Britain's vaunted productive apparatus was aging, with costs that were out of line with much of the competition from Europe and America, a process already under way before 1914. Just as American business managers during the

1960s and 1970s were slow to recognize the growing competitive threat from the improving productivity of manufacturers in Japan and Europe, British management in the early 1920s was hesitant about changing its ways. In 1924, British exports were running 25 percent below prewar levels. In addition to the resulting disappointments in export performance, Britain's difficulties were compounded further by strong demand for imports—back up to prewar levels—loss of overseas income, and the failure of shipping and insurance income to revive.

If Britain were to revert to the gold standard at Isaac Newton's longstanding metric, which had worked out to $4.86 per pound sterling for Americans in the prewar era, that $4.86 was not going to buy anywhere near as much in the Britain of the 1920s as $4.86 had bought in the past. Thus, it was clear that the stubborn character of the adverse trends in the balance of trade might well create unmanageable pressures on the gold stock. If, however, some lesser value were chosen for the pound as a means of helping the trade position, Britain's coveted credibility would be compromised and doubt would persist as to any kind of stability to British money for the indefinite future. Foreigners long accustomed to using the City of London as a banking center would flee elsewhere—New York or Paris, for example—and the pound would never look sterling again.

Although the debate swung back and forth all the way up to the 1925 deadline, informed opinion remained in firm support of $4.86. The obstacles appeared small compared to the magnitude of the victory that appeared to lie ahead. "Sacrifice" became a buzzword. As one contemporary expert, Sir Charles Addis, expressed it, "Admitting a sacrifice even though we may differ as to the amount, I think it would not be too high a price to pay for the substantial benefit to the trade of [the nation's] working classes, and also, although I put it last, for the recovery by the City of London of its former position as the world's financial center."[7]

Presiding over most of the major economic policy decisions and much of the debate over the pound was a mysterious and powerful man named Montagu Norman. Norman was elected Governor of the Bank of England for a record 24 years, serving twelve consecutive two-year terms from 1920 to 1944. According to his biographer Andrew Boyle, Norman's "reputation for godlike aloofness and for tantalizing omniscience" enabled him to exert with gusto every bit of the power that "the tremendous mystique surrounding the high office he held" placed in his hands.[8]

Gaunt, elegant, with a small beard and a grayish visage, Norman had descended from a family that had long been a part of the upper-class establishment of the City. He was alternately severe, austere, demanding, charming, and seductive, as well as given to periodic nervous breakdowns that kept him out of the office for extended periods of time. Brilliant in finance but unshakable in his conservative ideologies, he was, in Boyle's words, "the high priest of the City's dogma that the power of Britain had been founded on gold. . . . an article of faith as unassailable as the universal belief of mankind before the time of Copernicus and Galileo that it was the sun which moved, not the earth. . . . [Gold] was also a mystical symbol of all that was finest in the struggle of mankind to better its lot on earth."[9] When it came to views on sound money, Norman walked in the path that Ricardo had laid out just one hundred years earlier after the Napoleonic Wars.

Despite the disparities of price levels between Britain and its major trading partners, Norman was convinced that he could manage to get the pound back to $4.86 without "quasi-catastrophic effects" but that Britain must look forward to "a long period of dear money."[10] "Dear money" means high interest rates; high interest rates in turn tend to produce subdued business activity, which in turn means higher unemployment. The high unemployment keeps wages in check, which keeps price increases in check, which tends to strengthen the foreign exchange value of the currency and bring gold to the nation's shores. The human consequences of this inevitable sequence of events did not disturb Norman. When he jacked up interest rates in 1920 in order to squelch a budding boom, nearly a million men were laid off within twelve months, an outcome that was fully to be expected. According to Norman, the human pain was a matter for the government to worry about, not the Bank of England, whose primary responsibility was to add to the precious collection of gold bricks accumulated in its vaults below the ground.

The final sequence of events leading to the return to gold at $4.86 in April 1925 would make a wonderful scene in grand opera. The voluble dramatic actor Winston Churchill, Chancellor of the Exchequer with ultimate responsibility for the fatal decision, would be the heroic tenor, wandering in a dark and unmapped forest. Montagu Norman, cool, commanding, and expecting to be Churchill's guide, would sing the baritone role; Benjamin Strong, Norman's close friend and President of the Federal Reserve Bank of New York, would provide a kind of baritone obbligato under Norman's arias, and both Norman and Strong would be costumed as druids.* Continually distracting Norman would be the peasant-born President of the Bank of France, Emile Moreau, sharpened scythe in hand and singing contrabasso in a language that none of the others chose to understand. The eminent economist John Maynard Keynes would appear with a voice close to castrato, costumed like a nervous monkey and singing piercing high notes as a lonely but articulate critic of Churchill's decision. There would be a chorus of City financiers in top hats and morning coats. The finale of the opera would be an encounter between Norman and Moreau on a field of cloth of gold, evoking the historic meeting between Henry VIII and Francis I almost exactly four hundred years earlier.

To initiate the process up to the April 1925 deadline for restoration of the gold standard, Norman crossed the Atlantic in late December 1924 to consult with the eponymous Strong, who, although in theory subject to the control of the Federal Reserve Board in Washington, was prepared to act independently at the helm of the New York Federal Reserve Bank when the circumstances suited him. Strong shared all of Norman's values and prejudices. Norman also took the occasion to sound out J. P. Morgan, Secretary of the Treasury Mellon, as well as other Federal Reserve officials. Norman would report back that they all agreed that the moment for resumption in Britain had arrived. He added that Strong in particular had assured him that there would be no Federal Reserve policy aimed at a "deliberate policy of deflation" and would attempt to lean on the expansionist side, to the extent that they could influence prices.[11] Strong's own report of the meetings concluded that failure to resume the gold standard in Britain would lead to "a long period of unsettled conditions too serious really to contemplate. . . . It would prove an incentive to all those who were advancing novel ideas

*In accordance with precedent set by the Bank of England, presidents of the Federal Reserve banks in those days had the title of "Governor."

for nostrums and expedients other than the gold standard to sell their wares."[12]

Strong did warn Norman that his wishes would not necessarily prevail against a national mood opposed to international financial commitments and, in particular, the provincial attitude of most members of the Board in Washington. The most ominous possibility suggested by Strong was that the Federal Reserve might at some point have no choice but to raise interest rates in the United States to discourage stock market speculation—referred to in our day as "irrational exuberance"—at which point domestic considerations would have to come first. This was all too accurate a prediction, although Strong was already dead by the time it was fulfilled.

Encouraged by Norman's report, Churchill notified the Prime Minister that "It will be easy to attain the gold standard, and indeed almost impossible to avoid making the decision." But it was *not* so easy to make the decision. Between the end of December and the deadline at the end of April, Churchill would spend a miserable four months trying to come to grips with the matter. "When I held other offices under the Crown," he complained to a friend, "I could always find out where I was. Here I'm lost and reduced to groping."[13] He also grumbled that "The Governor [Norman] shows himself perfectly happy in the spectacle of Britain possessing the finest credit in the world simultaneously with a million and a quarter unemployed."[14] A senior advisor, Otto Niemeyer of the Treasury, observed that "None of the witch-doctors see eye to eye and Winston cannot make up his mind from day to day whether he is a gold bug or a pure inflationist."[15]

Niemeyer and Montagu Norman were in fact two witch doctors who did see eye-to-eye. Together, they probably had the most influence in locking Churchill into the decision for $4.86 by April 1925. Niemeyer insisted that any other route or continuation of the prohibition against the circulation of gold would prove that Britain had never "meant business" about the gold standard in the first place, that Britain's nerve had failed, that foreigners and Britons themselves would withdraw capital to foreign shores, and that an inflationary spiral was the inevitable consequence of a currency unsupported by a gold standard. There appeared to him to be little risk of unemployment by restoring the gold standard. On the contrary, this was the only sure step to the revival of trade and British exports. Norman's accompanying memorandum wrapped up the matter by concluding that a gold reserve and the gold standard "were as necessary, and as dangerous to do without, as a police force and a tax collector."[16] Those were strong words for a Chancellor to oppose.

The decision was reached on March 20 and announced in Parliament on April 25; on May 14, the king's signature made it official. The gold reserve at the Bank stood at £153 million. Strong had arranged for a $200 million standby credit from the Federal Reserve, and Morgan joined in for an additional $100 million—a moment of fulfillment for the Morgan partners. As early as 1923, Russell Leffingwell, a senior Morgan partner, had declared that he would "sell his shirt to help England out of this mess. . . . Could anything be more heartening than for England and America to lock arms for honest money?" When Norman had visited J. P. Morgan himself in December 1924, Morgan warned him that centuries of moral authority would go down the tube if Britain failed to carry out the return to gold. The Morgan decision was also a source of satisfaction to Strong, because it provided political cover to his alliance with Norman.[17]

Churchill went before Parliament on May 4 to defend the decision. "I do not pose as a currency expert," he began. "It would be absurd if I did: no one would believe me." But he claimed to have had experience with weighing the arguments of experts and he gave great weight to the judgments of "the men who have managed the currency so well" and who told him it would have been impossible to manage it up to this point if they had not had the return to gold as their goal. He emphasized that the decision was essential "for the revival of international trade and inter-Imperial trade [and] for the financial center of the world." And then, in a fine Churchillian flourish, he finished with these ringing words: "If the English pound is not to be the standard which everyone knows and can trust . . . the business not only of the British Empire but of Europe as well might have to be transacted in dollars instead of pounds sterling. I think that would be a great misfortune."[18]

The Gold Standard Act of 1925 did not completely restore the old arrangements. Bank notes remained legal tender but were no longer convertible into gold coin at the Bank. In other words, the ancient right to bring gold to the bank for minting into coin was abolished. Nevertheless, the Bank would continue to sell gold on demand in the form of four-hundred-ounce bars—heavy things weighing 33.33 pounds—at the traditional price of £3 17*s* 10½*d*—or about £1700 a bar.* Keynes drew a sad moral from this step. Looking back from the vantage point of 1930, he eloquently pointed out that

> [Gold] no longer passes from hand to hand, and the touch of the metal has been taken away from men's greedy palms. The little household gods, who dwelt in purses and stockings and tin boxes, have been swallowed by a single golden image in each country, which lives underground and is not seen. Gold is out of sight—gone back again into the soil. But when gods are no longer seen in a yellow panoply walking the earth, we begin to rationalize them; and it is not long before there is nothing left.[19]

Keynes was a bit ahead of his time, but his prophecy would echo loudly down through the years since 1930.

A week after Parliament had acted, *The Economist* of May 2, 1925, claimed that an important landmark in Britain's financial history had been reached and that it was "the crowning achievement of Mr. Montagu Norman." And then *The Economist* (pp. 844–846) went on to proclaim with pride that "Great Britain has made its gesture to the world in the grand manner: We have the honour to pay in our accustomed manner if it so be that your account is in credit on our ledgers." The *Times* would echo these sentiments a few days later, pointing to the need "to face the dollar in the eye," an expression that immediately caught on throughout the British press. The *Times* went on to attack complaints by Labour members of Parliament by telling them that "You worry about the immediate present in neglecting the long-run future."[20] Some wag's comment a year earlier about "The Norman Conquest of $4.86" had come true.[21]

The moment was less propitious than the majestic statements made it appear. The *Times* had got it wrong: there was enough to worry about in the "immediate present" to overwhelm whatever benefits might have

*In order to accommodate the British return to gold after the Napoleonic Wars, Ricardo had proposed limiting the circulation of gold to bars rather than coins in 1819. For a full discussion, see Bonar, 1923.

developed over "the long-run future." True, the markets had pushed the value of the pound up toward the old parity, but in large part because the decision was widely expected. Over seven million men were unemployed at the beginning of the year, and the number would mount rapidly. Even *The Economist*, in its issue of December 19, 1925, admitted that the gap between prices in the United States and Britain was by no means closed, though it had narrowed. Meanwhile, prices on the Continent had fallen further and faster than Britain's, with the result that British prices were now more out of line with European competitors than with American prices.[22]

Finally, Keynes had pointed out a few months earlier that a return to gold would be "a dangerous proceeding," because it would put postwar Britain at the mercy of the Federal Reserve authorities in the United States. The U.S. gold stock was six times the size of Britain's, he pointed out, which meant that Americans could absorb swings up and down in their gold stock that would ricochet back onto Britain with six times the impact. In addition, Britain was now in debt to the United States instead of being one of the Americans' largest creditors.[23] This perceptive argument was not an immediate problem, because both economic conditions and policy in the United States were congenial in the short run. Ultimately, however, Keynes's warning would turn out to be the most serious of all.

The grimmest problem was the failure of the vaunted revival of international trade to make its appearance on schedule. The pressures on the domestic economy were intense. At the end of July, the coal-mining industry, with costs too high to be competitive in export markets, demanded that the miners either take a cut in wages or face losing their jobs. There had already been a sharp drop in coal exports, and the industry was losing £1 million a month.[24] Meanwhile the miners, still smarting from bitter struggles against the employers in 1921 and 1922, flatly refused to accept the pay cut. Protracted negotiations continued into spring 1926, including threats of strike and a lockout, a temporary government subsidy, and a court of inquiry. One well-known member of this tribunal saw little alternative to a firm stand by the industry; the strike threat, he said, could be explained "only by the immediate *and necessary* effects of the return to gold."[25]

Prime Minister Baldwin agreed. It was precisely the kind of situation that Bryan had warned against when he cried, "You shall not crucify mankind upon a cross of gold!" Baldwin summed up the position of the employers by demanding that "All workers of this country have got to take a reduction in wages to get this country on its feet." On May 1, when the leader of the miners, A. J. Cook, declared, "Not a penny off the pay, not a minute on the day," the owners proceeded to lock out a million men.[26] The central organization of British unions, the Trades Union Congress, declared a national strike in support of the mine workers. The General Strike of 1926, as it came to be called, paralyzed large parts of the country, but it also brought out countless numbers of volunteers who kept supplies moving and essential services operating. The General Strike petered out, but the unpleasantness at the coal mines dragged on until November. At that point, the miners were on the verge of starvation. They folded up their protests and accepted the lower wage rates. The more liberal and leftist members of British society were convinced that the miners had been betrayed by stupid and venal leaders. The famous sociologist (and socialist) Beatrice Webb referred to them as "mental defectives."[27] Distrust by the Left and Labour toward politicians, financiers, and foreigners grew both vocal and unyielding.

Blame for all the bad news soon landed on poor Churchill. The situation at the mines was dreadful enough, but there were more profound and distressing developments. Quite contrary to widespread hopes and expectations, world prices failed to move upward and, in fact, were drifting downward in most countries, including the United States, on which so much depended.

Keynes lost no time in leading the outcry. He mounted a spiteful but eloquent and powerfully constructed attack on the decision in three articles that appeared before the general public in the *Evening Standard* and were republished later under the title of "The Economic Consequences of Mr. Churchill." The title was a play on words. As a high-ranking Treasury official, Keynes had been Lloyd George's chief economic advisor at the Versailles Peace Conference. Horrified at the unmanageable and cruel Carthaginian terms being imposed on the Germans, he resigned in disgust and produced a remarkable polemic on the subject called *The Economic Consequences of the Peace*. The book was an immediate best-seller and established a high influential public reputation for Keynes that he would use to advantage all through the Great Depression and right up into World War II and the process of reconstruction that followed.

Emphasizing that his arguments were not "against the gold standard as such," Keynes nevertheless insisted that Churchill was "just asking for trouble [by] committing himself to force down money wages and all money values without any idea of how it was to be done. Why did he do such a silly thing? Partly, perhaps because he has no instinctive judgement to prevent him from making mistakes."[28] After that unkind personal cut at the man who one day would lead Britain into "her finest hour" against the Nazis, Keynes goes on to admit that Churchill was "deafened by the clamorous voices of conventional finance; and, most of all, because he was gravely misled by his experts"—primarily Niemeyer and Norman.

Keynes gives Churchill no credit for having pushed his experts to the limit to assure himself that he would be doing the right thing. In February, three months before the fatal day, Churchill had circulated to Norman, Niemeyer, and other experts an elaborate memorandum referred to in the Treasury files as "Mr. Churchill's Exercise"—an effort that was a clear reflection of Keynes's views. The document listed six powerful objections against making the move back to gold, including the remarkable observation that "A Gold Reserve and the Gold Standard are in fact survivals of rudimentary and transitional stages in the evolution of finance and credit." Another radical suggestion was to renounce efforts to restore the gold standard and instead ship £100 million of gold to New York to pay war debts, thereby provoking inflation in America and leading to a significant improvement in the value of the pound in foreign exchange markets.[29] This was the document that led to the reasoning submitted to Churchill by Norman and Niemeyer, cited above, that convinced him to proceed as planned.

The French return to gold made a striking contrast with what had transpired in Britain, fulfilling all the stereotypes of the 1920s about the difference between the two nations: the cold-blooded English leaders quietly discussing matters in extended deliberations with professors and monetary experts, while the hot-headed French politicians made so much noise shouting at one another that the voices of the experts were drowned by the sound and fury. The French experience was a mixture of farce, tragedy, vacillation, unrealistic expectations, and unremitting anxiety, as operatic in every way as the British experience had been.

The French lurched from one crisis to another in the search for enough breathing space to make any kind of resolution at all—although there was never any doubt that France would rejoin the gold standard club at some point. In fact, when all the shouting was over, the French turned out to have made a wiser and more realistic decision than the British and were a great deal happier with where they ended up. Once the franc was stabilized, a flood of foreign gold and capital rushed toward Paris. That these repercussions would cause serious problems for London was more of a source of satisfaction than of concern.

The French predicament was clear enough: a government splattered with red ink. In the wake of the war, the demands for rebuilding France's shattered industry, housing, and infrastructure appeared insatiable, but so were the insistent appeals of the millions of veterans for social assistance. At the same time, revenues accruing to the Treasury were depressed by the slow rate of economic recovery, to say nothing of the French habits and skills at dodging taxes. Up to 1926, taxes covered less than half of government outlays.

The French parliamentary system produced much weaker governments than in Britain; in times of crisis, the deep ideological rift between the squabbling parties led on most occasions to paralysis or meaningless measures. The Left fought for capital levies and higher income taxes on the wealthy, while the Right demanded reductions in social spending. With hard choices almost impossible to arrive at, premiers and finance ministers went in and out of office as through a revolving door. There were ten Ministers of Finance between September 1924 and July 1926.

The mess was not just in the yawning gap between government spending and tax revenues. The worst of the deficit was in finding some way to finance it. With the wealthy and the banks reluctant to lend to a Treasury that seemed incapable of putting its house in order, the government had no choice but to borrow from the Bank of France. Every time the government took that step, it was the equivalent of turning on the printing press. Then inflationary pressures intensified and the franc came under attack in the foreign exchange markets.

Both Left and Right stubbornly continued to hope that all these difficulties could be overcome if only Germany would take over the whole burden by paying up on the reparations guaranteed by the Versailles Treaty—"*le Boche paiera*" (the Hun will pay) was one slogan every French citizen liked.[30] After all, in 1815 the French had paid seven hundred million francs to the victors at Waterloo and then five billion marks to the Germans in 1871. The French were now determined to be on the receiving end.[31] In January 1923, in an effort to extract reparations by force, the French and Belgian armies invaded the Ruhr region of Germany, the heart of its coal, iron, and steel industries. German passive resistance succeeded in rendering this adventure fruitless, especially as the cost of the occupation force was adding to the woes of the French deficits. The Germans, with terrible domestic problems of their own, were just unable to meet the outsized demands that the Allies had placed upon them.

With the help of credits from the ever-helpful J. P. Morgan & Co., still trying to stabilize the world, the franc had been pegged after the Armistice at 5.4 to the dollar (18.5¢) and 25.22 to the pound. But when the Morgan loan matured in March 1919, the franc dropped in the foreign exchange markets to the point where a Frenchman had to pay eleven francs to buy a dollar; the following year it would go as high as twenty—which meant that an American could buy a franc for a nickel. The franc continued to swing up and down like a jumping-jack for the next four years, rising when prospects of constructive action improved and plummeting as each possibility went into reverse. At its worst, the franc would be the equivalent of about 2¢.

By March 1924, with the budget deficit bulging and a large amount of government debt about to come due, the markets refused all accommodation to the Treasury. Earlier efforts to stop the printing-press consequences of borrowing from the Bank of France had led to an agreement that now blocked off even that source of finance. Panic broke out on March 4, with Frenchmen as well as foreigners rushing to convert francs into dollars and sterling. There were rumors that the whole thing had been provoked by a secret conspiracy organized by the German government—and this was not the first time the French had been tempted to suspect that "strangers" were causing their troubles. Foreign tourists were attacked on the streets of Paris. The government took some halfhearted steps amounting to so little that they served only to intensify the drop into the abyss.[32]

The French in desperation turned once again to Morgan, asking for a loan of $50 million. The Morgan people thought that $50 million would be insufficient and offered twice that sum but with tough conditions: gold as collateral, a tax increase, a cutback on reconstruction, and no new spending programs. Even though this transaction stemmed the tide and started the franc moving back uphill, these conditions so angered the French populace that the government fell in the May elections. Nevertheless, the speculators against the franc took a ferocious beating, especially in Germany and Austria. Almost the entire Austrian banking community was involved. According to one newspaper, they were caught like "ants in the honey."[33]

The victory of the franc in 1924 was only transitory, as the Morgan credits ran out and the old political merry-go-round started whirling once again. In the midst of all that, future borrowings from the United States were essentially shut off by the State Department, which followed American popular opinion by expressing an informal objection "to loans to countries that had not reached a settlement of their obligations under war debts to the United States."[34]

By July 1926, the franc was trading at 49 to the dollar, just about 10 percent of its pegged value of 1918, while wholesale prices were climbing at a monthly rate of almost 15 percent. With the nation exhausted by all the political infighting, a determined Right-Center government under Raymond Poincaré now took over. Poincaré was convinced that the only solution was to persuade the nervous and fickle French who had shifted large fortunes abroad that the franc would now be stabilized. To that end, he promptly lowered income taxes on the rich and raised the taxes on consumer goods that the masses paid—a politically tricky move that accomplished its strategic purpose.

The impact in the marketplace was dramatic. The franc had lost about a third of its value in terms of pounds and dollars just between June and July, but by October it had risen by a third and then climbed by about another third by November to a level that it would hold, within narrow margins, for the next ten years. France was back on the gold standard on a *de facto* basis.

Poincaré's strategy was validated, for the French had picked a value that was irresistible to foreigners—at the expense of the British in particular but also of the Americans. The value was also irresistible to Frenchmen who had earlier speculated against the franc by sending their money to London to await this very moment. Capital poured back into France. After all the travail, France would run an uninterrupted surplus in its international transactions for the next four years.

All of this was hardly good news to London. The capital inflow had permitted the Bank of France to accumulate large sums to its credit in the City, from £5 million in November 1926 to £160 million by the end of May 1927.[35] This was money that the Bank of France could withdraw on demand and represented a heavy potential claim against Britain's stock of gold. The relative positions were in any case shifting rapidly. From a position of approximate equality with the gold reserve of the Bank of England in 1926, the Bank of France's gold holdings were double Britain's by 1929; two years later, the French hoard would be approaching five times the size of Britain's.[36]

One of the ironies of this period was the rise in Germany's gold stock, which swelled from $181 million at the end of 1924 to $569 million at the end of 1928, while Britain's stagnated between $700 million and $800 million.[37] Capital inflows from abroad, especially from the United States, poured into Germany, lured by the high interest rates maintained by the Reichsbank in the wake of the hyperinflation earlier in the decade.[38]

Britain was under constant pressure to hold onto its gold stock in the face of the gains being made by France and Germany. In February 1931, Norman would describe his situation as having been continuously "under the harrow"—a farmer's cultivating tool set with spikes for pulverizing the soil.

The growing financial tension between London and Paris turned into personal aggravation and frustration when Emile Moreau, former head of the Bank of Algiers, took over in June 1926 as the President of the Bank of France. Strongly patriotic, canny, and sophisticated in financial matters, Moreau was well aware of the power that the ownership of gold conveyed in the postwar monetary system. In terms of personality, however, he was a maverick, for he was a laconic provincial from Auvergne who lacked the traditional polish of the central banker. He had little interest in international concerns, disliked travel, and spoke no foreign languages.

It would be hard to imagine anyone less to the taste of the suave, aristocratic, and worldly Montagu Norman. Norman patronized Moreau without mercy. Although Norman spoke fluent French, he insisted on speaking English at his meetings with Moreau; this meant that Moreau always had to have an interpreter present. Norman, who had spent one period of his youth in Germany, was always partial to Germans and antagonistic toward the French; his warm friendship with the Reichsbank president, Hjalmar Horace Greeley Schacht, only added to the friction between him and Moreau.

Schacht was a powerful and brilliant financier who had been primarily responsible for ending the wild German hyperinflation of the early 1920s. In the later 1930s, he was both President of the Reichsbank and Minister of Economics under Hitler, but rivalry with Hermann Goering led to his dismissal in 1939. He was imprisoned after the assassination attempt on Hitler on July 20, 1944, and also faced the war crimes tribunal in Nürnberg after World War II—where he was acquitted. He died in 1970, at the age of 93.

At their first confrontation a month after Moreau's appointment, Norman made no effort to disguise his dislike for the French, although he did emphasize that most of his animosity was directed at the politicians. Norman's great goal, in fact, was to make an international club out of all the European central bankers, in which the Bank of England would be the first among equals. This vision held no appeal for Moreau, who had his own agenda for France's financial relationships with the rest of Europe and would come to resent Norman's independent contacts with the other European central banks. Where Norman equated the happiness of the world with Britain's power and prosperity, Moreau's single-minded focus was limited to the fortunes of France.

The fiercest scuffle between the two men developed in the course of 1927, as France's balances in London were climbing at a rapid rate. Moreau made noises about wanting to convert these balances into gold by drawing from the Bank of England's gold stock; he suggested that Norman could avoid that unpleasant outcome by raising interest rates to persuade Frenchmen to stop converting their pounds. Norman could do no such thing in view of the high unemployment plaguing Britain. Instead, he insisted that France should legally restore the fixed relationship between francs and gold to halt the speculation that the franc might become even more expensive in terms of pounds. Benjamin Strong intervened in the conflict at this point, agreeing to provide the French with U.S. gold in exchange for their sterling balances, thereby taking the pressure off London.

The arguments persisted, however. In July, Ogden Mills, the U.S. Secretary of the Treasury, organized a peace conference at his Long Island home, to which he invited Strong, Moreau, Norman, and Schacht. As usual, Moreau declined to travel and sent a high-level representative in his place. Strong took the opportunity once again to step forward to help, agreeing that the Federal Reserve should lower interest rates in America to take pressure off the pound while also making additional amounts of gold available to the French in exchange for French sales of sterling.

Strong's gesture on interest rates was not totally selfless, because the U.S. economy was weak at that time and commodity prices were falling rapidly. Hindsight would bring bitter criticism against this move by those who believed that the policy of easy money in 1927 had fueled the most violent stages of the boom on Wall Street, leading to catastrophically restrictive actions little more than one year later. In March 1929, Leffingwell of Morgan, hearing that Norman was becoming agitated about overheated speculation in the stock market, observed that "Monty and Ben sowed the wind. I expect we shall have to reap the whirlwind. . . . We are going to have a world credit crisis."[39] Herbert Hoover, in scathing terms, would refer to Strong as a "mental annex to Europe."[40]

Despite Strong's earnest interventions, Norman and Moreau remained at loggerheads, with Moreau increasingly indignant about Norman's "imperialism." He complained to Poincaré in February 1928 that Britain had been "the first European country to reestablish a stable and secure money [and] had used that advantage to establish a basis for putting Europe under veritable financial domination. . . . Are we to let this continue?" And then he noted with satisfaction that "M. Poincaré's interest seems to be thoroughly aroused."[41] Taking his lead from the Premier, Moreau was charged up enough to actually cross the English

Channel "to offer Norman war or peace." Upon his arrival at the Bank, he was politely informed that Norman was indisposed. That did not stop Moreau, who proceeded to negotiate a set of congenial agreements with Norman's staff. But that did not stop Norman. He accomplished a miraculous recovery the instant Moreau had departed and lost no time in repudiating the agreements.

Norman's mental and physical troubles were by no means over, however. Moreau noted (with some pleasure?) in his diary in April that, "M. Norman [is] in a state of sickly neurosis as a result of the incidents in recent months."[42] Norman would receive another personal blow when his beloved friend Benjamin Strong succumbed to tuberculosis in October 1928. Norman would miss Strong, but the atmosphere at the Federal Reserve was already in the process of shifting even before Strong's final illness.

Indeed, in the United States, domestic considerations were now taking priority over international issues, as the authorities watched with increasing concern the thundering momentum of the bull market on Wall Street. Like the late 1990s, each breathtaking rise in stock prices served only to whet investors' appetite for more. The Dow Jones Industrial Average had doubled between the end of 1924 and the beginning of 1928, a three-year achievement that had occurred only four times in the history of the market, the latest of which had been in 1905. The market jumped another 50 percent in the second half of 1928. Then, after going nowhere in the first five months of 1929, it roared upward by 25 percent over the next three months before making its final top in August 1929. In late 1928, when John J. Raskob, Director of General Motors, friend of the DuPonts, and Chairman of the Democratic Committee, wrote in the *Ladies' Home Journal* that "Everybody Ought to Be Rich," he evidently had plenty of believers.[43]

It is fair to ask why the unfolding miracles in the stock market were of any concern to the Federal Reserve, which had been established in 1913 to supervise commercial banks and to provide liquidity for the economy as needed. The concern was not misplaced. Much of the boiling stock market was being financed by people who borrowed money to buy their stocks, often at interest rates well over 10 percent. Banks began to lose their taste for financing anything except this speculative binge. Even worse, a flood of capital from other parts of the economy began to surge toward Wall Street. Stock-market finance—technically, brokers' loans—at banks grew from $1.5 billion in 1925 to $2.6 billion in 1928 and even higher before the market peaked out. But at the same time, loans from nonbank sources jumped from only $1.0 billion to $6.6 billion at the peak, including a substantial amount from abroad.[44] Loans to brokers—payable on demand—by 1928 earned a lot more than normal commercial lending.[45]

The Federal Reserve authorities entered into an extended period of internal wrangling over what to do about all this. The Federal Reserve Board in Washington wanted the twelve regional Federal Reserve banks to use "direct pressure" on any commercial bank making "speculative loans" by denying that bank access to credit at its local Federal Reserve bank. The presidents of the regional banks, and the Federal Reserve Bank of New York in particular, were strongly opposed, insisting that this proposal was both illegal and impossible to administer—how do you identify beyond question a "speculative loan"? George Harrison, Strong's successor as President of the New York Federal Reserve, argued in favor of an earlier suggestion of Strong's to take "sharp, incisive action" to raise interest rates high enough to kill off the speculation, to be followed immediately by a decline in rates in order to avoid killing off the business prosperity. Strong had even persuaded Norman to support this notion, although Norman realized that any increase in rates in the United States would put further pressure on the Bank of England's gold stock. Central banks throughout Europe had been raising their interest rates all during the year.[46]

In a series of steps, the Federal Reserve did start raising the Discount Rate—the rate they charged commercial banks—from 3 percent in 1925 to 5 percent in 1928. In February 1929, the Federal Reserve Bank of New York began to press for a further increase to 6 percent. Washington refused. Ten additional and emphatic efforts by Harrison were also turned back. It would be August 1929 before Washington caved in and the Discount Rate would finally move to 6 percent. That was the zenith of the bull market.

These decisions have remained a subject of controversy ever since, but the sequence of events is clear enough. The Federal Reserve rate was so far below what could be earned by lending to speculators that it failed in its purpose of serving as a serious deterrent. Its success, instead, was in rising high enough to contribute to weakness in the general economy; industrial production had already been falling for a few months before the big crash hit the stock market in October. Nor were the consequences of these moves limited to the United States The vital flow of American lending to Europe, and especially to Germany, was unable to survive the rapid rise in domestic interest rates. By the time the stock market touched its peak, American lending abroad had essentially dried up to zero.[47] In fact, a rising stream of European capital had for some time been flowing to New York to join in the fun.

The outflow was no fun in the countries from which the capital moved, however, where interest rates shot upward in an effort to keep capital from leaving. Britain, Germany, Italy, and Austria were already on their way into depression at the moment the stock market crashed in October; German unemployment alone had quadrupled between the summer of 1928 and the end of 1929.[48]

Gold played no role in the Federal Reserve's struggle with the stock-market boom during 1928–1929, but this was one of the few occasions in the postwar years when gold was not the dominant consideration in policy decisions. Gold would soon return to center stage after the Great Crash, as all the stubborn maladjustments and unresolved dilemmas of the 1920s were thrown into sharp relief: the whole mess of unpaid war debts and reparations, the overvaluation of sterling and the undervaluation of the franc, falling commodity prices, and overextended banks.

The immediate impact of the cataclysmic events of 1929 was to intensify the worship of gold and to move it to an even more exalted position. As a result, appalling economic, financial, and human damage would tear across Europe and the United States before anyone in authority would stop to recall Churchill's rumination that perhaps gold might be a survivor of "rudimentary and transitional stages in the evolution of finance and credit." It was not just labor who was about to be crucified on the cross of gold.

18

The End of the Epoch

In the early days after the crash of 1929, Andrew Mellon—then Secretary of the Treasury and one of the wealthiest men in the United States—gave the following advice to President Hoover: "Liquidate labor, liquidate stocks, liquidate the farmers, liquidate real estate . . . purge the rottenness out of the system."[1] At about the same time, Russell Leffingwell of Morgan offered his prescription for how to get the economy out of the depression: "The remedy is for people to stop watching the ticker, listening to the radio, drinking bootleg gin, and dancing to jazz . . . and return to the old economics and prosperity based upon saving and working."[2]

The sins of the speculators were to be laid upon the children, as the Shakespearean proverb goes,[3] but in this case they were also to be laid upon the sinners themselves, to say nothing of the millions of innocents caught up in the whirlwind by circumstances beyond their control. No one was to be allowed to escape the choking grip that the process of deflation *cum* moral redemption was to impose.

Mellon and Leffingwell were far from alone in expressing these themes. On the contrary, their views encapsulated the conventional wisdom of the times: the rallying cry for deflation and purge would recur in many variations but with a terrible and oppressive monotony. That was by no means the worst. The policymakers—the central bankers as well as the leading politicians—would actually *follow* this advice as they faithfully translated these grim turns of phrase into policy decisions at every level and in every country. When viewed from the perspective of the past sixty years, these people seemed to be speaking the language of another planet.

There were a few brave souls who were convinced that it was the entire economic system that suffered from looming maladjustments, not the morals of the players in the stock market. These men argued that the way out of the Depression was to attempt to short-circuit the misery, not intensify it. They sought means to reliquefy the tottering banking system and somehow put money into people's pockets so that they would be both willing and able to go out and spend it. They found themselves either talking to a brick wall or facing such vigorous opposition that in time they gave up and retired from the fray.

One of these was Herbert Hoover himself. Hoover was shocked by Mellon's advice, especially as "Mellon was not hard-hearted. In fact he was generous and sympathetic with all the suffering."[4] Mellon's error, Hoover wisely pointed out, was his insistence that this was "just an ordinary boom-slump," which led him to underestimate the seriousness of the European situation. Nevertheless, Hoover's efforts to be pro-active were far too modest in scale to stem the cyclone sweeping around the world. Nor did he ever abandon the conventional notion that people could not look to government to solve their problems, no matter how helpless they felt. Sounding rather like Ronald Reagan fifty years later—under radically different circumstances—Hoover reminded his audience in a radio address on February 12, 1931, that:

> The evidence of our ability to solve great problems outside of government action and the degree of moral strength with which we emerge from this period will be determined by whether the individuals and local communities continue to meet their responsibilities. . . . Victory . . . will be won by the resolution of our people to fight their own battles . . . by stimulating their ingenuity to solve their own problems, by taking new courage to be masters of their own destiny in the struggle of life.[5]

Another believer in positive action was George Harrison, Benjamin Strong's successor at the Federal Reserve Bank of New York.* Within

*As a young staffer at the Federal Reserve Bank of New York during 1940–1942, I had occasion to meet with Harrison in person on a number of occasions. He was married to Woodrow Wilson's widow. What impressed me most about him was his $50,000 annual salary; mine was $125 a month.

days of the crash, Harrison proposed that the Federal Reserve banks should buy government securities in the open market to inject some liquidity into the system. Harrison believed this strategy was essential in order to satisfy the insatiable demand for money—the only asset that households, corporations, and financial institutions wanted to own in the panic environment. Bank lending had been clamped shut, forcing commodity prices to collapse, which led in turn to proliferating bankruptcies and bank failures.[6] As jobs were vanishing by the millions, Harrison did make a few brief efforts on his own to conduct open-market purchases at the New York Federal Reserve, but once again the Washington authorities and the presidents of the other Federal Reserve banks frustrated Harrison and his staff by calling a halt to such "inflationary" activities.

Poor Harrison—when the United States began to lose gold during the autumn of 1931, even he abandoned his expansionary views and fell into line with the mainstream views. Now he promptly agreed with his colleagues that the only proper policy under such conditions was to raise interest rates—and to raise them by a lot. Eugene Meyer, Chairman of the Federal Reserve Board in Washington and one of Harrison's few supporters in his earlier notions, hastened to agree, declaring that the sharp increase in interest rates "was called for by every known rule, and that . . . foreigners would regard it as a lack of courage if the rate were not advanced."[7]

At this moment, wholesale prices in the United States were already 24 percent below 1929, unemployment was climbing to over 15 percent of the labor force, and three thousand banks had failed. There was no such thing as deposit insurance in those days, which meant that depositors lost every dollar that they had on deposit at every bank that failed. This money simply disappeared into thin air. As the Federal Reserve drove interest rates even higher, prices would drop by another 10 percent, unemployment would reach 25 percent of the labor force, and over three thousand more banks would fail.[8]

Meyer was without doubt correct: the contractionary policy was called for by every *known* rule. Meyer's analysis reveals how profoundly the basic mindsets of the gold standard dominated policymakers far into the Depression—a situation that even Herbert Hoover recognized as something never before confronted in all of history. Politicians, monetary authorities, business leaders and bankers, and even most academics continued to genuflect before the gold bricks as though these gleaming hoards were all that mattered. They forgot that this was also the stuff that the Parthians had poured down the throat of Crassus after he had been defeated in battle.

The resulting infectious epidemic of disasters only strengthened the obstinate faith in the traditional approach. Indeed, as export trade shriveled in country after country, there seemed to be no choice but to restrain demand in order to hold down imports. Failure to act along those lines would be certain to lead to the most dreaded result: losses of gold to other nations. The vivid example of how gold had tortured the British economic system into deflation since 1925 was there for all to see, but Britain's path appeared to be the sole available roadmap to follow in managing the cataclysm of the 1930s. Although deflationary pressures were coming down so hard on Germany that Adolf Hitler would one day come roaring into power, and although mounting unemployment and spreading bank and business failures throughout the world were tearing into the deepest roots of the capitalist system, these horrors served only to strengthen the determination to preserve gold reserves above all else. The known rules defined the one safe policy when everything else was out of control.

Events during the first year after the Great Crash were disturbing, but 1930 in retrospect looks in many ways like the calm before the storm. On March 7, President Hoover reported that "All the evidence indicates that the worst effects of the Crash upon unemployment will have passed during the next sixty days."[9] This was not a bad forecast under the circumstances. The domino effect of a major crisis would not make itself felt until the end of 1930, first with the failure of Caldwell & Co., a bank in Tennessee that brought down industrial companies, insurance companies, and small commercial banks in its wake, and then with the failure of a small New York bank with a big name, the Bank of United States. Some 2300 banks would follow suit over the next few months.[10] In Britain, the primary consequence was a series of significant losses of gold. On January 13, Norman had already warned the Chancellor of the Exchequer that he could no longer postpone the unpleasant task of raising interest rates.

The fuses were in place. They were lit on May 11 when the explosive news of the failure of the Creditanstalt Bank in Vienna stunned the world. This was Austria's largest commercial bank by far, holding more than half of all Austrian bank deposits. Today we would call the Creditanstalt an institution too large to fail. It was too large to fail in 1931, too, and the Austrian government had to bail it out. But to no avail. The Creditanstalt failure, in the words of the British Treasury official Ralph Hawtrey, "sent a terrible spasm of panic through the financial centers of the world."[11] The spasm first ignited a run on the other Austrian banks and then panic hit the schilling in the foreign exchange markets. In desperation, the Austrian National Bank tried to borrow foreign exchange from other central banks. The Bank of France insisted that no loans would be possible unless the Austrians renounced their intention to form a customs union with Germany, which the Austrian government refused to do. Meanwhile, the Bank of France, busy substituting gold for deposits in foreign central banks, acquired $539 million of gold—about 25 percent more than the entire year's production of gold at the mines.[12] Nevertheless, Montagu Norman, still fighting his personal war against the French, succeeded in infuriating his enemy once more by going ahead with a loan to the Austrians from the Bank of England.

It was too late. Everything was now focused on protecting the golden stockpiles from further damage. Norman's modest efforts would prove to be nothing more than a transitory stopgap. In short order, the run on Austria provoked runs on Hungary, Czechoslovakia, Romania, and Poland. These panics were sufficient to disseminate alarm to still other countries, with the most serious repercussions coming down on Germany.

The knee-jerk response by the German Chancellor, Heinrich Brüning, was to slash government spending. Brüning tried to offset the fury unleashed by the additional unemployment and deflationary pressure he was creating by proclaiming that Germany had reached the limit of its ability to pay reparations. His statement may have been welcome at home, but it led the flight from the reichsmark to begin in earnest. The crisis became so threatening that on June 19 President Hoover, at Leffingwell's suggestion, proposed a one-year moratorium on both

German reparation payments and payments by the Allies to the United States for war debts. The French were furious at this concession to the Germans and refused at first to take part in any discussions. Although temporary credits were arranged for Germany, the haggling went on for so long over the Hoover proposal that the panic started up all over again and the German hemorrhage of gold and foreign exchange accelerated. In an effort to contain the damage, the Germans began the imposition of a system of controls on foreign exchange transactions that became so tight and so complex that by 1932 Germany effectively ceased to be on the gold standard.

The crisis in central Europe rapidly communicated itself to the pound, in large part due to the actions of the French. Britain now began to suffer sharp losses of gold and heavy withdrawals of foreign-owned sterling balances. The sterling crisis was all the more remarkable because prices in Britain had already fallen 38 percent from the level in 1925 when the gold standard had been reestablished.[13] The situation appeared to be so desperate that Winston Churchill, on vacation in Biarritz, blurted out, "Everybody I meet seems to be vaguely alarmed that something terrible is going to happen financially. I hope we shall hang Montagu Norman if it does. I shall certainly turn King's evidence against him."[14]

Norman, in fact, seemed to be as lost as anyone. When Harrison at the New York Federal Reserve Bank cabled him on July 15 that "We are concerned and surprised at sudden drop in sterling today," Norman's response was, "I cannot explain this drop. It was sudden and unexpected."[15]

One can only wonder at the way Norman ducked Strong's query. Two days earlier, the publication of the final report of the findings of a special governmental committee had disclosed the alarming deterioration in the condition of Britain's foreign trade position, with imports exceeding exports by an ever-widening margin. An even more immediate source of trouble was also coming to a head. London financiers had been borrowing at low interest rates in Paris and lending the proceeds to the Germans at much higher rates of interest, but now French financiers uneasy about the outlook for the pound were demanding repayment of their loans to London. The shocking sum of some £750 million was involved.[16]

A week later, the situation had reached a point where Norman made the extraordinary decision to dispatch one of the Bank directors to ask the Bank of France for an immediate loan. The French were willing if the British government—in effect, the British taxpayers—would guarantee the loan. The Cabinet refused, the negotiations broke down, and the pound resumed its slide.*

This turn of events was too much for Norman. On July 28, exhausted by the sequence of defeats to all his hopes and dreams, he went home from the Bank "feeling queer."[17] After a week in bed, he sailed to Canada for a vacation of total rest. The last act of the drama that he had largely written and directed was about to play itself out without him. We will never know whether he was too sick to deal with the crisis or just unable to face the total failure of his efforts that loomed just ahead.

Two days later, the Treasury issued an alarming report on the state of the government's burgeoning budget deficit. The deficit for 1932 was now projected to be £170 million, which was £50 million above the previous estimate. The news shook the entire financial world. No one understood why the report had to be published at that most sensitive moment; Keynes characterized it as "the most foolish document I have ever had the misfortune to read."[18]

As the exodus of Britain's stock of gold persisted, sentiment was building for the government to take drastic action to put its financial house in order. The state of the economy made the task extremely disagreeable: by August, nearly one in four workers was unemployed, up from one in six a year earlier, while prices and wages continued to fall. *The Economist* of August 22 chose this moment to declare that Britain was living beyond its means, that the budget must be balanced, and that "every extravagance in dole [relief payments to the unemployed] and other expenditures should be eliminated." That kind of talk had gone on intermittently ever since the war, but this time it was not just talk. Nevertheless, with the Labour Party in power, headed by Ramsay MacDonald, the decision to cut the dole was turning out to be even

*With too little and too late, the French did participate in loans to Britain in late August, as the crisis was reaching a climax.

more agonizing than if the Tories had been leading the government. Another emergency effort was undertaken to borrow from French and American bankers, including J. P. Morgan, but the bankers refused further credits without the imposition of budget cuts deeper than the government could accept, especially in the dole. Word of the bankers' conditions caused "pandemonium" in the Cabinet room.[19]

Yet something had to be done. On August 24, King George invited MacDonald to form a National Government, a coalition of Labour, Liberal, and Conservative parties, to make the pain of the budget cuts more politically palatable. The torment suffered by the country's leaders is vividly illustrated by a letter dated September 12 from the King to the Prime Minister, which MacDonald read aloud to Parliament in an emergency session. His Majesty expressed the desire "in the grave financial situation with which the country is confronted personally to participate in the movement for the reduction of national expenditure." The King proposed to forgo £50,000 a year in his annual allowance, a reduction of about 10 percent. Hailing the King's offer—and evoking the noble sacrifice of Dickens's Sidney Carton—MacDonald proclaimed that "It is far, far better for all of us to go with tight belts into stability than with loose ones into confusion." He went on to express his determination to perform in accordance with this credo by assuring the country that he would keep Parliament in emergency session until "the world is convinced once again that sterling is unassailable."[20]

It was a good thing that no one bothered to hold MacDonald to his promise. If they had, Parliament would still be sitting in that same emergency session.

Keynes's was a lonely voice in opposition to the mainstream thinking that only thrift could cure the world's awful economic diseases. "Suppose we were to stop spending our incomes altogether and were to save the lot," he suggested in a radio broadcast in January 1931. "Why, everyone would be out of work. . . . Therefore, oh patriotic housewives, sally out tomorrow early into the streets and go to the wonderful sales which are everywhere advertised. You will do yourselves good—for never were things so cheap. . . . And have the added joy that you are increasing employment [and] adding to the wealth of the country because you are setting on foot useful activities."[21]

Keynes's logic may have made sense to the patriotic housewives, but it had no effect on the intentions of the nation's political leaders. The

National Government's Budget and Economy Bill provided for a £70 million reduction in government spending and a tax increase of £86 million. Keynes lost no time in characterizing this legislation as "replete with folly and injustice." Nevertheless, the Government was convinced that the defense of sterling was the primary objective, regardless of human cost in Britain. As a further lure to foreigners to hold sterling, the Bank Rate—the rate charged by the Bank of England to banks needing immediate credit—had been raised in a giant leap to 6 percent from 2½ percent in June. The combination of higher taxes, reduced spending, and higher interest rates was lethal. The economy sank even lower and unemployment rose even higher, pulling tax revenues down along with the shrinking payrolls and profits. In the end, the government was left with a much larger deficit than the experts had predicted.

Before the Economy Bill had much opportunity to rescue the pound, a bizarre but shocking event occurred while the debate on the legislation was under way, a strange echo of the invasion of Fishguard in February 1797. A small contingent of sailors at the British navy station of Invergordon went on strike against the pay cuts that were part of the proposed legislation. The press, both at home and abroad, gave the pocket mutiny huge black headlines. Foreigners received the news in a state of high alarm: if such a thing could occur in the British navy, of all places, the whole country must be on the verge of revolution. Nearly £40 million of gold was swept out of the Bank's vaults in a single week; £200 million had been lost since the middle of July.

By the third week of September, the jig was up. The Bank of England asked the government to relieve it at once of the obligation to provide gold bullion on demand, an obligation that had been in place a mere six years. The requisite legislation passed the House on September 21. *The Economist* announced "The End of an Epoch." Unwilling to admit the consequences of the Norman Conquest of $4.86, the magazine put the blame on "the slump that followed the extravagances of the American boom [which] showed up in all their crudity the various defects which have prevented the gold standard from working properly and led to trade depression." Keynes's observations on September 27 were more to the point; he looked forward rather than backward. "There are few Englishmen," he wrote, "who do not rejoice at the breaking of the golden fetters. We feel that we have at last a free hand to do what is sensible. . . . I believe that the great events of the last week may open a new chapter in the world's monetary history. I have a hope that they may break down barriers which have seemed impassable."*[22] The most poignant comment came from Tom Johnson, a former Labour Minister, who said, "They never told us they could do that."[23]

A few days before these events, feeling much improved and ready to go back to work, Norman had sailed from Canada on a ship bound for home; he was totally unaware of the grand denouement of all his endeavors that lay just ahead. His colleagues at the Bank felt obliged to let him know about the momentous decision that was about to go into effect in his absence, but they did not want the news to leak out ahead of time. On the Saturday before the Monday on which the official announcement was to be made, and referring to the Old Lady of Threadneedle Street—the favorite nickname of the Bank of England—they cabled Norman, "Old Lady goes off on Monday." Poor Norman was so spaced out that he thought they were referring to his mother's plans for a vacation.[24] Did he get a shock when the ship landed at Southampton!

The pound, no longer convertible into gold, took a steep tumble in the foreign exchange markets during the next three months. Foreigners who held sterling on September 21, the day that Britain broke loose, could now convert their pounds into only $3.75 instead of $4.86—a major loss; in December it would touch $3.25. Central bankers around the world rapidly lost their appetite for holding their reserves in the currencies of other countries, even the almighty dollar itself. *There were to be no substitutes for gold.*

Twenty-four out of the 47 nations on the gold standard immediately raced down the path that Britain had just blazed through the thickets of economic chaos: they suspended convertibility into gold within days of the British action. A year later, only the United States, France,

*This superb essay deserves reading in full, both for its analysis of the past and the accuracy of its predictions for the future.

Switzerland, Holland, and Belgium remained on the gold standard; six years later, not a single country permitted their citizens to convert their currency or bank deposits into gold.[25] The golden hoards were to be defended by rendering them inactive!

The dash toward gold hit America hard. This urgency to get out of dollars was a surprise, for the official U.S. gold stock at that moment amounted to $4.5 billion—over 40 percent of the gold reserves of all central banks and treasuries around the world and 65 percent larger than France's gold holdings.[26] Nevertheless, on September 22, 1931, the Belgian national bank pulled $106 million in gold from New York in one fell swoop; France took $50 million on that day and another $70 million a few weeks later. From the end of September to the end of October, a total of $755 million in gold flowed out of the United States, of which nearly half went to France and the rest mainly to Belgium, Switzerland, and the Netherlands. About one in every seven gold bricks in the vaults of the Federal Reserve banks had departed.[27] The panic induced by this news led Americans to follow suit by making massive withdrawals from commercial banks in the form of currency and gold coin, leading almost at once to another eight hundred bank failures.

The prescription for dealing with this crisis was once again the conventional one: deflate and create unemployment. The Federal Reserve lost no time in more than doubling the Discount Rate, boosting it in one giant step from 1½ percent to 3½ percent. The prescription performed as expected. The gold outflow ceased—for the moment. Deflation and the creation of additional unemployment were also successfully achieved. Manufacturing production, already down by a third from 1929, sank by an additional 25 percent over the next nine months. Unemployment doubled from a worrisome 10 percent of the labor force to well over 20 percent, while wholesale prices dropped by 25 percent and would end up in 1932 almost 40 percent below their 1929 levels.

At this point, hoarding of currency and coin by the public was restricting even further the ability of the banks to provide credit to their customers. In the middle of 1930, Americans had held $11 in bank deposits for every dollar of currency in their pockets and cash registers, but this ratio dropped over the next twelve months to only $6 in deposits per dollar of currency.[28] President Hoover then invited Colonel Frank Knox of Chicago to conduct an educational campaign to discourage the hoarding; Knox must have been quite a salesman, for his pitch served at least to slow the rate of decline in the ratio for a while.*[29]

The savage deterioration in economic conditions forced the Federal Reserve authorities to conclude that they had pressed the policy of deflation far enough. Positive action could no longer be postponed. In the spring of 1932, the Reserve banks bought $1 billion of government securities, a move that Ralph Hawtrey, the British Treasury economist, characterized as "heroic."[30] Although the May 30, 1932, issue of *Time* magazine had placed a photograph of Federal Reserve Chairman Eugene Meyer on the cover (and included a surprisingly technical discussion of Federal Reserve operations in the government securities market), the billion-dollar purchase would prove to be little help to the economy. A fresh wave of anxiety and uncertainty broke out, prompted by concerns that the Federal Reserve was acting to promote inflation. The heroic step simply led to a renewed outflow of gold.

Now began a chilling replay of the events that had led to the final crisis of the British government in 1931: frantic efforts to extinguish a swelling budget deficit as tax revenues shriveled while the demand for government assistance to the unemployed increased in urgency. A deficit of $2 billion was estimated for the fiscal year ending in June 1932, over 3 percent of the total national output (an astonishing number for its time); the actual figure would exceed that amount.[31] Following dutifully in the footsteps of Brüning and MacDonald, Hoover pressed Congress to act to reduce this forbidding deficit by cutting expenditures and raising taxes. "Rigid economy is a real road to relief to home owners, farmers, workers, and every element of our population," he assured Congress. "Our first duty as a nation is to put our governmental house in order."[32]

Hoover's determination in this matter was inexhaustible, but Congress was less motivated than the President for such noble objectives. Their spending cuts and tax increases were well below what Hoover sought. Nevertheless, the economic impact of these measures added to the prevailing deflationary pressures and led to an even greater budget deficit in 1933.

*Knox, Secretary of War during World War II, was famous for his remark about the Japanese when he put his arm around the shoulder of T. V. Tsoong, the Chinese Ambassador: "Don't worry, T. V., we'll lick those yellow bastards yet."

And so matters wobbled along until the election of November 1932, when the Democratic candidate, Franklin D. Roosevelt, defeated Herbert Hoover in a landslide. The moment for action to revive the economy had not yet arrived, however, because in those days the inauguration took place on March 4 rather than January 20. A lame-duck President and Congress continued in place for four long months.

Despite untiring efforts to induce Roosevelt to work with him, Hoover complained again and again to the public about Roosevelt's flat-out refusal to cooperate in any measure whatsoever until Roosevelt had been inaugurated and was in power.[33] One of Hoover's most protracted efforts to engage Roosevelt's participation concerned plans for a major international economic conference on the world depression and the war debts. Hoover pleaded with Roosevelt:

> Ever since the storm began in Europe, the United States has held staunchly to the gold standard. . . . We have . . . maintained the one Gibraltar of stability in the world and contributed to checking the movement of chaos. . . . [A] mass of gold dashing hither and yon from one nation to another, seeking maximum safety, has acted like a cannon loose on the deck of the world in a storm. . . . Confidence cannot be reestablished by the abandonment of gold as a standard in the world.[34]

Even these strong words failed to persuade Roosevelt to cooperate. As a result, it was a rough four months up to the inauguration, with uncertainty growing as to what actually would lie ahead after the new president was installed. Roosevelt's campaign promise that the government would provide jobs for all the unemployed had the perverse effect of creating a new wave of unemployment by businessmen frightened by fears of socialism and reckless government spending.

Rumors were soon circulating that the new administration would begin "tinkering" with the currency. On January 2, 1933, thirty prominent economists expressed their alarm and insisted that "The gold standard of present weight and fineness should be unflinchingly maintained . . . agitation and experiments would impair confidence and retard recovery."[35] In a clear state of alarm, the famous financier Bernard Baruch, who had supported Roosevelt, told a Senate committee on February 13 that inflation was the road to ruin and that "If you start talking about [devaluation] you would not have a nickel's worth of gold in the Reserve System day after tomorrow."[36]

These exhortations only added to the spreading fear, but the litany on maintaining the gold standard resumed in the press, among leading members of Congress, and from George Harrison of the New York Federal Reserve himself. On January 31, however, Henry Wallace, who had been mentioned as a member of the new Cabinet, flew in the face of orthodoxy by declaring that "The smart thing would be to go off the gold standard a little further than England has." On February 18, the press announced that Senator Glass, one of the foremost experts on gold and currency in the Congress, had refused Roosevelt's invitation to be Secretary of the Treasury because the President-elect would not give him satisfactory assurances on maintaining the gold standard.[37]

Frightened Americans now joined agitated foreigners in seeking safety by moving their capital abroad or into gold. A renewed run on the U.S. gold stock resulted in $160 million leaving for foreign climes in February 1933 and another $160 million in the first four days of March that led up to Roosevelt's inauguration. The mounting panic included withdrawals of gold coin from the commercial banks, with over $80 million going out in the last ten days of February and over $200 million during the first four days of March.[38]

A dramatic incident occurred in Cambridge, Massachusetts, when one of the best-known members of the Harvard Business School faculty, Professor Arthur Dewing, marched into the Harvard Trust Company office on Harvard Square, withdrew his substantial bank account in gold coin, and placed the coins in his safe deposit box. When the crowds inside the bank reported Dewing's action to the people on the street, a mob gathered on the Square, fighting to get into the bank to follow the example set by the distinguished professor. Dewing was subsequently called on the carpet by the dean of the Business School for setting such an example of unpatriotic behavior. Dewing left the faculty soon afterward.*

*I heard this story as a Harvard undergraduate in the late 1930s; Professor Paul Samuelson of MIT was good enough to confirm it in personal correspondence.

The Harvard Trust Company survived, but thousands of other banks hit by runs on their deposits did not. Over ten thousand banks disappeared from the scene during 1933, by which time the total number of banks in the United States had fallen to fewer than ten thousand from thirty thousand in 1925 and about 25,000 in 1929.[39] The frantic liquidation of bank accounts had driven the ratio of bank deposits to currency in circulation into a precipitous drop from $6 of deposits for every dollar of currency in circulation at the end of 1932 to only $4 for every dollar of currency in March 1933—just about one-third of what this ratio had been before 1929.[40]

Where was the Federal Reserve while all of this was going on? The eminent economists Milton Friedman and Anna Schwartz provide an answer to this question in their monumental monetary history of the United States: "The System was demoralized [and] participated in the general atmosphere of panic that was spreading in the financial community and the community at large. The leadership which an independent central banking system was supposed to give to the market . . . [was] conspicuous by [its] absence."[41]

On March 5, the day after the inauguration, the new Secretary of the Treasury assured the country that the gold standard was inviolate. Over the next couple of days, the press both at home and abroad joined in repeating these sentiments. On March 8, Roosevelt held his first press conference and declared that the gold standard was safe.

So much for that. On March 9, Roosevelt pushed the Emergency Banking Act of 1933 through both houses of Congress, authorizing him to regulate or prohibit the export or hoarding of gold or silver and empowering the Secretary of the Treasury to require the surrender of all gold coin, bullion, and certificates (paper notes fully secured by gold) held by the public.[42] The public perceived the March 9 legislation as temporary! Anxiety eased, and gold and paper currency started to return to the banking system.

Everything seemed just fine for a few weeks, until the market began to suspect that Roosevelt really did plan to cut the gold value of the dollar. He had made no secret of his intention to stem the deflationary cycle and start prices back upward, because he was confident that bold steps in that direction would encourage business to start rehiring and increase the depressed level of production. As the rumors about gold proliferated, the run on the dollar resumed, and with good reason: on April 18, legislation was passed giving the President wide powers over the economy, including a reduction in the gold content of the dollar.

Hoover's memoirs are unsparing in their slashing attack on Roosevelt's policies. Hoover claimed that abandonment of the convertible gold standard was the first step toward "communism, fascism, socialism, statism, planned economy." Gold, he argued, is essential to prevent governments from "confiscating the savings of the people by manipulation of inflation and deflation." He goes on at length in this vein; in a footnote, he quotes an old proverb: "We have gold because we cannot trust Governments."[43]

Roosevelt was determined to proceed. On April 5, only a month after his inauguration and acting under the authority of the Trading with the Enemy Act of 1917 and the Emergency Banking Act passed in March, he issued an executive order requiring all persons to deliver all gold coin, gold certificates, and bullion to the banks in exchange for paper currency or bank deposits, and for the banks to deliver the gold to the Federal Reserve. According to Hoover, only about $400 million in gold came into the banks, adding less than 10 percent to the existing gold stock.

Further enabling legislation in April gave the President the authority, among other things, to fix the weight of gold in the dollar at not less than 50 percent or more than 60 percent below the weight that had established an ounce of gold at $20.67 in 1837, nearly one hundred years earlier. This act prompted Lewis Douglas, Director of the Budget, to predict that "This is the end of Western civilization."[44] There was more to come. Further congressional action on June 5 provided that any clause in any contract that provided for payment in gold was now abrogated—even including obligations of the U.S. government.

The cancellation of the gold clause in U.S. government obligations resulted in a rash of lawsuits that ended up in the Supreme Court. The Court agreed that Congress had no right to cancel the promise to redeem its debts in gold at the option of the holder. But then the justices went on to declare that, since the private ownership of gold coin was no longer legal, the plaintiff's demand for damages equal to the change in the gold value of the dollar from $20.67 to $35.00 was without merit![45]

On July 3, Roosevelt issued a statement—which came to be known as the "bombshell" message—declaring that efforts to stabilize exchange rates by going back to rigid relationships to gold were "old fetishes of so-called international bankers" and that exchange-rate stability was "a specious fallacy."[46] The statement scandalized most conservative politicians, financiers, and academic experts, but the President did find one supporter when John Maynard Keynes proclaimed "Roosevelt magnificently right!" Raymond Moley, one of the President's chief advisors, subsequently quipped, "Magnificently *left*, Keynes means."[47]

The dollar was now varying from day to day in the foreign exchange markets as Secretary of the Treasury Morgenthau followed Roosevelt's order to gradually reduce the amount of gold a dollar could buy—or, stated differently, to increase the number of dollars required to buy an ounce of gold. Secretary Morgenthau's diaries recite a famous anecdote from this period, as he and two other officials would meet each morning in the President's bedroom to set the price for gold for the day:

> Franklin Roosevelt would lie comfortably on his old-fashioned three-quarter mahogany bed. . . . The actual price [of gold] on any given day made little difference. Our object was simply to keep the trend gradually upward, hoping that commodity prices would follow. One day, when I must have come in more than usually worried about the state of the world [Hitler had just recently come to power in Germany], we were planning an increase of from 19 to 22 cents. Roosevelt took one look at me and suggested a rise of 21 cents. "It's a lucky number," the president said with a laugh, "because it's three times seven. . . ."
>
> He rather enjoyed the shock his policy gave to the international bankers. Montagu Norman of the Bank of England, whom FDR called "old pink whiskers," wailed across the ocean, "This is the most terrible thing that has happened. The whole world will be put into bankruptcy." The president and I looked at each other, picturing foreign bankers with every one of their hairs standing on end with horror. I began to laugh. FDR roared.[48]

For once, Keynes sided with his traditional adversary Norman and refused to join in the fun. He described the gyrations of the dollar "like a gold standard on the booze."[49]

The game came to an end on January 30, 1934, when an executive order fixed the price of gold at $35.00 an ounce, an increase of 69 percent from the old value. That price would prevail without interruption for 37 years, which was three years longer than the *de jure* value of $20.67 set in the Gold Standard Act of 1900. Although many other factors were at work, it is worth noting that from 1933 to 1937 industrial production jumped by 60 percent and wholesale prices climbed 31 percent while unemployment fell from 25 percent to 14 percent. By early 1937, the Dow Jones Industrial Average stood at 200, a mighty surge from its nadir at 40 touched during the darkest days of 1932. Happy Days were here again!

Except for the French, the Swiss, the Dutch, and the Belgians, who remained nailed to the cross well into the 1930s. The Dutch and the Belgians clung to their 1913 parities right up into World War II. The French franc, which had once made French goods look so cheap relative to British goods after it was stabilized in 1925, appeared increasingly expensive after the pound broke loose from gold in 1931. The French then caught a bad case of the deflationary disease from which the rupture from gold had liberated Britain and the United States. Prices in France fell by nearly 25 percent between 1931 and 1935, while French national income dropped by a third.[50]

By 1936, the horrors had reached the stage where France was besieged by angry sit-down strikes. The political chaos led to the formation of a Popular Front government that included Communists and Socialists—not the most appropriate combination to restore international confidence in the franc. The break from gold and the devaluation of the franc occurred in September under cover of a Tripartite Agreement with Britain and the United States. This agreement added up to little in the way of action but did at least restore international cooperation to something better than the endless friction and backbiting that had characterized international financial relations since the end of World War I.[51]

Meanwhile, something strange was happening to gold. As each currency broke away from gold and was devalued, a unit of each currency bought less gold than before—that is, the price of gold went up, as it had risen from \$20.67 to \$35.00 in the United States. In contrast, the prices of goods and services in all countries had fallen by substantial amounts. The result was that an ounce of gold in the mid-1930s could buy twice as many goods and services as that same ounce could have bought in 1929.[52]

In a world in which production was deeply depressed for just about everything that people desperately wanted but could not afford—food, clothing, housing—this leap in the price of gold was a bonanza for gold miners and the equivalent of a whole new gold rush for the world economy. Gold production soared. This new gold came primarily from South Africa, although, as in the past, Russia remained an important producer. In addition, Asia—beset by the Great Depression like everyone else—for the first time in history dishoarded gold and shipped about \$100 million westward. In 1932, the two million tons of gold coming out of the world's gold mines amounted to nearly half of all monetary gold accumulated from the beginning of time to the middle of the nineteenth century. In 1938, output was up another 50 percent from 1932.[53]

The gold reserves of the central banks and related government funds jumped from about forty million tons in 1929 (\$10 billion at \$20.67 per ounce) to sixty million tons (\$25 billion at \$35.00 per ounce) ten years later.[54] The growth in monetary gold around the world was so vast that by 1939 there was enough gold in the monetary reserves of the world to replace all ordinary currency 100 percent with gold coin.[55]

This was one rare moment when there seemed to be so much gold in existence that nobody knew what to do about it. Only one solution seemed acceptable: send the gold across the oceans to New York, where the United States stood ready to buy everything at \$35 an ounce. Consequently, most of this new gold crossed the oceans to New York, along with a lot of old gold. Two contemporary economists, Frank Graham and Charles Whittlesey, described what happened as a "Golden Avalanche." From 1900 to 1913, the rise in monetary gold in the United States had averaged around \$70 million at \$20.67 (\$122 million at \$35). From 1934 to 1939, the *smallest* increase in American gold reserves was \$1.1 billion.[56] Total U.S. imports of gold from 1934 to 1939 added up to the stupendous sum of \$9.6 billion, \$3.3 billion more than the greatly expanded production of gold during those years; about 20 percent of this inflow came from France, but, in the pain of the Depression, even India was now exporting gold to the United States.[57] When World War II broke out, some \$20 billion, or 60 percent of the world's monetary gold, was lodged in the United States compared with a share of only 38 percent in 1929 and 23 percent in 1913.[58] This massive hoard weighed more than fifteen thousand tons and was equal to twelve years' worldwide gold production at the time. What a pile it must have been! Atahualpa's chamber, when filled with gold, contained only six tons—and even that was greater than the total annual output of gold in Europe in the early 1500s.

What could explain such a phenomenal migration of gold from the whole world to the United States? The mountain of new production did raise questions about whether the price of gold might actually fall, along with the rest of the world's commodities, in which case the best strategy was to sell as much as possible to the United States at $35 as long as the opportunity persisted. But the more significant motivation was political: these were frightening days in Europe. Hitler was on the march, with Mussolini and the emperor of Japan rattling their swords by his side. Hitler rejected the provisions of the Treaty of Versailles, sent German troops back into the demilitarized Rhineland in 1935—touching the French border—and mounted a vigorous and undisguised program of rearmament almost immediately after he assumed the leadership of Germany. While most other countries were still floundering in the mess of the Depression, Hitler's heavy spending on arms succeeded in pulling Germany out of the Depression as rapidly as Roosevelt's new policies had promoted recovery in the United States. Italy invaded Abyssinia (now Ethiopia) in 1935. The Nazis invaded Austria in 1938 and Czechoslovakia in early 1939; Hitler made off with their gold reserves as soon as his troops entered Vienna and Prague. Meanwhile, the Communist system was thriving in Russia, where output and employment kept rising all during the 1930s.

In this alarming environment, shipping capital across the Atlantic to America seemed to make good sense, especially in the form of gold. The United States, alone in the world, stood ready to buy gold in unlimited amounts at the fixed price of $35.00. Other countries had either stopped buying gold or paid a varying price depending upon the exchange rate of their currencies against the dollar. The dollar/gold relationship was like a fixed star in the heavens to which all other stars and constellations were irresistibly attracted.

But the strangest thing of all was that the United States absorbed those billions of dollars' worth of gold without any sign of some natural force to throw the process in reverse. What had happened to David

Hume's authoritative observation back in 1752 that "It is impossible to heap up money, more than any other fluid, beyond its proper level"? (See p. 160.) None of the necessary steps to fulfill Hume's prediction occurred. The bank deposits received by those who exported gold to the United States sat idle or were invested at interest rates of less than 1 percent per annum. It was no time for taking risks. The banks whose reserves were swelled by the golden imports felt the same way: nothing in those days was as beautiful to behold as a nice, fat pile of cash. In short, money continued to heap up in America far beyond its proper level just to sit quietly until the storms had blown over. The process came to be known as a "liquidity trap." The accumulations of cash would be put to use only later when the pressures of wartime spending demanded it.

And so the great Victorian gold standard died an ugly, painful, and protracted death, a process that reached all the way back to the prohibitions on convertibility that were put in place after the outbreak of World War I. The old structure was never completely revived after 1918. The remarkable aspect of the story is that so many people believed they could revive that system in a world that the war had altered beyond recognition.

It is easy to understand the nostalgia for the prewar world that encouraged the struggle to return to gold. It is easy to understand the desire for a system whose simplicity and elegance was unmatched in the history of money. It is easy to understand the fascination with gold—a fascination that had never wavered from the times of Moses and Jason and Croesus and Pizarro right up to the times of Montagu Norman.

But it is not so easy to understand that men could make such mighty decisions on the basis of obsolete visions rather than objective analysis, with their minds shut tight against consideration of any other solution to the problem at hand.[59] It is most difficult to understand how so few seemed to learn—until it was too late—the lessons provided by Britain's example of how the simple decision could lead to unparalleled economic agony. The notion that gold would make everything come out all right was a notion that was upside down: gold would make everything come out all right *only when everything was all right in the first place*. That was the real meaning behind Disraeli's assertion in 1895 that Britain's gold standard was the consequence, rather than the cause, of her commercial prosperity.

As so often happens, the errors became increasingly clear after the fact. P. J. Grigg, who was Churchill's principal private secretary, has related that "Winston has almost come to believe [in his later years] that the decision to go back on gold was the greatest blunder of his life."[60] This was a striking judgment on Churchill's part in view of the nightmare of his key role as First Lord of the Admiralty in the disaster at Gallipoli in 1915.[61]

What about Norman himself? In correspondence with Norman in 1944, Russell Leffingwell had observed, "How we labored together, you and Ben [Strong], my partners and I, to rebuild the world after the last war—and look at the damned thing now!"*[62] Norman agreed: "As I look back, it now seems that, with all the thought and work and good intentions which we provided, we achieved *absolutely nothing*. . . . By and large nothing that I did, and very little that old Ben did . . . produced any good effect."[63]

*Leffingwell regularly sent Norman food packages during World War II and carried on an active correspondence with his old friend.

19

The Transcending Value

When the bombings, the bloodshed, and the persecutions of World War II came to an end in the summer of 1945, Europe and Asia were a shambles. Industries, cities, and transportation systems were little more than piles of rubble; millions of people were homeless or jobless, including many who had been forcibly transported far from their own countries; currencies in most countries were worthless—in Germany, cigarettes or nylon stockings were the preferred form of payment. In addition to the United States, only Britain, the Soviet Union, and China had emerged from the war with surviving forms of government, and only Josef Stalin and Chiang Kai-shek were still in office among the wartime leaders. Winston Churchill was voted out of office by a Labour landslide within months after the fighting had stopped.

Yet within less than twenty years, every vestige of the ravages of war had vanished. By the early 1960s, even western Germany, the Soviet Union, and Japan, which had suffered the worst damage, were vibrant economies enjoying high rates of economic growth and broadly competitive with the one major nation that had emerged unscathed from the hostilities—the United States of America.

We are about to see how, despite this imposing progress, all the best-laid plans of both leaders and followers ended up far away from their announced destinations. The villain of the piece turned out to be gold. In the disruptions, conflicts, and unpleasant surprises that developed in the course of the 1960s, gold became the focal point and at many points the source of the trouble. The story includes many moments when gold was causing such a rumpus that most authorities wished it would go away and stop bothering them. But then we have noted many occasions in this history where people ended up a long way from where they had intended to end up. Where gold is involved, dreams seldom come true. As Ruskin reminds us, he who has gold is often had.

The leader most concentrated on gold was General Charles de Gaulle, who commanded the Free French forces against Germany in World War II and was President of France for most of the 1960s. Even twenty years after the fact, he was still smarting from what he considered the inexcusable insults to him and to France when Roosevelt and Churchill had excluded him from their most important consultations and their wartime meetings with Stalin. Nothing would have pleased de Gaulle more than to see the Anglo-Saxons on their knees before him. He was convinced he could accomplish that objective if the world were to follow his advice to restore gold as the primary international standard and means of payment—thereby uprooting the dollar from its current preeminence.

On February 4, 1965, he assembled one thousand journalists at the Elysées Palace, the official home of the President of France, and seated them in the gilded Salles des Fêtes. The ubiquitous gilding of this opulent setting, from the chairs to the walls, was appropriate, for the General had called the press conference to demand nothing less than a return to the nineteenth-century gold standard. "Indeed," he insisted, "there can be no other criterion, no other standard, than gold—gold that never changes, that can be shaped into ingots, bars, coins, that has no nationality, and that is eternally and universally accepted as the unalterable fiduciary value par excellence."[1]

He reminded his audience that "The kind of transcending value attributed to the dollar has lost its initial foundation, which was possession by America of the greatest part of the world's gold." His facts were indisputable. By early 1965, the U.S. stock of monetary gold had fallen to its lowest level since March 1937. The stock was down to $15 billion compared with its all-time peak of $25 billion in 1949; America's share of the world's total monetary gold stock had shrunk from 75 percent to less than 50 percent. By the end of the 1960s, the U.S. share would be under 30 percent.

Later that day, Jacques Rueff, a famous French economist and chief advisor on such matters to the President, declared that de Gaulle was the man of the moment, "the statesman who will restore true money." The present system was "absurd . . . a serious obstacle to social progress." Six days later, the French Minister of Finance, with the courtly name of Valery Giscard d'Estaing, delivered a lecture at the University of Paris to a standing-room audience of three thousand students, in which he called for "a solemn and unequivocal declaration" by the major financial powers to settle all international payments deficits with gold. This action, he contended, would "stop the decay of the world money system." He went on to announce that France was taking the lead by starting to convert all new accumulations of dollars into gold.[2]

The French would proceed to make their point in no uncertain terms. Most of the time, other nations cashing in dollars for gold left the new gold for safekeeping in the vaults of the Federal Reserve Bank of New York. The French authorities made front-page news by announcing that all increases in their gold stock would travel across the Atlantic on French ocean liners to the secure shores of *la patrie*.

What had gone wrong? The designers of the postwar era had had every reason to believe that they had neatly caged the golden monster that had wreaked so much havoc in the 1920s and 1930s. As General de Gaulle went to some pains to point out, however, gold was too mighty to remain a prisoner. The press conference in the Salles des Fêtes was just one of a sequence of events in the 1960s that seemed destined to put the dollar in the shade and to restore gold to its former grandeur. Worse was yet to come. Nevertheless, when the moment arrived for gold to break free from its shackles and soar to its zenith in a blaze of glory, the blaze would turn out to be too bright, too hot, too magnificent to be sustainable. In a strange and most unexpected fashion, the world has come full circle since the early 1960s, with the dollar once again the transcending value and with gold in the shade.

The story begins in the immediate aftermath of World War II, one of those rare moments in history when people make all the right decisions. Most of the world outside the United States was in such a chaotic mess that the framers of the postwar era had a unique opportunity to shape the new structure on a clean slate and make the dreams of the Enlightenment and the Victorian age finally come true. The broad outlines of what was necessary were easy to define: the cascade of tragic errors in the 1920s and 1930s provided the leaders of the second postwar era with a perfect blueprint of what *not* to do. As John Maynard Keynes put it, "In 1918, most people's only idea was to get back to pre-1914. No one today feels like that about 1939."[3]

Instead of exacting reparations, the Allies carried on vigorous financial and political efforts to bring Germany, Italy, and Japan into the mainstream of democratic society. Instead of insisting on repayments for the huge amounts of military aid that the United States had provided during the war, Americans gave only lip service to demanding payment. Instead, they converted most of their contribution to the Allied war effort into gifts—and then added the prodigious assistance of the Marshall Plan and other substantial aid programs on top of that. Instead of a world where each nation stubbornly pursued its own self-interest, the United Nations was created to manage a world of international cooperation and harmony; unlike the League of Nations, the plans for the United Nations featured the enthusiastic participation of the United States.

The plans for a new international economic system were worked out by 730 delegates from 44 countries who gathered in the White Mountain resort of Bretton Woods, New Hampshire, in 1944. Most of the final design came from John Maynard Keynes, representing the British Treasury, and his counterpart, Harry White of the U.S. Treasury Department.* The scheme that Keynes and White concocted seemed like an obvious one for the times.

Instead of an international economy where each nation was at the mercy of its stock of gold, the new system made the U.S. dollar the centerpiece of the structure. The almighty dollar was then supported by 75 percent of the world's stock of monetary gold. The huge U.S. economy had sustained no war damage and was more productive than ever

*Both men died before they could see the product of their work in full flower, Keynes in April 1946 and White in August 1948. Given the ultimate shape of the Bretton Woods system, there is reason to believe that White was the dominant partner, with Keynes—representing the poor relation—playing second fiddle.

before in its history. The Economic Report of the President of January 1947 declared that the country had made "the swiftest and most gigantic changeover that any nation has ever made from war to peace." Total production in 1947 was 30 percent above 1941, the last full year of peacetime output.

The new arrangements provided that the United States—blessed with that dominant proportion of the world's gold stock—would be the only nation with a currency freely convertible into gold at a fixed rate; as in prewar days, however, the privilege of conversion was limited to national treasuries and central banks, not to private parties. All other countries were obligated to do their best to make their currencies convertible into dollars by everyone, but they were not required to maintain convertibility into gold. The conversion rate between dollars and gold was set at $35 per ounce, and then the rest of the world defined their currencies in terms of the dollar rather than gold.

If that had been all there was to it, the new system would have left individual countries as much a prisoner of the dollar as once upon a time they had been prisoners of their gold stock. The Allied nations had few dollars left after paying for the monumental costs of the war, even with American aid; Britain owed massive debts to its imperial possessions; the enemy countries were flat broke. As a result, only the relationship between gold and the dollar at $35 an ounce was expected to be permanent—in cement, as in the old days—but different arrangements were established for the relationship between the dollar and all the other currencies. These relationships, known as "legal par values," were also expected to be fixed under the normal course of events, but provisions were established to provide for changes in the legal par values when a country's efforts to meet its international payment obligations ran into problems that were deemed more likely to be permanent than temporary. Setting these par values at a level that each country could manage to sustain was far from easy. Germany and Japan did not set theirs until 1953; Italy waited until 1960. Most of the original settings were changed more than once before the final breakdown of the system after 1971. Indeed, until well into the 1960s, Canada, Switzerland, and the United States were the only advanced countries that allowed uncontrolled outflows of capital to other countries.

Arrangements for changes in legal par values was not the only step that the framers of the system took to avoid the suffocating deflations and unemployment that blind adherence to the old gold standard had mandated in the past. In the more frequent instances when trouble was expected to be temporary, the supply of foreign exchange available to be borrowed to tide a nation over such periods was to be augmented by the creation of a brand-new institution called the International Monetary Fund. The IMF was to function as a lender to governments and central banks requiring short-term accommodation that was not available from conventional sources.

Nevertheless, gold was still very much in the picture. The resources that the IMF had available to lend out came from contributions by each of its member countries, in two forms. Seventy-five percent of the contributions consisted of the members' own currencies—the French paid in francs, the Dutch paid in guilders, the United States paid in dollars, and so on. The other 25 percent, however, had to be in gold, although a lesser percentage was permitted for countries that could not afford the payment. Over time, many transactions in gold took place between the Fund and its member countries.

The new scheme, with its unfamiliar set of international obligations, encountered opposition from those who were fearful of newfangled systems. Their attitude provoked Keynes to a passionate defense of this new structure to which he had contributed so much: "I have spent my strength to persuade my countrymen and the world at large to change their traditional doctrines. . . . Was it not I, when many of today's iconoclasts were still worshipping the Calf, who wrote that 'Gold is a barbarous relic'?"[4]

The rest of the story is downhill all the way.

A grand underlying assumption supported this entire framework: that the dollar would continue to appear invincible—as good as gold—and therefore always acceptable everywhere and under all circumstances. This was an assumption that few people had stopped to question during the process of creation, or for the first ten years or so after all these arrangements were set in motion. Yet no matter how omnipotent economically, politically, and militarily the world may have perceived the Americans to be in 1945, there was no reason to expect that state of affairs to last forever.

On the contrary. The whole scheme was contrived with the primary purpose of putting Europe and Japan back on their feet. Once that goal was achieved, the dynamic would undergo fundamental change. The spanking new European and Japanese industrial facilities would be competition for American industry. They would also be attractive areas for American investment. As a result, the Americans would end up spending increasing amounts of money on imports and investing in foreign countries to a point where their massive gold hoard would be drawn down below its original swollen levels and their debts to foreigners would increase above the levels of the 1940s.

The Americans happily obliged by engaging in a great spending spree. As the economies of Europe and Asia revived according to plan and in response to American aid, the lure of the profit motive drove massive amounts of private capital from the United States into thousands of enterprises across the seas and attracted rising imports of foreign merchandise to America's shores. The United States undertook an unprecedented level of international economic assistance, launched large-scale social programs at home, deployed American military might around the world, and fought two hot wars in Asia as well as the Cold War against the Russians. Before the game was over, Americans would find themselves besieged by their economic enemies and forced by gold onto their knees before their friends.

The impact of the process on America's international financial position was already visible by the end of the 1950s. The U.S. monetary gold stock, which had held steady at around $22 billion from 1950 to 1958, shrank by over $3 billion between the end of 1958 and the end of 1960. Meanwhile, as Americans spent their dollars abroad, foreign ownership of bank deposits in American banks and of short-term U.S. Treasury obligations increased from only $8 billion in 1950 to over $20 billion in 1960. If foreigners at that moment had decided to convert all their liquid dollar assets into gold, the U.S. gold stock would have been exhausted.[5]

On October 27, 1960, provoked by news that the liberal John F. Kennedy was probably going to defeat Richard Nixon in the presidential election in the following week, the price of gold jumped as high as $40 an ounce in the London gold market, where gold was freely bought and sold in the form of bullion, not coins, and where most of the new supply came from South Africa. Kennedy did win the election at home, but he was alarmed by the adverse verdict in the gold market. Right after his election, Kennedy told his advisors that he ranked the dollar problem among his highest-priority concerns.[6]

This was an odd moment for an incipient dollar crisis to appear on the scene. No one should have expected the enormous excess of U.S. gold over liabilities to foreigners that existed at the end of the Second World War—more than $20 billion in gold and less than $10 billion in liabilities—to last indefinitely. This was an imbalance inherited from the dismal days of the late 1930s and the wartime sacrifices made by the Allied nations to overcome Germany and Japan. With peace and reconstruction, a shift back to the more normal relationship of gold stocks smaller than liabilities to foreigners was inevitable.

There is a case to be made that the process was not so alarming as the press and the television commentators tried to make the public believe. Nobody was forcing foreigners to hold that huge volume of dollars. Foreign owners of dollars were acting quite rationally. Dollars were acceptable everywhere in payment of obligations and to settle up balances between countries and between business firms. No other nation could match the magnitude or the wide variety of financial instruments offered in the U.S. money markets. Unlike gold, the dollars were easy to transfer from one owner to another. Dollars also earned interest income while held, which made them more attractive than gold as a reserve. As long as the dollars continued to serve as the most acceptable means of payment everywhere, no one had any need, or even any incentive, to cash in the dollars and hoard gold or hold some other country's currency instead.

In effect, the United States was functioning as a bank for the rest of the world, just as Britain had served as a bank for the rest of the world in the years before World War I, and for the same reason. The Bank of England carried only a small gold stock relative to its liabilities, because sterling was the foreign exchange reserve of choice and the capital markets of the City provided ready liquidity in a wide variety of instruments. At the same time, the earnings on Britain's investments abroad furnished a constant return flow of foreign exchange to the home country. Thus, sterling served as a ready means of payment not only to English people but to the world at large. Most banks carry modest cash reserves relative to their deposit liabilities precisely because their customers have found that transferring those deposits back and forth among themselves—

by writing checks, in other words—serves as a far more convenient and efficient means of payment than withdrawing cash that they would then have to send off to their creditors.*

Inflation was the only force that should have threatened the viability of the dollar under these circumstances. And here is where questions began to be raised. True, the U.S. economy had been free of inflationary pressures, despite high rates of economic growth, during the first half of the 1950s; in fact, consumer prices had fallen during 1954. Signs of trouble first appeared in 1956–1957, as the business cycle approached its peak and inflation bubbled up to around 3 percent. Even that rate of inflation might have been tolerated in the late phases of an economic expansion, but the increase of 2.7 percent in consumer prices from the end of 1957 to the end of 1958 came as a shock. By then the boom was over, and a serious decline in business activity had begun. Unemployment had risen by over a million, pushing the unemployment rate close to 7 percent of the labor force.

Such a thing had never happened before. Prices had *always* fallen in recessions and depressions. The Federal Reserve was so alarmed that it jacked up the Discount Rate in short order from 1½ percent to 4 percent, a move that aborted the recovery from this recession just two years after it began. The Chairman of the Federal Reserve, William McChesney Martin, announced that he considered inflation as serious a threat as communism to the safety and future of the United States.

Martin's determined stand against his hated enemy seems to have turned the trick. Once the bad news of 1958 was out of the way, the increase in consumer prices during the recovery years of 1959–1960 was even smaller than in 1958. The Federal Reserve's aggressive policy even persuaded Westinghouse and General Electric employees to abandon the cost-of-living clauses in their contracts and the militant West Coast longshoremen to give their employers free rein in introducing labor-saving machinery. From 1958 to 1964, inflation averaged only

*See Despres et al., 1966. It is argued there that, like any bank, the United States was lending or investing abroad on long-term while borrowing short from foreigners. Those experts who were generating so much concern about the high rate of growth in U.S. short-term liabilities to foreigners were victims of an accounting illusion. "No bank could survive in such an analytical world [where] the owners of wealth . . . insist on what they consider a more 'ultimate' means of payment. If the bank is sound, the trouble comes from the depositors' irrationality."

1.4 percent a year though the economy was expanding at an annual rate of 5 percent. Between 1959 and 1971, the rate of inflation and the rate of growth in the money supply in the United States were lower than in any of the major European economies.[7]

Perhaps these inflation numbers would have sufficed to calm the worries over the dollar, but other significant U.S. economic statistics spurred an accelerating drawdown of the gold stock. Just during the five years 1960–1964, imports totaled more than $80 billion, $11 billion was spent by the government sustaining the armed forces outside the United States, American business spent $29 billion investing in companies in Europe and Asia or building up financial assets in other countries, while foreign travel, other services, and foreign aid consumed another $18 billion. On the one hand, the American capital and the crowds of open-handed American tourists were welcome; on the other hand, resentment over the conspicuous display of American wealth festered throughout the 1960s.* The French were most vocal in their concerns and were determined to clip the wings of the American juggernaut.

During the second half of the 1960s, the inflation problem assumed more serious proportions, as the unemployment rate fell from over 5 percent of the labor force in 1965 to only 3.5 percent by 1969. Prices rose 3.4 percent a year from 1965 to 1968 and then increased by 5.5 percent in 1969. That was bad enough, but prices then rose by 5.7 percent in the recession year of 1970, again violating historical precedent. Further indications of an overheated U.S. economy appeared as the towering excess of merchandise exports over imports that had prevailed since the end of World War II peaked out at $6.8 billion in 1964 and then fell to only $600 million by 1969. At the same time, the volume of American capital continued to flow into foreign business firms as heavily as ever.

The intensification of the U.S. commitment to the war in Vietnam was the primary source of inflationary pressure. Defense spending jumped by about 60 percent during the second half of the 1960s. The

*This attitude was still alive and well at the dawn of the new millennium.

federal government had run surpluses through 1966, but in 1967 the budget deficit amounted to over $8 billion, and that was followed by a $26 billion deficit in 1968. In a rare exhibit of almost complete unanimity, professional economists of all stripes urged President Johnson to finance the swelling volume of defense expenditures by an increase in taxes. Johnson refused to follow their advice. To make matters even more difficult, most of the proceeds of rising military expenditures in Vietnam were ending up in French banks.

Foreign governments had great difficulty navigating through this kind of corrosion in the American economy. Nobody wanted to flee the dollar: no other currency was so well equipped to serve as an international reserve and means of payment. On the contrary, a run on the dollar and a fall in its value in terms of all the other currencies would have meant enormous losses for the billions of dollars that foreigners now held. The impact could be total chaos. Yet, notwithstanding these misgivings, gold—as always—remained as a tempting alternative for at least a portion of the expanding foreign holdings of dollars.

Consequently, the U.S. gold stock continued to sink despite the establishment of a variety of elaborate arrangements for short-term credits so that the United States would have other currencies available to meet its obligations abroad instead of drawing down its gold stock. The Federal Reserve attempted to maintain short-term interest rates high enough to make dollars more attractive than deutsche marks or Swiss francs and surely preferable to gold that paid no interest. The government pushed business groups and labor unions into "voluntary" agreements to check domestic inflation by limiting price and wage increases.

There was more. In September 1964, a special tax called the Interest Equalization Tax was enacted to discourage American investment abroad by taxing interest earned on deposits and bonds held in foreign currencies. That tax was now supplemented by additional measures, as President Johnson announced on January 1, 1968, that he would put "all the muscle this administration has behind the dollar and to keep our financial house in order."[8] American investment in Continental European companies was curbed. Corporations were required to repatriate part of their profits earned overseas. Bank lending abroad was limited. American travelers were urged to stay home and explore the beauties of their own country instead of spending precious dollars touring in other peoples' countries. After Richard Nixon's victory in the presidential election of 1968, a 10 percent tax surcharge was enacted to narrow the budget deficit—a belated reversal of Lyndon Johnson's adamant opposition to such a move.

Nothing sufficed. The accumulation of productive and profitable foreign assets by American firms and investors seemed to count for little. The U.S. gold stock declined every year from 1958 to 1971, falling from $19 billion to $10 billion, while America's liquid liabilities to foreigners rose every year over the same period of time until they had expanded to over $60 billion.[9] As the French economist Jacques Rueff put it on October 20, 1967, when the gold stock was $12 billion and the liabilities were $33 billion, the United States had exhausted its ability to pay off its creditors in gold: "It is like telling a bald man to comb his hair. There isn't any there."[10]

The United States seemed unable to restore any equilibrium to its international position. The gold bricks continued to move from American ownership at Fort Knox to foreign ownership stored for safety in the vaults of the Federal Reserve Bank of New York (or, for the French, at the Bank of France). The Europeans gained gold, but the inflow failed to stimulate their demand for imports from the United States by enough to reverse the eastward movement of gold. Like the Asians in times past, Europe defied Adam Smith's prediction that "When the quantity of gold and silver imported into any country exceeds the effectual demand, no vigilance of government can prevent their exportation." The "effectual demand" in the 1960s seemed to have no limit.

What appeared to be an unending sequence of bad news for everyone else was great news to the pessimists who were convinced that gold was the only hedge in a hopeless situation. These gold bugs, as they came to be known, had been accumulating gold in the London market since the late 1950s. The major financial powers were concerned that this buying could push gold above the official price of $35 an ounce, provoking an uncontrollable rush into gold that could topple the entire system. Starting in 1961, the United States, Great Britain, Germany, France, Italy, Switzerland, Holland, and Belgium had joined together to pool their resources in an effort to beat down these speculators. The pool would sell gold in the market whenever the price showed signs of moving more than a few cents above $35.

At the beginning, with new production coming in large quantities into London, the pool was able to buy more gold at $35 than it had to sell. The struggle with the speculators became increasingly one-sided, however, after General de Gaulle started beating the drums for an increase in the price of gold. In fact, General de Gaulle had pulled France out of the gold pool during 1967. In early March 1968, the United States had to transfer $950 million in gold to London to keep the price close to $35; nearly $2.5 billion had been paid out from Fort Knox since November 18, 1967, when the British had devalued sterling for the second time since the end of World War II.

On March 17, 1968, after seven fruitless years of pouring their treasure into the maws of the speculators, the members of the gold pool decided the game was up. They announced that henceforth they would no longer supply gold to the London market, or any gold market, nor did they intend to buy any gold from those sources in the future. Official transactions in gold between central banks would continue at $35 an ounce; central banks would still be free to buy gold from the United States for dollars at that price. From that point forward, the price of gold in the free market would be left to private parties to determine.

This decision to dismantle the gold pool was not only long overdue; the pool never should have been organized. Until the American balance of international transactions could exhibit some fundamental improvement, the members of the pool were simply pouring their gold stocks into the London market in a pointless exercise in which the pool could only lose while the speculators were taking a risk that was hard to resist. With the United States setting a floor to the price of gold by standing ready to buy all gold offered at $35, and with the pool members continuing to offer sufficient gold to hold the free market price at around $35.20, the speculators stood to lose only the small difference between what they paid and $35. The potential profit, however, might be enormous.* The incessant demands of the speculators could in time deplete the official gold stocks of the pool members to a level at which the major currencies would no longer appear to have adequate gold back-

*In today's terminology, this trade-off between risk and reward would be called a free option.

ing. At that point, the authorities would have no choice but to increase the official price of gold by a substantial amount. Who could pass up a deal like that?

General de Gaulle now proceeded to call the whole gold-pool strategy a sham, merely a stopgap on the way to the ultimate devaluation of the dollar. His blunt statements might have been considered just another of his long series of efforts to damn the dollar if William McChesney Martin, the Chairman of the Federal Reserve, had not been so indiscreet as to echo de Gaulle's prediction. In a speech in Detroit on March 20, 1968, three days after the gold pool had been closed down, Martin expressed his opinion that "We are perhaps on the road to devaluation."[11] The excitement drove the London gold price as high as $41 during April and May. By the spring of 1969, the price was over $43.

At this point, another disturbing possibility came into view. The gold pool had been organized so that each member's contribution was specified, in order to control any selling of gold that one or another member might want to undertake. Now the pool had been dismantled and the gold price was above $40. What would prevent one or another of the central banks that were former members of the pool from cashing in their dollars for gold at $35 in New York and quietly feeding gold into the London market at a handsome profit? With the pool no longer in operation, the temptation to cheat might be irresistible.

The danger was clear, and something had to be done. There was never any confirmation of an official pact, but rumors suggested that an informal handshake had taken place to deal with the problem. The European members of the pool agreed among themselves that they would refrain from converting any dollar balances into gold at least for the duration of the Vietnam War. That was the cutoff point, after which the Americans were expected at long last to come to grips with the gaping imbalance between the receipts from other countries and their payments abroad. The precedent for these arrangements had been set by the Germans a year earlier, when they had publicly forsworn any further redemption of dollar holdings into gold.

The willingness of the Europeans to play ball did not come for free. In return, the Americans were obliged to swallow the old-fashioned medicine of budget discipline and higher interest rates that had been routine in the 1920s and early 1930s. President Nixon was prevailed upon to support the 10 percent surcharge on all income taxes, which went into effect in 1969, his first year in office, and created a small but transitory budget surplus. The Federal Reserve raised the Discount Rate in a series of steps from 4 percent at the end of 1967 to 6 percent by the middle of 1969. The result was the mild recession of 1970, but even that accomplished little in the way of cooling the inflationary fevers as the rate of price increases showed no signs of subsiding.

While all this was going on, General de Gaulle was busy. He was determined to restore France to the days of *la gloire* and assail the Anglo-Saxons wherever possible. He twice vetoed Britain's entry into the European Common Market, the second time vetoing even negotiation on entry. He called for "a complete change in the structure of Canada," with Quebec elevated "to the rank of a sovereign state," for Quebec must "stand up to the invasion of the United States."[12] He rallied the descendants of the French in Louisiana to place their heritage above their American nationality. He limited his cooperation with the North Atlantic Treaty Organization (NATO) and expressed his determination to build an independent French nuclear capability. He decried the increasing ownership of French industry by Americans who were disbursing their dollars in such quantity into his great country.

Backed by the intellectual firepower provided by Jacques Rueff, de Gaulle and his associates called for an increase in the price of gold to $70, which would have doubled the dollar value of all the monetary gold in the world. This step would have been a juicy benefit for the French, who held the largest share of monetary gold outside the United States. Rueff went on to argue that the United States would have to give up its profit from this windfall by using its gold to pay down what he considered to be its bloated liabilities to foreigners. From that point forward, countries spending more abroad than they received in payments from foreigners would have to settle the difference by transfers of gold.

De Gaulle's ultimate objective was to bring an end to the special position of the United States, in which Americans could offset the deficit in their international transactions simply by paying over dollars—their own currency—to foreigners, while everyone else had to settle up with some other country's currency or in gold. De Gaulle was far from alone in resenting a process in which only the United States could finance its spending abroad by what amounted essentially to printing dollars, while the rest of the world had to "earn" their foreign currency or gold by running a surplus in their transactions with foreign nations.

It was de Gaulle's recommended solution that drew no support. The authorities in the other leading financial nations rejected his trial balloon. Quite aside from the inflationary potential in a doubling of the world's monetary base, this gain created by a stroke of the pen would have been a bonanza for the world's two largest gold producers, South Africa and the Soviet Union, neither of which would have won any popularity contests among the Western nations at that time.

This effort would turn out to be the General's last gasp. In April 1968, the authoritative French newspaper *Le Monde* reported that "The weakness of the [French] position stemmed from the absence of complex counterproposals to the lax but coherent system of the Americans and their European allies."[13] *Le Monde* up to that time had been ardent in its harassment of the dollar. Its defection from that position was a loud signal that de Gaulle's campaign was beginning to crumble.

The final blow came in May 1968, when a wild swirl of rioting and strikes broke loose in France. The tumultuous uproar was similar in intensity to the passionate uprisings that occurred in the United States at the same time, but the French were motivated by demands for higher wages rather than by protests over the Vietnam War. The strikes delivered a major blow to the French economy, cost over 750 million working hours, and resulted in a sharp increase in labor costs, which led in turn to rising expectations of a devaluation of the franc. The shocking violence of the uprising provoked a flight of capital reminiscent of the panics of the 1920s, accompanied by strong upward pressure on the deutsche mark and the Swiss franc as the most appropriate safe havens of the moment. By the time the dust had settled, de Gaulle had risked his tenure on a popular referendum that forced him to resign from power—and that decision ignited an even greater panic in the markets for the franc.[14]

So much for the General's campaign to force the dollar back to the old gold standard.

The events of 1968 were a turning point in history. The impact on gold was just part of a profound shift in the entire political, economic, and social scene.

The year 1968 was marked by radical demonstrations and social turmoil at a level not seen since the 1930s, and not only in the United States and France. In the United States, 1968 also produced the first Republican election victory since 1956. In the fruitless pursuit of victory in Vietnam, the postwar succession of innovative social programs climaxed by Lyndon Johnson's Great Society came to a quiet end. Instead, political leaders around the world became engaged in a great battle against the threats and disruptions of accelerating inflation—a struggle that would last for more than a decade and that would lead to revolutionary changes in the role of government, in the structure and institutions of financial systems, and in the fundamental character of the capitalist system itself.

The turning point for gold was in the decision on March 17, 1968, to close down the gold pool. From that point forward, the associated governments warned the speculators and the hedgers that gold was theirs to play with on their own. Now there would be neither floor nor ceiling to the price of gold in the free markets. Although aimed only at the public markets, this threat would turn out to be the beginning of the end for gold as the monetary standard. The concept was already tattered, as we have seen, but the dollar as the fulcrum of the financial system was still officially tied to gold at the old price of $35 an ounce. The problem was that the dollar itself was so tattered, and U.S. gold reserves so depleted, that the system was heading toward a climax from which something quite different would emerge. Once the authorities gave up any control over the price of gold in the free markets, the politicians had no choice but to join forces to break free of the golden fetters. For a long time, the politicians were ahead of the financial markets in this endeavor.

There was a lesson in all this, foretold by General de Gaulle's poignant but significant defeat. De Gaulle reminds us of poor King Midas, who turned his beloved daughter into a golden statue when he embraced her—or of Montagu Norman, whose blind faith in gold made him, as Churchill reminded us, "perfectly happy in the spectacle of Britain possessing the finest credit in the world simultaneously with a million and a quarter unemployed."

De Gaulle's driving ambition had been to take revenge on the Anglo-Saxons and bring them to their knees before France. His weapon of choice was "gold that never changes . . . that is eternally and universally accepted." As his mentor, Jacques Rueff, had insisted, any system other than a pure gold standard would be "a serious obstacle to social progress." Yet in the end, it was France's hoard of gold that was the obstacle to social progress and that drove the General into retirement from the public arena. While General de Gaulle was looking down his oversized nose at the U.S. dollar and gloating over all the gold that France was proudly shipping across the Atlantic, Americans consumed much delicious French food, drank many bottles of fabulous French wine, titillated themselves with haunting French perfumes, and, not incidentally, became owners of prime French companies such as the computer manufacturer Machines Bull. Had the citizens of France and the rest of Europe been the same kind of free-spenders as the Americans, the sequence of events would have been entirely different.

Disappointment, disillusion, and defeat have overcome everyone in this history who was so blinded in the pursuit of a hoard of gold that they could not comprehend the difference between useless metal and real wealth. That lesson seems to have been learned by the political leaders of the three decades that have followed the 1960s. Let us now see how the disturbances of 1968 started gold down the road to the place it occupies in the world today.

20

World War Eight and the Thirty Ounces of Gold

As inflation gathered steam during the course of 1968, the gold-based Bretton Woods system of fixed exchange rates loomed as an intolerable restraint on politicians struggling to finance rising costs of government. The result was renewed interest in gold among the public as a safe haven destined to fulfill the proverb that Herbert Hoover had thrown at President-Elect Roosevelt in 1933: "We have gold because we cannot trust Governments."

Yet governments were limited in what they could do if the value of their currencies in the foreign exchange markets were to remain rigidly fixed, as the Bretton Woods regime prescribed. Higher government spending tends to stimulate domestic demand, which often raises prices and sucks in imports, the very conditions that make people want to flee a currency and shift to countries with a more conservative style of managing their economic and financial affairs—or to gold. The more that governments tried to find wriggle room around the constraints of the Bretton Woods system, the more the public and the speculators followed Hoover's dictum and turned to gold as the ultimate hedge against the irresponsibility of governments.

Indeed, nobody was satisfied with the way conditions evolved. The creators of the postwar system had produced an artful design, but economic depression and deflation were the dominant influences on their work. The turbulent economic environment spawned by the overoptimism and aggressive governmental policies of the 1960s was still too novel for anyone to even suggest designing a replacement for Bretton Woods. Once the inflationary genie was out of the bottle, the system had no comfortable way to stuff it back in.

After 1968, inflation became a self-fulfilling prophecy that added momentum to the fundamental inflationary forces at work in the system. Employee compensation in the United States increased at annual rates of more than 7 percent during 1970 in the face of an unemployment rate that rose from 3.5 percent to over 6 percent of the labor force. The unions were convinced they had to keep wages climbing faster than inflation, while business managements were convinced they had to keep prices rising in order to cover the increased labor costs. The whole process developed a dynamic of its own, pushing on regardless of the unemployment rate, the profit rate, the interest rate, the tax rate, or any force that in other circumstances would have tamed it. These stubborn inflationary pressures only added to the tension over the dollar problem and the diminishing gold stock.

The Nixon administration could see just two ways out of these dilemmas. The first alternative, the traditional one, was etched in agony by the British in 1931: raise taxes and interest rates so high that the economy would be pushed into a serious recession, not just a pause as in 1970. That step might kill off the inflation mentality and rescue the dollar, but at an unacceptable human cost, to say nothing of the consequences for an elected politician who selected such a strategy.

The other choice, attempting a direct attack on rising prices, would involve the government in administering a system of controls to keep both wage and price increases in check. By controlling wages, the policy could assure business firms that they could function without constantly raising their prices to protect their profits; by controlling prices, the policy could assure employees that inflation in the cost of living would no longer erode the purchasing power of their earnings. This route, which was known euphemistically as "incomes policy," appeared to many to be the preferable choice. If controls could suppress inflation, there would be no need to crush the business expansion and drive up the unemployment rate. Lower inflation might also take heat off the dollar and the gold stock. Controls would mean interference with the free-market system, but they still appeared to offer the best of all possible worlds. This path had been advocated by many Democrats, but now more conservative support began to develop. In August 1970, Congress enacted legislation that gave the President discretionary authority to impose comprehensive wage and price controls.

Nixon, however, had no enthusiasm for the idea. Wartime experience as an employee of the Office of Price Administration in World War II had given him a good lesson in how challenging both the economics and the politics of wage and price controls could be. At first, he made nothing more than a token move toward controls with a number of meaningless but high-sounding measures such as appointing a National Commission on Productivity or ordering the Council of Economic Advisors to issue "inflation alerts" that were statistical and analytical rather than recommendations for direct action.

Despite his misgivings, the President recognized that conditions were backing him into a corner. In December, he took a major step toward a more active policy when he appointed John Connally as Secretary of the Treasury. Connally was a former governor of Texas who had gained national attention when he was wounded while riding in the car when President Kennedy was assassinated in Dallas. A skilled political operator, he was a handsome silver-haired man of commanding presence. He also had no preconceptions about policy. One of his favorite expressions was, "I can play it round or I can play it flat, just tell me how to play it."[1] Connally was just the man to overcome Nixon's reluctance to make spectacular moves in economic policy. Furthermore, as Secretary of the Treasury, the deteriorating international financial position of the United States was Connally's primary responsibility, and here the United States could not postpone action much longer.

Nixon and Connally decided to consider a two-pronged move. Its two elements appeared at first glance to have no clear relationship to each other; as matters worked out, they neatly combined into an integrated program.[2]

The first move was designed to solve the gold problem for the United States once and for all. The Treasury would simply shut down the gold window, which would mean refusing to sell gold at $35 an ounce to governments or central banks coming to the Treasury to exchange their dollars. This radical step would be the grand finale of the convertibility of the dollar into gold that had been in effect, with only the Civil War hiatus, for nearly two hundred years. The dollar would finally be liberated from the golden fetters, like all the other currencies of the world. Without any fixed anchor, the dollar would be free to "float" in the foreign exchange markets.

It is important to understand the full meaning of this expression. All foreign exchange rates are set in the first instance in a market where supply and demand determine the price of a currency, just as in the markets for common stocks, wheat, or oil. Suppose that a French commercial bank is accumulating more dollars than it needs because American tourists are exchanging large amounts in dollar traveler's checks for francs. There is a market where the bank can sell those excess dollars to foreign exchange dealers or to individuals or institutions willing to buy the dollars and pay for them with French francs. That fresh supply of dollars in the market may cause the price of the dollar to fall in terms of francs. That is, sellers of dollars will now receive fewer francs; however, buyers of dollars will have to pay fewer francs.

If the dollar is convertible into gold at a fixed price, however, the Bank of France may buy the unwanted dollars from the commercial bank, because the Bank can convert those dollars into gold at the U.S. Treasury at a price that will not decline—which means dollars are as good as gold. Under those conditions, the dollar–franc exchange rate will tend to be stable instead of deteriorating in response to the increased supply of dollars for sale.

But what happens when a currency is not convertible into gold, when the gold window in Washington is no longer available? Then no automatic limits exist for how low or how high the currency's exchange rate can go relative to the values of other currencies. The currency is floating. The only way to prevent the dollar from falling under these conditions is for the Bank of France to buy those dollars and just hold them, or for the U.S. Treasury to sell French francs from its reserves (a policy called "dirty floating"). If the Bank of France steps aside, however, or if the U.S. Treasury has too few francs in reserve to meet the demand, the dollar will depreciate and the value of the franc will appreciate.

If the gold window were shut, Nixon and Connally would force the foreign central banks to face a nasty set of alternatives. It was like a game of hearts, in which the Americans had passed the queen of spades to their opponents. The foreign central banks could continue to buy all dollars offered for sale, but that would only swell their already substantial dollar positions—in Wall Street parlance, the dollar was overowned. If they held back from buying, however, the dollar would decline in price in terms of other currencies. That would mean heavy losses to their citizens who had acquired dollars or dollar-denominated assets in the past and were still holding them. Furthermore, if French francs now cost Americans more dollars than before, Americans would tend to buy less French perfume and wine; at the same time, the French would now have to pay fewer francs to buy $1000 worth of American goods and services, which would give a boost to imports into France from the United States.

This was the precise outcome that Nixon and Connally hoped to achieve. All of that would be good for American business and jobs. Furthermore, by making American exports more attractive and foreign imports less attractive, the devaluation of the dollar might tend to be self-correcting as American demands for foreign currencies diminished and foreign demands for dollars picked up.

The second part of the Connally–Nixon strategy was designed to suppress the potentially inflationary consequences of this stimulus to business. In order to persuade the world (including Americans themselves) that the finale to gold convertibility was not also the last step on the sure road to runaway inflation, Nixon and Connally recognized they would have to package the shattering of the link to gold with price and wage controls that would confirm their dedication to fighting inflation.

Nixon was convinced that the time for half measures was past. He intended to stifle all criticism of pussyfooting by moving, as he described it, to "leapfrog them all."[3] He anticipated little difficulty. The combination of abandoning the gold standard and adopting mandatory price and wage controls made a perfect fit. The economic attractions were strong, but both Nixon and Connally appreciated even more the political appeal of this new policy: conservatives liked the free market implications of the break with gold while liberals liked the activist policy of wage and price controls.

The last straw came during the week of August 9, in a note of extraordinary irony, when the British economic representative came in person to the Treasury and asked for $3 billion in gold. On the following Friday, the 13th, the President abruptly ordered the sixteen major economic policymakers of the administration to accompany him by helicopter to Camp David. The President made certain that no leaks about the proceedings would occur by cutting the group off from all communication with the outside world. Herbert Stein, Chairman of the Council of Economic Advisors at the time, described the occasion as "one of the most exciting and dramatic events in the history of economic policy."[4]

The group brought forth what they dubbed a New Economic Policy, which combined the closing of the gold window with a mandatory and comprehensive freeze on prices and wages. The freeze was for ninety days, but the expectation was that this initial step would be followed by voluntary restraints by business and labor. In addition to the decisions on controls and gold, the new policy included recommendations for tax cuts for business, reductions in government spending, and a 10 percent surcharge on about half of all U.S. imports. The import surcharge was the equivalent of a devaluation of the dollar, even without any change in the foreign exchange markets, because it automatically made those imports more expensive for Americans.

All the participants agreed that the announcement of the New Economic Policy should be designed to have major impact around the world. The President was urged to make a public statement on prime-time television that Sunday evening. By making his decisions known before the markets opened on Monday morning, no leaks or rumors would be able to dilute the force of his words. Nixon demurred. he hesitated to make his speech on Sunday evening, for fear of irritating the public by preempting *Bonanza*, one of the most popular programs of the era.[5]

Under pressure from his advisors, Nixon managed to put the national interest ahead of the well-being of *Bonanza* fans. The news of his prime-time address broke with banner headlines on Monday morning's newspapers. The President minced no words:

> I have directed the Secretary of the Treasury to defend the dollar against the speculators. . . . Now the other nations are economically strong, and the time has come for them to bear their fair share of the burden of defending freedom around the world. The time has come

> for exchange rates to be set straight. . . . There is no longer any need for the United States to compete with one hand behind its back. . . . We are not about to ease up and lose the economic leadership of the world.[6]

"They've really shot both barrels," observed the President of Bankers Trust Company on Monday morning. Paul Samuelson, the Nobel Prize–winning economist, asserted in an article for the *New York Times* that "The President had no real choice. His hand was forced by the massive hemorrhage of dollar reserves of recent weeks. . . . For more than a decade the American dollar has been an overvalued currency. . . . [The new policy] also helps Japan . . . since it is foolish for Japan to give away goods without being repaid for them in equivalent goods." On Wall Street, one salesman exulted, "All brokers are the happiest people in the world today," as bond prices soared, the stock market boomed by nearly 4 percent, and trading volume was the highest on record up to that date.[7]

There were a few sour reactions. The only declared candidate for the Democratic presidential nomination, George McGovern, was unhappy: "It is a disgrace for a great nation like ours to end in this way the convertibility of the dollar. . . . By this act we will become the economic pariahs of the world."[8] The AFL–CIO (American Federation of Labor and Congress of Industrial Organizations), speaking for the labor unions and bristling at the prospect of controls on wage increases, announced that they had "absolutely no faith in the ability of President Nixon to successfully manage the economy of this nation."[9]

The negative views missed the whole point. Since the end of World War II, the Americans had locked themselves into a golden prison that only postponed the day of reckoning. They had tried every which way to preserve the tie to gold even as they spent enormous sums of money on imports and investments in foreign countries. They borrowed from and wheedled their friends, they taxed their citizens, they warred on speculators, and they raised bars against their corporations' investing abroad. The one step that might have allowed them to hold onto their gold—the traditional policy of pushing down on the economy and increasing unemployment—was unacceptable in the postwar world.

The only other alternative would have been to abandon gold much sooner than in 1971. A few oddballs dared to suggest that solution, but they were shouted down. Foreigners wanted the gold window kept open so that they could cash in their dollar balances for gold at will. Hubris blocked the American leaders from taking drastic action until the very last moment. At the same time, the Europeans and the Japanese feared a devaluation of the dollar because it would have been bad for their business and would have produced big losses for their citizens who had accumulated dollars and dollar-denominated assets in the past. Dollar devaluation would also have meant fewer exports to America and greater competition from imports from America. Yet only dollar devaluation was likely to convert the reluctant foreigners into buying more American goods and services and bring balance back into the system.

With the golden anchor torn loose, once and for all, the New Economic Policy created instant pandemonium abroad. In contrast to Wall Street, foreign stock markets plummeted. In Tokyo, the market suffered a genuine panic, as the *New York Times* described it, "with sell-at-any-price orders sending prices down sharply."[10] One American who wanted to buy a loaf of bread in Paris and offered a dollar bill to the baker was told, "That's not worth anything any more."[11]

The only alternative to a fall in the value of the dollar against the world's currencies would have been for foreign governments and central banks to stand ready to buy all dollars offered for sale by private parties who could no longer see any reason to continue taking the risk of holding dollars. While the authorities cogitated over what action to take, foreign exchange markets were shut down; no trading was permitted. Only Japan remained open, but after absorbing $4 billion in the two weeks after August 15, the Tokyo government let go and watched the yen appreciate against the dollar. Other markets opened on the 23rd, with similar results. The dollar had been devalued.

The flood of dollar selling provoked foreign governments to demand a prompt return to some kind of system of fixed exchange rates. Even the Americans had to admit that such volatile exchange rates created uncertainty for all kinds of business decisions. A long series of negotiations culminated in a meeting in December 1971 at the Smithsonian

Institution in Washington to reestablish order in the foreign exchange markets. A new set of parities was agreed upon, recognizing part of the depreciation of the dollar that had occurred in the markets over the past four months, and the United States withdrew the 10 percent import surcharge. A new official dollar price of gold was set at $38—the equivalent of a formal 7.9 percent devaluation of the dollar—although by that time gold in the London market was trading at between $43 and $44, about $5 higher than on August 15. With a preposterous degree of hyperbole, Nixon characterized this agreement as "the most significant monetary agreement in the history of the world."[12]

The new arrangements were incapable of surviving the intensifying inflationary pressures gathering all around the world. A series of crises led to another set of negotiations that produced an approved increase in the official dollar price of gold to $42.22 (which is the price still in use by the United States, 27 years later), but even this step failed to ward off a final breakdown in the efforts to sustain fixed exchange relationships among the major currencies. To make matters worse, OPEC (Organization of Petroleum Exporting Countries), a consortium of major oil-producing countries, joined together in October 1973 to restrict their production until the price of oil had jumped from $2.11 a barrel to over $10, igniting additional powerful and irrepressible inflationary impulses throughout the world economy.

All of this was too much for the U.S. system of price and wage controls. The administration had no choice but to abandon these arrangements in the face of the tremendous leap in the price of oil combined with the devaluation of the dollar, which automatically raised the price to Americans of most foreign goods and services.

Then, in November 1973, only a month after the OPEC countries had roiled the world economy, the central banks threw in the sponge on their 1968 decision to refrain from trading in gold except among themselves. Now the central banks could buy and sell in the London market at prices far above the official price of $42.22, and several loans from one government to another were collateralized by gold valued at more than $40. The French soon began valuing all their gold reserves at the market price, although others refused to follow their lead and left the French once again as outliers.

Beginning in 1975, tentative steps were taken to liberate the monetary system even further from gold. In January and June 1975, and again in 1978 and 1979, the U.S. Treasury auctioned a total of about 6 percent of its total gold stock, motivated by the belief that "Neither gold nor any other commodity provides a suitable base for monetary arrangements."[13] Then in August, an International Monetary Fund committee reached two momentous decisions: they agreed to abolish the official price for gold, and they also decided to auction a portion of the Fund's gold holdings. The proceeds of the auction were to be used for the benefit of developing countries and also to return to member countries some of the money they had originally contributed to the Fund. After one hundred years in which hoarding gold was the fashion among the central banks, all of a sudden hoarding was out and dishoarding was in.

The speculating public was unimpressed with both the words and the deeds of the governments and official agencies. If governments wanted to play games with gold at artificial values, or auction off nominal quantities of gold, that was their problem. None of the international agreements to manage exchange-rate volatility seemed to hold up. Inflation in all countries was eating away at the values of stocks, bonds, and cash. Inflation was most intense in Britain, France, and the United States among the developed countries, but even Germany's inflation averaged 5 percent from 1974 to 1981 and included episodes above 7 percent. Consequently, many speculators were only too happy to buy gold from central banks that insisted on behaving as though gold was just a barbarous relic and not worth owning any longer.

The soaring demand for gold as a safe haven for wealth and as a hedge against inflation drove the price in the London market from $46 an ounce at the beginning of 1972 to $64 an ounce at the end of the year. The price broke through $100 during 1973; from 1974 to 1977, gold fluctuated between $130 and $180. A second OPEC oil price increase to $30 a barrel in 1978 created a frenzy that ignited a new and precipitous climb in the gold markets: the price of gold hit $244 an ounce before the year was out and then doubled to $500 in 1979. In the spirit of the times, the famous comedienne Bette Midler, about to depart on a European tour, demanded on July 3, 1978, that her $600,000 fee be paid in South African gold coins instead of in U.S. dollars.[14]

The headline on the cover of the March 12, 1979, issue of *Business Week* magazine read "The Decline of U.S. Power" and showed a close-up of the face of the Statue of Liberty with a tear running down her cheek. There was plenty to cry about in the U.S. economy, with most of the trouble homegrown. America had become the victim of her own success. At the end of World War II, American business was so far ahead of the ruined economies in the rest of the world that American managements were convinced they had all the answers. Corporate executives belittled change and played down the competitive pressures that were steadily building beyond the national borders of the United States as Europe and Asia recovered from the war. While a new generation of business management abroad achieved high rates of economic growth and technological innovation, American business continued to suffer from economic hardening of the arteries.

The tragic loss of competitive position by the American economy in the 1970s was the equivalent of a major military defeat. Inflation appeared out of control, unemployment remained stubbornly high, fiscal policy was a mess, the dollar was approaching a major crisis at the end of the decade, and America's share of world markets was shrinking at a distressing rate.

In October 1979, inflation in the United States was running over 12 percent—a significant increase from the distressing figure of 8 percent a year earlier—while the dollar was at bay in the foreign exchange markets. Paul Volcker, the Chairman of the Federal Reserve System, was now confronted by his agitated counterparts in the major European countries and Japan, who feared that the whole world would succumb to a crisis as devastating as the 1930s unless the United States took strong and decisive steps to mend its ways. Volcker pledged the Federal Reserve to bring the surging U.S. money supply under control, even if it meant pushing interest rates up to levels never before seen in history. The Federal Reserve was about to swallow the conventional medicine.

Volcker's strategy was ultimately victorious in the long battle against inflation, but the immediate impact of his policies unleashed another torrent of turbulence in the financial markets. Nobody knew for certain how measures as tough as this would play out over time. The major concern was that the blow to the economy might be so severe, with widespread bankruptcies, plunging production, and soaring unemployment, that the policy would have to be completely reversed, unleashing a whole new wave of inflationary pressures.

The United States was not the only country facing chaotic conditions at that moment. Inflation in most countries at the end of 1979 was running in double digits and even Germany was up to 6 percent. Political conditions were perhaps even more frightening. Iranian radicals in November 1979 took over the U.S. embassy in Tehran and held the entire staff as hostages, initiating a crisis that would endure for more than four hundred days. At the same time, the Russians were building up their strength in southern Yemen near Saudi Arabia, near Afghanistan's border with Iran, and near Bulgaria's border with Yugoslavia—at a moment when Yugoslavia's 87-year-old Marshal Tito was in poor health.

January 1980 in the gold market turned out to be one of the wildest months in the history of any market, anywhere, any time. The price of gold jumped by $110 an ounce to $634 in just the first two business days of the month, while the value of the dollar in terms of German marks fell to a record low. A London branch bank reported that its inventory of one thousand gold sovereigns had sold out in the course of the two days. A precious metals trader for one of the Swiss banks, in a master understatement, told a reporter from the *New York Times* that "The market shows that people don't trust the governments and they don't trust paper money either."[15]

All of a sudden the central banks began to make noises about restoring gold to its traditional role in the monetary system, a complete reversal of recent policies of selling gold out of their reserves. The U.S. Undersecretary of the Treasury declared before Congress that "Gold remains a significant part of the reserves of the central banks available in time of need. This is unlikely to change in the foreseeable future."[16] No wonder: the stunning increase in the price of gold since 1978 had swollen the market value of the gold reserves to more than three times their total holdings of foreign currencies.

Then Treasury Secretary G. William Miller held a news conference at which he announced that the Treasury would hold no further gold auctions. "At the moment," he told the press, "it doesn't seem an appropriate time to sell our gold." With 220 million ounces (about seven thousand tons) of gold stored away at Fort Knox, gold hoarding was regaining some traditional respectability. This was a curious observation in light of the auctions of gold that the Treasury had conducted at much lower prices since they had begun the practice five years earlier. Most investors aim to buy low and sell high, but the U.S. Treasury apparently was more attracted to selling low than high: the last auction before these events, just two months earlier, had produced an average price of only $372.30.[17]

Within thirty minutes of Miller's remarks, the gold price shot up $30 an ounce to $715. The next day it was up to $760. The day after, gold hit $820. The manager of the precious metals department of a New York bank specializing in the gold trade was ecstatic: "Certificates, bullion, coins, bars, you name it, our business has been very brisk. Americans are catching the gold fever. As for the international bullion market, which represents the bulk of our business, it's become a zoo."[18]

Not everyone was caught up in the panic. Unlike Secretary Miller, many common citizens thought selling high was kind of a good idea. The *New York Times* for January 12 carried an article that began with these words: "They came clutching all manner of objects precious to them, from heirloom silver to gold coins and jewelry, hoping to turn their old gold and silver into new, fresh [dollar] bills." One prominent dealer's waiting room was described as resembling an airport lounge at peak holiday season rather than a company in the business of purchasing old metal objects. Five days later, when the price in the gold market was at $760 an ounce, a similar article reported, "On 47th Street the dealers were predicting the price would hit $1,000 an ounce by July, but no one seemed to be waiting."

The price touched its record high of $850 on January 21. James Sinclair, a commodities broker, summed it up when he commented that "We're in World War Eight, if you believe the market."[19] Late that afternoon, President Carter announced that the United States would have to "pay whatever price is required to remain the strongest nation in the world." His comment seemed to cool tempers in the gold and foreign exchange markets—the price of gold was down $50 by the close of trading.

Indeed, the temper of the marketplace did a 180-degree turn with extraordinary abruptness. On January 22, the price plunged by $145. The high in 1981 was $599 an ounce. By 1985, gold was down to around $300. The subsequent high, touched only briefly, was $486, in the wake of the stock market crash of 1987. At the end of 1997, gold broke below

$300. It had fallen by more than 60 percent in the course of less than eight years.

That fantastic bull market in gold from $35 in 1868 to $850 in the climax of January 1980 is an extraordinary episode in financial history. It represented a gain of 30 percent a year over twelve years, far in excess of the inflation rate of 7.5 percent from 1968 to 1980. Even the greatest bull markets in stock market history pale by comparison. The highest total annual return (including income) in the stock market over a twelve-year period was 19 percent, from the middle of 1949 to the middle of 1961. In 1959, the amount invested in gold was about one-fifth of the market value of all U.S. common stocks; in 1980, the $1.6 trillion invested in gold *exceeded* the market value of $1.4 trillion in U.S. stocks.[20] If only Croesus, Charlemagne, and Pizarro had lived to see such a triumphant march in the value of their precious gold!

Nevertheless, the raw data exaggerate the happiness that these zooming prices brought to the gold bugs. Few people who bought at $35, or even under $100, held on to sell at $850. Most of the early buyers undoubtedly took their profits and bailed out long before the peak, for the path to $850 was volatile all the way. The likelihood is that many more people were sucked into the gold market as it approached $850—and shortly afterward—than those who were farsighted enough to go in when the price was fussing around $40.

The rush into the gold markets in the early 1980s produced much the same kinds of results as the gold rush to the Klondike eighty years earlier, where only about four hundred people out of one hundred thousand prospectors hit it rich. Indeed, it is ironic that the State of Alaska Retirement System bought a ton of gold bullion in 1980 at $651 an ounce, and then a second ton at the end of 1980 for which they paid $575. In March 1983, the state sold out at $414.[21] Thus, the real winners at the end were the sellers—an opportunity that the U.S. Treasury chose to pass up.

In 1981, the U.S. monetary gold stock amounted to approximately eight thousand tons, a little more than a third of the 1949 peak, only 50 percent more than in 1933, and equal to about a quarter of world monetary gold stocks. At the official price of $42.22, the stock was carried at a mere $11 billion, although the stock was worth $120 billion at the 1981 average market price of $460 an ounce. Liabilities to foreigners, however, were now over $300 billion, an astonishing increase of nearly tenfold over the level that had so agitated General de Gaulle thirteen years earlier.[22]

Donald Regan, the Secretary of the Treasury, decided that the situation required a thorough examination. As David Ricardo in 1810 had called for the creation of a "SELECT COMMITTEE to enquire into the Cause of the High Price of GOLD BULLION, and to take into consideration the State of the CIRCULATING MEDIUM, and of the EXCHANGES between Great Britain and Foreign Parts," Regan appointed a Gold Commission in June 1981 to "conduct a study to assess and make recommendations . . . concerning the role of gold in domestic and international monetary systems." The Commission included members of Congress, representatives from the Federal Reserve Board, leading economists, one well-known academic, and two individuals active in the gold markets.

After nine meetings and 23 witnesses, the Commission issued a report that features an extraordinary number of footnotes drafted by individual members, indicating the depth of the disagreements over their understanding of what had happened to gold in the recent past and the appropriate course of action that the Commission should recommend for the immediate future. The report contains an admirable history of gold in monetary systems and a cornucopia of useful historical statistics, but its recommendations hold little interest because they fell so far short of unanimity in support among the members. The Regan Commission of 1981 has passed into anonymity, while the Bullion Committee Report of 1810 continues to be an important element in the study of money and banking. Just about the only vestige of the Regan Commission's recommendations that remains is the small number of gold coins minted after they were authorized by President Reagan in December 1985. Most of these handsome coins now reside in the hands of collectors.[23]

Quite aside from the failure of the Gold Commission to speak loudly and clearly with one voice, fundamental economic trends in the early 1980s were finally shoving gold away from center stage. Bond yields were in double digits and common stocks were providing a flow of dividend income as high as 6 percent. As gold pays no income and incurs storage costs, owning gold was expensive indeed compared to alternative investment opportunities.

Gold would still have made sense in spite of these hurdles if people had expected inflation to remain out of control. The whole story of the 1980s, however, was the growing recognition, around the world, that the virulent inflation of the 1970s had been beaten back at long last and that the prices of goods and services for the foreseeable future would rise at a more moderate and manageable pace. It is indeed remarkable that U.S. inflation fell from such precipitous heights at the end of the 1970s to as low as 3 percent by 1985, but similar trends were at work in most countries, even in such areas as Italy, Latin America, and the Middle East, where inflation had been a chronic problem. Holding gold can make little sense if inflation is dead or dying, because then there is little hope of recouping the storage costs and offsetting the lost income.

During the two decades after 1980, the ups and downs in the price of gold followed the ups and downs—mostly downs—in the rate of inflation. The price of gold fell absolutely, however, while the prices of goods and services continued to rise, albeit at a slower pace. The cost of living doubled from 1980 to 1999—an annual inflation rate of about 3.5 percent—but the price of gold fell by some 60 percent. In January 1980, one ounce of gold could buy a basket of goods and services worth $850. In 1999, the same basket would cost five ounces of gold.

The stock market offers an even more striking comparison. By some remarkable coincidence, the Dow Jones Industrial Average of stock prices was at just about 850 when gold touched its $850 peak.* Thus, an ounce of gold would have bought one share of the Average at that moment. When gold was down to the $300 area in the autumn of 1999, however, the Dow Jones was around 10,000. Now more than thirty ounces of gold would be needed to buy one share of the Average.

*The Average closed out January 1980 at 860.34.

One little-noted recommendation of the Regan Commission of 1981 involved the appropriate size of the government's stock of gold. Although an initial majority vote concluded that "Under circumstances as those that presently exist, the stock should be maintained at its present value," the final report recommends that "While no precise level for the gold stock is necessarily 'right,' the Treasury [should] retain the right to conduct sales of gold at its discretion, provided adequate levels are maintained for contingencies."[24] Despite the double-talk in the final phrase, this recommendation set the tone for the environment for gold for the rest of the 1980s and throughout the 1990s.

The lower the price of gold fell, the greater became the prospects of official sales, not just from the United States but from other countries and the International Monetary Fund itself. As the gold price rose from $375 in 1982 to nearly $500 after the stock-market crash of 1987, few central bank sales were executed. As the price then drifted downward toward $350 in 1992, about five hundred tons were disposed of. From 1992 to 1999, however, as the price sank below $300, the central bankers sold off three thousand tons, or about four hundred tons a year.[25] One does not have to be an amateur investor to sell low.

As the central banks were liquidating their gold, over two thousand tons a year of additional gold came into the markets from new mine production, about double the level of production before the price of gold broke free from the old $35 price. Sales of four hundred tons from the central banks sound small relative to the two thousand tons of supply forthcoming from the mines. Nevertheless, the volume of total central bank and official *holdings* was still so large—over thirty thousand tons—that the overhang loomed like a black cloud over the markets. Who could say how much of that hoarded treasure might come to market?

A loud thunderclap along these lines hit the markets in October 1997, when a team of Swiss experts issued a report recommending an amendment to the Swiss constitution that would result in a radical restructuring of the Swiss currency system. "Gold has lost its monetary function," the experts declared. "The gold parity is strictly an accounting tool. . . . A return to gold standards today is impossible. . . . The proposed draft of the new constitutional article does not contain any connection of the [Swiss] franc to gold. Paragraph 5 of article E-BV, which mandates the Swiss National Bank to hold adequate currency reserves, should replace the confidence inspiring gold coverage and ensure that the public's trust in the state currency remains."[26]

The experts were not quite ready to go all the way in abandoning gold, however. "Many depositors," they point out, "conceive of gold as the only asset that held its value over the millennia." They therefore recommended that the central bank continue to hold nearly half of its total gold stock and that "the separated portion of gold is to be sold in small steps."[27] Despite this bow to potential popular anxieties, the entire spirit of the report rests in its unquestioning confidence that the forecasting and managerial skills of the directors and staff of the central bank would perform a better job than obeisance to the gold stock in "the priority of maintaining price stability."

This view was by no means revolutionary doctrine in 1997—on the contrary, it represented mainstream thinking. Nevertheless, this was the *Swiss*, not the British or the Americans or some minor-league country. The Swiss were legendary in their attachment to gold and in their aversion to holding currencies of countries whose devotion to the constant struggle to keep inflation in check was less passionate than theirs. The "gnomes of Zurich" had been famous for their speculative attacks on the dollar and sterling during the crises of the 1970s. Now all that was forgotten.

Two years later, the British took a similar step with their gold stock, once upon a time the pride of British power. In May 1999, the British Treasury announced its intention of selling 415 tons out of its 715-ton stockpile. The price of gold promptly lost 4 percent of its value.

The central banks would soon catch on: their enemy was themselves. The overhang of gold held by central banks meant that every time an official sale hit the headlines, the gold price would fall and the proceeds of the sale would be diminished.

The authorities had already made some effort to talk up the price of gold. Six weeks after the report of the Swiss experts had been published, the vice chairman of the Swiss National Bank asserted that "We are convinced that gold will continue to play a role as a currency reserve, especially in times of crisis." In April 1998, the annual report of the Bank of France of 1997 sounded like old times: "Gold remains an element of long-term confidence in the currency. . . . Above all, holding gold is, from the political point of view, a sign of monetary sovereignty [and] an insurance policy against a major breakdown in the international monetary system." About the same time, a former managing director of the International Monetary Fund affirmed that "Gold remains at the heart of a collective belief in the credibility of an international economy . . . a sort of 'war chest,' indispensable for a tomorrow whose needs we can only guess at."[28] When the new European Central Bank opened in 1998 to manage Europe's new currency, the euro, 15 percent of the bank's reserves were held in gold.

But all of this was mostly talk or just symbolic. Few people were taken in by it.

How times had changed! In the 1960s, the major central banks had organized the gold pool to sell whatever amount of gold was necessary to keep the speculators from driving the price upward. In September 1999, owning nearly half of all gold held by central banks and other official institutions, they were in a position identical to Ruskin's man who strapped his golden wealth to himself as his ship was sinking and promptly sank to the bottom of the ocean. If the central banks all moved at the same time to sell off their hoards of gold, the price would run away from them on the downside and their sales would be a disaster.

They therefore agreed to limit their annual sales to four hundred tons of gold over the next five years—about the same as the annual average liquidated over the previous eight years. The IMF announced that it would "abide" by the spirit of the agreement. Australia and South Africa joined in an informal affiliation, bringing the amount of official gold covered up to 85 percent of the total. The central banks also resolved to limit their lending transactions with the mining companies. The agreement covered the thirteen hundred tons in the pipeline for the Swiss to sell and 365 tons for Britain, leaving only 335 tons for any other country that wants to liquidate gold over the five-year period covered by the arrangements.

William Duisberg, the President of the European Central Bank, was honest enough to refrain from describing these decisions as a move back toward restoring gold to its former glory. He was blunt about the matter: the objective was to protect the value of central bank reserves by "[keeping] the value of gold where it is. . . . The purpose of this action is to give certainty to the gold market."[29]

The central banks were not the only important sellers in the market, but they had been eager cooperators with the other major group: the mining companies. We would expect the mining companies to be sellers, because that is what they are in business for. During the 1990s, concerned like so many others about the future outlook for gold, the mining companies began to sell more than their current production. In effect, they mortgaged their future output at the prevailing price in order to avoid having to sell at a lower price later on. Buyers, however, want delivery when they contract to buy. The mining companies enlisted the central banks for this purpose: the miners borrowed gold from the central banks at a nominal rate of interest, secured by the promise to pay off the loan from future production, and then delivered that gold to the buyers. The central banks were delighted to earn anything at all on what was once the glory of their economic power but that they now considered a barren asset. This arrangement worked well—as long as the price of gold was falling. On the occasions when the price of gold went up, however, the central banks became more reluctant lenders and the mining companies got squeezed. As their current production was smaller than the amounts they had borrowed, they had to go into the market and join the other buyers there in order to make their promised deliveries to people who had bought gold from them. The result was an added impetus to the upward movement in the gold price.

While all of this was going on, the worldwide demand for gold remained vigorous. Gold consumption doubled in the course of the 1990s, and for good reason.[30] The price of gold was falling while the price of everything else was rising. As a result, gold was perceived as relatively inexpensive. The quantity of gold consumed in the production of jewelry—by far the most important component of demand—and in the electronics industry at the end of the 1990s was more than 50 per cent higher than in 1980 and about a third higher than in 1994.[31] Jewelry production alone was one hundred times larger than it had been in 1850, when Chevalier had warned that European demand of 25 tons for jewelry would be "an atom in comparison with total production" in the face of the glut of gold that the California discoveries were about to rain about the world.*

*These data provide a striking insight into the broad improvement in world living standards over the past 150 years. While jewelry production has increased one hundredfold, population has expanded only fivefold. Per capita jewelry consumption, therefore, has increased by twenty times.

The Asians, as in the past, continued to absorb large quantities of gold. *The Economist* reported in January 1999 that "The Indian lust for gold remains unabated. . . . Gold jewelery [*sic*] is the only form of wealth that many women can claim as their own."[32] At that moment, the total amount of gold in India, estimated at around nine thousand tons, exceeded even the great hoard stowed away in Fort Knox, Kentucky.[33]

Meanwhile, in response to the deteriorating economics of the business, mine production and scrap supplies from old gold increased at a much slower rate than demand. With new supply lagging and the basic demand for gold growing, the price of gold should have been expected to rise. Instead, the price fell. Was this surprising outcome due to the shrinking demand for gold as a hedge against inflation, combined with the persistent selling by banks and mining companies? Perhaps, but nothing in economics is that simple. We have no way of knowing whether the demand for jewelry in particular would have increased so much if the price of gold had not fallen so low and made gold jewelry look like a bargain.

How can we derive meaning from this long story, when its last chapter is such a dramatic break with all that had gone before? How could such a thing happen? Is gold now nothing more than a commodity, a beautiful and symbolic bauble, in a class with diamonds and platinum? Or will gold one day regain its grandeur? The time has come to look at the grand illusion of gold in light of these questions.

Epilogue: The Supreme Possession?

Over the centuries, gold has stirred the passions for power and glory, for beauty, for security, and even for immortality. Gold has been an icon for greed, a vehicle for vanity, and a potent constraint as a monetary standard. No other object has commanded so much veneration over so long a period of time.

God selected gold for the tabernacle where humans should come to worship. Jason saw the Golden Fleece as the key to establishing his dynasty. For the Egyptian pharaohs, gold would confirm their magnificence even in the Afterlife. Croesus coined his golden staters and bribed the Oracle of Delphi with gold to assure himself of the security of his rule. Crassus thought gold could buy him military glory and ended with molten gold in his throat. The Byzantines clung to gold as an instrument of power and to ward off their many enemies. The Arabs used gold, along with their military zeal, to humble the world with their business skills. The Genoese, Venetians, and Florentines coined gold to articulate their financial power. The survivors of the Black Death festooned themselves with gold to celebrate their survival.

Columbus thought gold could get people into Heaven. The Spaniards despoiled the New World's gold in a vain attempt to dominate the Old. Asians sponged up gold to protect themselves from the unknown. Isaac Newton, a scientist who spent years at alchemy, thought he understood the golden guinea and grossly underestimated its importance. The English, and then all the Europeans and the Americans, built complex financial systems on the bedrock of gold, expecting it to defend their wealth from the depredations of government and the impatient poor. The Forty-Niners ravaged Johann Sutter's farm in search of the life of kings. John Stewart MacArthur expected cyanidation to bring him great wealth and was foiled by others who were even greedier. Charles de Gaulle saw gold as a weapon to bring his rivals to their knees so that the world could enjoy the order that France would bestow upon it. The gnomes of Switzerland and the speculators in the frenzy of the early 1980s fled to gold for an invincible shield against the irrationality of the state.

But all of that is history. At the dawn of the new millennium, gold is no longer at the center of the universe. The last vestiges of the golden fetters were discarded by Richard Nixon in 1971. When the golden Humpty-Dumpty fell off that wall, no one had much interest in wanting to put him back together again. Dispossessed from its power over the world of money, gold has been emasculated. Now greed and the lust for power run down different channels. We have relegated gold to its traditional role in jewelry and adornment, although small amounts of gold fly into space and speed the motion of electronic blips. In an even more novel capacity, 22-carat flakes of gold have been sprinkled atop sashimi salads, roast lamb, and other pricey dishes.*

Has the glorious history of gold come to an end?

To answer that question, we must look back to the beginning of the story.

Throughout history, gold has played two roles—adornment and money—that have strengthened and supported each other. Gold con-

*See Neil Shister, "Let Them Eat Gold," *Boston Globe*, November 13, 1999, p. D1. Shister's eloquent article observes further that "It may not be surprising that in these times of excess and extreme wealth, 'Let them eat cake' has become 'Let them eat gold'—this time addressed to peers of the rich, not their underlings." Apparently, not everyone appreciates the opportunity: Julia Child, the high priestess of the art of cooking, commented that "I've vaguely heard about it, but I've never eaten gold and don't think I care to."

veyed power because of its unquenchable lustre, but it spoke more loudly of power as it acquired increasing importance as money.

Yet the seeds of gold's ultimate demise as money were sown far back in the story. Hien Tsung's inadvertent innovation of paper money in the ninth century was the first step down this path. Even more effective substitutes for hard money evolved during the Middle Ages from the increasing use of credit money such as bills of exchange, along with the associated development of banking. From the seventeenth century onward, the accelerating growth in trade and production stimulated an urgent expansion in the need for money. Gold in time became a hurdle rather than a doorway to financial transactions.

The gold standard that emerged, almost by accident, in the nineteenth century explicitly recognized this shift in the function of gold. Gold traveled less frequently from hand to hand. Now most of the monetary gold resided instead in bank vaults as the supreme collateral for the paper monies and bank deposits employed in the burgeoning volume of economic and financial transactions. Gold was enshrined as the absolute standard and as the impregnable barrier—as an unbreakable promise that the politicians would not run riot creating the more abstract forms of money and inflationary wildness that had characterized so many episodes in the past. In 1928, George Bernard Shaw, no conservative, summed up this attitude perfectly in *The Intelligent Woman's Guide to Capitalism and Socialism*: "You have to choose between trusting to the natural stability of gold and the honesty and intelligence of members of the government. And, with due respect for these gentlemen, I advise you, as long as the capitalist system lasts, to vote for gold."[1]

Even that critically important role for gold was doomed almost from the start. The impatience of politicians was by no means the only force that ultimately buried gold. The outcome was predestined by the increasing complexity and magnitude of world financial activity in general and the functions of government in particular. It appeared increasingly irrational to manage a global financial system with a metal whose supplies were arbitrarily determined by nature and whose major sources were in uncomfortable places such as Russia and South Africa. Gold became an anachronism.

Measured from the 1870s to the moment in 1971 when Richard Nixon cut the last vestigial tie to gold as the barrier and the standard, the gold standard had prevailed no more than half as long as the bezant of the Byzantines. Christopher Columbus, John Locke, David Ricardo, and Montagu Norman would have been astonished to discover that their eternal verities were not so eternal as they thought.

And yet we cannot be certain that that is the end of the story. In 1875, as we have seen, the distinguished English economist Stanley Jevons warned that "So unaccountable are the prejudices of men on the subject of currency that it is not well to leave anything to discretionary management."[2] Yet discretionary management is precisely the system that the world has chosen to replace the constraints of gold. Freed at long last from the golden fetters, all the countries in the world now function with monetary systems convertible into nothing except from one nation's money into another nation's money, all of which is costlessly produced with the touch of a computer's keyboard. We no longer have money that can be tested with a touchstone to determine whether it is the genuine stuff.

Many people believe that the dollar is the glue that holds the system together, as gold did in the past. Today, in other words, the U.S. dollar appears to be playing the same role in the international arena that Britain played in the nineteenth century. But after World War II, Britain's gold stock had been long since exhausted, and as the supply of pounds sterling far outran the demand for them, their value sank.

The dollar is no more metal than sterling was and no different from any other nation's currency. It just happens to be the kingpin of the system at the end of the twentieth century. No kingpin has survived forever, not even gold.

There is a perception that the dollar has ruled the roost not just because of America's stunning economic power but also because of the extraordinary skill of the money managers at the helm of the American central bank—the Federal Reserve System. An article by Floyd Norris in the *New York Times* of May 14, 1999, carried a headline that read, "Who Needs Gold When We Have Greenspan?" This headline reflected a widely held view of the era.

We must recall once again Benjamin Disraeli's observation in 1895: "Our gold standard is not the cause, but the consequence of our commercial prosperity." In the same way, perhaps the central bankers of all the major countries around the world looked good during the 1980s and 1990s because the basic economic conditions of those years made them look good. There were no major international wars to ignite the fires of inflation. The inflationary impulses that stemmed from the welfare state had been stifled by the shredding of social safety nets and the obsession to compress budget deficits, not just in the United States but in Europe and much of Latin America and Asia as well. The world economy was fiercely competitive, and American corporations were the most triumphantly competitive of all. Discovered resources to produce oil were vastly larger than in the early 1970s. In short, as the twentieth century was coming to an end, no overwhelming force had come along to test the true skills of the central bankers or to rock the dollar from its perch at the zenith.

Remember what Marco Polo had to say about Kublai Khan's currency? "[Kublai Khan's] mint," he wrote, "is so organized that you might well say that he has mastered the art of alchemy. . . . The procedure of issue is as formal and authoritative as if they were made of pure gold or silver. . . . The money is authentic. . . . Of this money the Khan has such a quantity made that with it he could buy all the treasure of the world." If Marco Polo were around today, he would no doubt comment on the remarkable resemblances between the dollar and the output of Kublai Khan's mint. Yet we have no assurance that the dollar's hegemony is any more permanent than the sometime dominance of Kublai Khan's paper money, Offa's penny, the bezant, the dinar, the ducat, or the pound sterling. In the frantic inflationary fevers of the late 1970s and early 1980s, frightened and even sophisticated people turned to gold from dollars. In the inevitable moment when such turbulence reappears, that history might well repeat itself. Well-developed markets for gold are alive and well.

As Robert Mundell, the Nobel Laureate in Economics, pointed out in December 1999 as he accepted the Prize, "The main thing we miss today is universal money, a standard of value, the link between the past and the future and the cement linking remote parts of the human race to one another." He went on to remind his audience that gold had filled this role from the time of Augustus to 1914 and that "The absence of gold as an intrinsic part of our monetary system today makes our century, the one that has just passed, unique in several thousand years."[3] Mundell overstates his case, but the absence of universal money will continue to plague the world economy for as long as such a shortcoming endures.

In March 1997, long before he knew he would be honored with the Nobel Prize, Mundell had predicted that "Gold will be part of the international monetary system in the twenty-first century."[4] This was a bold and controversial statement, and perhaps an ominous one. Gold may again serve as the ultimate hedge in chaotic conditions. Its return to its traditional role as universal money is unlikely, however, unless the time should come when the dollar, the euro, and the yen have all failed to function as acceptable means of payment across international borders.

The story of gold has a deeper message, one that has none of the transitory qualities of what we choose to use as money. Seen in this broader sense, the story of gold has no ending.

The most striking feature of this long history is that gold led most of the protagonists of the drama into the ditch. Over and over again, the characters have been like Ruskin's passenger who drowned while clutching his gold and discovered, all too late, that the gold possessed him instead of the other way around. Midas, Jason, Croesus, the emperors of Byzantium, the survivors of the Black Death, Pizarro and his Emperor Charles V, MacArthur the chemist, Montagu Norman and Benjamin Strong, Charles de Gaulle, and the gold bugs of the 1980s—all were fools for gold, chasing an illusion. None ended up where they had hoped.

Those who believed that gold was a hedge against the uncertainties of life failed to understand that the pursuit of eternity is not to be satisfied by gold, or by anything else we choose to replace gold—dollars, euros, whatever. Gold as an end in itself is meaningless. Hoarding does not create wealth. Gold and its surrogates make sense only as a means to an end: to beautify, to adorn, to exchange for what we need and really want.

Perhaps the wisest heroes of our story were the simple natives of Jenne and Timbuktu who silently swapped gold for the precious salt that would keep them alive.

Notes

Prologue

1. Ruskin, 1862, p. 86.
2. Crosby, 1997, p. 71, citing *Journals and Other Documents on the Life and Voyages of Christopher Columbus*, Samuel Eliot Morison, trans. New York: Heritage Press, 1963, p. 383.
3. Pindar, 1927, p. 613.
4. See Ruskin, 1982, p. 86.
5. Jevons, 1875, p. 202.
6. *International Wildlife Magazine*, May–June 1998.
7. Marx, 1978, pp. 8–9.
8. Green, 1993, p. 14.
9. Herrington et al., p. 28.
10. Exodus, 25, 11.

Chapter 1 Get Gold at All Hazards

1. Chamber of Mines of South Africa and Sutherland, 1959, p. 12.
2. Bartlett, John, 1943. *Familiar Quotations*, 11th ed., Christopher Morley, ed. Boston: Little, Brown & Co. This line came from Will Rogers's last dispatch to the press, sent from Fairbanks and published on August 15, 1935, the day he died in an airplane crash.
3. World Gold Council.
4. Job, 31, 24–25.
5. Sutherland, 1959, p. 57.
6. Ibid., p. 57.
7. Ibid., p. 57.
8. Marx, 1978, p. 236.

9. *Encyclopedia Britannica* On-Line, Egypt: History: The New Kingdom: The 18th Dynasty.
10. Marx, 1978, pp. 48–53.
11. Jacob, 1831, p. 55.
12. Ibid., pp. 50–59.
13. Marx, 1978, p. 44.
14. Jacob, 1831, p. 56.
15. Marx, 1978, p. 193.
16. Green, 1993, pp. 405–407.
17. Ibid., p. 17.
18. For the whole story, see Schwab, 1946, pp. 86–102.
19. Schwab, 1946, p. 87.
20. Ibid., p. 122.

Chapter 2 Midas's Wish and the Creatures of Pure Chance

1. Jacob, 1831, p. 313.
2. Davies, 1995, p. 43.
3. Furness, 1910, pp. 92–100.
4. Marx, 1978, p. 44.
5. Ibid., pp. 138–139.
6. Herodotus, 1992, pp. 5–35. *The Histories* were written about 450 BC to 430 BC.
7. Tassel, 1998, p. 58. This exciting article is well worth reading in full.
8. Herodotus, 1992, p. 77.
9. Burns, 1927, pp. 561 and 140.
10. Herodotus, 1992, p. 11.
11. Ibid., pp. 11–13.
12. Ibid., p. 35.
13. Ibid., p. 35.
14. Marx, 1978, p. 140.
15. Davies, 1995, p. 62.
16. See Burns, 1927, pp. 320–321.
17. Head (no date), pp. 10–13.
18. Davies, 1995, p. 63, and Burns, 1927, p. 43.
19. Tassel, 1998, p. 60.
20. Head (no date), pp. 18–19.
21. Burns, 1927, pp. 321–322.
22. Head (no date), p. 20.
23. Herodotus, 1992, pp. 17–18.
24. Ibid., pp. 18–19.

25. Ibid., p. 33.
26. Galbraith, 1954, p. 2.

Chapter 3 Darius's Bathtub and the Cackling of the Geese

1. Burns, 1927, p. 348.
2. Marx, 1978, p. 147.
3. Ibid., p. 163.
4. The material about Philip and Alexander is from Davies, 1995, pp. 78–86.
5. Ibid., p. 87.
6. Sutherland, 1959, pp. 84–88.
7. Gibbon, 1804, Vol. I, p. 8.
8. Ibid., footnote 35.
9. Sutherland, 1959, p. 90.
10. Marx, 1978, p. 197.
11. Jacob, 1831, p. 25.
12. *Encyclopedia Britannica* On-Line: Carrhae, Battle of.
13. World Gold Council.
14. Kemmerer, 1944, p. 9.
15. Davies, 1995, p. 97.
16. Gibbon, 1804, Vol. I, pp. 411–412.
17. Davies, 1995, pp. 105–106.
18. Ibid., p. 106.
19. Marx, 1978, p. 235.

Chapter 4 The Symbol and the Faith

1. Sutherland, 1959, p. 107.
2. *Encyclopedia Britannica* On-Line: Irene.
3. Ibid.: Nicephorus.
4. Marx, 1978, p. 242.
5. *Encyclopedia Britannica* On-Line: Basil III.
6. Marx, 1978, pp. 241–242.
7. Ibid., pp. 231–232.
8. Cherry, 1992, especially Figs. 20, 59, and 60.
9. Langer, 1952, p. 150.
10. Marx, 1978, p. 231.
11. Ibid., p. 232.
12. Lopez, 1951, p. 228.

13. Ibid., p. 232.
14. Ibid., pp. 224–260.
15. Ibid., p. 209.
16. Sutherland, 1959, pp. 113–115.
17. Lopez, 1951, p. 211.
18. Ibid., p. 214.
19. *Encyclopedia Britannica* On-Line: Leo III and the Age of Iconoclasm.
20. Ibid.: Irene.
21. Ibid.: Coinage in the Byzantine Empire.
22. Lopez, 1951, p. 214.
23. Ibid., p. 215.
24. Ibid., p. 221.
25. Ibid., p. 221.

Chapter 5 Gold, Salt, and the Blessed Town

1. Marx, 1978, p. 248.
2. Ibid., p. 246.
3. Ibid., pp. 243–248.
4. Sutherland, 1959, p. 113.
5. Ibid., pp. 113–115.
6. Ibid., pp. 114–116.
7. Vilar, 1976, p. 46.
8. Bovill, 1958, p. 10.
9. Tracy, 1990, Table 10.5, p. 329.
10. Ibid., p. 342.
11. Bovill, 1958, p. 48.
12. Ibid., p. 68.
13. Ibid., p. 141.
14. Ibid., p. 195.
15. Ibid., p. 236.
16. Ibid., p. 119.
17. Ibid., p. 103.

Chapter 6 The Legacy of Eoba, Babba, and Udd

1. Crosby, 1997, p. 69, citing St. Thomas Aquinas, *Summa Theologiae*.

2. For a detailed and illuminating description of hoarding in the Middle Ages and into the Renaissance, see North, 1990. This volume discusses a lot more than hoarding, but hoarding is a frequent subject *inter alia*.

3. Bloch, 1933, p. 8. Marc Bloch was one of the most brilliant young French economists of the 1930s. As a soldier in the French army in World War II, he was caught in the general Allied retreat during the German offensive of May 1940. He escaped to Britain in the massive evacuation from Dunkirk while the Germans besieged the port. Bloch voluntarily returned to France a few weeks later to fight in the underground. A Jew, he was captured and murdered in one of the death camps.

4. Fischer, 1996, p. 16.
5. Marx, 1978, p. 254.
6. Davies, 1995, p. 123.
7. Feaveryear, 1963, p. 9.
8. Ibid., pp. 123–126.
9. Lacey and Danziger, 1999, p. 68.
10. Langer, 1952, p. 155.
11. Marx, 1978, pp. 233–234.
12. Miskimin, 1977.
13. Davies, 1995, and information supplied by Professor Benjamin Friedman of the Harvard Economics Department.
14. Kindleberger, 1993, p. 22.
15. Feaveryear, 1963, p. 96.
16. Davies, 1995, p. 145.
17. Ibid., pp. 145–146.
18. Ibid., p. 139.
19. Gibbon, 1804, Vol. I, pp. 352–353.
20. Ibid., p. 164.

Chapter 7 The Great Chain Reaction

1. Fischer, 1996, p. 13.
2. Ibid., p. 16.
3. See Becker et al., 1999.
4. Bryant, 1962, p. 309.
5. Watson, 1976, pp. 9–10.
6. Ibid., p. 10.
7. See Vilar, 1976, p. 34, and Watson, 1976, pp. 7–8.
8. Lopez, 1956, p. 239.
9. Langer, 1952, p. 211.
10. Lopez, 1956, p. 237.
11. Ibid., p. 230.
12. Ibid., pp. 233–234.
13. Cipolla, 1956, p. 26.

14. Lopez, 1956, p. 219.
15. *Merchant of Venice*, Act III, Scene 1.
16. Fischer, 1996, p. 25.
17. Feaveryear, 1963, pp. 22–29.
18. Tuchman, 1978, p. 96.
19. Feaveryear, 1963, p. 24.

Chapter 8 The Disintegrating Age and the Kings' Ransoms

1. Tuchman, 1978, pp. xiii–xiv.
2. Ibid., p. 41.
3. Miskimin, 1977, Table 1, p. 21, and Tuchman, 1978, p. 94.
4. Tuchman, 1978, pp. 96–100.
5. Langer, 1952, p. 222.
6. Fischer, 1996, p. 41.
7. Bainton, 1952, p. 12.
8. Tuchman, 1978, p. 353.
9. Miskimin, 1989, VII, p. 486.
10. Ibid., pp. 484–485.
11. Miskimin, 1977, pp. 20–21.
12. Day, 1987, p. 191.
13. Miskimin, 1989, VII, p. 487.
14. Day, 1987, p. 191; see also Miskimin, 1989, VII, p. 488.
15. Tuchman, 1978, p. 123.
16. Miskimin, 1989, VII, pp. 488–489.
17. Davies, 1995, p. 164.
18. Feaveryear, 1963, pp. 33–34.
19. Davies, 1995, p. 162.
20. Tuchman, 1978, p. 378.
21. Marx, 1978, pp. 256–259.
22. Tuchman, 1978, p. 130.
23. Ibid., p. 144.
24. Ibid., p. 150.
25. Ibid., p. 152.
26. Ibid., p. 151.
27. Bryant, 1964, p. 139.
28. Tuchman, 1978, p. 189.
29. Ibid., p. 191.
30. Ibid., p. 191.
31. Tuchman, 1978, p. 198.

32. Davies, 1995, p. 165, says three million gold crowns were equal to £500,000. Feaveryear, 1963, p. 21, comments that laborers earned 1*s* 8*d* per week, and that both one sheep and six gallons of ale fetched the same amount.
33. Leary, 1959, p. 343.
34. Miskimin, 1977, p. 21.
35. The population number is from Vilar, 1976, p. 49.
36. See Kindleberger, 1993, p. 24.
37. One metric ton = 32,150 oz. Four metric tons = 129,000 oz. 129,000 × 28.35 = 3,646,000 grams. 3,646,000 ÷ 3.5 = 1,042,000 ducats.
38. Day, 1978, p. 9.
39. Kindleberger, 1993, p. 24.
40. Vilar, 1976, p. 19.
41. Day, 1978, p. 13.
42. Ibid., p. 15.
43. Ibid., p. 16.
44. Challis, 1992, pp. 198–201.
45. Day, 1978, p. 60.
46. Kindleberger, 1993, p. 24. See also Davies, 1995, p. 184.
47. Day, 1978, p. 142. See also Davies, 1995, pp. 184–186.
48. Vilar, 1976, p. 45.
49. Fischer, 1996, p. 51.
50. Feaveryear, 1963, Appendix II.
51. Davies, 1995, p. 175.
52. Vilar, 1976, p. 64.

Chapter 9 The Sacred Thirst

1. Brimelow, 1998.
2. Austen, 1990, in Tracy, 1990, Tables 10.1 and 10.6, pp. 315 and 332–333.
3. Wright, 1970, pp. 15–16.
4. Ibid., p. 41.
5. Vilar, 1976, p. 55.
6. Ibid., pp. 55–56.
7. Wright, 1970, pp. 57–59.
8. Ibid., p. 62.
9. Ibid., pp. 60–68.
10. Marx, 1978, p. 300.
11. Vilar, 1976, p. 63.
12. Marx, 1978, p. 323.
13. Ibid., p. 323.

14. Green, 1993, p. 11.
15. Ibid., pp. 329–330.
16. Prescott, 1847, p. 91.
17. Ibid., p. 91.
18. Emmerich, 1965, p. 79.
19. Wright, 1970, p. 229; see footnote.
20. Emmerich, 1965, p. 42, says 3.5 million to 7.0 million.
21. Wright, 1970, p. 236.
22. Prescott, 1847, p. 199.
23. Ibid., p. 203.
24. Ibid., p. 206.
25. Ibid., p. 207.
26. Ibid., p. 207.
27. Ibid., p. 207.
28. Ibid., p. 213.
29. Page 100.
30. Emmerich, 1965, pp. 173–174.
31. Ibid., pp. 25–40.
32. Vilar, 1976, p. 91, ascribes this measurement to Jean Bodin's work of 1578, *Response to Malestroit*, and says that the figures appear to be genuine.
33. Emmerich, 1965, pp. 43, 48.
34. Each peso was equal to 3.5 grams; there are 1000 grams in a metric ton. Therefore, 1,326,529 *pesos d'oro* weighed 4,642,887 grams, or 4.6 metric tons. A metric ton is equal to 1.102 U.S. tons. Therefore, 4.6 metric tons is equal to 5.0 tons, or 10,000 pounds avoirdupois. If the output of the mines was 190 tons, the gold in the chamber was the equivalent of about twenty years' production from the mines.
35. Prescott, 1847, p. 241.
36. Smith, 1776, p. 421.
37. Emmerich, 1965, p. 154.
38. Gibbon, 1804, Vol. I, p. 179.

Chapter 10 The Fatal Poison and Private Money

1. Brace, 1910, p. 9, quoting Jacob, 1831.
2. Parry, 1967, pp. 200–201, in Rich and Wilson, 1967.
3. Ibid., pp. 127, 137.
4. Sutherland, 1959, p. 135.
5. See both Andrews, 1978, and Andrews, 1984, for a full discussion of the role of piracy in the development of British, French, and Dutch interests in the riches of the New World.

6. Hamilton, 1934, p. 19.
7. Parry, 1967, p. 202.
8. Andrews, 1978, pp. 19–31.
9. *Encyclopedia Britannica* On-Line: Drake, Sir Francis.
10. Sutherland, 1959, p. 139. See also Wright, 1970, pp. 307–327.
11. Marx, 1978, p. 364.
12. Hamilton, 1934, Table 3, p. 42.
13. Kindleberger, 1989, p. 28.
14. Vilar, 1976, pp. 166–168.
15. Ibid., p. 160.
16. See Mauro, 1990, in Tracy, 1990, pp. 279 *et seq*.
17. Boyer-Xambeu et al., 1994, p. 116.
18. Ibid., p. 116.
19. Vilar, 1976, p. 149.
20. Kindleberger, 1989, pp. 30–31.
21. Ibid., p. 47.
22. For a discussion of the impact of this innovation on business practice, and the admirable monk Luca Paccioli who introduced it, see Bernstein, 1996, pp. 41–43.
23. Feaveryear, 1963, pp. 51–52.
24. Marx, 1978, p. 296.
25. Ibid., p. 292.
26. Sutherland, 1959, p. 142.
27. *Encyclopedia Britannica* On-Line: Francis I.
28. Hackett, 1929, p. 12.
29. Ibid., p. 113.
30. Bowle, 1964, pp. 96–99.
31. Hackett, 1929, p. 112.
32. Bowle, 1964, p. 99.
33. Fischer, 1996, pp. 65–91. See also the full text of Braudel and Spooner, 1967, in Rich and Wilson, 1967.
34. Fischer, 1996, p. 74.
35. Davies, 1995, p. 211.
36. Hamilton, 1934, pp. 291–292.
37. Miskimin, 1977, p. 21.
38. Fischer, 1996, p. 73.
39. Ibid., p. 334.
40. Kindleberger, 1989, p. 6.
41. Feaveryear, 1963, p. 52.
42. Cited in Hamilton, 1934, p. 283.
43. Vilar, 1976, p. 91.
44. Wilkie, 1994, p. 3.

45. Kindleberger, 1989, Tables 1 and 2, pp. 13–15. See also Morineau, 1985, for a full-scale attack on the notion that the peak was reached before 1600.

46. Schwartz, 1973.

47. Vilar, 1976, p. 174.

48. Ibid., p. 174.

49. Feaveryear, 1963, Appendix II, p. 347.

50. Gould, 1976, p. 272.

51. Smith, 1776, p. 333.

52. See Boyer-Xambeu et al., 1994, pp. 68–95; Kindleberger, 1989, pp. 39–41; Kindleberger, 1993, p. 37; and citations covering many localities in Postan and Habakkuk, 1952.

53. Mauro, 1990, pp. 263–266.

54. Boyer-Xambeu et al., 1994, Table 5.2, pp. 114–115.

55. Crosby, 1997, p. 202.

56. See Boyer-Xambeu et al., 1994, and Kindleberger, 1993, pp. 41–43.

57. Kindleberger, 1989, p. 10.

58. Boyer-Xambeu et al., 1994, p. 93.

59. Ibid., the whole book, but especially pp. 3–16 and 104–129.

Chapter 11 The Asian Necropolis and Hien Tsung's Inadvertent Innovation

1. Kindleberger, 1989, pp. 15–18.

2. Ibid., p. 78.

3. Hume, 1752, p. 334.

4. Mun, c. 1620, p. 49. For an authoritative analysis of this fascinating man, his times, his importance, and his role in the development of theories of trade and foreign exchange, see Kindleberger, 1990.

5. Kindleberger, 1989, p. 25.

6. Hume, 1752, p. 335.

7. Ibid., p. 335.

8. Kindleberger, 1989, p. 31.

9. Hamilton, 1934, p. 302.

10. *The Economist*, January 15, 1998, p. 67.

11. Polo, 1289, p. 123.

12. Ibid., p. 122.

13. Ibid., p. 125.

14. All quotations regarding Japan are from ibid., p. 244.

15. Vilar, 1976, p. 94.

16. Polo, 1289, p. 178.

17. Ibid., p. 187.
18. Vilar, 1976, p. 94.
19. Ibid., p. 97.
20. Davies, 1995, p. 56, and Kindleberger, 1989, p. 69.
21. Cribb et al., 1990, pp. 198–206.
22. Davies, 1995, pp. 180–181.
23. Ibid., pp. 182–183.
24. Polo, 1289, p. 147.
25. Ibid., p. 147.
26. Ibid., pp. 147–148.
27. Ibid., p. 148.
28. Ibid., p. 148.
29. Kindleberger, 1989, p. 58.
30. Marx, 1978, p. 302.
31. Cribb et al., 1990, p. 208.
32. Kindleberger, 1996b.
33. Smith, 1776, p. 183.
34. Ibid., p. 183.
35. Kindleberger, 1986, p. 55.
36. Smith, 1776, p. 75.
37. Ibid., p. 78.

Chapter 12 The Great Recoinage and the Last of the Magicians

1. Jacob, 1831, p. 322.
2. Challis, 1992, p. 16.
3. Davies, 1995, p. 241.
4. For a detailed description of the moneyers' elaborate and time-consuming methods, see Challis, 1992, pp. 305–307.
5. Ibid., Table 34, pp. 309–311.
6. Ibid., p. 302.
7. Davies, 1995, pp. 241–242.
8. Ibid., p. 242. See also Quinn, 1996, p. 480.
9. Challis, 1992, p. 362.
10. Feaveryear, 1963, pp. 89–90.
11. See Davies, 1995, pp. 241–243 regarding this whole discussion.
12. Feaveryear, 1963, p. 111.
13. Li, 1963, p. 56, citing Haynes's manuscript, *Brief Memoire Relating to the Silver and Gold Coins of England*, written between 1700 and 1702. This work is

a major source for much of the known data about the coinage during these years.

14. Challis, 1992, p. 380.
15. Feaveryear, 1963, p. 120.
16. Supple, 1959, quoting the contemporary observer Edward Misselden.
17. Li, 1963, p. 58.
18. Feaveryear, 1963, p. 115.
19. Kindleberger, 1993, p. 190.
20. Ibid., pp. 191–192.
21. Feaveryear, 1963, pp. 119–121.
22. Ibid., p. 121.
23. Ibid., pp. 122–123.
24. Li, 1963, p. 98.
25. Ibid., p. 64.
26. Ibid., pp. 104–105.
27. Cited by Haynes in his *Memoire*; see Li, 1963, p. 89.
28. Ibid., p. 92.
29. Ibid., p. 170.
30. Feaveryear, 1963, pp. 123–124.
31. Li, 1963, p. 114.
32. Ibid., pp. 114–115.
33. Challis, 1992, Table 55, p. 384.
34. White, 1977, p. 260.
35. Feaveryear, 1963, p. 129.
36. Challis, 1992, p. 387.
37. Feaveryear, 1963, p. 130.
38. Li, 1963, p. 138.
39. Feaveryear, 1963, p. 136.
40. White, 1977, p. 3.
41. Unless otherwise specified, all the following Newton biographical material is from White, 1977.
42. Ibid., p. 52.
43. Ibid., p. 227.
44. Ibid., p. 227.
45. Ibid., p. 253.
46. Li, 1963, p. 127.
47. McCulloch, 1856, p. 274.
48. Ibid., p. 277.
49. Ibid., p. 277.
50. Ibid., pp. 278–279.
51. Green, 1993, p. 19.
52. Li, 1963, p. 161.

CHAPTER 13 THE TRUE DOCTRINE AND THE GREAT EVIL

1. Davies, 1995, p. 298.
2. Feaveryear, 1963, pp. 212–213.
3. Ibid., p. 170.
4. Cannan, 1919, p. xi, and Table II on p. xliv.
5. Feaveryear, 1963, pp. 168–178.
6. Cannan, 1919, p. xvii.
7. Li, 1963, p. 173.
8. Jastram, 1977, p. 32, and Wilkie, 1994, p. 3.
9. For a detailed description of how the English system of money and banking evolved, see Feaveryear, 1963, pp. 160–174.
10. Cannan, 1919, p. xii.
11. Jevons, 1875, p. 68.
12. Menias, 1969, p. 18.
13. See Friedman, 1992, p. 135, and also Bordo and White, 1991, which argues that Britain's greater financial credibility permitted the British to carry on the war with a high volume of debt finance, while France's poor reputation forced reliance on taxation.
14. Wilkie, 1994, p. 3.
15. Cannan, 1919, p. xliv.
16. Ibid., p. 5.
17. See Friedman, 1992, p. 59.
18. Ricardo, 1809, p. 5.
19. The succeeding details of Ricardo's life are from Heilbroner, 1953, Chapter IV, pp. 67–95.
20. Ibid., p. 79.
21. Ibid., p. 80.
22. Ibid., p. 80.
23. Cannan, 1919, p. 3.
24. Ibid., p. xlii.
25. Ibid., p. xxii.
26. Davies, 1995, p. 300.
27. Ibid., p. 300.
28. Cannan, 1919, p. xxii.
29. Ibid., p. 6.
30. Ricardo, 1809, p. 23.
31. Cannan, 1919, p. 11.
32. Ibid., p. 16.
33. Ibid., p. 21.
34. Ibid., p. 17.
35. Ricardo, 1811b, p. 38.

36. Cannan, 1919, p. 10.
37. Green, 1993, p. 22.
38. Cannan, 1919, p. 32.
39. Ibid., p. 33.
40. Ibid., p. 34.
41. Neal, 1998, p. 55.
42. Jevons, 1875, pp. 231–232; for a full account of Jevons and his contributions to economic thought, see Bernstein, 1996, pp. 190–192.
43. Cannan, 1919, p. 47.
44. Ibid., p. 48.
45. Ibid., p. 53.
46. Ibid., pp. 52–53.
47. Ricardo, 1811b, p. 6.
48. Cannan, 1919, p. 69.
49. Ibid., text of resolutions, Resolution #14.
50. Ibid., Resolution #16.
51. Feaveryear, 1963, pp. 186–187.
52. Ibid., p. 213.
53. Davies, 1995, p. 302.
54. Feaveryear, 1963, p. 190, and Davies, 1995, p. 303.
55. Green, 1993, p. 23.

Chapter 14 The New Mistress and the Cursed Discovery

1. Brace, 1910, pp. 14–15.
2. Chevalier, 1859, pp. 54–56.
3. Brace, 1910, pp. 39, 53.
4. Vilar, 1976, p. 19.
5. Green, 1993, pp. 24–25.
6. Ibid., pp. 24–25.
7. Martin, 1977, p. 644.
8. Green, 1993, p. 30, and World Gold Council.
9. Gudde, 1936, pp. 184–186.
10. Ibid., p. 186.
11. Ibid., p. 192.
12. Ibid., p. 195.
13. Ibid., p. 198.
14. Ibid., p. 208.
15. Ibid., p. 227.
16. Hughes, 1987, p. 561.
17. Ibid., p. 561.

18. Ibid., p. 562.
19. Friedman, 1992, p. 40.
20. Hughes, 1987, pp. 564–565.
21. Ibid., p. 565.
22. Ibid., p. 564.
23. Ibid., p. 571.
24. King, 1997.
25. Rosenthal, 1970, p. 212.
26. Fivaz, 1988, p. 312.
27. See Fivaz, 1988, p. 311, and Rosenthal, 1970, p. 215.
28. Ibid., p. 311.
29. Barsky and DeLong, 1991, p. 823.
30. Fivaz, 1988, p. 313.
31. Ibid., Table 1, p. 313. 120 metric tons = 3,858,438 oz. @ $20.67/oz. = $79,753,913 = £16,410,270.
32. Rosenthal, 1970, p. 217.
33. High Court of South Africa, 1896, p. 244.
34. Fivaz, 1988, p. 317.
35. For more complete information on Chevalier, see Kindleberger, 1978, pp. 25–30.
36. Jastram, 1977, Table 2, p. 32. See also Martin, 1977, p. 645.
37. Chevalier, 1859, p. 23. Martin, 1977, p. 650, cites a number of sources supporting the notion that cyclical economic factors and military activities also influenced the rise in commodity prices.
38. Chevalier, 1859, p. 85.
39. Ibid., p. 106.
40. Ibid., p. 94.
41. Ibid., p. 95.
42. Ibid., p. 95.
43. Ibid., p. 96.
44. Ibid., p. 97.
45. Ibid., p. 98.
46. Ibid., p. 106.
47. Ibid., p. 107.
48. Ibid., p. 108.
49. Ibid., p. 109.
50. Ibid., p. 110.
51. Ibid., p. 109.
52. Ibid., pp. 113–114.
53. Jastram, 1977, Table 2, p. 32.
54. Friedman and Schwartz, 1971, pp. 34–35.
55. Bureau of the Census, 1975, Series M76, p. 588.

56. Fay, 1951, p. 30.
57. See Barsky and DeLong, 1991, for an extended discussion of informed opinion and the behavior of prices, the financial markets, and gold production from 1870 to 1914.
58. Chevalier, 1859, p. 104.
59. Ibid., p. 104.

Chapter 15 The Badge of Honor

1. Gallarotti, 1995, p. 143
2. Ibid., p. 144.
3. Ibid., p. 144.
4. Ibid., p. 144.
5. Flandreau, 1996, p. 873.
6. Ibid., p. 886.
7. Gallarotti, 1995, p. 147.
8. Ibid., pp. 31–32.
9. Boyle, 1967, p. 128.
10. Officer, 1996, p. 36, and Table 5.2, pp. 54–55.
11. *Wall Street Journal*, Op-Ed page, December 10, 1999.
12. Gallarotti, 1995, Table 5.1, p. 135.
13. Ibid., p. 115.
14. Cannan, 1919, pp. 11, 21.
15. Jevons, 1875, pp. 231–232.
16. See Friedman, 1992, p. 151n.
17. Redish, 1990, p. 805.
18. Bloch, 1933, p. 3.
19. Friedman, 1992, p. 153.
20. Hawtrey, 1947, p. 79.
21. Hamilton, 1791, p. 576.
22. Ibid., p. 576.
23. Ibid., p. 578.
24. Flandreau, 1996, p. 864.
25. Friedman, 1992, p. 133.
26. Chevalier, 1836, Letter 6, January 5, quoted in Kindleberger, 1978.
27. Friedman, 1992, pp. 55–57.
28. Martin, 1977, p. 650.
29. Ibid., especially pp. 656–657.
30. Holtfrerich, 1999, p. 187.
31. Flandreau, 1996.

32. Gallarotti, 1995, Table 6.3, p. 167.
33. Noyes, 1898, p. 157.
34. Ibid., p. 157.
35. Wirth, 1893, p. 218.
36. Ibid., p. 218.
37. See, especially, Wirth, 1893, pp. 219–229, for a vivid description of the derrings-do.
38. Pressnell, 1968, p. 217; the quoted diary was by Sir Edward Hamilton.
39. Wirth, 1893, p. 232.
40. Eichengreen, 1992, pp. 49–50.
41. Pressnell, 1968, p. 199.
42. Eichengreen, 1992, p. 49.
43. Ibid., pp. 49–50.
44. Pressnell, 1968, p. 203.
45. Kindleberger, 1996a, p. 139.
46. Ibid., p. 139.
47. See Kindleberger, 1993, p. 67; this is a good story.
48. Eichengreen, 1996, p. 33.
49. See Ibid., p. 31.
50. Gallarotti, 1995, p. 145.

Chapter 16 The Most Stupendous Conspiracy and the Endless Chain

1. Harvey, 1894, p. 215.
2. Bureau of the Census, 1975, Table 433, pp. 994–995.
3. Ibid., Table 424, pp. 994–995.
4. Friedman and Schwartz, 1971, p. 44.
5. Bureau of the Census, 1975, Table 52, p. 201.
6. Ibid., Table 52, p. 201, and Table 495, p. 1004.
7. Friedman, 1992, p. 51.
8. See Rockoff, 1990.
9. Friedman, 1992, pp. 62–63.
10. All the information in this paragraph is from Harvey, 1894, p. 39, who cites many sources.
11. Noyes, 1898, pp. 54–59.
12. Ibid., p. 160.
13. Ibid., p. 173.
14. Ibid., pp. 188–191.
15. Ibid., p. 220.

16. Niedringhaus, 1998, p. 19.
17. Noyes, 1898, p. 232.
18. Ibid., p. 232.
19. Ibid., p. 233.
20. Chernow, 1990, p. 74.
21. Ibid., p. 74.
22. Ibid., p. 75.
23. Ibid., p. 75.
24. Noyes, 1898, p. 237.
25. Chernow, 1990, p. 76.
26. Noyes, 1898, p. 236.
27. Ibid., p. 241.
28. Ibid., p. 253.
29. Friedman, 1992, p. 106.
30. Chernow, 1990, p. 78.
31. Quoted in Michael Kazin, "Where's the Outrage?" *New York Times Magazine*, June 7, 1998, p. 79.
32. Hicks, 1931, pp. 439–444.
33. Boorstin, 1966, pp. 593–604. This text includes useful background on Bryan by Richard Hofstadter.
34. Noyes, 1898, p. 266.
35. Ibid., pp. 266–267. He cites the *New York Financial Chronicle* for October 31 and November 7.
36. Ibid., pp. 264–266.
37. Friedman, 1992, pp. 104–125.
38. Ibid., p. 109, citing Henry Steele Commager.

Chapter 17 The Norman Conquest

1. All quotes except for *The Economist* from Moggridge, 1972, p. 10.
2. Eichengreen, 1992, p. 104.
3. Kindleberger, 1993, Table 16.4, p. 298.
4. Hawtrey, 1947, Appendix.
5. Jastram, 1977, pp. 32, 146.
6. Mayhew, 1999, p. 202.
7. Moggridge, 1972, p. 28.
8. Boyle, 1967, p. 133.
9. Ibid., p. 128.
10. Moggridge, 1972, pp. 26–27.

11. Ibid., p. 40.
12. Boyle, 1967, p. 185.
13. Ibid., p. 189.
14. Mayhew, 1999, p. 214.
15. Moggridge, 1972, p. 53.
16. Ibid., p. 49.
17. Chernow, 1990, pp. 274–275.
18. Kindleberger, 1993, p. 330.
19. Keynes, 1931, pp. 183–184, from *Auri Sacra Fames* (Accursed Greed for Gold).
20. Kindleberger, 1993, pp. 327, 331.
21. Moggridge, 1972, p. 81.
22. Keynes, 1931, p. 246, from "The Economic Consequences of Mr. Churchill."
23. Ibid., pp. 233–235, from "The Speeches of the Bank Chairmen."
24. Smith, 1996.
25. Boyle, 1967, pp. 195–196. My italics.
26. Ibid., p. 196.
27. Ibid., p. 207.
28. Keynes, 1931, pp. 248–249.
29. Moggridge, 1972, pp. 45–46.
30. Kindleberger, 1993, p. 335.
31. See Kindleberger, 1986, p. 18.
32. For an extended and vivid description of these events, see Kindleberger, 1993, pp. 339–340.
33. Ibid., p. 343.
34. Ibid., p. 344.
35. Ibid., p. 332.
36. Eichengreen, 1996, Table 3.1, p. 65.
37. Hawtrey, 1947, Appendix.
38. Eichengreen, 1996, p. 66.
39. Chernow, 1990, p. 313.
40. Kindleberger, 1993, p. 334.
41. Boyle, 1967, pp. 231–232.
42. Ibid., pp. 233–234.
43. Galbraith, 1954, p. 57.
44. Bureau of the Census, 1975, Tables 548–550, p. 1009, and Kindleberger, 1986, Table 9, p. 100.
45. Bureau of the Census, 1975, Tables 445 and 447, p. 1001.
46. Kindleberger, 1986, pp. 100–102.
47. Eichengreen, 1996, p. 71.
48. Kindleberger, 1993, pp. 355, 358.

Chapter 18 The End of the Epoch

1. Hoover, 1952, p. 30.
2. Chernow, 1990, p. 322.
3. See *The Merchant of Venice*, Act III, Scene 2.
4. Hoover, 1952, p. 31.
5. Ibid., p. 53.
6. See Kindleberger, 1986, Tables 11, 13, and 14, pp. 113, 138, 139.
7. Friedman and Schwartz, 1971, p. 382.
8. Bureau of the Census, 1975, Tables 40, 9, and 588 (pp. 200, 126, and 1021).
9. Chernow, 1990, p. 323.
10. See Kindleberger, 1986, p. 130, and Hawtrey, 1947, p. 161.
11. Ibid., p. 145.
12. Ibid., p. 128.
13. Ibid., p. 165.
14. Boyle, 1967, p. 263.
15. Ibid., pp. 263–264.
16. Ibid., p. 264.
17. Ibid., p. 267.
18. Ibid., p. 266.
19. Ibid., pp. 272–273.
20. *The Economist*, September 12, 1931.
21. Keynes, 1931, "Saving and Spending," pp. 152–153.
22. Ibid., "The End of the Gold Standard," pp. 288, 294.
23. Moggridge, 1972, p. 9.
24. Boyle, 1967, p. 268.
25. Eichengreen, 1996, p. 48, and Hawtrey, 1947, p. 161.
26. Hawtrey, 1947, Appendix.
27. Kindleberger, 1993, pp. 370–371.
28. Friedman and Schwartz, 1971, p. 333.
29. Hoover, 1952, p. 120.
30. Hawtrey, 1947, p. 188.
31. Bureau of the Census, 1975, Table 493, p. 1117.
32. Hoover, 1952, p. 133.
33. Ibid., Chapters 17 and 18.
34. Ibid., p. 191.
35. Ibid., p. 199.
36. Ibid., p. 202.
37. Ibid., p. 204.
38. Ibid., pp. 201–202, and Eichengreen, 1992, p. 328.
39. Federal Reserve data.

40. Friedman and Schwartz, 1971, p. 333.
41. Ibid., p. 391.
42. Eichengreen, 1992, pp. 329–330.
43. Hoover, 1952, pp. 390–391.
44. Ibid., p. 395.
45. U.S. Supreme Court, *Perry* v. *United States*, No. 532, dated February 18, 1935.
46. Eichengreen, 1992, p. 333.
47. Hoover, 1952, p. 367.
48. Ibid., p. 398.
49. Ibid., p. 399.
50. Kindleberger, 1993, p. 385.
51. See Ibid., p. 387.
52. Jastram, 1977, Tables 3 and 8, pp. 34, 147.
53. Graham and Whittlesey, 1939, pp. 6–7.
54. Ibid., p. 9.
55. Ibid., p. 14.
56. Ibid., p. 14.
57. Ibid., p. 23.
58. Ibid., p. 20.
59. See Moggridge, 1972, pp. 81–90, for a full discussion of this view.
60. Boyle, 1967, p. 190.
61. Ibid., p. 190.
62. Chernow, 1990, p. 475.
63. Boyle, 1967, pp. 327–328.

Chapter 19 The Transcending Value

1. de Gaulle, 1965.
2. All above quotations are from the *New York Times*.
3. Moggridge, 1980, p. 229.
4. Ibid., p. 230.
5. From Triffin, 1960, Table 2, p. 5.
6. Personal reminiscence of Robert Roosa.
7. Eichengreen, 1996, p. 131.
8. Weil and Davidson, 1970, p. 62.
9. U.S. Treasury Department, 1982, p. 84.
10. *New York Times,* October 21, 1967.
11. Ibid., March 21, 1968.
12. Ibid., November 28, 1967.

13. Weil and Davidson, 1970, p. 100.
14. For details, see Ibid., pp. 143–147.

Chapter 20 World War Eight and the Thirty Ounces of Gold

1. Stein, 1984, p. 162.
2. This whole story is from Stein, 1984, pp. 162–180.
3. Ibid., p. 166.
4. Ibid., p. 176.
5. Ibid., p. 177.
6. *New York Times*, August 16, 1971.
7. All quotations in this paragraph are from the *New York Times*, August 17, 1971.
8. Ibid., August 16, 1971.
9. Ibid., August 20, 1971.
10. Ibid., August 19, 1971.
11. Ibid., August 17, 1971.
12. Eichengreen, 1996, p. 133.
13. U.S. Treasury Department, 1982, p. 93.
14. *New York Times Abstracts*, 1978, p. 30, col. 5.
15. *New York Times*, January 4, 1980.
16. Ibid., January 6, 1980.
17. This entire paragraph is from the *New York Times*, January 16, 1980.
18. Ibid., January 18, 1980.
19. Ibid., January 22, 1980.
20. Ibbotson and Siegel, 1983, Tables 1 and 3.
21. *Pensions & Investments*, March 12, 1979, October 13, 1980, and April 18, 1983. For further details about this episode, see Clowes, 2000.
22. U.S. Treasury Department, 1982, pp. 84, 199, 205.
23. *New York Times*, December 19, 1985.
24. U.S. Treasury Department, 1982, p. 13.
25. International Monetary Fund data.
26. Swiss Expert Group, 1997, p. 2.
27. Ibid., p. 7.
28. Advertisement of the World Gold Council in the *New York Times*, September 8, 1998.
29. *New York Times*, September 28, 1999.
30. Bankers Trust Research, Global Economics, *Commodity Focus*, June 27, 1997.
31. World Gold Council.

32. *The Economist*, January 16, 1999.

33. Mitsui Global Precious Metals, Presentation at Bank Credit Analyst Conference, February 12, 1999.

EPILOGUE

1. Shaw, 1928, p. 263.
2. Jevons, 1875, pp. 231–232.
3. *Wall Street Journal*, Op-Ed page, December 10, 1999.
4. From a lecture delivered at Saint Vincent College, Latrobe, Pa., on March 13, 1997.

Bibliography

Andrews, Kenneth, 1978. *The Spanish Caribbean: Trade and Plunder, 1530–1630.* New Haven, CT: Yale University Press.

Andrews, Kenneth, 1984. *Trade, Plunder and Settlement: Maritime Enterprise and the Genesis of the British Empire, 1480–1630.* Cambridge: Cambridge University Press.

Arnon, Arie, 1991. *Thomas Tooke: Pioneer of Monetary Theory.* Ann Arbor: University of Michigan Press.

Attman, Artur, 1962. *American Bullion in the European World Trade, 1600–1800.* Goteborg: Kungl. Vetenskaps- och Vitterhets-Samhallet. (I drew on the information in this book as provided in Kindleberger, 1989.)

Austen, Ralph A., 1990. "Marginalization, Stagnation, and Growth: The Trans-Saharan Caravan Trade in the Era of European Expansion, 1500–1900." In Tracy, 1990.

Bainton, Roland, 1952. *The Reformation of the Sixteenth Century.* Boston: Beacon Press.

Bank for International Settlements. Various annual reports.

Barnes, James A., 1937. "Myths of the Bryan Campaign." *Mississippi Valley Historical Review*, 34 (Dec.), pp. 367–400.

Barsky, Robert, and Bradford DeLong, 1991. "Forecast Pre–World War I Inflation: The Fisher Effect and the Gold Standard." *Quarterly Journal of Economics,* 106, pp. 815–836.

Bayoumi, Tamim, Barry Eichengreen, and Mark Taylor, eds., 1996. *Modern Perspectives on the Gold Standard.* Cambridge: Cambridge University Press.

Becker, Gary S., Edward Glaeser, and Ken Murphy, 1999. "Population and Economic Growth." *American Economic Review*, 89, no. 2 (May), pp. 145–149.

Bernstein, Peter L., 1968. *A Primer on Money, Banking and Gold*, 2nd edition. New York: Random House.

Bernstein, Peter L., 1970. *Economist on Wall Street.* New York: Macmillan.

Bernstein, Peter L., 1996. *Against the Gods: The Remarkable Story of Risk.* New York: John Wiley & Sons.

Bloch, Mark, 1933. "Le problème de l'or au moyen age." *Annales d'histoire économique et sociale*, no. 19, January 31, pp. 1–33.

Bloomfield, Arthur, 1959. *Monetary Policy Under the Gold Standard, 1800–1914.* Federal Reserve Bank of New York.

Bonar, J., 1923. "Ricardo's Ingot Plan." *Economic Journal*, XXXIII, pp. 281–304.

Boorstin, Daniel, ed., 1966. *An American Primer.* New York: Penguin Books.

Bordo, Michael, 1986. "Money, Deflation and Seigniorage in the Fifteenth Century: A Review Essay." *Journal of Monetary Economics*, 18, no. 3, pp. 337–346.

Bordo, Michael, and Tamim Bayoumi, 1999. "Getting Pegged: Comparing the 1879 and 1925 Gold Resumptions." Cambridge, MA: National Bureau of Economic Research, Working Paper 5497.

Bordo, Michael, and Forrest Capie, eds., 1993. *Monetary Regimes in Transition.* Cambridge: Cambridge University Press.

Bordo, Michael, and Barry Eichengreen, 1998. "The Rise and Fall of a Barbarous Relic: The Role of Gold in the International Monetary System." Cambridge, MA: National Bureau of Economic Research, Working Paper 6436.

Bordo, Michael, and Ronald MacDonald, 1997. "Violations of 'Rules of the Game' and the Credibility of the Classic Gold Standard, 1890–1914." Cambridge, MA: National Bureau of Economic Research, Working Paper 6115.

Bordo, Michael, and Hugh Rockoff, 1996. "The Gold Standard as the Good Housekeeping Seal of Approval." Cambridge, MA: National Bureau of Economic Research, Working Paper 5340.

Bordo, Michael, and Anna Schwartz, 1984. *A Retrospective on the Classical Gold Standard, 1921–1931.* Chicago: University of Chicago Press.

Bordo, Michael, and Eugene White, 1991. "A Tale of Two Currencies: British and French Finance During the Napoleonic Wars." *Journal of Economic History*, 51, no. 2 (June), pp. 303–316.

Bordo, Michael, Ehsan Choudri, and Anna Schwartz, 1999. "Was Expansionary Monetary Policy Feasible During the Great Contraction?" Cambridge, MA: National Bureau of Economic Research, Working Paper 7125.

Bovill, E. W., 1958. *The Golden Trade of the Moors.* London: Oxford University Press.

Bowle, John, 1964. *Henry VIII: A Study of Power in Action.* New York: Dorset Press.

Boyer-Xambeu, Marie-Thérèse, Ghislain Deleplace, and Lucien Gillard, 1994. *Private Money & Public Currencies: The 16th Century Challenge.* Translated by Azizeh Azodi. Armonk, NY: M. E. Sharpe.

Boyle, Andrew, 1967. *Montagu Norman: A Biography.* London: Cassell.

Brace, Harrison H., 1910. *Gold Production and Future Prices: An Inquiry into the Increased Production of Gold and Other Causes of Price Changes with a View to Determining the Future of Prices.* New York: The Bankers Publishing Co.

Braudel, F., and F. Spooner, 1967. "Prices in Europe from 1450 to 1570." In Rich and Wilson, 1967.

Brimelow, Peter, 1998. "Human Capital." *Forbes*, July 6, pp. 52–62.

Bryan, William Jennings, 1896. *The First Battle.* Chicago: W. B. Conkey.

Bryant, Arthur, 1962. *Makers of England*. Garden City: Doubleday & Co.

Bryant, Arthur, 1964. *The Age of Chivalry*. Garden City: Doubleday & Co.

Bureau of the Census, U.S. Department of Commerce, 1975. *Historical Statistics of the United States: Colonial Times to 1970*.

Burns, Arthur R., 1927. *Money and Monetary Policy in Early Times*. New York: Alfred A. Knopf.

Cannan, Edwin, ed., 1919. *The Paper Pound of 1797–1821*. Contains a reprint of the Bullion Committee Report. Reprinted in 1969 by Augustus Kelley, New York.

Challis, Christopher, 1978. *The Tudor Coinage*. Manchester: Manchester University Press (reviewed in Gould, 1979).

Challis, Christopher, ed., 1992. *A New History of the Royal Mint*. Cambridge: Cambridge University Press.

Chernow, Ron, 1990. *The House of Morgan*. New York: Atlantic Monthly Press.

Cherry, John, 1992. *Medieval Craftsmen: Goldsmiths*. Toronto: University of Toronto Press.

Chevalier, Michel, 1836. "Lettres sur l'Amérique du Nord." See Kindleberger, 1978.

Chevalier, Michel, 1859. *On the Probable Fall in the Value of Gold: The Commercial and Social Consequences Which May Ensue, and the Measures Which It Invites*. Trans. Richard Cobden. Reprinted by Greenwood Press, New York, 1968.

Cipolla, Carlo, 1956. *Money, Prices and Civilization in the Mediterranean World: 5th to 17th Centuries*. Princeton: Princeton University Press.

Cipolla, Carlo, 1993. *Before the Industrial Revolution: European Society and Economy, 1000–1700,* 3rd edition. London and New York: Routledge. Originally published 1976 by W. W. Norton in New York.

Clay, Sir Henry, 1957. *Lord Norman*. London: Macmillan.

Clowes, Mike, 2000. *The Money Flood: A History of Pension Fund Investing*. New York: John Wiley & Sons.

Court, W. H. B., 1964. *A Concise Economic History of Great Britain: 1750 to Recent Times*. Cambridge: Cambridge University Press.

Cribb, Joe, Barrie Cook, and Ian Carradice, 1990. *The Coin Atlas: The World of Coinage from Its Origins to the Present Day*. New York: Facts on File.

Crone, G. R., 1937. *The Voyages of Cadamosto and Other Documents on Western Africa in the Second Half of the Fifteenth Century*. London: Hakluyt Society.

Crosby, Alfred W., 1997. *The Measure of Reality: Quantification and Western Society,* 1250–1600. Cambridge: Cambridge University Press.

Davies, Glyn, 1995. *A History of Money from Ancient Times to the Present Day*. Cardiff: University of Wales Press.

Day, John, 1978. "The Great Bullion Famine of the Fifteenth Century." *Past and Present*, 79 (May), pp. 3–54.

Day, John, 1987. *Medieval Market Economy*. Oxford: Blackwell.

Debeir, Jean-Claude, 1978. "La crise du franc de 1924: Un exemple de speculation 'internationale.' " *Relations internationales*, no. 13, pp. 29–49.

de Gaulle, Charles, 1965. "Discours et messages, 1962–1965." Paris: Plon.

Despres, Emile, Charles P. Kindleberger, and Walter S. Salant, 1966. "The Dollar and World Liquidity: A Minority View." *The Economist*, 218, no. 6389 (February 5).

Dobbs, Betty Jo Teeter, 1992. *The Janus Faces of Genius: The Role of Alchemy in Newton's Thought*. Cambridge: Cambridge University Press.

Drake, Louis S. 1985. "Reconstruction of a Bimetallic Price Level." *Explorations in Economic History*, 22, pp. 194–219.

Eichengreen, Barry, 1986. "The Bank of France and the Sterilization of Gold." *Explorations in Economic History*, 23, pp. 56–84.

Eichengreen, Barry, 1987. "Conducting the International Orchestra: Bank of England Leadership Under the Classical Gold Standard, 1880–1913." *Journal of International Money and Finance*, 6.

Eichengreen, Barry, 1992. *Golden Fetters*. New York: Oxford University Press.

Eichengreen, Barry, 1996. *Globalizing Capital: A History of the International Monetary System*. Princeton: Princeton University Press.

Eichengreen, Barry, and Ian McLean, 1994. "The Supply of Gold Under the Pre-1914 Gold Standard." *Economic History Review*, 47.

Emmerich, Andre, 1965. *Sweat on the Sun and Tears of the Moon: Gold and Silver in Precolombian Art*. Seattle: University of Washington Press.

Encyclopedia Britannica On-Line (www.eb.com).

Fay, C. R., 1951. *Huskisson and His Age*. London: Longmans Green & Co.

Feaveryear, A., 1963. *The Pound Sterling*. Oxford: Clarendon Press.

Federal Reserve Board, 1943. Banking and Monetary Statistics.

Fischer, David Hackett, 1996. *The Great Wave: Price Revolutions and the Rhythm of History*. New York: Oxford University Press.

Fivaz, C. E., 1988. "How the MacArthur–Forrest Cyanidation Process Ensured South Africa's Golden Future." *Journal of the South African Institute of Mining and Metallurgy*, September, pp. 309–318.

Flandreau, Marc, 1996. "The French Crime of 1873: An Essay on the Emergence of the International Gold Standard, 1870–1880." *Journal of Economic History*, 56, no. 4 (Dec.), pp. 862–897.

Flandreau, Marc, 1996. "As Good as Gold? Bimetallism in Equilibrium, 1848–1873." In Lawrence Officer, ed., *Monetary Standards in History*. London: Routledge.

Fraser, Russell, 1973. *The Dark Ages & the Age of Gold*. Princeton: Princeton University Press.

Friedman, Milton, 1992. *Money Mischief: Episodes in Monetary History*. New York: Harcourt Brace.

Friedman, Milton, and Anna Schwartz, 1971. *A Monetary History of the United States, 1867–1960*. Princeton: National Bureau of Economic Research and Princeton University Press.

Furness, William Henry, 1910. *The Island of Stone Money: Uap and the Carolines.* Philadelphia: J. B. Lippincott.

Galbraith, John Kenneth, 1954. *The Great Crash: 1929.* New York: Houghton Mifflin.

Gallarotti, Giulio M., 1995. *The Anatomy of an International Monetary Regime: The Classical Gold Standard 1880–1914.* New York: Oxford University Press.

Gibbon, Edward, 1804. *The History of the Decline and Fall of the Roman Empire.* Originally published 1782. The citations herein, kindness of Charles Kindleberger, are from an edition of eight volumes that was published in 1804 in Philadelphia by William Y. Birch and Abraham Small.

Goldsmith, Raymond W., 1985. *Comparative National Balance Sheets: A Study of Twenty Countries, 1688–1978.* Chicago: University of Chicago Press.

Gould, John D., 1970. *The Great Debasement.* Oxford: Clarendon Press.

Gould, John D., 1976. "How It All Began." *Economic History Review,* XXIX, no. 2 (May).

Gould, John D., 1979. Review of C. E. Challis, *The Tudor Coinage. The Economic History Review,* XXXII, no. 2 (May), pp. 271–272.

Graham, Frank D., and Charles R. Whittlesey, 1939. *The Golden Avalanche.* Princeton: Princeton University Press.

Green, Timothy, 1993. *The World of Gold: The Inside Story of Who Mines, Who Markets, Who Buys Gold.* London: Rosendale Press.

Gudde, Erwin G., 1936. *Sutter's Own Story: The Life of General John Augustus Sutter and the History of New Helvetia in the Sacramento Valley.* New York: G. P. Putnam's Sons.

Habashi, Fathi, 1987. "One Hundred Years of Cyanidation." *Historical Metallurgy Notes,* 80, no. 905, pp. 108–114.

Hackett, Francis, 1929. *Henry VIII.* New York: Horace Liveright. Reprinted September 1945.

Hamilton, Alexander, 1791. *Report on the Establishment of a Mint.* Originally published in Philadelphia. Reprinted in Harold Syrett, ed., *The Papers of Alexander Hamilton.* New York: Columbia University Press, 1965.

Hamilton, Earl, 1934. *American Treasure and the Price Revolution in Spain, 1501–1650.* Cambridge, MA. Reprinted by Octagon Books, New York, 1970.

Hanke, Louis, 1951. *Bartolome de las Casas: An Interpretation of His Life and Writings.* The Hague: Nijhoff.

Harvey, Wiliam H., 1894. *Coin's Financial School.* Reprint edited by Richard Hofstadter. Cambridge, MA: Harvard University Press, 1963.

Hawtrey, R. G., 1947. *The Gold Standard in Theory & Practice,* 5th edition. London: Longmans, Green & Co. Originally published 1927.

Head, Barclay Vincent. *The Coinage of Lydia.* San Diego: Pegasus Publishing (no date).

Heilbroner, Robert L., 1953. *The Worldly Philosophers.* New York: Simon & Schuster.

Heilbroner, Robert L., 1956. *The Quest for Wealth.* New York: Simon & Schuster.

Helleiner, Karl F., 1967. *The Population of Europe from the Black Death to the Eve of the Vital Revolution.* In Rich and Wilson, 1967.

Hellferich, Karl, 1927. *Money.* New York: The Adelphi Company.

Hemming, John, 1970. *The Conquest of the Incas.* San Diego: Harcourt Brace & Co.

Herodotus, 1992. *The Histories.* Translated by Walter Blanco. New York: W. W. Norton.

Herrington, Richard, Chris Stanley, and Robert Symes. *Gold.* London: The Natural History Museum. Forthcoming.

Hicks, John, 1931. *The Populist Revolt.* Minneapolis: University of Minnesota Press.

High Court of South Africa, 1986. *Official Reports: Hay v. African Gold Recovery Co.*, pp. 244–301.

Hofstadter, Richard, 1948. *The American Political Tradition and the Men Who Made It.* New York: Knopf.

Holtfrerich, Carl Ludwig, 1999. *Frankfurt as a Financial Centre: From Medieval Trade Fair to European Banking Centre.* Munich: Verlag C. H. Beck.

Hoover, Herbert, 1952. *The Memoirs of Herbert Hoover: The Great Depression, 1929–41.* New York: Macmillan.

Hughes, Robert, 1987. *The Fatal Shore: A History of the Transportation of Convicts to Australia, 1787–1868.* New York: Alfred A. Knopf.

Hume, David, 1752. "Of the Balance of Trade." In *Essays, Moral, Political, and Literary*, vol. I, 1898 edition. London: Longmans Green, pp. 330–345.

Ibbotson, Roger, and Laurence Siegel, 1983. "The World Market Wealth Portfolio." *Journal of Portfolio Management*, 9, no. 2 (winter), pp. 5–17.

Jacob, William, 1831. *An Historical Inquiry into the Production and Consumption of the Precious Metals.* London: John Murray.

Jastram, Roy, 1977. *The Golden Constant: The English & American Experience, 1560–1976.* New York: John Wiley & Sons.

Jevons, W. Stanley, 1875. *Money and the Mechanism of Exchange.* New York: Appleton. Reprinted 1896.

Kaye, Joel, 1998. *Economy and Nature in the Fourteenth Century: Money, Market Exchange, and the Emergence of Scientific Thought.* Cambridge: Cambridge University Press.

Kemmerer, Edward, 1944. *Gold and the Gold Standard.* New York: McGraw-Hill.

Keynes, John Maynard, 1923. *A Tract on Monetary Reform.* London: Macmillan.

Keynes, John Maynard, 1931. *Essays in Persuasion.* London: Macmillan.

Kindleberger, Charles, 1978. "Chevalier, 1806–1870, The Economic de Tocqueville." Unpublished manuscript reprinted as Chapter 2 in Kindleberger, 1985.

Kindleberger, Charles, 1985. *Keynesianism versus Monetarism and Other Essays in Financial History.* London: George Allen & Unwin.

Kindleberger, Charles, 1986. *The World in Depression*, 2nd edition. Berkeley: University of California Press. Original edition 1973.

Kindleberger, Charles, 1989. "Spenders and Hoarders: The World Distribution of Spanish American Silver, 1550–1750." Singapore: Institute of Southeast Asian Studies. Reprinted in Kindleberger, 1990, pp. 35–85.

Kindleberger, Charles, 1990. *Historical Economics: Art or Science?* Berkeley: University of California Press.

Kindleberger, Charles, 1993. *A Financial History of Western Europe*. New York: Oxford University Press.

Kindleberger, Charles, 1996a. *Manias, Panics, and Crashes: A History of Financial Crises*, 3rd edition. New York: John Wiley & Sons.

Kindleberger, Charles, 1996b. "The French Crime of 1871: A Comment." Unpublished manuscript.

Kindleberger, Charles, 1996c. *World Economic Primacy, 1500–1990*. New York: Oxford University Press.

Kindleberger, Charles, 1998. *Economic and Financial Crises and Transformations in Sixteenth Century Europe*. Princeton: Department of Economics, Princeton University.

King, Gail, 1997. "A Mother Lode of Klondike Lore." *Wall Street Journal*, July 17, Op-Ed page.

Krooss, Herman E., 1969. *Documentary History of Banking & Currency in the U.S.* New York: Chelsea House Publishers. Contains Alexander Hamilton's report on the establishment of a mint.

Lacey, Robert, and Danny Danziger, 1999. *The Year 1000: What Life Was Like at the Turn of the First Millennium*. Boston: Little, Brown.

Lane, Frederic, and Reinhold Mueller, 1985. *Money & Banking in Medieval and Renaissance Venice*, vol. I, *Coins and Money of Account*. Baltimore: Johns Hopkins University Press.

Langer, William, 1952. *An Encyclopedia of World History*. Boston: Houghton Mifflin. A revision and update of Ploetz, 1883.

Leary, Francis, 1959. *The Golden Longing*. New York: Charles Scribner's Sons.

Li, Ming-Hsun, 1963. *The Great Recoinage of 1696–1699*. London: Wiedenfeld & Nicholson.

Lopez, Robert S., 1951. "The Dollar of the Middle Ages." *Journal of Economic History*, 11, pp. 209–234.

Lopez, Robert S., 1956. "Back to Gold, 1252." *Economic History Review*, 2nd series, 9, pp. 219–240.

Martin, David, 1977. "The Impact of Mid-Nineteenth Century Gold Depreciation Upon Western Monetary Standards." *Journal of European Economic History*, 6, no. 3, pp. 641–658.

Marx, Jenifer, 1978. *The Magic of Gold*. New York: Doubleday.

Mauro, Frédéric, 1990. "Merchant Communities, 1350–1750." In Tracy, 1990.

Mayhew, Nicholas J., 1992. "From Regional to Central Mining, 1158–1464." In Challis, 1992.

Mayhew, Nicholas J., 1999. *Sterling: The Rise and Fall of a Currency*. London: Allen Lane/Penguin Press.

McCulloch, John R., ed., 1856. *A Select Collection of Scarce and Valuable Tracts on Money*. London: Political Economy Club. Reprinted 1966 by August M. Kelley, New York.

Menias, G.-P., 1969. *Napoleon et l'Argent*. Paris: Editions de l'Epargne.

Metropolitan Museum, New York, 1985. *The Art of Precolumbian Gold*.

Miskimin, Harry, 1963. *Money Prices and Foreign Exchange in Fourteenth Century France*. New Haven: Yale University Press.

Miskimin, Harry A., 1977. *The Economy of Later Renaissance Europe: 1460–1600*. Cambridge: Cambridge University Press.

Miskimin, Harry, 1984. *Money and Power in Fifteenth Century France*. New Haven: Yale University Press.

Miskimin, Harry A., 1989. *Cash, Credit, and Crisis in Europe, 1300–1600*. London: Variorum Reprints.

Moggridge, Donald, 1969. *The Return to Gold 1925: The Foundation of Economic Policy and Its Critics*. Cambridge: Cambridge University Press.

Moggridge, Donald, 1972. *British Monetary Policy, 1924–31: The Norman Conquest of $4.86*. Cambridge: Cambridge University Press.

Moggridge, Donald, 1980. *The Collected Writings of John Maynard Keynes*, vol. XXVI, "Activities." London: Macmillan.

Morineau, Michel, 1985. *Incroyables gazettes et faubuleux métaux: Les retours des trésors américains d'après les gazettes hollandaises (XVIe–XVIIIe siècles)*. Paris: Cambridge University Press.

Mun, Thomas, c. 1620. *England's Treasure by Foreign Trade*. Reproduced in *Early English Tracts on Commerce*, J. R. McCulluch, ed., Cambridge: Cambridge University Press, 1954.

Neal, Larry, 1998. "The Financial Crisis of 1825 and the Restructuring of the British Financial System." *Review of the Federal Reserve Bank of St. Louis*, 80, no. 3 (May/June), pp. 53–76.

Niedringhaus, Lee I., 1998. "The Panic of 1893." *Financial History*, winter, pp. 16–23.

North, Michael, 1990. *Geldumlauf und Wirtschaftskonjunktur im südluchen Ostseeraum an der Wende zur Neuzeit (1440–1570)*. Sigmaringen: Jan Thorbecke Verlag.

Noyes, Alexander Dana, 1898. *Forty Years of American Financial History*. New York: Putnam.

Officer, Lawrence, 1996a. *Between the Dollar-Sterling Gold Points*. Cambridge: Cambridge University Press.

Officer, Lawrence, 1996b. *Monetary Standards in History*. London: Routledge.

O'Leary, Paul M., 1960. "The Scene of the Crime of 1873 Revisited: A Note." *Journal of Political Economy*, 68, August, pp. 398–392.

Parry, J. H., 1967. "Transport and Trade Routes." In Rich and Wilson, 1967.

Phillips, Carla Rahn, 1986. *Six Galleons for the King of Spain: Imperial Defense in the Early Seventeenth Century*. Baltimore: Johns Hopkins University Press.

Pindar, 1927. *The Odes of Pindar Including the Principal Fragments*. Sir John Sandys.

Ploetz, Carl, 1883. *Epitome of Ancient, Medieval, and Modern History*. Translated by William H. Tillinghast. Boston: Houghton, Mifflin & Co.

Polo, Marco, 1289. *The Travels of Marco Polo*. Translated by Ronald Latham. London: Penguin Books, 1958.

Postan, M. M., and H. J. Habakkuk, 1952. *The Cambridge Economic History of Europe*, vol. II: *Trade and Industry in the Middle Ages*. Cambridge: Cambridge University Press.

Prescott, William H., 1847. *History of the Conquest of Peru*. Boston: Harper & Brothers. Republished 1957 by The Heritage Press, New York, from which the citations herein are taken.

Pressnell, L. S., 1968. "Gold Reserves, Banking Reserves, and the Barings Crisis of 1890," in C. R. Whittlesey and J. S. G. Wilson, eds., *Essays in Honour of R. S. Sayers*. Oxford: Clarendon Press, pp. 167–288.

Quinn, Stephen, 1996. "Gold, Silver, and the Glorious Revolution: Arbitrage Between Bills of Exchange and Bullion." *Economic History Review*, XLIX, no. 3, pp. 473–490.

Ramage, Andrew, and Paul Craddock, 2000. *King Croesus' Gold: Excavations at Sardis and the History of Gold Refining*. London: British Museum Publications.

Redish, A., 1990. "The Evolution of the Gold Standard in England." *Journal of Economic History*, Vol. L, pp. 789–806.

Ricardo, David, 1809. *The Price of Gold*. Reprinted by The Johns Hopkins Press, Baltimore, 1903, Jacob Hollander, ed.

Ricardo, David, 1811a. "Reply to Mr. Bosanquet's Practical Observations on the Report of the Bullion Committee." In *Economic Essays*, E. C. K. Gonner, ed. London: G. Bell & Sons, 1923, pp. 63–149.

Ricardo, David, 1811b. "The High Price of Bullion and the Depreciation of Bank Notes." In *Economic Essays*, E. C. K. Gonner, ed. London: G. Bell & Sons, 1923, pp. 3–60.

Ricardo, David, 1816. "Proposals for an Economical and Secure Currency; with Observations on the Profit of the Bank of England, as They Regard the Public and the Proprietors of the Bank of England." In *Economic Essays*, E. C. K. Gonner, ed. London: G. Bell & Sons, 1923, pp. 63–149.

Rich, E. E., and C. H. Wilson, eds., 1967. *The Cambridge Economic History of Europe*, vol. IV: *The Economy of Expanding Europe in the Sixteenth and Seventeenth Centuries*. Cambridge: Cambridge University Press.

Robertson, Dennis H., 1929. *Money*. New York: Harcourt, Brace & Co.

Rockoff. Hugh, 1990. "The Wizard of Oz as a Monetary Allegory." *Journal of Political Economy*, 98 (August), pp. 739–760.

Roll, Eric, 1995. *Where Did We Go Wrong: From the Gold Standard to Europe.* London: Faber & Faber.

Rolnick, Arthur J., and Warren E. Weber, 1986. "Gresham's Law or Gresham's Fallacy." *Journal of Political Economy*, 94 (February), pp. 185–199.

Rolnick, A. J., F. R. Velde, and W. E. Weber, 1996. "The Debasement Puzzle: An Essay on Medieval Monetary History." *Journal of Economic History*, December.

Rosenthal, Eric, 1970. *Gold. Gold. Gold.* London and New York: Macmillan.

Rousseau, Peter L., and Richard Sylla, 1999. "Emerging Financial Markets and Early U.S. Growth." Cambridge, MA: National Bureau of Economic Research, Working Paper 7448.

Rueff, Jacques, 1972. *The Monetary Sin of the West.* New York: Macmillan.

Ruskin, John, 1862 [1982]. *"Unto This Last": Four Essays on the First Principles of Political Economy.* London: Smith, Elder & Co. These interesting essays also appear in *The Complete Works of John Ruskin*, vol. XVII, E. T. Cook and Alexander Wedderburn, eds. London: George Allen, 1905.

Schubert, Aurel, 1991. *The Credit-Anstalt Crisis in 1931.* Cambridge: Cambridge University Press.

Schuker, Stephen A., 1976. *The End of French Predominance in Europe: The Financial Crisis of 1924 and the Adoption of the Dawes Plan.* Chapel Hill: The University of North Carolina Press.

Schwab, Gustav, 1946. *Gods and Heroes: Myths & Epics of Ancient Greece.* Translated from German by Olga Marx and Ernst Morwitz. New York: Pantheon Books.

Schwartz, Anna, 1973. "Secular Price Change in Historical Perspective." *Journal of Money, Credit & Banking*, 5, pp. 243–269.

Select Committee of the House of Commons on the High Price of Gold Bullion (The Bullion Committee Report of 1810). London: P. S. King, 1925.

Shaw, Bernard, 1928. *The Intelligent Woman's Guide to Socialism and Capitalism.* Reprinted by New Transaction Books, New Brunswick, NJ, 1984.

Skousen, Mark, 1977. *Economics of a Pure Gold Standard.* Irvington-on-Hudson: The Foundation for Economic Education.

Smith, Adam, 1776. *The Wealth of Nations.* Amherst, NY: Prometheus Press, 1991.

Smith, Martin, 1996. *Bookwatch: The General Strike.* International Socialism, March (from www.google.com).

Sraffa, P., *The Works and Correspondence of David Ricardo.* Cambridge: Cambridge University Press.

Stein, Herbert, 1984. *Presidential Economics: The Making of Economic Policy from Roosevelt to Reagan and Beyond.* New York: Simon & Schuster.

Stigler, Stephen, 1977. "Eight Centuries of Sampling Inspection: The Trial of the Pyx." *Journal of the American Statistical Association*, 72, pp. 493–500.

Supple, B. E., 1959. *Commercial Crisis and Change in England, 1600–1642.* Cambridge: Cambridge University Press.

Sutherland, C. H. V., 1959. *Gold: Its Beauty, Power, and Allure.* London: Thames & Hudson.

Swiss Expert Group, 1997. "Der Neue Geld-Und Währungsartikel in der Bundesverfassung." Press release dated October 24.

Tallman, Ellis, 1998. "Gold Shocks, Liquidity, and the United States Economy During the National Banking Era." *Explorations in Economic History*, 35, pp. 381–404.

Tassel, Janet, 1998. "The Search for Sardis." *Harvard Magazine*, April, pp. 51–60, 95–96.

Temin, Peter, 1989. *Lessons from the Great Depression.* Cambridge, MA: MIT Press.

Tracy, James D., ed., 1990. *The Rise of Merchant Empires: Long-Distance Trade in the Early Modern World, 1350–1750.* Cambridge: Cambridge University Press.

Triffin, Robert, 1960. *Gold and the Dollar Crisis.* New Haven: Yale University Press.

Tuchman, Barbara W., 1978. *A Distant Mirror: The Calamitous 14th Century.* New York: Ballantine Books.

U.S. House Committee on Foreign Affairs, 1961. "Gold and the U.S. Balance of Payment Deficits."

U.S. House of Representatives, Committee on Banking and Currency, Report No. 31, Forty-first Congress, Second Session. 1870. "The New York Gold Conspiracy."

U.S. Treasury Department, 1982. "Report to Congress on the Role of Gold in the Domestic and International Monetary Systems."

Vilar, Pierre, 1976. *A History of Gold and Money, 1450–1920.* London: New Left Books.

Watson, Andrew M., 1967. "Back to Gold—and Silver." *Economic History Review*, 2nd series, 20, pp. 1–34.

Weil, Gordon, and Ian Davidson, 1970. *The Gold War: The Story of the Monetary Crisis.* New York: Holt Rinehart.

Wheatcroft, Geoffrey, 1985. *The Randlords.* London: Atheneum.

White, Michael, 1977. *Isaac Newton: The Last Sorceror.* Reading, MA: Addison-Wesley.

Wilkie, A. D., 1994. "The Risk Premium on Ordinary Shares." A presentation to the Faculty of Actuaries and the Institute of Actuaries, London.

Wimmer, Larry, 1975. "The Gold Crisis of 1869: Stabilizing or Destabilizing Speculation Under Floating Exchange Rates." *Explorations in Economic History*, 12, pp. 105–122.

Wirth, Max, 1893. "The Crisis of 1890." *Journal of Political Economy*, 1, no. 2, pp. 214–235.

Wright, Louis B., 1970. *Gold, Glory, and the Gospel: The Adventurous Lives and Times of the Renaissance Explorers.* New York: Atheneum.

Index